Learning Python

Learning Python

Mark Lutz and David Ascher

O'REILLY®

Beijing · Cambridge · Farnham · Köln · Paris · Sebastopol · Taipei · Tokyo

Learning Python
by Mark Lutz and David Ascher

Published by O'Reilly & Associates, Inc., 1005 Gravenstein Highway North, Sebastopol, CA 95472.

Editor: Frank Willison

Production Editor: Mary Anne Weeks Mayo

Printing History:

March 1999:   First Edition.

ISBN: 1-56592-464-9
[M]   [2/03]

Table of Contents

Preface

About This Book

This book provides a quick introduction to the Python programming language. Python is a popular object-oriented language used for both standalone programs and scripting applications in a variety of domains. It's free, portable, powerful, and remarkably easy to use. Whether you're new to programming or a professional developer, this book's goal is to bring you up to speed on the core Python language in a hurry. Before we jump into details, we'd like to use this preface to say a few words about the book's design.

This Book's Scope

Although this text covers the essentials of the Python language, we've kept its scope narrow in the interest of speed and size. Put another way, the presentation is focused on core concepts and is sometimes deliberately simplistic. Because of that, this book is probably best described as both an introduction and a stepping stone to more advanced and complete texts.

For example, we won't say anything about Python/C integration—a big, complicated topic, with lots of big, complicated examples, which is nevertheless central to many Python-based systems. We also won't talk much about the Python community, Python's history, or some of the philosophies underlying Python development. And popular Python applications such as GUIs, system tools, network scripting, and numeric programming get only a short survey at the end (if they are mentioned at all). Naturally, this misses some of the big picture.

By and large, Python is about raising the quality bar a few notches in the scripting world. Some of its ideas require more context than can be provided here, and we'd be remiss if we didn't recommend further study after you finish this text. We hope that most readers of this book will eventually go on to gain a deeper and more complete understanding, from texts such as O'Reilly's *Programming Python*. The rest of the Python story requires studying examples that are more realistic than there is space for here.*

But despite its limited scope (and perhaps because of it), we think you'll find this to be a great first book on Python. You'll learn everything you need to get started writing useful standalone Python programs and scripts. By the time you've finished this book, you will have learned not only the language itself, but also how to apply it to day-to-day tasks. And you'll be equipped to tackle more advanced topics as they come your way.

This Book's Style

Much of this book is based on training materials developed for a three-day hands-on Python course. You'll find exercises at the end of most chapters, with solutions in Appendix C. The exercises are designed to get you coding right away, and are usually one of the highlights of the course. We strongly recommend working through the exercises along the way, not only to gain Python programming experience, but also because some exercises raise issues not covered elsewhere in the text. The solutions at the end should help if you get stuck (we encourage you to cheat as much and as often as you like). Naturally, you'll need to install Python to run the exercises; more on this in a moment.

Because this text is designed to introduce language basics quickly, we've organized the presentation by major language features, not examples. We'll take a bottom-up approach here: from built-in object types, to statements, to program units, and so on (in fact, if you've seen Appendix E in *Programming Python*, parts of this book may stir up feelings of déjà vu). Each chapter is fairly self-contained, but later chapters use ideas introduced in earlier ones (e.g., by the time we get to classes, we'll assume you know how to write functions), so a linear reading probably makes the most sense. From a broader perspective, this book is divided into three sections:

Part I: The Core Language

This part of the book presents the Python language, in a bottom-up fashion. It's organized with one chapter per major language feature—types, functions, and so forth—and most of the examples are small and self-contained (some might also

---

* See *http://www.ora.com* and *http://www.python.org* for details on supplemental Python texts. *Programming Python* was written by one of this book's authors. As its title implies, it discusses practical programming issues in detail.

call the examples in this section artificial, but they illustrate the points we're out to make). This section represents the bulk of the text, which tells you something about the focus of the book.

Chapter 1, *Getting Started*

We begin with a quick introduction to Python and then look at how to run Python programs so you can get started coding examples and exercises immediately.

Chapter 2, *Types and Operators*

Next, we explore Python's major built-in object types: numbers, lists, dictionaries, and so on. You can get a lot done in Python with these tools alone.

Chapter 3, *Basic Statements*

The next chapter moves on to introduce Python's statements—the code you type to create and process objects in Python.

Chapter 4, *Functions*

This chapter begins our look at Python's higher-level program structure tools. Functions turn out to be a simple way to package code for reuse.

Chapter 5, *Modules*

Python modules let you organize statements and functions into larger components, and this chapter illustrates how to create, use, and reload modules on the fly.

Chapter 6, *Classes*

Here we explore Python's object-oriented programming (OOP) tool, the class. As you'll see, OOP in Python is mostly about looking up names in linked objects.

Chapter 7, *Exceptions*

We wrap up the section with a look at Python's exception handling model and statements. This comes last, because exceptions can be classes if you want them to be.

Part II: The Outer Layers

In this section, we sample Python's built-in tools, and put them to use in a more or less random collection of small example programs.

Chapter 8, *Built-in Tools*

This chapter presents a selection of the modules and functions that are included in the default Python installation. By definition, they comprise the minimum set of modules you can reasonably expect any Python user to have access to. Knowing the contents of this standard toolset will likely save you weeks of work.

Chapter 9, *Common Tasks in Python*

> This chapter presents a few nontrivial programs. By building on the language core explained in Part I and the built-in tools described in Chapter 8, we present many small but useful programs that show how to put it all together. We cover three areas that are of interest to most Python users: basic tasks, text processing, and system interfaces.

Chapter 10, *Frameworks and Applications*

> This final chapter shows how real applications can be built, leveraging on more specialized libraries that are either part of the standard Python distribution or freely available from third parties. The programs in this chapter are the most complex, but also the most satisfying to work through. We close with a brief discussion of JPython, the Java port of Python, and a substantial JPython program.

Part III: Appendixes

The book ends with three appendixes that list Python resources on the Net (Appendix A), give platform-specific tips for using Python on Unix, Windows, and Macintosh-based machines (Appendix B), and provide solutions to exercises that appear at the end of chapters (Appendix C). Note: the index can be used to hunt for details, but there are no reference appendixes in this book per se. The *Python Pocket Reference* from O'Reilly (*http://www.ora.com*), as well as the free Python reference manuals maintained at *http://www.python.org*, will fill in the details.

Prerequisites

There are none to speak of, really. This is an introductory-level book. It may not be an ideal text for someone who has never touched a computer before (for instance, we're not going to spend a lot of time explaining what a computer is), but we haven't made many assumptions about your programming background or education. On the other hand, we won't insult readers by assuming they are "dummies" either (whatever that means); it's easy to do useful things in Python, and we hope to show you how. The text occasionally contrasts Python with languages such as C, C++, and Pascal, but you can safely ignore these comparisons if you haven't used such languages in the past.

One thing we should probably mention up front: Python's creator, Guido van Rossum, named it after the BBC comedy series *Monty Python's Flying Circus*. Because of this legacy, many of the examples in this book use references to that show. For instance, the traditional "foo" and "bar" become "spam" and "eggs" in the Python world. You don't need to be familiar with the series to make sense of the examples (symbols are symbols), but it can't hurt.

Book Updates

Improvements happen (and so do mis^H^H^H typos). Updates, supplements, and corrections for this book will be maintained (or referenced) on the Web, at one of the following sites:

- *http://www.oreilly.com* (O'Reilly's site)
- *http://rmi.net/~lutz* (Mark's site)
- *http://starship.skyport.net/~da* (David's site)
- *http://www.python.org* (Python's main site)

If we could be more clairvoyant, we would, but the Web tends to change faster than books.

Font Conventions

This book uses the following typographical conventions:

Italic

For email addresses, filenames, URLs, for emphasizing new terms when first introduced, and for some comments within code sections.

`Constant width`

To show the contents of files or the output from commands and to designate modules, methods, statements, and commands.

`Constant width bold`

In code sections to show commands or text that would be typed.

`Constant width italic`

To mark replaceables in code sections.

 The owl icon designates a note, which is an important aside to the nearby text.

About the Programs in This Book

This book, and all the program examples in it, are based on Python Version 1.5. But since we'll stick to the core language here, you can be fairly sure that most of what we have to say won't change very much in later releases of Python.* Most of this book applies to earlier Python versions too, except when it doesn't; naturally, if you try using extensions added after the release you've got, all bets are off. As a rule of thumb, the latest Python is the best Python. Because this book focuses on the core language, most of it also applies to JPython, the new Java-based Python implementation.

Source code for the book's examples, as well as exercise solutions, can be fetched from O'Reilly's web site *http://www.oreilly.com/catalog/lpython/*.

So how do you run the examples? We'll get into start-up details in a few pages, but the first step is installing Python itself, unless it's already available on your machine. You can always fetch the latest and greatest Python release from *http://www.python.org*, Python's official web site. There, you'll find both prebuilt Python executables (which you just unpack and run) and the full source-code distribution (which you compile on your machine). You can also find Python on CD-ROMs, such as those sold by Walnut Creek, supplied with Linux distributions, or shipped with bigger Python books. Installation steps for both executable and source forms are well documented, so we won't say much more about this beyond a cursory overview in Chapter 1 (see *Programming Python* for install details).

How to Contact Us

Please address comments and questions concerning this book to the publisher:

> O'Reilly & Associates
> 101 Morris Street
> Sebastopol, CA 95472
> 1-800-998-9938 (in United States or Canada)
> 1-707-829-0515 (international or local)
> 1-707-829-0104 (fax)

You can also send us messages electronically. To be put on the mailing list or request a catalog, send email to *info@oreilly.com*.

To ask technical questions or comment on the book, send email to *bookquestions@oreilly.com*.

---

* Well, probably. Judging from how *Programming Python* has stayed current over the last few years, the language itself changes very little over time, and when it does, it's still usually backward compatible with earlier releases (Guido adds things, but rarely changes things that are already there). Peripheral tools such as the Python/C API and the Tkinter GUI interface seem to be more prone to change, but we'll mostly ignore them here. Still, you should always check the release notes of later versions to see what's new.

Acknowledgments

We'd like to express our gratitude to all the people who played a part in developing this book, but this is too short a book to list them all. But we'd like to give a special thanks to our editor, Frank Willison, and O'Reilly in general, for supporting another Python book. Thanks also to everyone who took part in the early review of this book—Eric Raymond, Guido van Rossum, Just van Rossum, Andrew Kuchling, Dennis Allison, Greg Ward, and Jennifer Tanksley. And for creating such an enjoyable and useful language, we owe an especially large debt to Guido, and the rest of the Python community; like most freeware systems, Python is the product of many heroic efforts.

Mark Also Says:

Since writing *Programming Python*, I've had the opportunity to travel around the country teaching Python to beginners. Besides racking up frequent flyer miles, these courses helped me refine the core language material you'll see in the first part of this book. I'd like to thank the early students of my course, at Badger, Lawrence Livermore, and Fermi Labs, in particular. Your feedback played a big role in shaping my contributions to this text. I also want to give a special thanks to Softronex, for the chance to teach Python in Puerto Rico this summer (a better perk would be hard to imagine).

Finally, a few personal notes of thanks. To coauthor David Ascher, for his hard work and patience on this project. To the people I worked with at Lockheed Martin while writing this book. To the late Carl Sagan, for inspiration. To Lao Tzu, for deep thoughts. To the Denver Broncos, for winning the big one. And most of all, to my wife Lisa, and my kids—a set which now consists of Michael, Samantha, and Roxanne—for tolerating yet another book project. I owe the latter bunch a trip to Wally World.

November 1998
Longmont, Colorado

David Also Says:

In addition to the thanks listed above, I'd like to extend special thanks to several people.

First, thanks to Mark Lutz for inviting me to work with him on this book and for supporting my efforts as a Python trainer. Belated thank yous go to the Python folks who encouraged me in my early days with the language and its tools, especially Guido, Tim Peters, Don Beaudry, and Andrew Mullhaupt.

Like Mark, I've developed a course in which I teach Python and JPython. The students in these courses have helped me identify the parts of Python that are the trickiest to learn (luckily, they are rare), as well as remind me of the aspects of the language that make it so pleasant to use. I thank them for their feedback. I would also like to thank those who have given me the chance to develop these courses: Jim Anderson (Brown University), Cliff Dutton (then at Distributed Data Systems), Geoffrey Philbrick (Hibbitt, Karlsson & Sorensen, Inc.), Paul Dubois (Lawrence Livermore National Labs), and Ken Swisz (KLA-Tencor).

Thanks to my scientific advisors, Jim Anderson, Leslie Welch, and Norberto Grzywacz, who have all kindly supported my efforts with Python in general and this book in particular, not necessarily understanding why I was doing it but trusting me nonetheless.

The first victims of my Python evangelization efforts deserve gold stars for tolerating my most enthusiastic (some might say fanatical) early days: Thanassi Protopapas, Gary Strangman, and Steven Finney. Thanassi also gave his typically useful feedback on an early draft of the book.

Finally, thanks to my family: my parents JacSue and Philippe for always encouraging me to do what I want to do; my brother Ivan for reminding me of some of my early encounters with programming; my wife Emily for her constant support and utter faith that writing a book was something I could do. I thank our son Hugo for letting me use the keyboard at least some of the time, and only learning how to turn the computer off in the last phase of this project. He was three days old when I received the first email from Mark about this book. He's eighteen months old now. It's been a great year and a half.

To the reader of this book, I hope you enjoy the book and through it, the Python language. Through Python, I've learned more than I ever thought I'd want to about many aspects of computing that once seemed foreboding. My aim in helping write this book was to allow others the same experience. If your aim in learning Python is to work on a specific problem, I hope that Python becomes so transparent that it becomes invisible, letting you focus your efforts on the issues you're dealing with. I suspect, however, that at least a few readers will have the same reaction that I had when discovering Python, which was to find in Python itself a world worth learning more about. If that's the case for you, be aware that exploring Python is not necessarily a short-term project. After countless hours, I'm still poking around, and still having fun.

November 1998
San Francisco, California

I

The Core Language

In this first section, we study the Python language itself. We call this part "The Core Language," because our focus will be on the essentials of Python programming: its built-in types, statements, and tools for packaging program components. By the time you finish reading this section and working through its exercises, you'll be ready to write scripts of your own.

We also use the word "Core" in the title on purpose, because this section isn't an exhaustive treatment of every minute detail of the language. While we may finesse an obscurity or two along the way, the basics you'll see here should help you make sense of the exceptions when they pop up.

1

Getting Started

This chapter starts with a nontechnical introduction to Python and then takes a quick look at ways to run Python programs. Its main goal is to get you set up to run Python code on your own machine, so you can work along with the examples and exercises in the later chapters. Along the way, we'll study the bare essentials of Python configuration—just enough to get started. You don't have to work along with the book on your own, but we strongly encourage it if possible. Even if you can't, this chapter will be useful when you do start coding on your own.

We'll also take a quick first look at Python module files here. Most of the examples you see early in the book are typed at Python's interactive interpreter command-line. Code entered this way goes away as soon as you leave Python. If you want to save your code in a file, you need to know a bit about Python modules, so module fundamentals are introduced here. We'll save most module details for a later chapter.

Why Python?

If you've bought this book, chances are you already know what Python is, and why it's an important tool to learn. If not, you probably won't be sold on Python until you've learned the language by reading the rest of this book. But before jumping into details, we'd like to use a few pages to briefly introduce some of the main reasons behind Python's popularity. (Even if you don't care for nontechnical overviews, your manager might.)

An Executive Summary

Python is perhaps best described as an object-oriented scripting language: its design mixes software engineering features of traditional languages with the usability of scripting languages. But some of Python's best assets tell a more complete story.

It's object-oriented

Python is an object-oriented language, from the ground up. Its class model supports advanced notions such as polymorphism, operator overloading, and multiple inheritance; yet in the context of Python's dynamic typing, object-oriented programming (OOP) is remarkably easy to apply. In fact, if you don't understand these terms, you'll find they are much easier to learn with Python than with just about any other OOP language available.

Besides serving as a powerful code structuring and reuse device, Python's OOP nature makes it ideal as a scripting tool for object-oriented systems languages such as C++ and Java. For example, with the appropriate glue code, Python programs can subclass (specialize) classes implemented in C++ or Java. Of equal significance, OOP is an option in Python; you can go far without having to become an object guru all at once.

It's free

Python is freeware—something which has lately been come to be called *open source software*. As with Tcl and Perl, you can get the entire system for free over the Internet. There are no restrictions on copying it, embedding it in your systems, or shipping it with your products. In fact, you can even sell Python, if you're so inclined.

But don't get the wrong idea: "free" doesn't mean "unsupported." On the contrary, the Python online community responds to user queries with a speed that most commercial software vendors would do well to notice. Moreover, because Python comes with complete source code, it empowers developers and creates a large team of implementation experts. Although studying or changing a programming language's implementation isn't everyone's idea of fun, it's comforting to know that it's available as a final resort and ultimate documentation source.

It's portable

Python is written in portable ANSI C, and compiles and runs on virtually every major platform in use today. For example, it runs on Unix systems, Linux, MS-DOS, MS-Windows (95, 98, NT), Macintosh, Amiga, Be-OS, OS/2, VMS, QNX, and more. Further, Python programs are automatically compiled to portable *bytecode*, which runs the same on any platform with a compatible version of Python installed (more on this in the section "It's easy to use").

What that means is that Python programs that use the core language run the same on Unix, MS-Windows, and any other system with a Python interpreter. Most

Python ports also contain platform-specific extensions (e.g., COM support on MS-Windows), but the core Python language and libraries work the same everywhere.

Python also includes a standard interface to the Tk GUI system called Tkinter, which is portable to the X Window System, MS Windows, and the Macintosh, and now provides a native look-and-feel on each platform. By using Python's Tkinter API, Python programs can implement full-featured graphical user interfaces that run on all major GUI platforms without program changes.

It's powerful

From a features perspective, Python is something of a hybrid. Its tool set places it between traditional scripting languages (such as Tcl, Scheme, and Perl), and systems languages (such as C, C++, and Java). Python provides all the simplicity and ease of use of a scripting language, along with more advanced programming tools typically found in systems development languages. Unlike some scripting languages, this combination makes Python useful for substantial development projects. Some of the things we'll find in Python's high-level toolbox:

Dynamic typing
> Python keeps track of the kinds of objects your program uses when it runs; it doesn't require complicated type and size declarations in your code.

Built-in object types
> Python provides commonly used data structures such as lists, dictionaries, and strings, as an intrinsic part of the language; as we'll see, they're both flexible and easy to use.

Built-in tools
> To process all those object types, Python comes with powerful and standard operations, including concatenation (joining collections), slicing (extracting sections), sorting, mapping, and more.

Library utilities
> For more specific tasks, Python also comes with a large collection of precoded library tools that support everything from regular-expression matching to networking to object persistence.

Third-party utilities
> Because Python is freeware, it encourages developers to contribute precoded tools that support tasks beyond Python's built-ins; you'll find free support for COM, imaging, CORBA ORBs, XML, and much more.

Automatic memory management
> Python automatically allocates and reclaims ("garbage collects") objects when no longer used, and most grow and shrink on demand; Python, not you, keeps track of low-level memory details.

Programming-in-the-large support

Finally, for building larger systems, Python includes tools such as modules, classes, and exceptions; they allow you to organize systems into components, do OOP, and handle events gracefully.

Despite the array of tools in Python, it retains a remarkably simple syntax and design. As we'll see, the result is a powerful programming tool, which retains the usability of a scripting language.

It's mixable

Python programs can be easily "glued" to components written in other languages. In technical terms, by employing the Python/C integration APIs, Python programs can be both extended by (called to) components written in C or C++, and embedded in (called by) C or C++ programs. That means you can add functionality to the Python system as needed and use Python programs within other environments or systems.

Although we won't talk much about Python/C integration, it's a major feature of the language and one reason Python is usually called a scripting language. By mixing Python with components written in a compiled language such as C or C++, it becomes an easy-to-use frontend language and customization tool. It also makes Python good at rapid prototyping: systems may be implemented in Python first to leverage its speed of development, and later moved to C for delivery, one piece at a time, according to performance requirements.

Speaking of glue, the PythonWin port of Python for MS-Windows platforms also lets Python programs talk to other components written for the COM API, allowing Python to be used as a more powerful alternative to Visual Basic. And a new alternative implementation of Python, called JPython, lets Python programs communicate with Java programs, making Python an ideal tool for scripting Java-based web applications.

It's easy to use

For many, Python's combination of rapid turnaround and language simplicity make programming more fun than work. To run a Python program, you simply type it and run it. There are no intermediate compile and link steps (as when using languages such as C or C++). As with other interpreted languages, Python executes programs immediately, which makes for both an interactive programming experience and rapid turnaround after program changes.

Strictly speaking, Python programs are compiled (translated) to an intermediate form called *bytecode*, which is then run by the interpreter. But because the compile step is automatic and hidden to programmers, Python achieves the develop-

ment speed of an interpreter without the performance loss inherent in purely interpreted languages.

Of course, development cycle turnaround is only one aspect of Python's ease of
use. It also provides a deliberately simple syntax and powerful high-level built-in
tools. Python has been called "executable pseudocode": because it eliminates
much of the complexity in other tools, you'll find that Python programs are often a
fraction of the size of equivalent programs in languages such as C, C++, and Java.

It's easy to learn

This brings us to the topic of this book: compared to other programming languages, the core Python language is amazingly easy to learn. In fact, you can
expect to be coding significant Python programs in a matter of days (and perhaps
in just hours, if you're already an experienced programmer). That's good news
both for professional developers seeking to learn the language to use on the job,
as well as for end users of systems that expose a Python layer for customization or
control.*

Python on the Job

Besides being a well-designed programming language, Python is also useful for
accomplishing real-world tasks—the sorts of things developers do day in and day
out. It's commonly used in a variety of domains, as a tool for scripting other components and implementing standalone programs. Some of Python's major roles
help define what it is.

System utilities

Python's built-in interfaces to operating-system services make it ideal for writing portable, maintainable system-administration tools (sometimes called shell scripts).
Python comes with POSIX bindings and support for the usual OS tools: environment
variables, files, sockets, pipes, processes, threads, regular expressions, and so on.

GUIs

Python's simplicity and rapid turnaround also make it a good match for GUI programming. As previously mentioned, it comes with a standard object-oriented
interface to the Tk GUI API called Tkinter, which allows Python programs to
implement portable GUIs with native look and feel. If portability isn't a priority,

---

* So, you might ask, how in the world do Python trainers get any business? For one thing, there are still
challenges in Python beyond the core language that will keep you busy beyond those first few days. As
we'll see, Python's collection of libraries, as well as its peripheral tools (e.g., the Tkinter GUI and Python/
C integration APIs) are a big part of real Python programming.

you can also use MFC classes to build GUIs with the PythonWin port for MS Windows, X Window System interfaces on Unix, Mac toolbox bindings on the Macintosh, and KDE and GNOME interfaces for Linux. For applications that run in web browsers, JPython provides another GUI option.

Component integration

Python's ability to be extended by and embedded in C and C++ systems makes it useful as a glue language, for scripting the behavior of other systems and components. For instance, by integrating a C library into Python, Python can test and launch its components. And by embedding Python in a product, it can code on-site customizations without having to recompile the entire product (or ship its source code to your customers). Python's COM support on MS-Windows and the JPython system provide alternative ways to script applications.

Rapid prototyping

To Python programs, components written in Python and C look the same. Because of this, it's possible to prototype systems in Python initially and then move components to a compiled language such as C or C++ for delivery. Unlike some prototyping tools, Python doesn't require a complete rewrite once the prototype has solidified; parts of the system that don't require the efficiency of a language such as C++ can remain coded in Python for ease of maintenance and use.

Internet scripting

Python comes with standard Internet utility modules that allow Python programs to communicate over sockets, extract form information sent to a server-side CGI script, parse HTML, transfer files by FTP, process XML files, and much more. There are also a number of peripheral tools for doing Internet programming in Python. For instance, the HTMLGen and pythondoc systems generate HTML files from Python class-based descriptions, and the JPython system mentioned above provides for seamless Python/Java integration.*

Numeric programming

The NumPy numeric programming extension for Python includes such advanced tools as an array object, interfaces to standard mathematical libraries, and much more. By integrating Python with numeric routines coded in a compiled language

---

* We say more about JPython and other systems in Chapter 10, *Frameworks and Applications*. Among other things, JPython can compile Python programs to Java virtual machine code (so they may run as client-side applets in any Java-aware browser) and allows Python programs to talk to Java libraries (for instance, to create AWT GUIs on a client).

for speed, NumPy turns Python into a sophisticated yet easy-to-use numeric programming tool.

Database programming

Python's standard pickle module provides a simple object-persistence system: it allows programs to easily save and restore entire Python objects to files. For more traditional database demands, there are Python interfaces to Sybase, Oracle, Informix, ODBC, and more. There is even a portable SQL database API for Python that runs the same on a variety of underlying database systems, and a system named *gadfly* that implements an SQL database for Python programs.

And more: Image processing, AI, distributed objects, etc.

Python is commonly applied in more domains than can be mentioned here. But in general, many are just instances of Python's component integration role in action. By adding Python as a frontend to libraries of components written in a compiled language such as C, Python becomes useful for scripting in a variety of domains.

For instance, image processing for Python is implemented as a set of library components implemented in a compiled language such as C, along with a Python frontend layer on top used to configure and launch the compiled components. The easy-to-use Python layer complements the efficiency of the underlying compiled-language components. Since the majority of the "programming" in such a system is done in the Python layer, most users need never deal with the complexity of the optimized components (and can get by with the core language covered in this text).

Python in Commercial Products

From a more concrete perspective, Python is also being applied in real revenue-generating products, by real companies. For instance, here is a partial list of current Python users:

- Red Hat uses Python in its Linux install tools.

- Microsoft has shipped a product partially written in Python.

- Infoseek uses Python as an implementation and end-user customization language in web search products.

- Yahoo! uses Python in a variety of its Internet services.

- NASA uses Python for mission-control-system implementation.

- Lawrence Livermore Labs uses Python for a variety of numeric programming tasks.

- Industrial Light and Magic and others use Python to produce commercial-grade animation.

There are even more exciting applications of Python we'd like to mention here, but alas, some companies prefer not to make their use of Python known because they consider it to be a competitive advantage. See Python's web site (*http://www. python.org*) for a more comprehensive and up-to-date list of companies using Python.

Python Versus Similar Tools

Finally, in terms of what you may already know, people sometimes compare Python to languages such as Perl, Tcl, and Java. While these are also useful tools to know and use, we think Python:

- Is more powerful than Tcl, which makes it applicable to larger systems development

- Has a cleaner syntax and simpler design than Perl, which makes it more readable and maintainable

- Doesn't compete head-on with Java; Python is a scripting language, Java is a systems language such as C++

Especially for programs that do more than scan text files, and that might have to be read in the future by others (or by you!), we think Python fits the bill better than any other scripting language available today. Of course, both of your authors are card-carrying Python evangelists, so take these comments as you may.

And that concludes the hype portion of this book. The best way to judge a language is to see it in action, so now we turn to a strictly technical introduction to the language. In the remainder of this chapter, we explore ways to run Python programs, peek at some useful configuration and install details, and introduce you to the notion of module files for making code permanent. Again, our goal here is to give you just enough information to run the examples and exercises in the rest of the book; we won't really start programming until Chapter 2, *Types and Operators*, but make sure you have a handle on the start-up details shown here before moving on.

How to Run Python Programs

So far, we've mostly talked about Python as a programming language. But it's also a software package called an *interpreter*. An interpreter is a kind of program that executes other programs. When you write Python programs, the Python interpreter reads your program, and carries out the instructions it contains.* In this section we explore ways to tell the Python interpreter which programs to run.

When the Python package is installed on your machine, it generates a number of components. Depending on how you use it, the Python interpreter may take the form of an executable program, or a set of libraries linked into another program. In general, there are at least five ways to run programs through the Python interpreter:

- Interactively

- As Python module files

- As Unix-style script files

- Embedded in another system

- Platform-specific launching methods

Let's look at each of these strategies in turn.

Other Ways to Launch Python Programs

Caveat: to keep things simple, the description of using the interpreter in this chapter is fairly generic and stresses lowest-common-denominator ways to run Python programs (i.e., the command line, which works the same everywhere Python runs). For information on other ways to run Python on specific platforms, flip ahead to Appendix B, *Platform-Specific Topics*. For instance, Python ports for MS-Windows and the Macintosh include graphical interfaces for editing and running code, which may be more to your taste.

Depending on your platform and background, you may also be interested in seeing a description of the new IDLE Integrated Development Environment for Python—a graphical interface for editing, running, and debugging Python code that runs on any platform where Python's Tk support is installed (IDLE is a Python program that uses the Tkinter extension we'll meet in Part II). You can find this description in Appendix A, *Python Resources*. Emacs users can also find support at Python's web site for launching Python code in the Emacs environment; again, see Appendix A for details.

---

* Technically, Python programs are first compiled (i.e., translated) to an intermediate form—byte-code—which is then scanned by the Python interpreter. This byte-code compilation step is hidden and automatic, and makes Python faster than a pure interpreter.

The Interactive Command Line

Perhaps the simplest way to run Python programs is to type them at Python's interactive command line. Assuming the interpreter is installed as an executable program on your system, typing `python` at your operating system's prompt without any arguments starts the interactive interpreter. For example:

```
% python
>>> print 'Hello world!'
Hello world!
>>> lumberjack = "okay"
>>>                                    # Ctrl-D to exit (Ctrl-Z on some platforms)
```

Here `python` is typed at a Unix (or MS-DOS) prompt to begin an interactive Python session. Python prompts for input with >>> when it's waiting for you to type a new Python statement. When working interactively, the results of statements are displayed after the >>> lines. On most Unix machines, the two-key combination Ctrl-D (press the Ctrl key, then press D while Ctrl is held down) exits the interactive command-line and returns you to your operating system's command line; on MS-DOS and Windows systems, you may need to type Ctrl-Z to exit.

Now, we're not doing much in the previous example: we type Python `print` and assignment statements, which we'll study in detail later. But notice that the code we entered is executed immediately by the interpreter. For instance, after typing a `print` statement at the >>> prompt, the output (a Python string) is echoed back right away. There's no need to run the code through a compiler and linker first, as you'd normally do when using a language such as C or C++.

Because code is executed immediately, the interactive prompt turns out to be a handy place to experiment with the language, and we'll use it often in this part of the book to demonstrate small examples. In fact, this is the first rule of thumb: if you're ever in doubt about how a piece of Python code works, fire up the interactive command line and try it out. That's what it's there for.

The interactive prompt is also commonly used as a place to test the components of larger systems. As we'll see, the interactive command line lets us import components interactively and test their interfaces rapidly. Partly because of this interactive nature, Python supports an experimental and exploratory programming style you'll find convenient when starting out.

A word on prompts: we won't meet compound (multiple-line) statements until Chapter 3, *Basic Statements*, but as a preview, you should know that when typing lines two and beyond of a compound statement interactively, the prompt changes to ... instead of >>>. At the ... prompt, a blank line (hitting the Enter key) tells Python that you're done typing the statement. This is different from compound statements typed into files, where blank lines are simply ignored. You'll see why this matters in Chapter 3. These two prompts can also be changed (in Part II, we'll see that they are attributes in the built-in **sys** module), but we'll assume they haven't been in our examples.

Running Module Files

Although the interactive prompt is great for experimenting and testing, it has one big disadvantage: programs you type there go away as soon as the Python interpreter executes them. The code you type interactively is never stored in a file, so you can't run it again without retyping it from scratch. Cut-and-paste and command recall can help some here, but not much, especially when you start writing larger programs.

To save programs permanently, you need Python *module files*. Module files are simply text files containing Python statements. You can ask the Python interpreter to execute such a file by listing its name in a **python** command. As an example, suppose we start our favorite text editor and type two Python statements into a text file named *spam.py*:

```
import sys
print sys.argv                    # more on this later
```

Again, we're ignoring the syntax of the statements in this file for now, so don't sweat the details; the point to notice is that we've typed code into a file, rather than at the interactive prompt. Once we've saved our text file, we can ask Python to run it by listing the filename as an argument on a **python** command in the operating system shell:

```
% python spam.py -i eggs -o bacon
['spam.py', '-i', 'eggs', '-o', 'bacon']
```

Notice that we called the module file *spam.py*; we could also call it simply *spam*, but for reasons we'll explain later, files of code we want to import into a client have to end with a *.py* suffix. We also listed four command-line arguments to be used by the Python program (the items after **python spam.py**); these are passed to the Python program, and are available through the name **sys.argv**, which works like the C argv array. By the way, if you're working on a Windows or MS-DOS platform, this example works the same, but the system prompt is normally different:

```
C:\book\tests> python spam.py -i eggs -o bacon
['spam.py', '-i', 'eggs', '-o', 'bacon']
```

Running Unix-Style Scripts

So far, we've seen how to type code interactively and run files of code created with a text editor (modules). If you're going to use Python on a Unix, Linux, or Unix-like system, you can also turn files of Python code into executable programs, much as you would for programs coded in a shell language such as *csh* or *ksh*. Such files are usually called *scripts*; in simple terms, Unix-style scripts are just text files containing Python statements, but with two special properties:

Their first line is special

Scripts usually start with a first line that begins with the characters #!, followed by the path to the Python interpreter on your machine.

They usually have executable privileges

Script files are usually marked as executable, to tell the operating system that they may be run as top-level programs. On Unix systems, a command such as chmod +x file.py usually does the trick.

Let's look at an example. Suppose we use our favorite text editor again, to create a file of Python code called *brian*:

```
#!/usr/local/bin/python
print 'The Bright Side of Life...'          # another comment here
```

We put the special line at the top of the file to tell the system where the Python interpreter lives. Technically, the first line is a Python comment. All comments in Python programs start with a # and span to the end of the line; they are a place to insert extra information for human readers of your code. But when a comment such as the first line in this file appears, it's special, since the operating system uses it to find an interpreter for running the program code in the rest of the file.

We also called this file simply *brian*, without the *.py* suffix we used for the module file earlier. Adding a *.py* to the name wouldn't hurt (and might help us remember that this is a Python program file); but since we don't plan on letting other modules import the code in this file, the name of the file is irrelevant. If we give our file executable privileges with a chmod +x brian shell command, we can run it from the operating system shell as though it were a binary program:

```
% brian
The Bright Side of Life...
```

A note for Windows and MS-DOS users: the method described here is a Unix trick, and may not work on your platform. Not to worry: just use the module file technique from the previous section. List the file's name on an explicit **python** command line:

```
C:\book\tests> python brian
The Bright Side of Life...
```

In this case, you don't need the special #! comment at the top (though Python just ignores it if it's present), and the file doesn't need to be given executable privileges. In fact, if you want to run files portably between Unix and MS-Windows, your life will probably be simpler if you always use the module file approach, not Unix-style scripts, to launch programs.

 On some systems, you can avoid hardcoding the path to the Python interpreter by writing the special first-line comment like this: #!/ usr/bin/env python. When coded this way, the **env** program locates the **python** interpreter according to your system search-path settings (i.e., in most Unix shells, by looking in all directories listed in the **PATH** environment variable). This **env**-based scheme can be more portable, since you don't need to hardcode a Python install path in the first line of all your scripts; provided you have access to **env** everywhere, your scripts will run no matter where **python** lives on your system.

Embedded Code and Objects

We've seen how to run code interactively, and how to launch module files and Unix-style scripts. That covers most of the cases we'll see in this book. But in some specialized domains, Python code may also be run by an enclosing system. In such cases, we say that Python programs are embedded in (i.e., run by) another program. The Python code itself may be entered into a text file, stored in a database, fetched from an HTML page, and so on. But from an operational perspective, another system—not you—may tell Python to run the code you've created.

For example, it's possible to create and run strings of Python code from a C program by calling functions in the Python runtime API (a set of services exported by the libraries created when Python is compiled on your machine):

```
#include <Python.h>
. . .
Py_Initialize();
PyRun_SimpleString("x = brave + sir + robin");
```

In this code snippet, a program coded in the C language (`somefile.c`) embeds the Python interpreter by linking in its libraries and passes it a Python assignment statement string to run. C programs may also gain access to Python objects, and process or execute them using other Python API tools.

This book isn't about Python/C integration, so we won't go into the details of what's really happening here.* But you should be aware that, depending on how your organization plans to use Python, you may or may not be the one who actually starts the Python programs you create. Regardless, you can still use the interactive and file-based launching techniques described here, to test code in isolation from those enclosing systems that may eventually use it.

Platform-Specific Startup Methods

Finally, depending on which type of computer you are using, there may be more specific ways to start Python programs than the general techniques we outlined above. For instance, on some Windows ports of Python, you may either run code from a Unix-like command-line interface, or by double-clicking on Python program icons. And on Macintosh ports, you may be able to drag Python program icons to the interpreter's icon, to make program files execute. We'll have more to say about platform-specific details like this in an appendix to this book.

What You Type and Where You Type It

With all these options and commands, it's easy for beginners to be confused about which command is entered at which prompt. Here's a quick summary:

Starting interactive Python
> The Python interpreter is usually started from the system's command line:
>
> ```
> % python
> ```

Entering code interactively
> Programs may be typed at Python's interactive interpreter command line:
>
> ```
> >>> print X
> ```

Entering code in files for later use
> Programs may also be typed into text files, using your favorite text editor:
>
> ```
> print X
> ```

Starting script files
> Unix-style script files are started from the system shell:
>
> ```
> % brian
> ```

---

* See *Programming Python* for more details on embedding Python in C/C++.

Starting program (module) files

Module files are run from the system shell:

```
% python spam.py
```

Running embedded code

When Python is embedded, Python code may be entered in arbitrary ways.

When typing Python programs (either interactively or into a text file), be sure to start all your unnested statements in column 1. If you don't, Python prints a "SyntaxError" message. Until the middle of Chapter 3, all our statements will be unnested, so this includes everything for now. We'll explain why later—it has to do with Python's indentation rules—but this seems to be a recurring confusion in introductory Python classes.

A First Look at Module Files

Earlier in this chapter, we saw how to run module files (i.e., text files containing Python statements) from the operating-system shell's command line. It turns out that we can also run module files from Python's interactive command line by importing or reloading them, as we'd normally do from other system components. The details of this process are covered in Chapter 5, *Modules*, but since this turns out to be a convenient way to save and run examples, we'll give a quick introduction to the process.

The basic idea behind importing modules is that importers may gain access to names assigned at the top level of a module file. The names are usually assigned to services exported by the modules. For instance, suppose we use our favorite text editor to create the one-line Python module file *myfile.py*, shown in the following code snippet. This may be one of the world's simplest Python modules, but it's enough to illustrate basic module use:

```
title = "The Meaning of Life"
```

Notice that the filename has a *.py* suffix: this naming convention is required for files imported from other components. Now we can access this module's variable `title` in other components two different ways, either by importing the module as a whole with an **import** statement and qualifying the module by the variable name we want to access:

```
% python                 Start Python
>>> import myfile         Run file, load module as a whole
>>> print myfile.title    Use its names: '.' qualification
The Meaning of Life
```

or by fetching (really, copying) names out of a module with `from` statements:

```
% python                          Start Python
>>> from myfile import title      Run file, load its names
>>> print title                   Use name directly: no need to qualify
The Meaning of Life
```

As we'll see later, `from` is much like an `import`, with an extra assignment to names in the importing component. Notice that both statements list the name of the module file as simply *myfile*, without its *.py* suffix; when Python looks for the actual file, it knows to include the suffix.

Whether we use `import` or `from`, the statements in the module file *myfile.py* are executed, and the importing component (here, the interactive prompt) gains access to names assigned at the top level of the file. There's only one such name in this simple example—the variable `title`, assigned to a string—but the concept will be more useful when we start defining objects such as functions and classes. Such objects become services accessed by name from one or more client modules.

When a module file is imported the first time in a session, Python executes all the code inside it, from the top to the bottom of the file. Because of this, importing a module interactively is another way to execute its code all at once (instead of, for instance, running it from the system shell with a command such as `python myfile.py`). But there's one catch to this process: Python executes a module file's code only the first time it's imported. If you import it again during the same interactive session, Python won't reexecute the file's code, even if you've changed it with your editor. To really rerun a file's code without stopping and restarting the interactive interpreter, you can use the Python `reload` function, as follows:

```
% python                          Start Python
>>> import myfile                 Run/load module
>>> print myfile.title            Qualify to fetch name
The Meaning of Life
```

Change myfile.py in your text editor

```
>>> import myfile                 Will NOT rerun the file's code
>>> reload(myfile)                WILL rerun the file's (current) code
```

While this scheme works, `reload` has a few complications, and we suggest you avoid it for now (just exit and reenter the interpreter between file changes). On the other hand, this has proven to be a popular testing technique in Python classes, so you be the judge.

A First Look at Namespace Inspection

Another trick that has proven popular is using the `dir` built-in function to keep track of defined names while programming interactively. We'll have more to say about it later, but before we turn you loose to work on some exercises, here is a brief introduction. If you call the `dir` function without arguments, you get back a Python list (described in Chapter 2) containing all the names defined in the interactive namespace:

```
>>> x = 1
>>> y = "shrubbery"
>>> dir()
['__builtins__', '__doc__', '__name__', 'x', 'y']
```

Here, the expression `dir()` is a *function call*; it asks Python to run the function named `dir`. We'll meet functions in Chapter 4, *Functions*; but for now, keep in mind that you need to add parenthesis after a function name to call it (whether it takes any arguments or not).

When `dir` is called, some of the names it returns are names you get "for free": they are built-in names that are always predefined by Python. For instance, `__name__` is the module's filename, and `__builtins__` is a module containing all the built-in names in Python (including `dir`). Other names are variables that you've assigned values to (here, `x` and `y`). If you call `dir` with a module as an *argument*, you get back the names defined inside that module:[*]

```
% cat threenames.py
a = 'dead'
b = 'parrot'
c = 'sketch'
% python
>>> import threenames
>>> dir(threenames)
['__builtins__', '__doc__', '__file__', '__name__', 'a', 'b', 'c']
>>> dir(__builtins__)
```
All the names Python predefines for you

Later, we'll see that some objects have additional ways of telling clients which names they expose (e.g., special attributes such as `__methods__` and `__members__`). But for now, the `dir` function lets you do as much poking around as you'll probably care to do.

Python Configuration Details

So far, we've seen how to make the Python interpreter execute programs we've typed. But besides the interpreter, a Python installation also comes with a collec-

---

[*] Technically, in the module's *namespace*—a term we'll soon use so often that you'll probably get tired of hearing it. Since we're being technical anyhow, the interactive command line is really a module too, called `__main__`; code you enter there works as if it were put in a module file, except that expression results are printed back to you. Notice that the result of a `dir` call is a list, which could be processed by a Python program. For now, hold that thought: namespaces can be fetched in other ways too.

tion of utility programs, stored in the Python source library. Moreover, the Python interpreter recognizes settings in the system shell's environment, which let us tailor the interpreter's behavior (where it finds the source-code files, for example). This section talks about the environment settings commonly used by Python programmers, peeks at Python installation details, and presents an example script that illustrates most of the configuration steps you'll probably need to know about. If you have access to a ready-to-run Python, you can probably skip much of this section, or postpone it for a later time.

Environment Variables

The Python interpreter recognizes a handful of environment variable settings, but only a few are used often enough to warrant explanation here. Table 1-1 summarizes the main Python variable settings.

Table 1-1. Important Environment Variables

Role	Variable
System shell search path (for finding "python")	PATH (or path)
Python module search path (for imports)	PYTHONPATH
Path to Python interactive startup file	PYTHONSTARTUP
GUI extension variables (Tkinter)	TCL_LIBRARY, TK_LIBRARY

These variables are straightforward to use, but here are a few pointers:

- The PATH setting lists a set of directories that the operating system searches for executable programs. It should normally include the directory where your Python interpreter lives (the python program on Unix, or the *python.exe* file on Windows). You don't need to set this on the Macintosh (the install handles path details).

- The PYTHONPATH setting serves a role similar to PATH: the Python interpreter consults the PYTHONPATH variable to locate module files when you import them in a program. This variable is set to a list of directories that Python searches to find an imported module at runtime. You'll usually want to include your own source-code directories and the Python source library's directory (unless it's been preset in your Python installation).

- If PYTHONSTARTUP is set to the pathname of a file of Python code, Python executes the file's code automatically whenever you start the interactive interpreter, as though you had typed it at the interactive command line. This is a handy way to make sure you always load utilities whenever you're working interactively.

- Provided you wish to use the Tkinter GUI extension (see Chapter 10, *Frameworks and Applications*), the two GUI variables in Table 1-1 should be set to the name of the source library directories of the Tcl and Tk systems (much like `PYTHONPATH`).

Unfortunately, the way to set these variables and what to set them to depends on your system's configuration. For instance, on Unix systems the way to set variables depends on the shell; under the *csh* shell, you might set this to the Python module search path:

```
setenv PYTHONPATH .:/usr/local/lib/python:/usr/local/lib/python/tkinter
```

which tells Python to look for imported modules in three directories: the current directory (.), the directory where the Python source library is installed on your machine (here, */usr/local/lib/python*), and the `tkinter` source library subdirectory, where the Python GUI extension support code resides. But if you're using the ksh shell, the setting might instead look like this:

```
export PYTHONPATH=".:/usr/local/lib/python:/usr/local/lib/python/tkinter"
```

And if you're using MS-DOS, an environment configuration could be something very different still:

```
set PYTHONPATH=.;c:\python\lib;c:\python\lib\tkinter
```

Since this isn't a book on operating system shells, we're going to defer to other sources for more details. Consult your system shell's manpages or other documentation for details. And if you have trouble figuring out what your settings must be, ask your system administrator (or other local guru) for help.

An Example Startup Script

The code below, call it *runpy*, pulls some of these details together in a simple Python startup script. It sets the necessary environment variables to reasonable values (on Mark's machine, at least) and starts the Python interactive interpreter. To use it, type runpy at your system shell's prompt.

```
#!/bin/csh
# Give this file executable privileges (chmod +x runpy).
# Put this info in your .cshrc file to make it permanent.

# 1) Add path to command-line interpreter
set path = (/usr/local/bin $path)

# 2) Set python library search paths (unless predefined)
# add your module file directories to the list as desired
setenv PYTHONPATH \
     .:/usr/local/lib/python:/usr/local/lib/python/tkinter

# 3) Set tk library search paths for GUIs (unless predefined)
```

```
setenv TCL_LIBRARY /usr/local/lib/tcl8.0
setenv TK_LIBRARY  /usr/local/lib/tk8.0

# 4) Start up the interactive command-line
python
```

runpy illustrates a typical Python configuration, but it has a few drawbacks:

- It's written to only work under the *csh* shell, a command-line processor common on Unix and Linux platforms; you'll need to interpolate if you're not a *csh* user.

- The settings it illustrates are usually made once in your shell's startup file (*~/.cshrc* for *csh* users), instead of each time you run Python.

- Depending on how your Python was built, you may not need to list the paths to standard source libraries, since they might be hardwired into your installation.

A note for MS-Windows users: a similar configuration can be created in a MS-DOS batch file, which might look something like this, depending on which Windows port of Python you've installed:

```
PATH c:\python;%PATH%
set PYTHONPATH=.;c:\python\lib;c:\python\lib\tkinter
set TCL_LIBRARY=c:\Program Files\Tcl\lib\tcl8.0
set TK_LIBRARY=c:\Program Files\Tcl\lib\tk8.0
python
```

A GUI Test Session

If you or your administrator have installed Python with the Tkinter GUI extension, the following interactive session shows one way to test your Python/GUI configuration. (You can skip this section if you won't be using Tkinter.)

```
% runpy
Version/copyright information...
>>> from Tkinter import *
>>> w = Button(text="Hello", command='exit')
>>> w.pack()
>>> w.mainloop()
```

Type *runpy* at the system shell and then all the Python code shown after the Python >>> prompts. Ignore the details in the example's code for now; we study Tkinter in Chapter 10. If everything is set up properly, you should get a window on your screen that looks something like Figure 1-1 (shown running on a MS-Windows machine; it looks slightly different on the X Window System or a Macintosh, since Tkinter provides for native look and feel).

If this test doesn't work, start checking your environment variable path settings, and/or the Python install. Tkinter is an optional extension that must be explicitly enabled, so make sure it's in your version of Python. Also make sure you have

Figure 1-1. Tkinter GUI test screen

access to the Tcl/Tk source libraries; they're required by the current Python Tkinter implementation. See the *README* files in the Python source distribution and the Python web site for more details.

Installation Overview

In the interest of completeness, this section provides a few pointers on the Python installation process. When you're just getting started with Python, you normally shouldn't need to care about Python installation procedures. Hopefully, someone else—perhaps your system administrator—has already installed Python on your platform, and you can skip most of the information here.

But this isn't always the case, and even if Python is already installed on your machine, installation details may become more important as your knowledge of Python grows. In some scenarios, it's important to know how to build Python from its source code, so you can bind in extensions of your own statically. But again, this isn't a book on Python/C integration, so if Python has already been installed for you, you may want to file this section away for future reference.

Python comes in binary or C source-code forms

You can get Python as either a prebuilt binary executable (which runs "out of the box") or in its C source-code form (which you must compile on your machine before it can run). Both forms can be found in a variety of media— the Python web/FTP sites (see Appendix A), CDs accompanying Python books, independent CD distributors, Linux distributions, and so on. Naturally, if you go for the binary format, you must get one that's compatible with your machine; if you use the C source-code distribution, you'll need a C compiler/ build system on your machine. Both forms are usually distributed as compressed archive files, which means you usually need utilities such as `gzip` and `tar` to unpack the file on your computer (though some Windows ports install themselves).

C source code configures/builds automatically

Although getting Python in binary form means you don't need to compile it yourself, it also means you have little control over what extensions are enabled; you'll get the extensions that the person who built the binary happened to think were important. Moreover, besides the Python binary itself, you need to get and install the Python source library, which may or may not be included in a Python binary package. For more control, fetch the full Python C source-code distribution and compile it on your machine. We won't list the compile commands here, but the source-code build procedure is largely automatic; Python configures its own `makefiles` according to your platform, and Python compiles without a glitch on just about any platform you might mention.

Don't build from source unless you've used a C compiler before

Having said that, we should note that even automated C compiles of a large system like Python are not to be taken lightly. If you've never used a C compiler before, we suggest you try to obtain a Python binary package for your platform first, before falling back on building Python from its source-code on your machine. And as usual, you can always ask a local C guru for assistance with the build or install.

Prebuilt Python binaries exist for most platforms now, including MS-Windows, the Macintosh, and most flavors of Unix; see Python's web site for links. We should also note that the full C source-code distribution contains the entire Python system, and is true freeware; there are no copyright constraints preventing you from using it in your products. Although hacking an interpreter's source code isn't everybody's cup of tea, it's comforting to know that you have control over all the source code in your Python system.

For more details on installing and building Python, see the *README* files in the C source-code distribution, the Python web site, and other Python texts such as *Programming Python*. And for pointers to various Python distributions, see the URLs listed in Appendix A.

Summary

In this chapter, we've explored ways to launch Python programs, the basics of Python module files and namespace inspection, and Python configuration and installation details. Hopefully, you should now have enough information to start interacting with the Python interpreter. In Chapter 2, we explore basic object types in Python, before looking at statements and larger program components.

Exercises

Okay: time to start doing a little coding on your own. This session is fairly simple, but a few of these questions hint at topics to come in later chapters. Remember, check Appendix C, *Solutions to Exercises*, for the answers; they sometimes contain supplemental information not discussed in the chapters. In other words, you should peek, even if you can manage to get all the answers on your own.

1. *Interaction.* Start the Python command line, and type the expression: `"Hello World!"` (including the quotes). The string should be echoed back to you. The purpose of this exercise is to get your environment configured to run Python. You may need to add the path to the `python` executable to your **PATH** environment variable. Set it in your *.cshrc* or *.kshrc* file to make Python permanently available on Unix systems; use a *setup.bat* or *autoexec.bat* file on Windows.

2. *Programs.* With the text editor of your choice, write a simple module file—a file containing the single statement: `print 'Hello module world!'`. Store this statement in a file named *module1.py*. Now, run this file by passing it to the Python interpreter program on the system shell's command line.

3. *Modules.* Next, start the Python command line and import the module you wrote in the prior exercise. Does your **PYTHONPATH** setting include the directory where the file is stored? Try moving the file to a different directory and importing it again; what happens? (Hint: is there still a file named *module1.pyc* in the original directory?)

4. *Scripts.* If your platform supports it, add the `#!` line to the top of your *module1.py* module, give the file executable privileges, and run it directly as an executable. What does the first line need to contain?

5. *Errors.* Experiment with typing mathematical expressions and assignments at the Python command line. First type the expression: `1 / 0`; what happens? Next, type a variable name you haven't assigned a value to yet; what happens this time? You may not know it yet, but you're doing exception processing, a topic we'll explore in depth in Chapter 7, *Exceptions*. We'll also see Python's source debugger, `pdb`, in Chapter 8, *Built-in Tools*; if you can't wait that long, either flip to that chapter, or see other Python documentation sources. Python's default error messages will probably be as much error handling as you need when first starting out.

6. *Breaks.* At the Python command line, type:

```
L = [1, 2]
L.append(L)
L
```

What happens? If you're using a Python version older than 1.5.1, a Ctrl-C key combination will probably help on most platforms. Why do you think this occurs? What does Python report when you type the Ctrl-C key combination? *Warning:* if you have a Python older than release 1.5.1, make sure your machine can stop a program with a break-key combination of some sort before running this test, or you may be waiting a long time.

2

Types and Operators

This chapter begins our tour of the Python language. From an abstract perspective, in Python we write programs that do *things with stuff.*[*] Programs take the form of statements, which we'll meet later. Here, we're interested in the *stuff* our programs do things to. And in Python, stuff always takes the form of *objects*. They may be built-in kinds of objects Python provides for us, or objects we create using Python or C tools. Either way, we're always doing things to objects in Python.

Naturally, there's more to Python development than doing things to stuff. But since the subjects of Python programs are the most fundamental notion in Python programming, we start with a survey of Python's built-in object types.

Python Program Structure

By way of introduction, let's first get a clear picture of how what we study in this chapter fits into the overall Python picture. From a more concrete perspective, Python programs can be decomposed into modules, statements, and objects, as follows:

1. Programs are composed of modules.

2. Modules contain statements.

3. Statements create and process *objects*.

---

* Pardon our formality: we're computer scientists.

26

Why Use Built-in Types?

If you've used lower-level languages such as C or C++, you know that much of your work centers on implementing objects—what some folks call *data structures*—to represent the components in your application's domain. You need to lay out memory structures, manage memory allocation, implement search and access routines, and so on. These chores are about as tedious (and error prone) as they sound, and usually distract from your programs' real goals.

In typical Python programs, most of this grunt work goes away. Because Python provides powerful object types as an intrinsic part of the language, there's no need to code object implementations before you start solving problems. In fact, unless you have a need for special processing that built-in types don't provide, you're almost always better off using a built-in object instead of implementing your own. Here are some reasons why:

Built-in objects make simple programs easy to write

> For simple tasks, built-in types are often all you need to represent the structure of problem domains. Because we get things such as collections (lists) and search tables (dictionaries) for free, you can use them immediately. You can get a lot of work done with just Python's built-in object types alone.

Python provides objects and supports extensions

> In some ways, Python borrows both from languages that rely on built-in tools (e.g., LISP), and languages that rely on the programmer to provide tool implementations or frameworks of their own (e.g., C++). Although you can implement unique object types in Python, you don't need to do so just to get started. Moreover, because Python's built-ins are standard, they're always the same; frameworks tend to differ from site to site.

Built-in objects are components of extensions

> For more complex tasks you still may need to provide your own objects, using Python statements and C language interfaces. But as we'll see in later chapters, objects implemented manually are often built on top of built-in types such as lists and dictionaries. For instance, a stack data structure may be implemented as a class that manages a built-in list.

Built-in objects are often more efficient than custom data structures

> Python's built-in types employ already optimized data structure algorithms that are implemented in C for speed. Although you can write similar object types on your own, you'll usually be hard-pressed to get the level of performance built-in object types provide.

In other words, not only do built-in object types make programming easier, they're also more powerful and efficient than most of what can be created from scratch.

Regardless of whether you implement new object types or not, built-in objects form the core of every Python program.

Table 2-1 previews the built-in object types in this chapter. Some will probably seem familiar if you've used other languages (e.g., numbers, strings, and files), but others are more general and powerful than what you may be accustomed to. For instance, you'll find that lists and dictionaries obviate most of the work you do to support collections and searching in lower-level languages.

Table 2-1. Built-in Objects Preview

Object Type	Example Constants/Usage
Numbers	`3.1415, 1234, 999L, 3+4j`
Strings	`'spam', "guido's"`
Lists	`[1, [2, 'three'], 4]`
Dictionaries	`{'food':'spam', 'taste':'yum'}`
Tuples	`(1,'spam', 4, 'U')`
Files	`text = open('eggs', 'r').read()`

Numbers

On to the nitty-gritty. The first object type on our tour is Python numbers. In general, Python's number types are fairly typical and will seem familiar if you've used just about any other programming language in the past. Python supports the usual numeric types (integer and floating point), constants, and expressions. In addition, Python provides more advanced numeric programming support, including a complex number type, an unlimited precision integer, and a variety of numeric tool libraries. The next few sections give an overview of the numeric support in Python.

Standard Numeric Types

Among its basic types, Python supports the usual suspects: both integer and floating-point numbers, and all their associated syntax and operations. Like C, Python also allows you to write integers using hexadecimal and octal constants. Unlike C, Python also has a complex number type (introduced in Python 1.4), as well as a long integer type with unlimited precision (it can grow to have as many digits as your memory space allows). Table 2-2 shows what Python's numeric types look like when written out in a program (i.e., as constants).

Table 2-2. Numeric Constants

Constant	Interpretation
`1234, -24, 0`	Normal integers (C longs)
`999999999999L`	Long integers (unlimited size)

Table 2-2. Numeric Constants (continued)

Constant	Interpretation
`1.23, 3.14e-10, 4E210, 4.0e+210`	Floating-point (C doubles)
`0177, 0x9ff`	Octal and hex constants
`3+4j, 3.0+4.0j, 3J`	Complex number constants

By and large, Python's numeric types are straightforward, but a few are worth highlighting here:

Integer and floating-point constants

Integers are written as a string of decimal digits. Floating-point numbers have an embedded decimal point, and/or an optional signed exponent introduced by an `e` or `E`. If you write a number with a decimal point or exponent, Python makes it a floating-point object and uses floating-point (not integer) math when it's used in an expression. The rules for writing floating-point numbers are the same as with C.

Numeric precision

Plain Python integers (row 1) are implemented as C `longs` internally (i.e., at least 32 bits), and Python floating-point numbers are implemented as C `doubles`; Python numbers get as much precision as the C compiler used to build the Python interpreter gives to `longs` and `doubles`. On the other hand, if an integer constant ends with an `l` or `L`, it becomes a Python long integer (not to be confused with a C `long`) and can grow as large as needed.

Hexadecimal and octal constants

The rules for writing hexadecimal (base 16) and octal (base 8) integers are the same as in C: octal constants start with a leading zero (0), and hexadecimals start with a leading `0x` or `0X`. Notice that this means you can't write normal base-ten integers with a leading zero (e.g., `01`); Python interprets them as octal constants, which usually don't work as you'd expect!

Complex numbers

Python complex constants are written as `real-part + imaginary-part`, and terminated with a `j` or `J`. Internally, they are implemented as a pair of floating-point numbers, but all numeric operations perform complex math when applied to complex numbers.

Built-in Tools and Extensions

Besides the built-in number types shown in Table 2-2, Python provides a set of tools for processing number objects:

Expression operators

`+, *, >>, **`, etc.

Built-in mathematical functions
    pow, abs, etc.

Utility modules
    rand, math, etc.

We'll meet all of these as we go along. Finally, if you need to do serious number-crunching, an optional extension for Python called *Numeric Python* provides advanced numeric programming tools, such as a matrix data type and sophisticated computation libraries. Because it's so advanced, we won't say more about Numeric Python in this chapter; see the examples later in the book and Appendix A, *Python Resources*. Also note that, as of this writing, Numeric Python is an optional extension; it doesn't come with Python and must be installed separately.

Python Expression Operators

Perhaps the most fundamental tool that processes numbers is the *expression*: a combination of numbers (or other objects) and operators that computes a value when executed by Python. In Python, expressions are written using the usual mathematical notation and operator symbols. For instance, to add two numbers X and Y, we say X + Y, which tells Python to apply the + operator to the values named by X and Y. The result of the expression is the sum of X and Y, another number object.

Table 2-3 lists all the operator expressions available in Python. Many are self-explanatory; for instance, the usual mathematical operators are supported: +, -, *, /, and so on. A few will be familiar if you've used C in the past: % computes a division remainder, << performs a bitwise left-shift, & computes a bitwise and result, etc. Others are more Python-specific, and not all are numeric in nature: the is operator tests object identity (i.e., address) equality, lambda creates unnamed functions, and so on.

Table 2-3. Python Expression Operators and Precedence

Operators	Description
x or y, lambda args: expression	Logical or (y is evaluated only if x is false), anonymous function
x and y	Logical and (y is evaluated only if x is true)
not x	Logical negation
<, <=, >, >=, ==, <>, !=, is, is not, in, not in	Comparison operators, identity tests, sequence membership
x | y	Bitwise or
x ^ y	Bitwise exclusive or
x & y	Bitwise and

Table 2-3. Python Expression Operators and Precedence (continued)

Operators	Description
x << y, x >> y	Shift x left or right by y bits
x + y, x - y	Addition/concatenation, subtraction
x * y, x / y, x % y	Multiplication/repetition, division, remainder/format
-x, +x, ~x	Unary negation, identity, bitwise complement
x[i], x[i:j], x.y, x(...)	Indexing, slicing, qualification, function calls
(...), [...], {...}, `...`	Tuple, list, dictionary, conversion to string

Table 2-3 is mostly included for reference; since we'll see its operators in action later, we won't describe every entry here. But there are a few basic points we'd like to make about expressions before moving on.

Mixed operators: Operators bind tighter lower in the table

As in most languages, more complex expressions are coded by stringing together operator expressions in the table. For instance, the sum of two multiplications might be written as: A * B + C * D. So how does Python know which operator to perform first? When you write an expression with more than one operator, Python groups its parts according to what are called *precedence* rules, and this grouping determines the order in which expression parts are computed. In the table, operators lower in the table have higher precedence and so bind more tightly in mixed expressions. For example, if you write X + Y * Z, Python evaluates the multiplication first (Y * Z), then adds that result to X, because * has higher precedence (is lower in the table) than +.

Parentheses group subexpressions

If the prior paragraph sounded confusing, relax: you can forget about precedence completely if you're careful to group parts of expressions with parentheses. When you parenthesize subexpressions, you override Python precedence rules; Python always evaluates parenthesized expressions first, before using their results in enclosing expressions. For instance, instead of X + Y * Z, write (X + Y) * Z, or for that matter X + (Y * Z) to force Python to evaluate the expression in the desired order. In the former case, + is applied to X and Y first; in the latter, the * is performed first (as if there were no parentheses at all). Generally speaking, adding parentheses in big expressions is a great idea; it not only forces the evaluation order you want, but it also aids readability.

Mixed types: Converted up just as in C

Besides mixing operators in expressions, you can also mix numeric types. For instance, you can add an integer to a floating-point number, but this leads to another dilemma: what type is the result—integer or floating-point? The answer is simple, especially if you've used almost any other language before: in mixed type expressions, Python first converts operands up to the type of the most complex operand, and then performs the math on same-type operands. Python ranks the complexity of numeric types like so: integers are simpler than long integers, which are simpler than floating-point numbers, which are simpler than complex numbers. So, when an integer is mixed with a floating-point, the integer is converted up to a floating-point value first, and then floating-point math yields the floating-point result. Similarly, any mixed-type expression where one operand is a complex number results in the other operand being converted up to a complex, and yields a complex result.

Preview: operator overloading

Although we're focusing on built-in numbers right now, keep in mind that all Python operators may be overloaded by Python classes and C extension types, to work on objects you implement. For instance, you'll see later that objects coded with classes may be added with + expressions, indexed with [i] expressions, and so on. Furthermore, some operators are already overloaded by Python itself: they perform different actions depending on the type of built-in objects being processed. For example, the + operator performs *addition* when applied to numbers, but (as we'll see in a moment) performs *concatenation* when applied to sequence objects such as strings and lists.*

Numbers in Action

Perhaps the best way to understand numeric objects and expressions is to see them in action. Let's fire up the interactive command line and type some basic, but illustrative operations.

Basic operations

First of all, let's exercise some basic math: addition and division. In the following interaction, we first *assign two variables* (a and b) to integers, so we can use them later in a larger expression. We'll say more about this later, but in Python, variables are created when first assigned; there is no need to predeclare the names a and b before using them. In other words, the assignments cause these variables to spring into existence automatically.

```
% python
>>> a = 3          # name created
>>> b = 4
```

---

* This is usually called *polymorphism*—the meaning of an operation depends on the type of objects being operated on. But we're not quite ready for object-oriented ideas like this yet, so hold that thought for now.

We've also used a *comment* here. These were introduced in Chapter 1, *Getting Started*, but as a refresher: in Python code, text after a # mark and continuing to the end of the line is considered to be a comment, and is ignored by Python (it's a place for you to write human-readable documentation for your code; since code you type interactively is temporary, you won't normally write comments there, but we've added them to our examples to help explain the code). Now, let's use our integer objects in expressions; variables are replaced with their values, and expression results are echoed back to us:

```
>>> b / 2 + a      # same as ((4 / 2) + 3)
5
>>> b / (2.0 + a)  # same as (4 / (2.0 + 3))
0.8
```

In the first expression, there are no parentheses, so Python automatically groups the components according to its precedence rules; since / is lower in Table 2-3 than +, it binds more tightly, and so is evaluated first. The result is as if we had parenthesized the expression as shown in the comment to the right of the code. Also notice that all the numbers are integers in the first expression; because of that, Python performs integer division and addition.

In the second expression, we add parentheses around the + part to force Python to evaluate it first (i.e., before the /). We also made one of the operands floating point by adding a decimal point: 2.0. Because of the mixed types, Python converts the integer referenced by a up to a floating-point value (3.0) before performing the +. It also converts b up to a floating-point value (4.0) and performs a *floating-point* division: (4.0 / 5.0) yields a floating-point result of 0.8. If this were *integer* division instead, the result would be a truncated integer zero.

Bitwise operations

Besides the normal numeric operations (addition, subtraction, and so on), Python supports most of the numeric expressions available in the C language. For instance, here it's at work performing bitwise shift and Boolean operations:

```
>>> x = 1          # 0001
>>> x << 2         # shift left 2 bits: 0100
4
>>> x | 2          # bitwise OR: 0011
3
>>> x & 1          # bitwise AND: 0001
1
```

In the first expression, a binary 1 (in base 2, 0001) is shifted left two slots to create a binary 4 (0100). The last two operations perform a binary or (0001 | 0010 = 0011), and a binary and (0001 & 0001 = 0001). We won't go into much more detail on bit-twiddling here. It's supported if you need it, but be aware that it's often not as important in a high-level language such as Python as it is in a low-level language such as C. As a rule of thumb, if you find yourself wanting to flip bits in Python, you should think long and hard about which language you're really using. In general, there are often better ways to encode information in Python than bit strings.*

Long integers

Now for something more exotic: here's a look at long integers in action. When an integer constant ends with an L (or lowercase l), Python creates a long integer, which can be arbitrarily big:

```
>>> 9999999999999999999999999999 + 1
OverflowError: integer literal too large
>>> 9999999999999999999999999999L + 1
10000000000000000000000000000L
```

Here, the first expression fails and raises an error, because normal integers can't accommodate such a large number. On the other hand, the second works fine, because we tell Python to generate a long integer object instead.

Long integers are a convenient tool. In fact, you can use them to count the national debt in pennies, if you are so inclined. But because Python must do extra work to support their extended precision, long integer math is usually much slower than normal integer math. If you need the precision, it's built in for you to use. But as usual, there's no such thing as a free lunch.

Complex numbers

Complex numbers are a recent addition to Python. If you know what they are, you know why they are useful; if not, consider this section optional reading.† Complex numbers are represented as two floating-point numbers—the *real* and *imaginary* parts—and are coded by adding a j or J suffix to the imaginary part. We can also write complex numbers with a nonzero real part by adding the two parts with a +. For example, the complex number with a real part of 2 and an imaginary part of −3 is written: 2 + −3j. Some examples of complex math at work:

```
>>> 1j * 1J
(-1+0j)
>>> 2 + 1j * 3
(2+3j)
```

---

* Usually. As for every rule there are exceptions. For instance, if you interface with C libraries that expect bit strings to be passed in, our preaching doesn't apply.

† One of your authors is quick to point out that he has never had a need for complex numbers in some 15 years of development work. The other author isn't so lucky.

```
>>> (2+1j)*3
(6+3j)
```

Complex numbers also allow us to extract their parts as attributes, but since complex math is an advanced tool, check Python's language reference manual for additional details.

Other numeric tools

As mentioned above, Python also provides both built-in functions and built-in modules for numeric processing. Here are the built-in **math** module and a few built-in functions at work; we'll meet more built-ins in Chapter 8, *Built-in Tools*.

```
>>> import math
>>> math.pi
3.14159265359
>>>
>>> abs(-42), 2**4, pow(2, 4)
(42, 16, 16)
```

Notice that built-in modules such as **math** must be imported and qualified, but built-in functions such as **abs** are always available without imports. Really, modules are external components, but built-in functions live in an implied namespace, which Python searches to find names used in your program. This namespace corresponds to the module called __builtin__. We talk about name resolution in Chapter 4, *Functions*; for now, when we say "module", think "import."

Strings

The next major built-in type is the Python *string*—an ordered collection of characters, used to store and represent text-based information. From a functional perspective, strings can be used to represent just about anything that can be encoded as text: symbols and words (e.g., your name), contents of text files loaded into memory, and so on.

You've probably used strings in other languages too; Python's strings serve the same role as character arrays in languages such as C, but Python's strings are a higher level tool. Unlike C, there is no **char** type in Python, only one-character strings. And strictly speaking, Python strings are categorized as *immutable sequences*—big words that just mean that they respond to common sequence operations but can't be changed in place. In fact, strings are representative of the larger class of objects called sequences; we'll have more to say about what this means in a moment, but pay attention to the operations introduced here, because they'll work the same on types we'll see later.

Table 2-4 introduces common string constants and operations. Strings support expression operations such as *concatenation* (combining strings), *slicing* (extracting sections), *indexing* (fetching by offset), and so on. Python also provides a set of utility modules for processing strings you import. For instance, the `string` module exports most of the standard C library's string handling tools, and the `regex` and `re` modules add regular expression matching for strings (all of which are discussed in Chapter 8).

Table 2-4. Common String Constants and Operations

Operation	Interpretation
s1 = ''	Empty string
s2 = "spam's"	Double quotes
block = """..."""	Triple-quoted blocks
s1 + s2, s2 * 3	Concatenate, repeat
s2[i], s2[i:j], len(s2)	Index, slice, length
"a %s parrot" % 'dead'	String formatting
for x in s2, 'm' in s2	Iteration, membership

Empty strings are written as two quotes with nothing in between. Notice that string constants can be written enclosed in either single or double quotes; the two forms work the same, but having both allows a quote character to appear inside a string without escaping it with a backslash (more on backslashes later). The third line in the table also mentions a triple-quoted form; when strings are enclosed in three quotes, they may span any number of lines. Python collects all the triple-quoted text into a multiline string with embedded newline characters.

Strings in Action

Rather than getting into too many details right away, let's interact with the Python interpreter again to illustrate the operations in Table 2-4.

Basic operations

Strings can be concatenated using the + operator, and repeated using the * operator. Formally, adding two string objects creates a new string object with the contents of its operands joined; repetition is much like adding a string to itself a number of times. In both cases, Python lets you create arbitrarily sized strings; there's

no need to predeclare anything in Python, including the sizes of data structures.*
Python also provides a `len` built-in function that returns the length of strings (and
other objects with a length):

```
% python
>>> len('abc')          # length: number items
3
>>> 'abc' + 'def'       # concatenation: a new string
'abcdef'
>>> 'Ni!' * 4           # like "Ni!" + "Ni!" + ...
'Ni!Ni!Ni!Ni!'
```

Notice that operator overloading is at work here already: we're using the same
operators that were called addition and multiplication when we looked at numbers. Python is smart enough to do the correct operation, because it knows the
types of objects being added and multiplied. But be careful; Python doesn't allow
you to mix numbers and strings in + and * expressions: `'abc' + 9` raises an error,
instead of automatically converting 9 to a string. As shown in the last line in
Table 2-4, you can also *iterate* over strings in loops using `for` statements and test
membership with the `in` expression operator:

```
>>> myjob = "hacker"
>>> for c in myjob: print c,    # step though items
...
h a c k e r
>>> "k" in myjob                # 1 means true
1
```

But since you need to know something about statements and the meaning of truth
in Python to really understand `for` and `in`, let's defer details on these examples
until later.

Indexing and slicing

Because strings are defined as an ordered collection of characters, we can access
their components by position. In Python, characters in a string are fetched by
indexing—providing the numeric offset of the desired component in square brackets after the string. As in C, Python offsets start at zero and end at one less than
the length of the string. Unlike C, Python also lets you fetch items from sequences
such as strings using negative offsets. Technically, negative offsets are added to the
length of a string to derive a positive offset. But you can also think of negative offsets as counting backwards from the end (or right, if you prefer).

---

* Unlike C character arrays, you don't need to allocate or manage storage arrays when using Python
strings. Simply create string objects as needed, and let Python manage the underlying memory space.
Internally, Python reclaims unused objects' memory space automatically, using a reference-count *garbage
collection* strategy. Each object keeps track of the number of names, data-structures, etc. that reference it;
when the count reaches zero, Python frees the object's space. This scheme means Python doesn't have
to stop and scan all of memory to find unused space to free; it also means that objects that reference
themselves might not be collected automatically.

```
>>> S = 'spam'
>>> S[0], S[-2]                    # indexing from front or end
('s', 'a')
>>> S[1:3], S[1:], S[:-1]          # slicing: extract section
('pa', 'pam', 'spa')
```

In the first line, we define a four-character string and assign it the name S. We then index it two ways: S[0] fetches the item at offset 0 from the left (the one-character string 's'), and S[-2] gets the item at offset 2 from the end (or equivalently, at offset (4 + -2) from the front). Offsets and slices map to cells as shown in Figure 2-1.

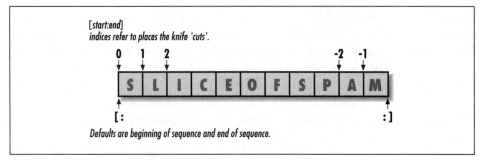

Figure 2-1. Using offsets and slices

The last line in the example above is our first look at slicing. When we index a sequence object such as a string on a pair of offsets, Python returns a new object containing the contiguous section identified by the offsets pair. The left offset is taken to be the lower bound, and the right is the upper bound; Python fetches all items from the lower bound, up to but not including the upper bound, and returns a new object containing the fetched items.

For instance, S[1:3] extracts items at offsets 1 and 2, S[1:] gets all items past the first (the upper bound defaults to the length of the string), and S[:-1] gets all but the last item (the lower bound defaults to zero). This may sound confusing on first glance, but indexing and slicing are simple and powerful to use, once you get the knack. Here's a summary of the details for reference; remember, if you're unsure about what a slice means, try it out interactively.

Indexing (S[i]):

- Fetches components at offsets (the first item is at offset zero)
- Negative indexes mean to count from the end (added to the positive length)
- S[0] fetches the first item
- S[-2] fetches the second from the end (it's the same as S[len(S) - 2])

Slicing (S[i:j]):

- Extracts contiguous sections of a sequence

- Slice boundaries default to zero and the sequence length, if omitted

- S[1:3] fetches from offsets 1 up to, but not including, 3

- S[1:] fetches from offsets 1 through the end (length)

- S[:-1] fetches from offsets 0 up to, but not including, the last item

Later in this chapter, we'll see that the syntax used to index by offset (the square brackets) is also used to index dictionaries by *key*; the operations look the same, but have different interpretations.

Why You Will Care: Slices

Throughout this part of the book, we include sidebars such as this to give you a peek at how some of the language features being introduced are typically used in real programs. Since we can't show much of real use until you've seen most of the Python picture, these sidebars necessarily contain many references to topics we haven't introduced yet; at most, you should consider them previews of ways you may find these abstract language concepts useful for common programming tasks.

For instance, you'll see later that the argument words listed on a command line used to launch a Python program are made available in the **argv** attribute of the built-in **sys** module:

```
% cat echo.py
import sys
print sys.argv

% python echo.py -a -b -c
['echo.py', '-a', '-b', '-c']
```

Usually, we're only interested in inspecting the arguments past the program name. This leads to a very typical application of slices: a single slice expression can strip off all but the first item of the list. Here, **sys.argv[1:]** returns the desired list, ['-a', '-b', '-c']. You can then process without having to accommodate the program name at the front.

Slices are also often used to clean up lines read from input files; if you know that a line will have an end-of-line character at the end (a '\n' newline marker), you can get rid of it with a single expression such as line[:-1], which extracts all but the last character in the line (the lower limit defaults to 0). In both cases, slices do the job of logic that must be explicit in a lower-level language.

Changing and formatting

Remember those big words—immutable sequence? The immutable part means that you can't change a string in-place (e.g., by assigning to an index). So how do we modify text information in Python? To change a string, we just need to build and assign a new one using tools such as concatenation and slicing:

```
>>> S = 'spam'
>>> S[0] = "x"
Raises an error!
>>> S = S + 'Spam!'        # to change a string, make a new one
>>> S
'spamSpam!'
>>> S = S[:4] + 'Burger' + S[-1]
>>> S
'spamBurger!'
>>> 'That is %d %s bird!' % (1, 'dead')      # like C sprintf
That is 1 dead bird!
```

Python also overloads the % operator to work on strings (it means remainder-of-division for numbers). When applied to strings, it serves the same role as C's `sprintf` function: it provides a simple way to format strings. To make it go, simply provide a format string on the left (with embedded conversion targets—e.g., %d), along with an object (or objects) on the right that you want Python to insert into the string on the left, at the conversion targets. For instance, in the last line above, the integer 1 is plugged into the string where the %d appears, and the string 'dead' is inserted at the %s. String formatting is important enough to warrant a few more examples:

```
>>> exclamation = "Ni"
>>> "The knights who say %s!" % exclamation
'The knights who say Ni!'
>>> "%d %s %d you" % (1, 'spam', 4)
'1 spam 4 you'
>>> "%s -- %s -- %s" % (42, 3.14159, [1, 2, 3])
'42 -- 3.14159 -- [1, 2, 3]'
```

In the first example, plug the string "Ni" into the target on the left, replacing the %s marker. In the second, insert three values into the target string; when there is more than one value being inserted, you need to group the values on the right in parentheses (which really means they are put in a *tuple*, as we'll see shortly).

Python's string % operator always returns a new string as its result, which you can print or not. It also supports all the usual C `printf` format codes. Table 2-5 lists the more common string-format target codes. One special case worth noting is that %s converts *any* object to its string representation, so it's often the only conversion code you need to remember. For example, the last line in the previous example converts integer, floating point, and list objects to strings using %s (lists are up next). Formatting also allows for a dictionary of values on the right, but since we haven't told you what dictionaries are yet, we'll finesse this extension here.

Table 2-5. String Formatting Codes

%s	String (or any object's print format)	%X	Hex integer (uppercase)
%c	Character	%e	Floating-point format 1[a]
%d	Decimal (int)	%E	Floating-point format 2
%i	Integer	%f	Floating-point format 3
%u	Unsigned (int)	%g	Floating-point format 4
%o	Octal integer	%G	Floating-point format 5
%x	Hex integer	%%	Literal %

[a] The floating-point codes produce alternative representations for floating-point numbers. See `printf` documentation for details; better yet, try these formats out in the Python interactive interpreter to see how the alternative floating-point formats look (e.g., `"%e %f %g" % (1.1, 2.2, 3.3)`).

Common string tools

As previously mentioned, Python provides utility modules for processing strings. The `string` module is perhaps the most common and useful. It includes tools for converting case, searching strings for substrings, converting strings to numbers, and much more (the Python library reference manual has an exhaustive list of string tools).

```
>>> import string             # standard utilities module
>>> S = "spammify"
>>> string.upper(S)           # convert to uppercase
'SPAMMIFY'
>>> string.find(S, "mm")      # return index of substring
3
>>> string.atoi("42"), `42`   # convert from/to string
(42, '42')
>>> string.join(string.split(S, "mm"), "XX")
'spaXXify'
```

The last example is more complex, and we'll defer a better description until later in the book. But the short story is that the `split` function chops up a string into a list of substrings around a passed-in delimiter or whitespace; `join` puts them back together, with a passed-in delimiter or space between each. This may seem like a roundabout way to replace `"mm"` with `"XX"`, but it's one way to perform arbitrary global substring replacements. We study these, and more advanced text processing tools, later in the book.

Incidentally, notice the second-to-last line in the previous example: the `atoi` function converts a string to a number, and backquotes around any object convert that object to its string representation (here, `42` converts a number to a string). Remember that you can't mix strings and numbers types around operators such as +, but you can manually convert before that operation if needed:

```
>>> "spam" + 42
Raises an error
>>> "spam" + `42`
'spam42'
>>> string.atoi("42") + 1
43
```

Later, we'll also meet a built-in function called **eval** that converts a string to *any* kind of object; `string.atoi` and its relatives convert only to numbers, but this restriction means they are usually faster.

String constant variations

Finally, we'd like to show you a few of the different ways to write string constants; all produce the same kind of object (a string), so the special syntax here is just for our convenience. Earlier, we mentioned that strings can be enclosed in single or double quotes, which allows embedded quotes of the opposite flavor. Here's an example:

```
>>> mixed = "Guido's"          # single in double
>>> mixed
"Guido's"
>>> mixed = 'Guido"s'          # double in single
>>> mixed
'Guido"s'
>>> mixed = 'Guido\'s'         # backslash escape
>>> mixed
"Guido's"
```

Notice the last two lines: you can also *escape* a quote (to tell Python it's not really the end of the string) by preceding it with a backslash. In fact, you can escape all kinds of special characters inside strings, as listed in Table 2-6; Python replaces the escape code characters with the special character they represent. In general, the rules for escape codes in Python strings are just like those in C strings.[*] Also like C, Python concatenates adjacent string constants for us:

```
>>> split = "This" "is" "concatenated"
>>> split
'Thisisconcatenated'
```

And last but not least, here's Python's triple-quoted string constant form in action: Python collects all the lines in such a quoted block and concatenates them in a single multiline string, putting an end-of-line character between each line. The end-of-line prints as a "\012" here (remember, this is an octal integer); you can

---

[*] But note that you normally don't need to terminate Python strings with a \0 null character as you would in C. Since Python keeps track of a string's length internally, there's usually no need to manage terminators in your programs. In fact, Python strings can contain the null byte \0, unlike typical usage in C. For instance, we'll see in a moment that file data is represented as strings in Python programs; binary data read from or written to files can contain nulls because strings can too.

also call it "\n" as in C. For instance, a line of text with an embedded tab and a line-feed at the end might be written in a program as python\tstuff\n (see Table 2-6).

```
>>> big = """This is
... a multi-line block
... of text; Python puts
... an end-of-line marker
... after each line."""
>>>
>>> big
'This is\012a multi-line block\012of text; Python puts\012an end-of-line
marker\012after each line.'
```

Python also has a special string constant form called *raw strings*, which don't treat backslashes as potential escape codes (see Table 2-6). For instance, strings r'a\b\ c' and R"a\b\c" retain their backslashes as real (literal) backslash characters. Since raw strings are mostly used for writing regular expressions, we'll defer further details until we explore regular expressions in Chapter 8.

Table 2-6. String Backslash Characters

\newline	Ignored (a continuation)	\n	Newline (linefeed)
\\	Backslash (keeps one \)	\v	Vertical tab
\'	Single quote (keeps ')	\t	Horizontal tab
\"	Double quote (keeps ")	\r	Carriage return
\a	Bell	\f	Formfeed
\b	Backspace	\0XX	Octal value XX
\e	Escape (usually)	\xXX	Hex value XX
\000	Null (doesn't end string)	\other	Any other char (retained)

Generic Type Concepts

Now that we've seen our first composite data type, let's pause a minute to define a few general type concepts that apply to most of our types from here on. One of the nice things about Python is that a few general ideas usually apply to lots of situations. In regard to built-in types, it turns out that operations work the same for all types in a category, so we only need to define most ideas once. We've only seen numbers and strings so far, but they are representative of two of the three major type categories in Python, so you already know more about other types than you think.

Types share operation sets by categories

When we introduced strings, we mentioned that they are immutable sequences: they can't be changed in place (the immutable part), and are ordered collections accessed by offsets (the sequence bit). Now, it so happens that all the sequences seen in this chapter respond to the same sequence operations we previously saw at work on strings—concatenation, indexing, iteration, and so on. In fact, there are three type (and operation) categories in Python:

- Numbers support addition, multiplication, etc.
- Sequences support indexing, slicing, concatenation, etc.
- Mappings support indexing by key, etc.

We haven't seen mappings yet (we'll get to dictionaries in a few pages), but other types are going to be mostly more of the same. For example, for any sequence objects X and Y:

- X + Y makes a new sequence object with the contents of both operands.
- X * N makes a new sequence object with N copies of the sequence operand X.

In other words, these operations work the same on any kind of sequence. The only difference is that you get back a new result object that is the same type as the operands X and Y (if you concatenate strings, you get back a new string, not a list). Indexing, slicing, and other sequence operations work the same on all sequences too; the type of the objects being processed tells Python which flavor to perform.

Mutable types can be changed in place

The immutable classification might sound abstract, but it's an important constraint to know and tends to trip up new users. If we say an object type is immutable, you shouldn't change it without making a copy; Python raises an error if you do. In general, immutable types give us some degree of integrity, by guaranteeing that an object won't be changed by another part of a program. We'll see why this matters when we study shared object references later in this chapter.

Lists

Our next stop on the built-in object tour is the Python *list*. Lists are Python's most flexible ordered collection object type. Unlike strings, lists can contain any sort of object: numbers, strings, even other lists. Python lists do the work of most of the collection data structures you might have to implement manually in lower-level languages such as C. In terms of some of their main properties, Python lists are:

Ordered collections of arbitrary objects

From a functional view, lists are just a place to collect other objects, so you can treat them as a group. Lists also define a left-to-right positional ordering of the items in the list.

Accessed by offset

Just as with strings, you can fetch a component object out of a list by indexing the list on the object's offset. Since lists are ordered, you can also do such
tasks as slicing and concatenation.

Variable length, heterogeneous, arbitrarily nestable

Unlike strings, lists can grow and shrink in place (they're variable length), and
may contain any sort of object, not just one-character strings (they're heterogeneous). Because lists can contain other complex objects, lists also support
arbitrary nesting; you can create lists of lists of lists, and so on.

Of the category mutable sequence

In terms of our type category qualifiers, lists can be both changed in place
(they're mutable) and respond to all the sequence operations we saw in action
on strings in the last section. In fact, sequence operations work the same on
lists, so we won't have much to say about them here. On the other hand,
because lists are mutable, they also support other operations strings don't,
such as deletion, index assignment, and methods.

Arrays of object references

Technically, Python lists contain zero or more references to other objects. If
you've used a language such as C, lists might remind you of arrays of pointers. Fetching an item from a Python list is about as fast as indexing a C array;
in fact, lists really are C arrays inside the Python interpreter. Moreover, references are something like pointers (addresses) in a language such as C, except
that you never process a reference by itself; Python always follows a reference to an object whenever the reference is used, so your program only deals
with objects. Whenever you stuff an object into a data structure or variable
name, Python always stores a reference to the object, not a copy of it (unless
you request a copy explicitly).

Table 2-7 summarizes common list object operations.

Table 2-7. Common List Constants and Operations

Operation	Interpretation
L1 = []	An empty list
L2 = [0, 1, 2, 3]	Four items: indexes 0 . . 3
L3 = ['abc', ['def', 'ghi']]	Nested sublists
L2[i], L3[i][j] L2[i:j], len(L2)	Index, slice, length
L1 + L2, L2 * 3	Concatenate, repeat
for x in L2, 3 in L2	Iteration, membership

Table 2-7, Common List Constants and Operations (continued)

Operation	Interpretation
`L2.append(4)`, `L2.sort()`, `L2.index(1)`, `L2.reverse()`	Methods: grow, sort, search, reverse, etc.
`del L2[k]`, `L2[i:j] = []`	Shrinking
`L2[i] = 1`, `L2[i:j] = [4,5,6]`	Index assignment, slice assignment
`range(4)`, `xrange(0, 4)`	Make lists/tuples of integers

Lists are written as a series of objects (really, expressions that return objects) in square brackets, separated by commas. Nested lists are coded as a nested square-bracketed series, and the empty list is just a square-bracket set with nothing inside.*

Most of the operations in Table 2-7 should look familiar, since they are the same sequence operations we put to work on strings earlier—indexing, concatenation, iteration, and so on. The last few table entries are new; lists also respond to *method calls* (which provide utilities such as sorting, reversing, adding items on the end, etc.), as well as *in-place change* operations (deleting items, assignment to indexes and slices, and so forth). Remember, lists get these last two operation sets because they are a mutable object type.

Lists in Action

Perhaps the best way to understand lists is to see them at work. Let's once again turn to some simple interpreter interactions to illustrate the operations in Table 2-7.

Basic operations

Lists respond to the + and * operators as with strings; they mean *concatenation* and *repetition* here too, except that the result is a new list, not a string. And as Forrest Gump was quick to say, "that's all we have to say about that"; grouping types into categories is intellectually frugal (and makes life easy for authors like us).

```
% python
>>> len([1, 2, 3])              # length
3
>>> [1, 2, 3] + [4, 5, 6]       # concatenation
[1, 2, 3, 4, 5, 6]
```

---

* But we should note that in practice, you won't see many lists written out like this in list-processing programs. It's more common to see code that processes lists constructed dynamically (at runtime). In fact, although constant syntax is important to master, most data structures in Python are built by running program code at runtime.

```
>>> ['Ni!'] * 4                    # repetition
['Ni!', 'Ni!', 'Ni!', 'Ni!']
>>> for x in [1, 2, 3]: print x,    # iteration
...
1 2 3
```

We talk about iteration (as well as **range** built-ins) in Chapter 3, *Basic Statements*. One exception worth noting here: + expects the same sort of sequence on both sides, otherwise you get a type error when the code runs. For instance, you can't concatenate a list and a string, unless you first convert the list to a string using backquotes or **%** formatting (we met these in the last section). You could also convert the string to a list; the **list** built-in function does the trick:

```
>>> `[1, 2]` + "34"        # same as "[1, 2]" + "34"
'[1, 2]34'
>>> [1, 2] + list("34")    # same as [1, 2] + ["3", "4"]
[1, 2, '3', '4']
```

Indexing and slicing

Because lists are sequences, indexing and slicing work the same here too, but the result of indexing a list is whatever type of object lives at the offset you specify, and slicing a list always returns a new list:

```
>>> L = ['spam', 'Spam', 'SPAM!']
>>> L[2]                        # offsets start at zero
'SPAM!'
>>> L[-2]                       # negative: count from the right
'Spam'
>>> L[1:]                       # slicing fetches sections
['Spam', 'SPAM!']
```

Changing lists in place

Finally something new: because lists are mutable, they support operations that change a list object in-place; that is, the operations in this section all modify the list object directly, without forcing you to make a new copy as you had to for strings. But since Python only deals in object references, the distinction between in-place changes and new objects can matter; if you change an object in place, you might impact more than one reference to it at once. More on that later in this chapter.

When using a list, you can change its contents by assigning to a particular item (offset), or an entire section (slice):

```
>>> L = ['spam', 'Spam', 'SPAM!']
>>> L[1] = 'eggs'               # index assignment
>>> L
['spam', 'eggs', 'SPAM!']
>>> L[0:2] = ['eat', 'more']    # slice assignment: delete+insert
>>> L                           # replaces items 0,1
['eat', 'more', 'SPAM!']
```

Index assignment works much as it does in C: Python replaces the object reference at the designated slot with a new one. Slice assignment is best thought of as
two steps: Python first deletes the slice you specify on the left of the =, and then
inserts (splices) the new items into the list at the place where the old slice was
deleted. In fact, the number of items inserted doesn't have to match the number of
items deleted; for instance, given a list L that has the value [1, 2, 3], the assignment L[1:2] = [4, 5] sets L to the list [1, 4, 5, 3]. Python first deletes the 2 (a
one-item slice), then inserts items 4 and 5 where 2 used to be. Python list objects
also support *method* calls:

```
>>> L.append('please')              # append method call
>>> L
['eat', 'more', 'SPAM!', 'please']
>>> L.sort()                        # sort list items ('S' < 'e')
>>> L
['SPAM!', 'eat', 'more', 'please']
```

Methods are like functions, except that they are associated with a particular object.
The syntax used to call methods is similar too (they're followed by arguments in
parentheses), but you *qualify* the method name with the list object to get to it.
Qualification is coded as a period followed by the name of the method you want;
it tells Python to look up the name in the object's *namespace*—set of qualifiable
names. Technically, names such as **append** and **sort** are called *attributes*—names
associated with objects. We'll see lots of objects that export attributes later in the
book.

The list **append** method simply tacks a single item (object reference) to the end of
the list. Unlike concatenation, **append** expects us to pass in a single object, not a
list. The effect of L.append(X) is similar to L+[X], but the former changes L in
place, and the latter makes a new list.* The **sort** method orders a list in-place; by
default, it uses Python standard comparison tests (here, string comparisons; you
can also pass in a comparison function of your own, but we'll ignore this option
here).

---

* Also unlike + concatenation, **append** doesn't have to generate new objects, and so is usually much
faster. On the other hand, you can mimic **append** with clever slice assignments: L[len(L):]=[X] is like
L.append(X), and L[:0]=[X] is like appending at the front of a list. Both delete an empty slice and
insert X, changing L in place quickly like **append**. C programmers might be interested to know that Python
lists are implemented as single heap blocks (rather than a linked list), and **append** is really a call to
realloc behind the scenes. Provided your heap manager is smart enough to avoid copying and re-mal-
locing, **append** can be very fast. Concatenation, on the other hand, must always create new list objects
and copy the items in both operands.

Here's another thing that seems to trip up new users: **append** and **sort** change the associated list object in-place, but don't return the list as a result (technically, they both return a value called **None**, which we'll meet in a moment). If you say something like L = **L.append(X)**, you won't get the modified value of L (in fact, you'll lose the reference to the list altogether); when you use attributes such as **append** and **sort**, objects are changed as a side effect, so there's no reason to reassign.

Finally, because lists are mutable, you can also use the **del** statement to delete an item or section. Since slice assignment is a deletion plus an insert, you can also delete sections of lists by assigning an empty list to a slice (L[i:j] = []); Python deletes the slice named on the left and then inserts nothing. Assigning an empty list to an index, on the other hand, just stores a reference to the empty list in the specified slot: L[0] = [] sets the first item of L to the object [], rather than deleting it (L winds up looking like [[],...]):

```
>>> L
['SPAM!', 'eat', 'more', 'please']
>>> del L[0]                    # delete one item
>>> L
['eat', 'more', 'please']
>>> del L[1:]                   # delete an entire section
>>> L                          # same as L[1:] = []
['eat']
```

Here are a few pointers before moving on. Although all the operations above are typical, there are additional list methods and operations we won't illustrate here (including methods for reversing and searching). You should always consult Python's manuals or the *Python Pocket Reference* for a comprehensive and up-to-date list of type tools. Even if this book was complete, it probably couldn't be up to date (new tools may be added any time). We'd also like to remind you one more time that all the in-place change operations above work only for mutable objects: they won't work on strings (or tuples, discussed ahead), no matter how hard you try.

Dictionaries

Besides lists, dictionaries are perhaps the most flexible built-in data type in Python. If you think of lists as ordered collections of objects, dictionaries are unordered collections; their chief distinction is that items are stored and fetched in dictionaries by key, instead of offset. As we'll see, built-in dictionaries can replace many of the searching algorithms and data-structures you might have to implement manually in lower-level languages. Dictionaries also sometimes do the work of records and symbol tables used in other languages. In terms of their main properties, dictionaries are:

Accessed by key, not offset

Dictionaries are sometimes called *associative arrays* or *hashes*. They associate a set of values with keys, so that you can fetch an item out of a dictionary using the key that stores it. You use the same indexing operation to get components in a dictionary, but the index takes the form of a key, not a relative offset.

Unordered collections of arbitrary objects

Unlike lists, items stored in a dictionary aren't kept in any particular order; in fact, Python randomizes their order in order to provide quick lookup. Keys provide the symbolic (not physical) location of items in a dictionary.

Variable length, heterogeneous, arbitrarily nestable

Like lists, dictionaries can grow and shrink in place (without making a copy), they can contain objects of any type, and support nesting to any depth (they can contain lists, other dictionaries, and so on).

Of the category mutable mapping

They can be changed in place by assigning to indexes, but don't support the sequence operations we've seen work on strings and lists. In fact, they can't: because dictionaries are unordered collections, operations that depend on a fixed order (e.g., concatenation, slicing) don't make sense. Instead, dictionaries are the only built-in representative of the mapping type category—objects that map keys to values.

Tables of object references (hash tables)

If lists are arrays of object references, dictionaries are unordered tables of object references. Internally, dictionaries are implemented as *hash tables* (data structures that support very fast retrieval), which start small and grow on demand. Moreover, Python employs optimized hashing algorithms to find keys, so retrieval is very fast. But at the bottom, dictionaries store object references (not copies), just like lists.

Table 2-8 summarizes some of the most common dictionary operations (see the library manual for a complete list). Dictionaries are written as a series of `key:value` pairs, separated by commas, and enclosed in curly braces.* An empty dictionary is an empty set of braces, and dictionaries can be nested by writing one as a value in another dictionary, or an item in a list (or tuple).

---

* The same note about the relative rarity of constants applies here: we often build up dictionaries by assigning to new keys at runtime, rather than writing constants. But see the following section on changing dictionaries; lists and dictionaries are grown in different ways. Assignment to new keys works for dictionaries, but fails for lists (lists are grown with `append`).

Table 2-8. Common Dictionary Constants and Operations

Operation	Interpretation
d1 = {}	Empty dictionary
d2 = {'spam': 2, 'eggs': 3}	Two-item dictionary
d3 = {'food': {'ham': 1, 'egg': 2}}	Nesting
d2['eggs'], d3['food']['ham']	Indexing by key
d2.has_key('eggs'), d2.keys(), d2.values()	Methods: membership test, keys list, values list, etc.
len(d1)	Length (number stored entries)
d2[key] = new, del d2[key]	Adding/changing, deleting

As Table 2-8 illustrates, dictionaries are indexed by *key*; in this case, the key is a string object ('eggs'), and nested dictionary entries are referenced by a series of indexes (keys in square brackets). When Python creates a dictionary, it stores its items in any order it chooses; to fetch a value back, supply the key that stores it.

Dictionaries in Action

Let's go back to the interpreter to get a feel for some of the dictionary operations in Table 2-8.

Basic operations

Generally, you create dictionaries and access items by key. The built-in **len** function works on dictionaries too; it returns the number of items stored away in the dictionary, or equivalently, the length of its keys list. Speaking of keys lists, the dictionary **keys** method returns all the keys in the dictionary, collected in a list. This can be useful for processing dictionaries sequentially, but you shouldn't depend on the order of the keys list (remember, dictionaries are randomized).

```
% python
>>> d2 = {'spam': 2, 'ham': 1, 'eggs': 3}
>>> d2['spam']                  # fetch value for key
2
>>> len(d2)                     # number of entries in dictionary
3
>>> d2.has_key('ham')           # key membership test (1 means true)
1
>>> d2.keys()                   # list of my keys
['eggs', 'spam', 'ham']
```

Changing dictionaries

Dictionaries are mutable, so you can change, expand, and shrink them in place without making new dictionaries, just as for lists. Simply assign a value to a key to change or create the entry. The `del` statement works here too; it deletes the entry associated with the key specified as an index. Notice that we're nesting a list inside a dictionary in this example (the value of key `"ham"`):

```
>>> d2['ham'] = ['grill', 'bake', 'fry']      # change entry
>>> d2
{'eggs': 3, 'spam': 2, 'ham': ['grill', 'bake', 'fry']}

>>> del d2['eggs']                            # delete entry
>>> d2
{'spam': 2, 'ham': ['grill', 'bake', 'fry']}

>>> d2['brunch'] = 'Bacon'                    # add new entry
>>> d2
{'brunch': 'Bacon', 'spam': 2, 'ham': ['grill', 'bake', 'fry']}
```

As with lists, assigning to an existing index in a dictionary *changes* its associated value. Unlike lists, whenever you assign a new dictionary key (i.e., one that hasn't been assigned before), you create a new entry in the dictionary, as done previously for `'brunch'`. This doesn't work for lists, because Python considers an offset out of bounds if it's beyond the end of a list. To expand a list, you need to use such tools as the `append` method or slice assignment instead.

A marginally more real example

Here is a more realistic dictionary example. The following example creates a table that maps programming language names (the keys) to their creators (the values). You fetch a creator name by indexing on language name:

```
>>> table = {'Python':  'Guido van Rossum',
...          'Perl':    'Larry Wall',
...          'Tcl':     'John Ousterhout' }
...
>>> language = 'Python'
>>> creator  = table[language]
>>> creator
'Guido van Rossum'
>>> for lang in table.keys(): print lang, '\t', table[lang]
...
Tcl      John Ousterhout
Python   Guido van Rossum
Perl     Larry Wall
```

Notice the last command. Because dictionaries aren't sequences, you can't iterate over them directly with a `for` statement, as for strings and lists. But if you need to step through the items in a dictionary it's easy: calling the dictionary `keys` method returns a list of all stored keys you can iterate through with a `for`. If needed, you can index from key to value inside the `for` loop as done previously. We'll talk about the `print` and `for` statements in more detail in Chapter 3.

Dictionary Usage Notes

Before we move on to more types, here are a few additional details you should be aware of when using dictionaries:

Sequence operations don't work

We're being redundant on purpose here, because this is another common question from new users. Dictionaries are mappings, not sequences; because there's no notion of ordering among their items, things like concatenation (an ordered joining) and slicing (extracting contiguous section) simply don't apply. In fact, Python raises an error when your code runs, if you try.

Assigning to new indexes adds entries

Keys can be created either when you write a dictionary constant (in which case they are embedded in the constant itself), or when you assign values to new keys of an existing dictionary object. The end result is the same.

Keys need not always be strings

We've been using strings as keys here, but other immutable objects (not lists) work just as well. In fact, you could use integers as keys, which makes a dictionary look much like a list (albeit, without the ordering). Tuples (up next) are sometimes used as dictionary keys too, allowing for compound key values. And class instance objects (discussed in Chapter 6, *Classes*) can be used as keys, as long as they have the proper protocol methods; they need to tell Python that their values won't change, or else they would be useless as fixed keys.

Tuples

The last collection type in our survey is the Python *tuple*. Tuples construct simple groups of objects. They work exactly like lists, except that tuples can't be changed in place (they're immutable) and are usually written as a series of items in parentheses, not square brackets. Tuples share most of their properties with lists. They are:

Ordered collections of arbitrary objects

Like strings and lists, tuples are an ordered collection of objects; like lists, they can embed any kind of object.

Accessed by offset

Like strings and lists, items in a tuple are accessed by offset (not key); they support all the offset-base access operations we've already seen, such as indexing and slicing.

Of the category immutable sequence

Like strings, tuples are immutable; they don't support any of the in-place change operations we saw applied to lists. Like strings and lists, tuples are sequences; they support many of the same operations.

Why You Will Care: Dictionary Interfaces

Besides being a convenient way to store information by key in your programs, some Python extensions also present interfaces that look and work the same as dictionaries. For instance, Python's interface to *dbm* access-by-key files looks much like a dictionary that must be opened; strings are stored and fetched using key indexes:

```
import anydbm
file = anydbm.open("filename")      # link to external file
file['key'] = 'data'                # store data by key
data = file['key']                  # fetch data by key
```

Later, we'll see that we can store entire Python objects this way too, if we replace "anydbm" in the above with "shelve" (shelves are access-by-key databases of persistent Python objects). For Internet work, Python's CGI script support also presents a dictionary-like interface; a call to *cgi.FieldStorage* yields a dictionary-like object, with one entry per input field on the client's web page:

```
import cgi
form = cgi.FieldStorage()           # parse form data (stdin, environ)
if form.has_key('name'):
    showReply('Hello, ' + form['name'].value)
```

All of these (and dictionaries) are instances of mappings. More on CGI scripts in Chapter 9, *Common Tasks in Python*.

Fixed length, heterogeneous, arbitrarily nestable

Because tuples are immutable, they can't grow or shrink without making a new tuple; on the other hand, tuples can hold other compound objects (e.g., lists, dictionaries, other tuples) and so support nesting.

Arrays of object references

Like lists, tuples are best thought of as object reference arrays; tuples store access points to other objects (references), and indexing a tuple is relatively quick.

Table 2-9 highlights common tuple operations. Tuples are written as a series of objects (really, expressions), separated by commas, and enclosed in parentheses. An empty tuple is just a parentheses pair with nothing inside.

Table 2-9. Common Tuple Constants and Operations

Operation	Interpretation
()	An empty tuple
t1 = (0,)	A one-item tuple (not an expression)
t2 = (0, 1, 2, 3)	A four-item tuple
t2 = 0, 1, 2, 3	Another four-item tuple (same as prior line)

Table 2-9. Common Tuple Constants and Operations (continued)

Operation	Interpretation
`t3 = ('abc', ('def', 'ghi'))`	Nested tuples

`t1[i], t3[i][j]`
`t1[i:j],`
`len(t1)`
	Index,
	slice,
	length

`t1 + t2` `t2 * 3`	Concatenate, repeat
`for x in t2,` `3 in t2`	Iteration, membership

The second and fourth entries in Table 2-9 merit a bit more explanation. Because parentheses can also enclose expressions (see the previous section "Numbers"), you need to do something special to tell Python when a single object in parentheses is a tuple object and not a simple expression. If you really want a single-item tuple, simply add a trailing comma after the single item and before the closing parenthesis.

As a special case, Python also allows us to omit the opening and closing parentheses for a tuple, in contexts where it isn't syntactically ambiguous to do so. For instance, in the fourth line of the table, we simply listed four items, separated by commas; in the context of an assignment statement, Python recognizes this as a tuple, even though we didn't add parentheses. For beginners, the best advice here is that it's probably easier to use parentheses than it is to figure out when they're optional.

Apart from constant syntax differences, tuple operations (the last three rows in the table) are identical to strings and lists, so we won't show examples here. The only differences worth noting are that the +, *, and slicing operations return new tuples when applied to tuples, and tuples don't provide the methods we saw for lists and dictionaries; generally speaking, only mutable objects export callable methods in Python.

Why Lists and Tuples?

This seems to be the first question that always comes up when teaching beginners about tuples: why do we need tuples if we have lists? Some of it may be historic. But the best answer seems to be that the immutability of tuples provides some integrity; you can be sure a tuple won't be changed through another reference elsewhere in a program. There's no such guarantee for lists, as we'll discover in a moment. Some built-in operations also require tuples, not lists; for instance, argument lists are constructed as tuples, when calling functions dynamically with built-ins such as `apply` (of course, we haven't met `apply` yet, so you'll have to take our word for it for now). As a rule of thumb, lists are the tool of choice for ordered collections you expect to change; tuples handle the other cases.

Files

Hopefully, most readers are familiar with the notion of files—named storage compartments on your computer that are managed by your operating system. Our last built-in object type provides a way to access those files inside Python programs. The built-in **open** function creates a Python file object, which serves as a link to a file residing on your machine. After calling **open**, you can read and write the associated external file, by calling file object methods.

Compared to types we've seen so far, file objects are somewhat unusual. They're not numbers, sequences, or mappings; instead, they export methods only for common file processing tasks. Technically, files are a prebuilt C extension type that provides a thin wrapper over the underlying C **stdio** filesystem; in fact, file object methods have an almost 1-to-1 correspondence to file functions in the standard C library.

Table 2-10 summarizes common file operations. To open a file, a program calls the **open** function, with the external name first, followed by a processing mode (**'r'** means open for input, **'w'** means create and open for output, **'a'** means open for appending to the end, and others we'll ignore here). Both arguments must be Python strings.

Table 2-10. Common File Operations

Operation	Interpretation
output = open('/tmp/spam', 'w')	Create output file ('w' means write)
input = open('data', 'r')	Create input file ('r' means read)
S = input.read()	Read entire file into a single string
S = input.read(N)	Read N bytes (1 or more)
S = input.readline()	Read next line (through end-line marker)
L = input.readlines()	Read entire file into list of line strings
output.write(S)	Write string S onto file
output.writelines(L)	Write all line strings in list L onto file
output.close()	Manual close (or it's done for you when collected)

Once you have a file object, call its methods to read from or write to the external file. In all cases, file text takes the form of *strings* in Python programs; reading a file returns its text in strings, and text is passed to the **write** methods as strings. Reading and writing both come in multiple flavors; Table 2-10 gives the most common.

Calling the file `close` method terminates your connection to the external file. We talked about *garbage collection* in a footnote earlier; in Python, an object's memory space is automatically reclaimed as soon as the object is no longer referenced anywhere in the program. When file objects are reclaimed, Python automatically closes the file if needed. Because of that, you don't need to always manually close your files, especially in simple scripts that don't run long. On the other hand, manual `close` calls can't hurt and are usually a good idea in larger systems.

Files in Action

Here is a simple example that demonstrates file-processing basics. We first open a new file for output, write a string (terminated with an end-of-line marker, `'\n'`), and close the file. Later, we open the same file again in input mode, and read the line back. Notice that the second `readline` call returns an empty string; this is how Python file methods tell us we've reached the *end of the file* (empty lines are strings with just an end-of-line character, not empty strings).

```
>>> myfile = open('myfile', 'w')          # open for output (creates)
>>> myfile.write('hello text file\n')     # write a line of text
>>> myfile.close()

>>> myfile = open('myfile', 'r')          # open for input
>>> myfile.readline()                     # read the line back
'hello text file\012'
>>> myfile.readline()                     # empty string: end of file
''
```

There are additional, more advanced file methods not shown in Table 2-10; for instance, `seek` resets your current position in a file, `flush` forces buffered output to be written, and so on. See the Python library manual or other Python books for a complete list of file methods. Since we're going to see file examples in Chapter 9, we won't present more examples here.

Related Python Tools

File objects returned by the `open` function handle basic file-interface chores. In Chapter 8, you'll see a handful of related but more advanced Python tools. Here's a quick preview of all the file-like tools available:

File descriptor-based files
   The `os` module provides interfaces for using low-level descriptor-based files.

DBM keyed files
   The `anydbm` module provides an interface to access-by-key files.

Persistent objects

> The `shelve` and `pickle` modules support saving entire objects (beyond simple strings).

Pipes

> The `os` module also provides POSIX interfaces for processing pipes.

Other

> There are also optional interfaces to database systems, B-Tree based files, and more.

General Object Properties

Now that we've seen all of Python's built-in types, let's take a quick look at some of the properties they share. Some of this section is a review of ideas we've already seen at work.

Type Categories Revisited

Table 2-11 classifies all the types we've seen, according to the type categories we introduced earlier. As we've seen, objects share operations according to their category—for instance, strings, lists, and tuples all share sequence operations. As we've also seen, only mutable objects may be changed in place. You can change lists and dictionaries in place, but not numbers, strings, or tuples.* Files only export methods, so mutability doesn't really apply (they may be changed when written, but this isn't the same as Python type constraints).

Table 2-11. Object Classifications

Object type	Category	Mutable?
Numbers	Numeric	No
Strings	Sequence	No
Lists	Sequence	Yes
Dictionaries	Mapping	Yes
Tuples	Sequence	No
Files	Extension	N/A

---

* You might think that number immutability goes without saying, but that's not the case in every programming language. For instance, some early versions of FORTRAN allowed users to change the value of an integer constant by assigning to it. This won't work in Python, because numbers are immutable; you can rest assured that 2 will always be 2.

> ## *Why You Will Care: Operator Overloading*
>
> Later, we'll see that objects we implement ourselves with classes can pick and choose from these categories arbitrarily. For instance, if you want to provide a new kind of specialized sequence object that is consistent with built-in sequences, code a class that overloads things like indexing, slicing, and concatenation:
>
> ```
> class MySequence:
>     def __getitem__(self, index):
>         # called on self[index], for x in self, x in self
>     def __getslice__(self, low, high):
>         # called on self[low:high]
>     def __add__(self, other):
>         # called on self + other
> ```
>
> and so on. You can also make the new object mutable or not, by selectively implementing methods called for in-place change operations (e.g., __setitem__ is called on self[index]=value assignments). Although this book isn't about C integration, it's also possible to implement new objects in C, as *C extension types*. For these, you fill in C function pointer slots to choose between number, sequence, and mapping operation sets. Python built-in types are really precoded C extension types; like Guido, you need to be aware of type categories when coding your own.

Generality

We've seen a number of compound object types (collections with components). In general:

- Lists, dictionaries, and tuples can hold any kind of object.
- Lists, dictionaries, and tuples can be arbitrarily nested.
- Lists and dictionaries can dynamically grow and shrink.

Because they support arbitrary structures, Python's compound object types are good at representing complex information in a program. For instance, the following interaction defines a tree of nested compound sequence objects; to access its components, we string as many index operations as required. Python evaluates the indexes from left to right, and fetches a reference to a more deeply nested object at each step. (This may be a pathologically complicated data structure, but it illustrates the syntax used to access nested objects in general.)

```
>>> L = ['abc', [(1, 2), ([3], 4)], 5]
>>> L[1]
[(1, 2), ([3], 4)]
>>> L[1][1]
```

```
([3], 4)
>>> L[1][1][0]
[3]
>>> L[1][1][0][0]
3
```

Shared References

We mentioned earlier that assignments always store references to objects, not copies. In practice, this is usually what you want. But because assignments can generate multiple references to the same object, you sometimes need to be aware that changing a mutable object in place may affect other references to the same object in your program. For instance, in the following, we create a list assigned to X and another assigned to L that embeds a reference back to list X. We also create a dictionary D that contains another reference back to list X:

```
>>> X = [1, 2, 3]
>>> L = ['a', X, 'b']
>>> D = {'x':X, 'y':2}
```

At this point, there are three references to the list we created first: from name X, from the list assigned to L, and from the dictionary assigned to D. The situation is sketched in Figure 2-2.

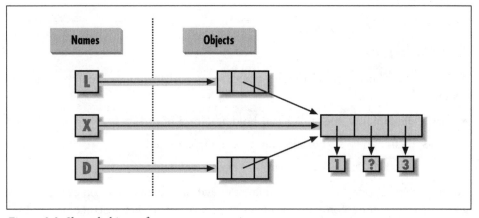

Figure 2-2. Shared object references

Since lists are mutable, changing the shared list object from any of the three references changes what the other two reference:

```
>>> X[1] = 'surprise'            # changes all three references!
>>> L
['a', [1, 'surprise', 3], 'b']
>>> D
{'x': [1, 'surprise', 3], 'y': 2}
```

One way to understand this is to realize that references are a higher-level analog of pointers in languages such as C. Although you can't grab hold of the reference itself, it's possible to store the same reference in more than one place

Comparisons, Equality, and Truth

All Python objects also respond to the comparisons: test for equality, relative magnitude, and so on. Unlike languages like C, Python comparisons always inspect all parts of compound objects, until a result can be determined. In fact, when nested objects are present, Python automatically traverses data structures and applies comparisons recursively. For instance, a comparison of list objects compares all their components automatically:

```
>>> L1 = [1, ('a', 3)]        # same value, unique objects
>>> L2 = [1, ('a', 3)]
>>> L1 == L2, L1 is L2        # equivalent?, same object?
(1, 0)
```

Here, L1 and L2 are assigned lists that are equivalent, but distinct objects. Because of the nature of Python references, there are two ways to test for equality:

The == operator tests value equivalence
> Python performs an equivalence test, comparing all nested objects recursively

The is operator tests object identity
> Python tests whether the two are really the same object (i.e., live at the same address).

In our example, L1 and L2 pass the == test (they have equivalent values because all their components are equivalent), but fail the is check (they are two different objects). As a rule of thumb, the == operator is used in almost all equality checks, but we'll see cases of both operators put to use later in the book. Relative magnitude comparisons are applied recursively to nested data structures too:

```
>>> L1 = [1, ('a', 3)]
>>> L2 = [1, ('a', 2)]
>>> L1 < L2, L1 == L2, L1 > L2    # less, equal, greater: a tuple of results
(0, 0, 1)
```

Here, L1 is greater than L2 because the nested 3 is greater than 2. Notice that the result of the last line above is really a *tuple* of three objects—the results of the three expressions we typed (an example of a tuple without its enclosing parentheses). The three values represent true and false values; in Python as in C, an integer 0 represents *false* and an integer 1 represents *true*. Unlike C, Python also recognizes any empty data structure as false and any nonempty data structure as true. Table 2-12 gives examples of true and false objects in Python.

Python also provides a special object called None (the last item in Table 2-12), which is always considered to be false. None is the only value of a special data type

Table 2-12. Example Object Truth Values

Object	Value
"spam"	True
" "	False
[]	False
{}	False
1	True
0.0	False
None	False

in Python; it typically serves as an empty placeholder, much like a NULL pointer in C. In general, Python compares the types we've seen in this chapter, as follows:

- Numbers are compared by relative magnitude.

- Strings are compared lexicographically, character-by-character ("abc" < "ac").

- Lists and tuples are compared by comparing each component, from left to right.

- Dictionaries are compared as though comparing sorted (key, value) lists.

In later chapters, we'll see other object types that can change the way they get compared. For instance, class instances are compared by address by default, unless they possess special comparison protocol methods.

Python's Type Hierarchies

Finally, Figure 2-3 summarizes all the built-in object types available in Python and their relationships. In this chapter, we've looked at the most prominent of these; other kinds of objects in Figure 2-3 either correspond to program units (e.g., functions and modules), or exposed interpreter internals (e.g., stack frames and compiled code).

The main point we'd like you to notice here is that everything is an object type in a Python system and may be processed by your Python programs. For instance, you can pass a stack frame to a function, assign it to a variable, stuff it into a list or dictionary, and so on. Even types are an object type in Python: a call to the built-in function type(X) returns the type object of object X. Besides making for an amazing tongue-twister, type objects can be used for manual type comparisons in Python.

Built-in Type Gotchas

In this and most of the next few chapters, we'll include a discussion of common problems that seem to bite new users (and the occasional expert), along with their

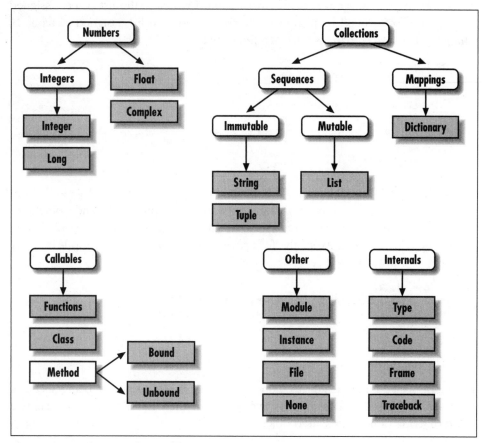

Figure 2-3. Built-in type hierarchies

solutions. We call these *gotchas*—a degenerate form of "got you"—because some may catch you by surprise, especially when you're just getting started with Python. Others represent esoteric Python behavior, which comes up rarely (if ever!) in real programming, but tends to get an inordinate amount of attention from language aficionados on the Internet (like us).* Either way, all have something to teach us about Python; if you can understand the exceptions, the rest is easy.

Assignment Creates References, Not Copies

We've talked about this earlier, but we want to mention it again here, to underscore that it can be a gotcha if you don't understand what's going on with shared

---

* We should also note that Guido could make some of the gotchas we describe go away in future Python releases, but most reflect fundamental properties of the language that are unlikely to change (but don't quote us on that).

references in your program. For instance, in the following, the list object assigned to name L is referenced both from L and from inside the list assigned to name M. Changing L in place changes what M references too:

```
>>> L = [1, 2, 3]
>>> M = ['X', L, 'Y']          # embed a reference to L
>>> M
['X', [1, 2, 3], 'Y']

>>> L[1] = 0                    # changes M too
>>> M
['X', [1, 0, 3], 'Y']
```

Solutions

This effect usually becomes important only in larger programs, and sometimes shared references are exactly what you want. If they're not, you can avoid sharing objects by copying them explicitly; for lists, you can always make a top-level copy by using an empty-limits slice:

```
>>> L = [1, 2, 3]
>>> M = ['X', L[:], 'Y']        # embed a copy of L
>>> L[1] = 0                    # only changes L, not M
>>> L
[1, 0, 3]
>>> M
['X', [1, 2, 3], 'Y']
```

Remember, slice limits default to 0 and the length of the sequence being sliced; if both are omitted, the slice extracts every item in the sequence, and so makes a top-level copy (a new, unshared object).[*]

Repetition Adds One-Level Deep

When we introduced sequence repetition, we said it's like adding a sequence to itself a number of times. That's true, but when mutable sequences are nested, the effect might not always be what you expect. For instance, in the following, X is assigned to L repeated four times, whereas Y is assigned to a list *containing* L repeated four times:

```
>>> L = [4, 5, 6]
>>> X = L * 4                   # like [4, 5, 6] + [4, 5, 6] + ...
>>> Y = [L] * 4                 # [L] + [L] + ... = [L, L,...]

>>> X
```

---

[*] Empty-limit slices still only make a top-level copy; if you need a complete copy of a deeply nested data structure, you can also use the standard copy module that traverses objects recursively. See the library manual for details.

```
[4, 5, 6, 4, 5, 6, 4, 5, 6, 4, 5, 6]
>>> Y
[[4, 5, 6], [4, 5, 6], [4, 5, 6], [4, 5, 6]]
```

Because L was nested in the second repetition, Y winds up embedding references back to the *original* list assigned to L, and is open to the same sorts of side effects we noted in the last section:

```
>>> L[1] = 0              # impacts Y but not X
>>> X
[4, 5, 6, 4, 5, 6, 4, 5, 6, 4, 5, 6]
>>> Y
[[4, 0, 6], [4, 0, 6], [4, 0, 6], [4, 0, 6]]
```

Solutions

This is really another way to trigger the shared mutable object reference issue, so the same solutions above apply here. And if you remember that repetition, concatenation, and slicing copy only the top level of their operand objects, these sorts of cases make much more sense.

Cyclic Data Structures Can't Be Printed

We actually encountered this gotcha in a prior exercise: if a compound object contains a reference to itself, it's called a *cyclic* object. In Python versions before Release 1.5.1, printing such objects failed, because the Python printer wasn't smart enough to notice the cycle (you'll keep seeing the same text printed over and over, until you break execution). This case is now detected, but it's worth knowing; cyclic structures may also cause code of your own to fall into unexpected loops if you're not careful. See the solutions to Chapter 1 exercises for more details.

```
>>> L = ['hi.']; L.append(L)    # append reference to same object
>>> L                           # before 1.5.1: a loop! (cntl-C breaks)
```

Solutions

Don't do that. There are good reasons to create cycles, but unless you have code that knows how to handle them, you probably won't want to make your objects reference themselves very often in practice (except as a parlor trick).

Immutable Types Can't Be Changed in Place

Finally, as we've mentioned plenty of times by now: you can't change an immutable object in place:

```
T = (1, 2, 3)
T[2] = 4            # error!
T = T[:2] + (4,)    # okay: (1, 2, 4)
```

Solutions

Construct a new object with slicing, concatenation, and so on, and assign it back to the original reference if needed. That might seem like extra coding work, but the upside is that the previous gotchas can't happen when using immutable objects such as tuples and strings; because they can't be changed in place, they are not open to the sorts of side effects that lists are.

Summary

In this chapter, we've met Python's built-in object types—numbers, strings, lists, dictionaries, tuples, and files—along with the operations Python provides for processing them. We've also noticed some of the themes underlying objects in Python along the way; in particular, the notions of operation overloading and type categories help to simplify types in Python. Finally, we've seen a few common pitfalls of built-in types.

Almost all the examples in this chapter were deliberately artificial to illustrate the basics. In the next chapter, we'll start studying statements that create and process objects and let us build up programs that do more realistic work.

Other Types in Python

Besides the core objects we've studied in this chapter, a typical Python installation has dozens of other object types available as linked-in C extensions or Python classes. We'll see examples of a few later in the book—regular expression objects, DBM files, GUI widgets, and so on. The main difference between these extra tools and the built-in types we've just seen is that the built-ins provide special language *creation syntax* for their objects (e.g., 4 for an integer, [1,2] for a list, the open function for files). Other tools are generally exported in a built-in module that you must first import to use. See Python's library reference for a comprehensive guide to all the tools available to Python programs.

Exercises

This session asks you to get your feet wet with built-in object fundamentals. As before, a few new ideas may pop up along the way, so be sure to flip to Appendix C when you're done (and even when you're not).

1. *The basics.* Experiment interactively with the common type operations found in this chapter's tables. To get you started, bring up the Python interactive

interpreter, type the expressions below, and try to explain what's happening in each case:

```
2 ** 16
2 / 5, 2 / 5.0

"spam" + "eggs"
S = "ham"
"eggs " + S
S * 5
S[:0]
"green %s and %s" % ("eggs", S)

('x',)[0]
('x', 'y')[1]

L = [1,2,3] + [4,5,6]
L, L[:], L[:0], L[-2], L[-2:]
([1,2,3] + [4,5,6])[2:4]
[L[2], L[3]]
L.reverse(); L
L.sort(); L
L.index(4)

{'a':1, 'b':2}['b']
D = {'x':1, 'y':2, 'z':3}
D['w'] = 0
D['x'] + D['w']
D[(1,2,3)] = 4
D.keys(), D.values(), D.has_key((1,2,3))

[[]], ["",[],(),{},None]
```

2. *Indexing and slicing.* At the interactive prompt, define a list named L that contains four strings or numbers (e.g., L=[0,1,2,3]). Now, let's experiment with some boundary cases.

    a. What happens when you try to index out of bounds (e.g., L[4])?

    b. What about slicing out of bounds (e.g., L[-1000:100])?

    c. Finally, how does Python handle it if you try to extract a sequence in reverse—with the lower bound greater than the higher bound (e.g., L[3:1])? Hint: try assigning to this slice (L[3:1] = ['?']) and see where the value is put. Do you think this may be the same phenomenon you saw when slicing out of bounds?

3. *Indexing, slicing, and del.* Define another list L with four items again, and assign an empty list to one of its offsets (e.g., L[2] = []): what happens? Then try assigning an empty list to a slice (L[2:3] = []): what happens now? Recall that slice assignment deletes the slice and inserts the new value where it used to be. The `del` statement deletes offsets, keys, attributes, and names: try using it on your list to delete an item (e.g., `del L[0]`). What happens if

you del an entire slice (del L[1:])? What happens when you assign a nonsequence to a slice (L[1:2] = 1)?

4. *Tuple assignment.* What do you think is happening to X and Y when you type this sequence? We'll return to this construct in Chapter 3, but it has something to do with the tuples we've seen here.

```
>>> X = 'spam'
>>> Y = 'eggs'
>>> X, Y = Y, X
```

5. *Dictionary keys.* Consider the following code fragments:

```
>>> D = {}
>>> D[1] = 'a'
>>> D[2] = 'b'
```

We learned that dictionaries aren't accessed by offsets; what's going on here? Does the following shed any light on the subject? (Hint: strings, integers, and tuples share which type category?)

```
>>> D[(1, 2, 3)] = 'c'
>>> D
{1: 'a', 2: 'b', (1, 2, 3): 'c'}
```

6. *Dictionary indexing.* Create a dictionary named D with three entries, for keys a, b, and c. What happens if you try to index a nonexistent key d (D['d'])? What does Python do if you try to assign to a nonexistent key d (e.g., D['d'] = 'spam')? How does this compare to out-of-bounds assignments and references for lists? Does this sound like the rule for variable names?

7. *Generic operations.* Run interactive tests to answer the following questions.

   a. What happens when you try to use the + operator on different/mixed types (e.g., string + list, list + tuple)?

   b. Does + work when one of the operands is a dictionary?

   c. Does the **append** method work for both lists and strings? How about the using the **keys** method on lists? (Hint: What does **append** assume about its subject object?)

   d. Finally, what type of object do you get back when you slice or concatenate two lists or two strings?

8. *String indexing.* Define a string S of four characters: S = "spam". Then type the following expression: S[0][0][0][0][0]. Any clues as to what's happening this time? (Hint: recall that a string is a collection of characters, but Python characters are one-character strings.) Does this indexing expression still work if you apply it to a list such as: ['s', 'p', 'a', 'm']? Why?

9. *Immutable types.* Define a string S of 4 characters again: S = "spam". Write an assignment that changes the string to "slam", using only slicing and concate-

nation. Could you perform the same operation using just indexing and concatenation? How about index assignment?

10. *Nesting*. Write a data-structure that represents your personal information: name
(first, middle, last), age, job, address, email ID, and phone number. You may
build the data structure with any combination of built-in object types you like:
lists, tuples, dictionaries, strings, numbers. Then access the individual components of your data structures by indexing. Do some structures make more
sense than others for this object?

11. *Files*. Write a script that creates a new output file called *myfile.txt* and writes
the string "Hello file world!" in it. Then write another script that opens
myfile.txt, and reads and prints its contents. Run your two scripts from the system command line. Does the new file show up in the directory where you ran
your scripts? What if you add a different directory path to the filename passed
to open?

12. *The dir function revisited*. Try typing the following expressions at the interactive prompt. Starting with Version 1.5, the dir function we met in Chapter 1
has been generalized to list all attributes of *any* Python object you're likely to
be interested in. If you're using an earlier version than 1.5, the __methods__
scheme has the same effect.

```
[].__methods__      # 1.4 or 1.5
dir([])             # 1.5 and later
{}.__methods__
dir({})
```

3

Basic Statements

Now that we've seen Python's fundamental built-in object types, we're going to move on in this chapter to explore its basic statement types. In simple terms, statements are the things you write to tell Python what your programs should do. If programs do *things* with *stuff*, statements are the way you specify what sort of *things* a program does. By and large, Python is a procedural, statement-based language; by combining statements, you specify a procedure Python performs to satisfy a program's goals.

Another way to understand the role of statements is to revisit the concept hierarchy we introduced in Chapter 2, *Types and Operators*. In that chapter we talked about built-in objects; now we climb the hierarchy to the next level:

1. Programs are composed of modules.

2. Modules contain *statements*.

3. Statements create and process objects.

Statements process the objects we've already seen. Moreover, statements are where objects spring into existence (e.g., in assignment statement expressions), and some statements create entirely new kinds of objects (functions, classes, and so on). And although we won't discuss this in detail until Chapter 5, *Modules*, statements always exist in modules, which themselves are managed with statements.

Table 3-1 summarizes Python's statement set. We've introduced a few of these already; for instance, in Chapter 2, we saw that the `del` statement deletes data structure components, the assignment statement creates references to objects, and so on. In this chapter, we fill in details that were skipped and introduce the rest of Python's basic procedural statements. We stop short when statements that have to do with larger program units—functions, classes, modules, and exceptions—are reached. Since these statements lead to more sophisticated programming ideas, we'll give them each a chapter of their own. More exotic statements like **exec** (which compiles and executes code we create as strings) and **assert** are covered later in the book.

Table 3-1. Python Statements

Statement	Role	Examples
Assignment	Creating references	`curly, moe, larry = 'good', 'bad', 'ugly'`
Calls	Running functions	`stdout.write("spam, ham, toast\n")`
Print	Printing objects	`print 'The Killer', joke`
If/elif/else	Selecting actions	`if "python" in text: print text`
For/else	Sequence iteration	`for x in mylist: print x`
While/else	General loops	`while 1: print 'hello'`
Pass	Empty placeholder	`while 1: pass`
Break, Continue	Loop jumps	`while 1:` `    if not line: break`
Try/except/ finally	Catching exceptions	`try: action()` `except: print 'action error'`
Raise	Triggering exception	`raise endSearch, location`
Import, From	Module access	`import sys; from sys import stdin`
Def, Return	Building functions	`def f(a, b, c=1, *d): return a+b+c+d[0]`
Class	Building objects	`class subclass: staticData = []`
Global	Namespaces	`def function(): global x, y; x = 'new'`
Del	Deleting things	`del data[k]; del data[i:j]; del obj.attr`
Exec	Running code strings	`exec "import " + modName in gdict, ldict`
Assert	Debugging checks	`assert X > Y`

Assignment

We've been using the Python assignment statement already, to assign objects to names. In its basic form, you write a target of an assignment on the left of an equals sign and an object to be assigned on the right. The target on the left may be a name or object component, and the object on the right can be an arbitrary expression that computes an object. For the most part, assignment is straightforward to use, but here are a few properties to keep in mind:

Assignments create object references

As we've already seen, Python assignment stores references to objects in names or data structure slots. It always creates *references* to objects, instead of copying objects. Because of that, Python variables are much more like pointers than data storage areas as in C.

Names are created when first assigned

As we've also seen, Python creates variable names the first time you assign them a value (an object reference). There's no need to predeclare names ahead of time. Some (but not all) data structure slots are created when assigned too (e.g., dictionary entries, some object attributes). Once assigned, a name is replaced by the value it references when it appears in an expression.

Names must be assigned before being referenced

Conversely, it's an error to use a name you haven't assigned a value to yet. Python raises an exception if you try, rather than returning some sort of ambiguous (and hard to notice) default value.

Implicit assignments: import, from, def, class, for, function arguments, etc.

In this section, we're concerned with the = statement, but assignment occurs in many contexts in Python. For instance, we'll see later that module imports, function and class definitions, for loop variables, and function arguments are all implicit assignments. Since assignment works the same everywhere it pops up, all these contexts simply bind names to object references at runtime.

Table 3-2 illustrates the different flavors of the assignment statement in Python.

Table 3-2. Assignment Statement Forms

Operation	Interpretation
spam = 'Spam'	Basic form
spam, ham = 'yum', 'YUM'	Tuple assignment (positional)
[spam, ham] = ['yum', 'YUM']	List assignment (positional)
spam = ham = 'lunch'	Multiple-target

The first line is by far the most common: binding a single object to a name (or data-structure slot). The other table entries represent special forms:

Tuple and list unpacking assignments

The second and third lines are related. When you use tuples or lists on the left side of the =, Python pairs objects on the right side with targets on the left and assigns them from left to right. For example, in the second line of the table, name **spam** is assigned the string `'yum'`, and name **ham** is bound to string `'YUM'`. Internally, Python makes a tuple of the items on the right first, so this is often called tuple (and list) unpacking assignment.

Multiple-target assignments

The last line shows the multiple-target form of assignment. In this form, Python assigns a reference to the same object (the object farthest to the right) to all the targets on the left. In the table, names **spam** and **ham** would both be assigned a reference to the string `'lunch'`, and so share the same object. The effect is the same as if you had coded **ham='lunch'**, followed by **spam=ham**, since **ham** evaluates to the original string object.

Here's a simple example of unpacking assignment in action. We introduced the effect of the last line in a solution to the exercise from Chapter 2: since Python creates a temporary tuple that saves the items on the right, unpacking assignments are also a way to swap two variables' values without creating a temporary of our own.

```
>>> nudge = 1
>>> wink  = 2
>>> A, B = nudge, wink          # tuples
>>> A, B
(1, 2)
>>> [C, D] = [nudge, wink]      # lists
>>> C, D
(1, 2)
>>> nudge, wink = wink, nudge   # tuples: swaps values
>>> nudge, wink                 # same as T=nudge; nudge=wink; wink=T
(2, 1)
```

Variable Name Rules

Now that we've told you the whole story of assignment statements, we should also get a bit more formal in our use of variable names. In Python, names come into existence when you assign values to them, but there are a few rules to follow when picking names for things in our program. Python's variable name rules are similar to C's:

Syntax: (underscore or letter) + (any number of letters, digits, or underscores)

Variable names must start with an underscore or letter, and be followed by any number of letters, digits, or underscores. **_spam**, **spam**, and **Spam_1** are legal names, but **1_Spam**, **spam$**, and **@#!** are not.

Case matters: SPAM is not the same as spam

Python always pays attention to case in programs, both in names you create and in reserved words. For instance, names **X** and **x** refer to two different variables.

Reserved words are off limits

Names we define cannot be the same as words that mean special things in the Python language. For instance, if we try to use a variable name like `class`, Python will raise a syntax error, but `klass` and `Class` work fine. The list below displays the reserved words (and hence off limits to us) in Python.

and	assert	break	class	continue
def	del	elif	else	except
exec	finally	for	from	global
if	import	in	is	lambda
not	or	pass	print	raise
return	try	while		

Before moving on, we'd like to remind you that it's crucial to keep Python's distinction between *names* and *objects* clear. As we saw in Chapter 2, objects have a type (e.g., integer, list), and may be mutable or not. Names, on the other hand, are just references to objects. They have no notion of mutability and have no associated type information apart from the type of the object they happen to be bound to at a given point in time. In fact, it's perfectly okay to assign the same name to different kinds of objects at different times:

```
>>> x = 0           # x bound to an integer object
>>> x = "Hello"     # now it's a string
>>> x = [1, 2, 3]   # and now it's a list
```

In later examples, we'll see that this generic nature of names can be a decided advantage in Python programming.*

Expressions

In Python, you can use expressions as statements too. But since the result of the expression won't be saved, it makes sense to do so only if the expression does something useful as a side effect. Expressions are commonly used as statements in two situations:

For calls to functions and methods

Some functions and methods do lots of work without returning a value. Since you're not interested in retaining the value they return, you can call such functions with an *expression statement*. Such functions are sometimes called *proce-*

---

* If you've used C++ in the past, you may be interested to know that there is no notion of C++'s `const` declaration in Python; certain objects may be immutable, but names can always be assigned. Or usually; as we'll see in later chapters, Python also has ways to hide names in classes and modules, but they're not the same as C++'s declarations.

dures in other languages; in Python, they take the form of functions that don't return a value.

For printing values at the interactive prompt

As we've already seen, Python echoes back the results of expressions typed at the interactive command line. Technically, these are expression statements too; they serve as a shorthand for typing `print` statements.

Table 3-3 lists some common expression statement forms in Python; we've seen most before. Calls to functions and methods are coded with a list of objects (really, expressions that evaluate to objects) in parentheses after the function or method.

Table 3-3. Common Python Expression Statements

Operation	Interpretation
spam(eggs, ham)	Function calls
spam.ham(eggs)	Method calls
spam	Interactive print
spam < ham and ham != eggs	Compound expressions
spam < ham < eggs	Range tests

The last line in the table is a special form: Python lets us string together magnitude comparison tests, in order to code chained comparisons such as *range* tests. For instance, the expression (A < B < C) tests whether B is between A and C; it's equivalent to the Boolean test (A < B and B < C) but is easier on the eyes (and keyboard). Compound expressions aren't normally written as statements, but it's syntactically legal to do so and can even be useful at the interactive prompt if you're not sure of an expression's result.

 Although expressions can appear as statements in Python, statements can't be used as expressions. For instance, unlike C, Python doesn't allow us to embed assignment statements (=) in other expressions. The rationale for this is that it avoids common coding mistakes; you can't accidentally change a variable by typing = when you really mean to use the == equality test.

Print

The `print` statement simply prints objects. Technically, it writes the textual representation of objects to the standard output stream. The standard output stream happens to be the same as the C `stdout` stream and usually maps to the window where you started your Python program (unless you've redirected it to a file in your system's shell).

In Chapter 2, we also saw file methods that write text. The `print` statement is similar, but more focused: `print` writes objects to the `stdout` stream (with some default formatting), but file `write` methods write strings to files. Since the standard output stream is available in Python as the `stdout` object in the built-in `sys` module (aka `sys.stdout`), it's possible to emulate `print` with file writes (see below), but `print` is easier to use.

Table 3-4 lists the `print` statement's forms.

Table 3-4. Print Statement Forms

Operation	Interpretation
`print spam, ham`	Print objects to `sys.stdout`, add a space between
`print spam, ham,`	Same, but don't add newline at end

By default, `print` adds a space between items separated by commas and adds a linefeed at the end of the current output line. To suppress the linefeed (so you can add more text on the same line later), end your `print` statement with a comma, as shown in the second line of the table. To suppress the space between items, you can instead build up an output string using the string concatenation and formatting tools in Chapter 2:

```
>>> print "a", "b"
a b
>>> print "a" + "b"
ab
>>> print "%s...%s" % ("a", "b")
a...b
```

The Python "Hello World" Program

And now, without further delay, here's the script you've all been waiting for (drum roll please)—the *hello world* program in Python. Alas, it's more than a little anticlimactic. To print a *hello world* message in Python, you simply print it:

```
>>> print 'hello world'               # print a string object
hello world

>>> 'hello world'                     # interactive prints
'hello world'

>>> import sys                        # printing the hard way
>>> sys.stdout.write('hello world\n')
hello world
```

Printing is as simple as it should be in Python; although you can achieve the same effect by calling the `write` method of the `sys.stdout` file object, the `print` statement is provided as a simpler tool for simple printing jobs. Since expression results are echoed in the interactive command line, you often don't even need to use a `print` statement there; simply type expressions you'd like to have printed.

Why You Will Care: print and stdout

The equivalence between the `print` statement and writing to `sys.stdout` is important to notice. It's possible to reassign `sys.stdout` to a user-defined object that provides the same methods as files (e.g., `write`). Since the `print` statement just sends text to the `sys.stdout.write` method, you can capture printed text in your programs by assigning `sys.stdout` to an object whose `write` method saves the text. For instance, you can send printed text to a GUI window by defining an object with a `write` method that does the routing. We'll see an example of this trick later in the book, but abstractly, it looks like this:

```
class FileFaker:
    def write(self, string):
        # do something with the string

import sys
sys.stdout = FileFaker()
print someObjects          # sends to the write method of the class
```

Python's built-in `raw_input()` function reads from the `sys.stdin` file, so you can intercept read requests in a similar way (using classes that implement file-like read methods). Notice that since `print` text goes to the stdout stream, it's the way to print HTML in CGI scripts (see Chapter 9, *Common Tasks in Python*). It also means you can redirect Python script input and output at the operating system's command line, as usual:

```
python script.py < inputfile > outputfile
python script.py | filter
```

---

if Tests

The Python `if` statement selects actions to perform. It's the primary selection tool in Python and represents much of the logic a Python program possesses. It's also our first *compound* statement; like all compound Python statements, the `if` may contain other statements, including other `ifs`. In fact, Python lets you combine statements in a program both *sequentially* (so that they execute one after another), and arbitrarily *nested* (so that they execute only under certain conditions).

General Format

The Python if statement is typical of most procedural languages. It takes the form of an if test, followed by one or more optional elif tests (meaning "else if"), and ends with an optional else block. Each test and the else have an associated block of nested statements indented under a header line. When the statement runs, Python executes the block of code associated with the first test that evaluates to true, or the else block if all tests prove false. The general form of an if looks like this:

```
if <test1>:              # if test
    <statements1>        # associated block
elif <test2>:            # optional elif's
    <statements2>
else:                    # optional else
    <statements3>
```

Examples

Here are two simple examples of the if statement. All parts are optional except the initial if test and its associated statements. Here's the first:

```
>>> if 1:
...     print 'true'
...
true
>>> if not 1:
...     print 'true'
... else:
...     print 'false'
...
false
```

Now, here's an example of the most complex kind of if statement—with all its optional parts present. The statement extends from the if line, through the else's block. Python executes the statements nested under the first test that is true, or else the else part. In practice, both the elif and else parts may be omitted, and there may be more than one statement nested in each section:

```
>>> x = 'killer rabbit'
>>> if x == 'roger':
...     print "how's jessica?"
... elif x == 'bugs':
...     print "what's up doc?"
... else:
...     print 'Run away! Run away!'
...
Run away! Run away!
```

If you've used languages like C or Pascal, you might be interested to know that there is no switch (or case) statement in Python. Instead, *multiway branching* is coded as a series of `if`/`elif` tests as done above, or by indexing dictionaries or searching lists. Since dictionaries and lists can be built at runtime, they're sometimes more flexible than hardcoded logic:

```
>>> choice = 'ham'
>>> print {'spam':  1.25,          # a dictionary-based 'switch'
...         'ham':   1.99,          # use has_key() test for default case
...         'eggs':  0.99,
...         'bacon': 1.10}[choice]
1.99
```

An almost equivalent `if` statement might look like the following:

```
>>> if choice == 'spam':
...         print 1.25
... elif choice == 'ham':
...         print 1.99
... elif choice == 'eggs':
...         print 0.99
... elif choice == 'bacon':
...         print 1.10
... else:
...         print 'Bad choice'
...
1.99
```

Dictionaries are good at associating values with keys, but what about more complicated actions you can code in `if` statements? We can't get into many details yet, but in Chapter 4, *Functions*, we'll see that dictionaries can also contain *functions* to represent more complex actions.

Python Syntax Rules

Since the `if` statement is our first compound statement, we need to say a few words about Python's syntax rules now. In general, Python has a simple, statement-based syntax. But there are a few properties you need to know:

Statements execute one after another, until you say otherwise

Python normally runs statements in a file or nested block from first to last, but statements like the `if` (and, as we'll see in a moment, loops) cause the interpreter to jump around in your code. Because Python's path through a program is called the *control flow*, things like the `if` that affect it are called control-flow statements.

Block and statement boundaries are detected automatically

There are no braces or begin/end delimiters around blocks of code; instead, Python uses the indentation of statements under a header to group the statements in a nested block. Similarly, Python statements are not normally terminated with a semicolon as in C; rather, the end of a line marks the end of most statements.

Compound statements = header, ':', indented statements

All compound statements in Python follow the same pattern: a header line terminated with a colon, followed by one or more nested statements indented under the header. The indented statements are called a *block* (or sometimes, a suite). In the `if` statement, the `elif` and `else` clauses are part of the `if`, but are header lines in their own right.

Spaces and comments are usually ignored

Spaces inside statements and expressions are almost always ignored (except in string constants and indentation). So are comments: they start with a # character (not inside a string constant) and extend to the end of the current line. Python also has support for something called documentation strings associated with objects, but we'll ignore these for the time being.

As we've seen, there are no variable type declarations in Python; this fact alone makes for a much simpler language syntax than what you may be used to. But for most new users, the lack of braces and semicolons to mark blocks and statements seems to be the most novel syntactic feature of Python, so let's explore what this means in more detail here.*

Block delimiters

As mentioned, block boundaries are detected by line indentation: all statements indented the same distance to the right belong to the same block of code, until that block is ended by a line less indented. Indentation can consist of any combination of spaces and tabs; tabs count for enough spaces to move the current column number up to a multiple of 8 (but it's usually not a good idea to mix tabs and spaces). Blocks of code can be nested by indenting them further than the enclosing block. For instance, Figure 3-1 sketches the block structure of this example:

```
x = 1
if x:
    y = 2
    if y:
        print 'block2'
    print 'block1'
print 'block0'
```

---

* It's probably more novel if you're a C or Pascal programmer. Python's indentation-based syntax is actually based on the results of a usability study of nonprogrammers, conducted for the ABC language. Python's syntax is often called the "what you see is what you get" of languages; it enforces a consistent appearance that tends to aid readability and avoid common C and C++ errors.

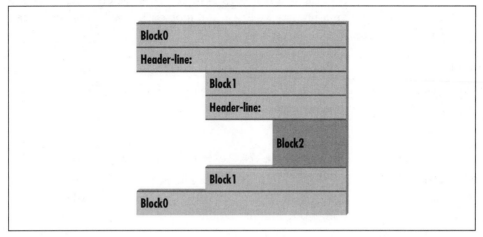

Figure 3-1. Nested code blocks

Notice that code in the outermost block must start in column 1, since it's unnested; nested blocks can start in any column, but multiples of 4 are a common indentation style. If this all sounds complicated, just code blocks as you would in C or Pascal, and omit the delimiters; consistently-indented code always satisfies Python's rules.

Statement delimiters

As also mentioned, statements normally end at the end of the line they appear on, but when statements are too long to fit on a single line, a few special rules may be used:

Statements may span lines if you're continuing an open syntactic pair

For statements that are too long to fit on one line, Python lets you continue typing the statement on the next line, if you're coding something enclosed in (), {}, or [] pairs. For instance, parenthesized expressions and dictionary and list constants can span any number of lines. Continuation lines can start at any indentation level.

Statements may span lines if they end in a backslash

This is a somewhat outdated feature, but if a statement needs to span multiple lines, you can also add a backslash (\) at the end of the prior line to indicate you're continuing on the next line (much like C #define macros). But since you can also continue by adding parentheses around long constructs, backslashes are almost never needed.

Other rules

Very long string constants can span lines arbitrarily. In fact, the triple-quoted string blocks in Chapter 2 are designed to do so. You can also terminate statements with a semicolon if you like (this is more useful when more than one statement appears on a line, as we'll see in a moment). Finally, comments can appear anywhere.

A few special cases

Here's what a continuation line looks like, using the open pairs rule; we can span delimited constructs across any number of lines:

```
L = ["Good",
    "Bad",
    "Ugly"]                          # open pairs may span lines
```

This works for anything in parentheses too: expressions, function arguments, functions headers (see Chapter 4), and so on. If you like using backslashes to continue you can, but it's more work, and not required:

```
if a == b and c == d and   \
   d == e and f == g:
   print 'olde'                      # backslashes allow continuations

if (a == b and c == d and
    d == e and e == f):
    print 'new'                      # but parentheses usually do too
```

As a special case, Python allows you to write more than one simple statement (one without nested statements in it) on the same line, separated by semicolons. Some coders use this form to save program file real estate:

```
x = 1; y = 2; print x                # more than 1 simple statement
```

And finally, Python also lets you move a compound statement's body up to the header line, provided the body is just a simple statement. You'll usually see this most often used for simple `if` statements with a single test and action:

```
if 1: print 'hello'                  # simple statement on header line
```

You can combine some of these special cases to write code that is difficult to read, but we don't recommend it; as a rule of thumb, try to keep each statement on a line of its own. Six months down the road, you'll be happy you did.

Truth Tests Revisited

We introduced the notions of comparison, equality, and truth values in Chapter 2. Since `if` statements are the first statement that actually uses test results, we'll expand on some of these ideas here. In particular, Python's Boolean operators are a bit different from their counterparts in languages like C. In Python:

- True means any nonzero number or nonempty object.

- False means not true: a zero number, empty object, or **None**.

- Comparisons and equality tests return 1 or 0 (true or false).

- Boolean **and** and **or** operators return a true or false operand object.

The last item here is new; in short, Boolean operators are used to combine the results of other tests. There are three Boolean expression operators in Python:

X and Y
> Is true if both X and Y are true

X or Y
> Is true if either X or Y are true

not X
> Is true if X is false (the expression returns 1 or 0)

Here, X and Y may be any truth value or an expression that returns a truth value (e.g., an equality test, range comparison, and so on). Unlike C, Boolean operators are typed out as words in Python (instead of C's &&, ||, and !). Also unlike C, Boolean **and** and **or** operators return a true or false object in Python, not an integer 1 or 0. Let's look at a few examples to see how this works:

```
>>> 2 < 3, 3 < 2       # less-than: return 1 or 0
(1, 0)
```

Magnitude comparisons like these return an integer 1 or 0 as their truth value result. But **and** and **or** operators always return an object instead. For **or** tests, Python evaluates the operand objects from left to right, and returns the first one that is true. Moreover, Python stops at the first true operand it finds; this is usually called *short-circuit* evaluation, since determining a result short-circuits (terminates) the rest of the expression:

```
>>> 2 or 3, 3 or 2     # return left operand if true
(2, 3)                 # else return right operand (whether true or false)
>>> [] or 3
3
>>> [] or {}
{}
```

In the first line above, both operands are true (2, 3), so Python always stops and returns the one on the left. In the other two tests, the left operand is false, so Python evaluates and returns the object on the right (that may have a true or false value). **and** operations also stop as soon as the result is known; in this case, Python evaluates operands from left to right and stops at the first false object:

```
>>> 2 and 3, 3 and 2   # return left operand if false
(3, 2)                 # else return right operand (whether true or false)
>>> [] and {}
[]
>>> 3 and []
[]
```

Both operands are true in the first line, so Python evaluates both sides and returns the object on the right. In the second test, the left operand is false ([]), so Python stops and returns it as the test result. In the last test, the left side is true (3), so Python evaluates and returns the object on the right (that happens to be false). The end result is the same as in C (true or false), but it's based on objects, not integer flags.[*]

while Loops

Python's `while` statement is its most general iteration construct. In simple terms, it repeatedly executes a block of indented statements, as long as a test at the top keeps evaluating to a true value. When the test becomes false, control continues after all the statements in the `while`, and the body never runs if the test is false to begin with.

The `while` statement is one of two looping statements (along with the `for`, which we'll meet next). We call it a *loop*, because control keeps looping back to the start of the statement, until the test becomes false. The net effect is that the loop's body is executed repeatedly while the test at the top is true. Python also provides a handful of tools that implicitly loop (iterate), such as the `map`, `reduce`, and `filter` functions, and the `in` membership test; we explore some of these later in this book.

General Format

In its most complex form, the `while` statement consists of a header line with a test expression, a body of one or more indented statements, and an optional `else` part that is executed if control exits the loop without running into a `break` statement (more on these last few words later). Python keeps evaluating the test at the top, and executing the statements nested in the `while` part, until the test returns a false value:

```
while <test>:           # loop test
    <statements1>       # loop body
else:                   # optional else
    <statements2>       # run if didn't exit loop with break
```

---

[*] One common way to use Python Boolean operators is to select from one or more objects with an `or`; a statement such as X = A or B or C sets X to the first nonempty (true) object among A, B, and C. Short-circuit evaluation is important to understand, because expressions on the right of a Boolean operator might call functions that do much work or have side effects that won't happen if the short-circuit rule takes effect.

Examples

To illustrate, here are a handful of simple while loops in action. The first just prints a message forever, by nesting a print statement in a while loop. Recall that an integer 1 means true; since the test is always true, Python keeps executing the body forever or until you stop its execution. This sort of behavior is usually called an *infinite loop* (and tends to be much less welcome when you don't expect it):

```
>>> while 1:
...     print 'Type Ctrl-C to stop me!'
```

The next example keeps slicing off the first character of a string, until the string is empty. Later in this chapter, we'll see other ways to step more directly through the items in a string.

```
>>> x = 'spam'
>>> while x:
...     print x,
...     x = x[1:]        # strip first character off x
...
spam pam am m
```

Finally, the code below counts from the value of a, up to but not including b. It works much like a C for loop; we'll see an easier way to do this with a Python for and range in a moment.

```
>>> a=0; b=10
>>> while a < b:          # one way to code counter loops
...     print a,
...     a = a+1
...
0 1 2 3 4 5 6 7 8 9
```

break, continue, pass, and the Loop else

Now that we've seen our first Python loop, we should introduce two simple statements that have a purpose only when nested inside loops—the break and continue statements. If you've used C, you can skip most of this section, since they work the same in Python. Since break and loop else clauses are intertwined, we'll say more about else here too. And while we're at it, let's also look at Python's empty statement—the pass, which works just like C's empty statement (a bare semicolon). In Python:

break

Jumps out of the closest enclosing loop (past the entire loop statement).

continue

Jumps to the top of the closest enclosing loop (to the loop's header line).

pass

Does nothing at all: it's an empty statement placeholder.

loop **else** *block*

Run if and only if the loop is exited normally—i.e., without hitting a **break**.

General loop format

When we factor in **break** and **continue** statements, the general format of the **while** loop looks like this:

```
while <test>:
    <statements>
    if <test>: break        # exit loop now, skip else
    if <test>: continue     # go to top of loop now
else:
    <statements>            # if we didn't hit a 'break'
```

break and **continue** statements can appear anywhere inside the **while** loop's body, but they are usually coded further nested in an **if** test as we've shown, to take action in response to some sort of condition.

Examples

Let's turn to a few simple examples to see how these statements come together in practice. The **pass** statement is often used to code an empty body for a compound statement. For instance, if you want to code an infinite loop that does nothing each time through, do it with a **pass**:

```
while 1: pass    # type Ctrl-C to stop me!
```

Since the body is just an empty statement, Python gets stuck in this loop, silently chewing up CPU cycles.* **pass** is to statements as **None** is to objects—an explicit nothing. Notice that the **while** loop's body is on the same line as the header above; as in the **if**, this only works if the body isn't a compound statement.

The **continue** statement sometimes lets you avoid statement nesting; here's an example that uses it to skip odd numbers. It prints all even numbers less than 10 and greater than or equal to 0. Remember, 0 means false, and **%** is the remainder-of-division operator, so this loop counts down to zero, skipping numbers that aren't multiples of two (it prints **8 6 4 2 0**):

```
x = 10
while x:
    x = x-1
    if x % 2 != 0: continue    # odd?--skip print
    print x,
```

---

* This probably isn't the most useful Python program ever written, but frankly, we couldn't think of a better pass example. We'll see other places where it makes sense later in the book (for instance, to define empty classes).

Because `continue` jumps to the top of the loop, you don't need to nest the `print` statement inside an `if` test; the `print` is only reached if the `continue` isn't run. If this sounds similar to a `goto` in other languages it should; Python has no `goto` per se, but because `continue` lets you jump around a program, all the warnings about readability you may have heard about `goto` apply. It should probably be used sparingly, especially when you're first getting started with Python.

The `break` statement can often eliminate the search status flags used in other languages. For instance, the following piece of code determines if a number `y` is prime, by searching for factors greater than one:

```
x = y / 2
while x > 1:
    if y % x == 0:                # remainder
        print y, 'has factor', x
        break                     # skip else
    x = x-1
else:                             # normal exit
    print y, 'is prime'
```

Rather than setting a flag to be tested when the loop is exited, insert a `break` where a factor is found. This way, the loop `else` can assume that it will be executed only if no factor was found; if you don't hit the `break`, the number is prime. Notice that a loop `else` is also run if the body of the loop is never executed, since you don't run a `break` in that event either; in a `while` loop, this happens if the test in the header is false to begin with. In the example above, you still get the `is prime` message if `x` is initially less than or equal to 1 (e.g., if `y` is 2).

for Loops

The `for` loop is a generic *sequence iterator* in Python: it can step through the items in any object that responds to the sequence indexing operation. The `for` works on strings, lists, tuples, and new objects we'll create later with classes. We've already seen the `for` in action, when we mentioned the iteration operation for sequence types in Chapter 2. Here, we'll fill in the details we skipped earlier.

General Format

The Python `for` loop begins with a header line that specifies an assignment target (or targets), along with an object you want to step through. The header is followed by a block of indented statements, which you want to repeat:

```
for <target> in <object>:    # assign object items to target
    <statements>             # repeated loop body: use target
else:
    <statements>             # if we didn't hit a 'break'
```

When Python runs a for loop, it assigns items in the sequence object to the *target*, one by one, and executes the loop body for each.* The loop body typically uses the assignment target to refer to the current item in the sequence, as though it were a cursor stepping through the sequence. Technically, the for works by repeatedly indexing the sequence object on successively higher indexes (starting at zero), until an index out-of-bounds exception is raised. Because for loops automatically manage sequence indexing behind the scenes, they replace most of the *counter* style loops you may be used to coding in languages like C.

The for also supports an optional else block, which works exactly as it does in while loops; it's executed if the loop exits without running into a break statement (i.e., if all items in the sequence were visited). The break and continue statements we introduced above work the same in the for loop as they do in the while too; we won't repeat their descriptions here, but the for loop's complete format can be described this way:

```
for <target> in <object>:      # assign object items to target
    <statements>
    if <test>: break           # exit loop now, skip else
    if <test>: continue        # go to top of loop now
else:
    <statements>               # if we didn't hit a 'break'
```

Examples

Let's type a few for loops interactively. In the first example below, the name x is assigned to each of the three items in the list in turn, from left to right, and the print statement is executed for each. Inside the print statement (the loop body), the name x refers to the current item in the list:

```
>>> for x in ["spam", "eggs", "ham"]:
...     print x,
...
spam eggs ham
```

The next two examples compute the sum and product of all the items in a list. In Chapter 8, *Built-in Tools*, we'll see built-ins that apply operations like + and * to items in a list, but it's usually just as easy to use a for:

```
>>> sum = 0
>>> for x in [1, 2, 3, 4]:
...     sum = sum + x
...
>>> sum
```

---

* The name used as the assignment target in a for header line is simply a (possibly new) variable in the namespace (scope) where the for statement is coded. There's not much special about it; it can even be changed inside the for loop's body, but it's automatically set to the next item in the sequence when control returns to the top of the loop again.

```
10
>>> prod = 1
>>> for item in [1, 2, 3, 4]: prod = prod * item
...
>>> prod
24
```

As mentioned, for loops work on strings and tuples too. One thing we haven't mentioned is that, if you're iterating through a sequence of tuples, the loop target can actually be a *tuple* of targets. This is just another case of tuple *unpacking* assignment at work; remember, the for assigns items in the sequence to the target, and assignment works the same everywhere:

```
>>> S, T = "lumberjack", ("and", "I'm", "okay")

>>> for x in S: print x,
...
l u m b e r j a c k

>>> for x in T: print x,
...
and I'm okay

>>> T = [(1, 2), (3, 4), (5, 6)]
>>> for (a, b) in T:                    # tuple assignment at work
...     print a, b
...
...
1 2
3 4
5 6
```

Now, let's look at something a bit more sophisticated. The next example illustrates both the loop else in a for and statement nesting. Given a list of objects (items) and a list of keys (tests), this code searches for each key in the objects list, and reports on the search's success:

```
>>> items = ["aaa", 111, (4, 5), 2.01]    # a set of objects
>>> tests = [(4, 5), 3.14]                # keys to search for
>>>
>>> for key in tests:                     # for all keys
...     for item in items:                # for all items
...         if item == key:               # check for match
...             print key, "was found"
...             break
...     else:
...         print key, "not found!"
...
(4, 5) was found
3.14 not found!
```

Since the nested if runs a break when a match is found, the loop else can assume that the search has failed. Notice the nesting here: when this code runs, there are two loops going at the same time. The outer loop scans the keys list, and the inner loop scans the items list for each key. The nesting of the loop `else` is critical; it's indented at the same level as the header line of the inner `for` loop, so it's associated with the inner loop (not the `if` or outer `for`). By the way, this example is easier to code if you employ the `in` operator from Chapter 2, to test *membership* for us; since `in` implicitly scans a list looking for a match, it replaces the inner loop:

```
>>> for key in tests:              # for all keys
...     if key in items:           # let Python check for a match
...         print key, "was found"
...     else:
...         print key, "not found!"
...
(4, 5) was found
3.14 not found!
```

In general, it's a good idea to let Python do the work like this. The next example performs a typical data-structure task with a `for`—collecting common items in two sequences (strings). It's roughly a simple set *intersection* routine; after the loop runs, `res` refers to a list that contains all the items found in both `seq1` and `seq2`:[*]

```
>>> seq1 = "spam"
>>> seq2 = "scam"
>>>
>>> res = []                       # start empty
>>> for x in seq1:                 # scan first sequence
...     if x in seq2:              # common item?
...         res.append(x)          # add to result end
...
>>> res
['s', 'a', 'm']
```

Unfortunately, this code is equipped to work only on two specific variables: `seq1` and `seq2`. It would be nice if this loop could be somehow generalized into a tool we could use more than once. As we'll see, that simple idea leads us to *functions*, the topic of our next chapter.

range and Counter Loops

The `for` loop subsumes most counter-style loops, so it's the first tool you should reach for whenever you need to step though a sequence. But there are also situations where you need to iterate in a more specialized way. You can always code unique iterations with a `while` loop, but Python also provides a way to specialize

---

[*] This isn't exactly what some folks would call set intersection (an item can appear more than once in the result if it appears more than once in `seq1`), but this isn't exactly a text on set theory either. To avoid duplicates, say if x in seq2 and x not in res inside the loop instead. Incidentally, this is a great example of how lists get built up dynamically (by program code), rather than being written out as a constant. As we mentioned before, most data structures are built, rather than written.

Why You Will Care: File Scanner Loops

In general, loops come in handy any place you need to repeat or process something more than once. Since files contain multiple characters and lines, they are one of the more typical uses for loops. For example it's common to see file scanning loops coded with a **while** and **breaks**, instead of end-of-file tests at the top:

```
file = open("name", "r")
while 1:
    line = file.readline()        # fetch next line, if any
    if not line: break            # exit loop on end-of-file (empty string)
    Process line here
```

The **for** loop comes in handy for scanning files too; the **readlines** file method introduced in Chapter 2 hands you a lines list to step through:

```
file = open("name", "r")
for line in file.readlines():      # read into a lines list
    Process line here
```

In other cases, you might scan byte-by-byte (using **while** and **file.read(1)**), or load the file all at once (e.g., **for char in file.read()**). We'll learn more about file processing later in the book.

---

indexing in a **for**; the built-in **range** function returns a list of successively higher integers, which can be used as indexes in a **for**.[*]

Examples

A few examples will make this more concrete. The **range** function is really independent of **for** loops; although it's used most often to generate indexes in a **for**, you can use it anywhere you need a list of integers:

```
>>> range(5), range(2, 5), range(0, 10, 2)
([0, 1, 2, 3, 4], [2, 3, 4], [0, 2, 4, 6, 8])
```

With one argument, **range** generates a list with integers from zero, up to but not including the argument's value. If you pass in two arguments, the first is taken as the *lower* bound. An optional third argument can give a *step*; if used, Python adds the step to each successive node in the result (steps default to one). Now, the easiest way to step through a sequence is with a simple **for**; Python handles most of the details for you:

```
>>> X = 'spam'
>>> for item in X: print item,        # simple iteration
```

---

[*] Python also provides a built-in called **xrange** that generates indexes one at a time instead of storing all of them in a list at once. There's no speed advantage to **xrange**, but it's useful if you have to generate a huge number of values.

```
...
s p a m
```

Internally, the `for` initializes an index, detects the end of the sequence, indexes the sequence to fetch the current item, and increments the index on each iteration. If you really need to take over the indexing logic explicitly, you can do it with a `while` loop; this form is as close to a C `for` loop as you can come in Python:

```
>>> i = 0
>>> while i < len(X):                    # while iteration
...     print X[i],; i = i+1
...
s p a m
```

And finally, you can still do manual indexing with a `for`, if you use **range** to generate a list of indexes to iterate through:

```
>>> for i in range(len(X)): print X[i],    # manual indexing
...
s p a m
```

But unless you have a special indexing requirement, you're always better off using the simple `for` loop form in Python. One situation where **range** does come in handy is for repeating an action a specific number of times; for example, to print three lines, use a **range** to generate the appropriate number of integers:

```
>>> for i in range(3): print i, 'Pythons'
...
0 Pythons
1 Pythons
2 Pythons
```

Common Coding Gotchas

Before we turn you lose on some programming exercises, we'd like to point out some of the most common mistakes beginners seem to make when coding Python statements and programs. You'll learn to avoid these once you've gained a bit of Python coding experience (in fact, Mark commonly gets into trouble because he uses Python syntax in C++ code!); but a few words might help you avoid falling into some of these traps initially.

Don't forget the colons

Don't forget to type a **:** at the end of compound statement headers (the first line of an `if`, `while`, `for`, etc.). You probably will at first anyhow (we did too), but you can take some comfort in the fact that it will soon become an unconscious habit.

Start in column 1

We mentioned this in Chapter 1, *Getting Started*, but as a reminder: be sure to start top-level (unnested) code in column 1. That includes unnested code typed into module files, as well as unnested code typed at the interactive prompt.

Blank lines matter at the interactive prompt

Blank lines in compound statements are always ignored in module files, but, when typing code, end the statement at the interactive prompt. In other words, blank lines tell the interactive command line that you've finished a compound statement; if you want to continue, don't hit the Return key at the ... prompt until you're really done.

Indent consistently

Avoid mixing tabs and spaces in indentation, unless you're sure what your editor does with tabs. Otherwise, what you see in your editor may not be what Python sees when it counts tabs as a number of spaces.

Don't code C in Python

A note to C/C++ programmers: you don't need to type parentheses around tests in `if` and `while` headers (e.g., `if (X==1): print X`), but you can if you like; any expression can be enclosed in parentheses. And remember, you can't use { } around blocks; indent nested code blocks instead.

Don't always expect a result

Another reminder: in-place change operations like the `list.append()` and `list.sort()` methods in Chapter 2 don't return a value (really, they return `None`); call them without assigning the result. It's common for beginners to say something like `list=list.append(X)` to try to get the result of an `append`; instead, this assigns `list` to `None`, rather than the modified list (in fact, you'll lose a reference to the list altogether).

Use calls and imports properly

Two final reminders: you must add parentheses after a function name to call it, whether it takes arguments or not (e.g., `function()`, not `function`), and you shouldn't include the file suffix in import statements (e.g., `import mod`, not `import mod.py`). In Chapter 4, we'll see that functions are simply objects that have a special operation—a call you trigger with the parentheses. And in Chapter 5, we'll see that modules may have other suffixes besides *.py* (a *.pyc*, for instance); hard-coding a particular suffix is not only illegal syntax, it doesn't make sense.

Summary

In this chapter, we explored Python's basic procedural statements:

- Assignments store references to objects.

- Expressions call functions and methods.

- `print` sends text to the standard output stream.

- `if/elif/else` selects between one or more actions.

- `while/else` loops repeat an action until a test proves false.

- `for/else` loops step through the items in a sequence object.

- `break` and `continue` jump around loops.

- `pass` is an empty placeholder.

We also studied Python's syntax rules along the way, looked at Boolean operators and truth tests, and talked a little about some general programming concepts in Python.

By combining basic statements, we are able to code the basic logic needed to process objects. In Chapter 4, we move on to look at a set of additional statements used to write functions, which package statements for reuse. In later chapters, we'll see more statements that deal with bigger program units, as well as exceptions. Table 3-5 summarizes the statement sets we'll be studying in the remaining chapters of this part of the book.

Table 3-5. Preview: Other Statement Sets

Unit	Role
Functions	Procedural units
Modules	Code/data packages
Classes	New objects
Exceptions	Errors and special cases

Exercises

Now that you know how to code basic program logic, this session asks you to implement some simple tasks with statements. Most of the work is in Exercise 4, which lets you explore coding alternatives. There are always many ways to arrange statements and part of learning Python is learning which arrangements work better than others.

   1. *Coding basic loops.*

      a. Write a `for` loop that prints the ASCII code of each character in a string named `S`. Use the built-in function `ord(character)` to convert each character to an ASCII integer (test it interactively to see how it works).

      b. Next, change your loop to compute the *sum* of the ASCII codes of all characters in a string.

    c. Finally, modify your code again to return a *new list* that contains the ASCII codes of each character in the string. Does this expression have a similar effect—`map(ord, S)`? (Hint: see Chapter 4, *Functions*.)

2. *Backslash characters.* What happens on your machine when you type the following code interactively?

```
for i in range(50):
    print 'hello %d\n\a' % i
```

Warning: this example beeps at you, so you may not want to run it in a crowded lab (unless you happen to enjoy getting lots of attention). Hint: see the backslash escape characters in Table 2-6.

3. *Sorting dictionaries.* In Chapter 2, we saw that dictionaries are *unordered* collections. Write a `for` loop that prints a dictionary's items in sorted (ascending) order. Hint: use the dictionary `keys` and list `sort` methods.

4. *Program logic alternatives.* Consider the following code, which uses a `while` loop and `found` flag to search a list of powers-of-2, for the value of 2 raised to the power 5 (32). It's stored in a module file called *power.py*.

```
L = [1, 2, 4, 8, 16, 32, 64]
X = 5

found = i = 0
while not found and i < len(L):
    if 2 ** X == L[i]:
        found = 1
    else:
        i = i+1

if found:
    print 'at index', i
else:
    print X, 'not found'
```

```
C:\book\tests> python power.py
at index 5
```

As is, the example doesn't follow normal Python coding techniques. Follow the steps below to improve it; for all the transformations, you may type your code interactively or store it in a script file run from the system command line (though using a file makes this exercise much easier).

    a. First, rewrite this code with a `while` loop `else`, to eliminate the `found` flag and final `if` statement.

    b. Next, rewrite the example to use a `for` loop with an `else`, to eliminate the explicit list indexing logic. Hint: to get the index of an item, use the list *index* method (`L.index(X)` returns the offset of the first X in list L).

c. Now, remove the loop completely by rewriting the examples with a simple `in` operator membership expression (see Chapter 2 for more details, or type this: `2 in [1,2,3]`).

d. Finally, use a `for` loop and the list **append** method to generate the powers-of-2 list (L), instead of hard-coding a list constant.

e. Deeper thoughts: (1) Do you think it would improve performance to move the `2**X` expression outside the loops? How would you code that? (2) As we saw in Exercise 1, Python also includes a `map(function, list)` tool that can generate the powers-of-2 list too, as follows: `map(lambda x: 2**x, range(7))`. Try typing this code interactively; we'll meet `lambda` more formally in Chapter 4.

4

Functions

In the last chapter, we looked at basic procedural statements in Python. Here, we'll move on to explore a set of additional statements that create functions of our own. In simple terms, functions are a device that groups a bunch of statements, so they can be run more than once in a program. Functions also let us specify parameters, which may differ each time a function's code is run. Table 4-1 summarizes the function-related statements we'll study in this chapter.

Table 4-1. Function-Related Statements

Statement	Examples
Calls	`myfunc("spam, ham, toast\n")`
`def, return`	`def adder(a, b, c=1, *d): return a+b+c+d[0]`
`global`	`def function(): global x, y; x = 'new'`

Why Use Functions?

Before we get into the details, let's get a clear picture of what functions are about. Functions are a nearly universal program-structuring device. Most of you have probably come across them before in other languages, but as a brief introduction, functions serve two primary development roles:

Code reuse

As in most programming languages, Python functions are the simplest way to package logic you may wish to use in more than one place and more than one time. Up to now, all the code we've been writing runs immediately; functions allow us to group and parametize chunks of code to be used arbitrarily many times later.

Procedural decomposition

Functions also provide a tool for splitting systems into pieces that have a well-defined role. For instance, to make a pizza from scratch, you would start by mixing the dough, rolling it out, adding toppings, baking, and so on. If you were programming a pizza-making robot, functions would help you divide the overall "make pizza" task into chunks—one function for each subtask in the process. It's easier to implement the smaller tasks in isolation than it is to implement the entire process at once. In general, functions are about procedure—how to do something, rather than what you're doing it to. We'll see why this distinction matters in Chapter 6, *Classes.*

Here, we talk about function basics, scope rules and argument passing, and a handful of related concepts. As we'll see, functions don't imply much new syntax, but they do lead us to some bigger programming ideas.

Function Basics

Although we haven't gotten very formal about it, we've already been using functions in earlier chapters. For instance, to make a file object, we call the built-in open function. Similarly, we use the len built-in function to ask for the number of items in a collection object.

In this chapter, we will learn how to write *new* functions in Python. Functions we write ourselves behave the same way as the built-ins we've already seen—they are called in expressions, are passed values, and return results. But writing functions requires a few new ideas; here's an introduction to the main concepts:

def creates a function object and assigns it to a name

Python functions are written with a new statement, the def. Unlike functions in compiled languages such as C, def is an executable statement—when run, it generates a new function object and assigns it to the function's name. As with all assignments, the function name becomes a reference to the function object.

return sends a result object back to the caller

When a function is called, the caller stops until the function finishes its work and returns control to the caller. Functions that compute a value send it back to the caller with a return statement.

global declares module-level variables that are to be assigned

By default, all names assigned in a function are local to that function and exist only while the function runs. To assign a name in the enclosing module, functions need to list it in a global statement.

Arguments are passed by assignment (object reference)

In Python, arguments are passed to functions by assignment (i.e., by object reference). As we'll see, this isn't quite like C's passing rules or C++'s reference parameters—the caller and function share objects by references, but there is no name aliasing (changing an argument name doesn't also change a name in the caller).

Arguments, return types, and variables are not declared

As with everything in Python, there are no type constraints on functions. In fact, nothing about a function needs to be declared ahead of time; we can pass in arguments of any type, return any sort of object, and so on. As one consequence, a single function can often be applied to a variety of object types.

Let's expand on these ideas and look at a few first examples.

General Form

The `def` statement creates a function object and assigns it a function name. As with all compound Python statements, it consists of a header line, followed by a block of indented statements. The indented statements become the function's body—the code Python executes each time the function is called. The header specifies a function name (which is assigned the function object), along with a list of *arguments* (sometimes called *parameters*), which are assigned to the objects passed in parentheses at the point of call:

```
def <name>(arg1, arg2,... argN):
    <statements>
    return <value>
```

The Python **return** statement can show up in function bodies; it ends the function call and sends a result back to the caller. It consists of an object expression that gives the function's result. The **return** is optional; if it's not present, a function exits when control flow falls off the end of the function body. Technically, a function without a **return** returns the `None` object automatically (more on this later in this chapter).

Definitions and Calls

Let's jump into a simple example. There are really two sides to the function picture: a definition (the `def` that creates a function) and a *call* (an expression that tells Python to run the function). A definition follows the general format above; here's one that defines a function called `times`, which returns the product of its two arguments:

```
>>> def times(x, y):        # create and assign function
...     return x * y        # body executed when called
...
```

When Python runs this `def`, it creates a new function object that packages the function's code and assigns it the name `times`. After the `def` has run, the program can run (call) the function by adding parentheses after the function name; the parenthesis may optionally contain one or more object *arguments*, to be passed (assigned) to the names in the function's header:

```
>>> times(2, 4)          # arguments in parentheses
8
>>> times('Ni', 4)       # functions are 'typeless'
'NiNiNiNi'
```

In the first line, we pass two arguments to `times`: the name `x` in the function header is assigned the value 2, `y` is assigned 4, and the function's body is run. In this case, the body is just a `return` statement, which sends back the result 8 as the value of the call expression.

In the second call, we pass in a string and an integer to `x` and `y` instead. Recall that `*` works on both numbers and sequences; because there are no type declarations in functions, you can use `times` to multiply numbers or repeat sequences. Python is known as a *dynamically typed* language: types are associated with objects at runtime, rather than declared in the program itself. In fact, a given name can be assigned to objects of different types at different times.[*]

Example: Intersecting Sequences

Here's a more realistic example that illustrates function basics. Near the end of Chapter 3, *Basic Statements*, we saw a `for` loop that collected items in common in two strings. We noted there that the code wasn't as useful as it could be because it was set up to work only on specific variables and could not be rerun later. Of course, you could cut and paste the code to each place it needs to be run, but this isn't a general solution; you'd still have to edit each copy to support different sequence names, and changing the algorithm requires changing multiple copies.

Definition

By now, you can probably guess that the solution to this dilemma is to package the `for` loop inside a function. By putting the code in a function, it becomes a tool that can be run as many times as you like. And by allowing callers to pass in arbitrary arguments to be processed, you make it general enough to work on any two sequences you wish to intersect. In effect, wrapping the code in a function makes it a general intersection utility:

---

[*] If you've used compiled languages such as C or C++, you'll probably find that Python's dynamic typing makes for an incredibly flexible programming language. It also means that some errors a compiler roots out aren't caught by Python until a program runs (adding a string to an integer, for instance). Luckily, errors are easy to find and repair in Python.

```
def intersect(seq1, seq2):
    res = []                        # start empty
    for x in seq1:                  # scan seq1
        if x in seq2:               # common item?
            res.append(x)           # add to end
    return res
```

The transformation from simple code to this function is straightforward; you've just nested the original logic under a `def` header and made the objects on which it operates parameters. Since this function computes a result, you've also added a `return` statement to send it back to the caller.

Calls

```
>>> s1 = "SPAM"
>>> s2 = "SCAM"

>>> intersect(s1, s2)               # strings
['S', 'A', 'M']

>>> intersect([1, 2, 3], (1, 4))    # mixed types
[1]
```

Again, we pass in different types of objects to our function—first two strings and then a list and a tuple (mixed types). Since you don't have to specify the types of arguments ahead of time, the `intersect` function happily iterates though any kind of sequence objects you send it.[*]

Scope Rules in Functions

Now that we've stepped up to writing our own functions, we need to get a bit more formal about what names mean in Python. When you use a name in a program, Python creates, changes, or looks up the name in what is known as a namespace—a place where names live. As we've seen, names in Python spring into existence when they are assigned a value. Because names aren't declared ahead of time, Python uses the assignment of a name to associate it with a particular namespace. Besides packaging code, functions add an extra namespace layer to your programs—by default, names assigned inside a function are associated with that function's namespace, and no other.

Here's how this works. Before you started writing functions, all code was written at the top-level of a module, so the names either lived in the module itself, or

---

[*] Technically, any object that responds to indexing. The `for` loop and `in` tests work by repeatedly indexing an object; when we study classes in Chapter 6, you'll see how to implement indexing for user-defined objects too, and hence iteration and membership.

were built-ins that Python predefines (e.g., **open**).* Functions provide a nested namespace (sometimes called a *scope*), which localizes the names they use, such that names inside the function won't clash with those outside (in a module or other function). We usually say that functions define a *local* scope, and modules define a *global* scope. The two scopes are related as follows:

The enclosing module is a global scope
> Each module is a global scope—a namespace where variables created (assigned) at the top level of a module file live.

Each call to a function is a new local scope
> Every time you call a function, you create a new local scope—a namespace where names created inside the function usually live.

Assigned names are local, unless declared global
> By default, all the names assigned inside a function definition are put in the local scope (the namespace associated with the function call). If you need to assign a name that lives at the top-level of the module enclosing the function, you can do so by declaring it in a `global` statement inside the function.

All other names are global or built-in
> Names not assigned a value in the function definition are assumed to be globals (in the enclosing module's namespace) or built-in (in the predefined names module Python provides).

Name Resolution: The LGB Rule

If the prior section sounds confusing, it really boils down to three simple rules:

- Name references search at most three scopes: local, then global, then built-in.
- Name assignments create or change local names by default.
- "Global" declarations map assigned names to an enclosing module's scope.

In other words, all names assigned inside a function **def** statement are locals by default; functions can use globals, but they must declare globals to change them. Python's name resolution is sometimes called the *LGB* rule, after the scope names:

- When you use an unqualified name inside a function, Python searches three scopes—the local (L), then the global (G), and then the built-in (B)—and stops at the first place the name is found.

---

* Remember, code typed at the interactive command line is really entered into a built-in module called __main__, so interactively created names live in a module too. There's more about modules in Chapter 5, *Modules.*

- When you assign a name in a function (instead of just referring to it in an expression), Python always creates or changes the name in the local scope, unless it's declared to be global in that function.

- When outside a function (i.e., at the top-level of a module or at the interactive prompt), the local scope is the same as the global—a module's namespace.

Figure 4-1 illustrates Python's three scopes. As a preview, we'd also like you to know that these rules only apply to simple names (such as spam). In the next two chapters, we'll see that the rules for qualified names (such as object.spam, called *attributes*) live in a particular object and so work differently.

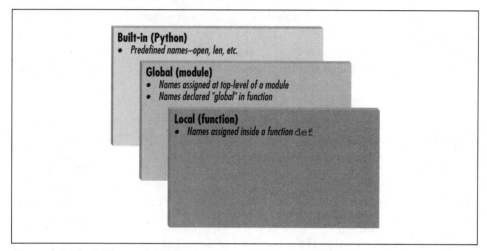

Figure 4-1. The LGB scope lookup rule

Example

Let's look at an example that demonstrates scope ideas. Suppose we write the following code in a module file:

```
# global scope
X = 99              # X and func assigned in module: global

def func(Y):        # Y and Z assigned in function: locals
    # local scope
    Z = X + Y       # X is not assigned, so it's a global
    return Z

func(1)             # func in module: result=100
```

This module, and the function it contains, use a number of names to do their business. Using Python's scope rules, we can classify the names as follows:

Global names: X, func

>   X is a global because it's assigned at the top level of the module file; it can be referenced inside the function without being declared global. func is global for the same reason; the def statement assigns a function object to the name func at the top level of the module.

Local names: Y, Z

>   Y and Z are local to the function (and exist only while the function runs), because they are both assigned a value in the function definition; Z by virtue of the = statement, and Y because arguments are always passed by assignment (more on this in a minute).

The whole point behind this name segregation scheme is that local variables serve as temporary names you need only while a function is running. For instance, the argument Y and the addition result Z exist only inside the function; they don't interfere with the enclosing module's namespace (or any other function, for that matter). The local/global distinction also makes a function easier to understand; most of the names it uses appear in the function itself, not at some arbitrary place in a module.*

The global Statement

The global statement is the only thing that's anything like a declaration in Python. It tells Python that a function plans to change global names—names that live in the enclosing module's scope (namespace). We've talked about global in passing already; as a summary:

*   global means "a name at the top-level of a module file."

*   Global names must be declared only if they are assigned in a function.

*   Global names may be referenced in a function without being declared.

The global statement is just the keyword global, followed by one or more names separated by commas. All the listed names will be mapped to the enclosing module's scope when assigned or referenced within the function body. For instance:

```
y, z = 1, 2          # global variables in module

def all_global():
    global x          # declare globals assigned
    x = y + z         # no need to declare y,z: 3-scope rule
```

---

* The careful reader might notice that, because of the LGB rule, names in the local scope may override variables of the same name in the global and built-in scopes, and global names may override built-ins. A function can, for instance, create a local variable called open, but it will hide the built-in function called open that lives in the built-in (outer) scope.

Here, x, y, and z are all globals inside function all_global. y and z are global because they aren't assigned in the function; x is global because we said so: we listed it in a global statement to map it to the module's scope explicitly. Without the global here, x would be considered local by virtue of the assignment. Notice that y and z are not declared global; Python's LGB lookup rule finds them in the module automatically. Also notice that x might not exist in the enclosing module before the function runs; if not, the assignment in the function creates x in the module.

Argument Passing

Let's expand on the notion of argument passing in Python. Earlier, we noted that arguments are passed by *assignment*; this has a few ramifications that aren't always obvious to beginners:

Arguments are passed by assigning objects to local names
>   Function arguments should be familiar territory by now: they're just another instance of Python assignment at work. Function arguments are references to (possibly) shared objects referenced by the caller.

Assigning to argument names inside a function doesn't affect the caller
>   Argument names in the function header become new, local names when the function runs, in the scope of the function. There is no aliasing between function argument names and names in the caller.

Changing a mutable object argument in a function may impact the caller
>   On the other hand, since arguments are simply assigned to objects, functions can change passed-in mutable objects, and the result may affect the caller.

Here's an example that illustrates some of these properties at work:

```
>>> def changer(x, y):
...     x = 2            # changes local name's value only
...     y[0] = 'spam'    # changes shared object in place
...
>>> X = 1
>>> L = [1, 2]
>>> changer(X, L)        # pass immutable and mutable
>>> X, L                 # X unchanged, L is different
(1, ['spam', 2])
```

In this code, the changer function assigns to argument name x and a component in the object referenced by argument y. Since x is a local name in the function's scope, the first assignment has no effect on the caller; it doesn't change the binding of name X in the caller. Argument y is a local name too, but it's passed a mutable object (the list called L in the caller); the result of the assignment to y[0] in

the function impacts the value of L after the function returns. Figure 4-2 illustrates
the name/object bindings that exist immediately after the function is called.

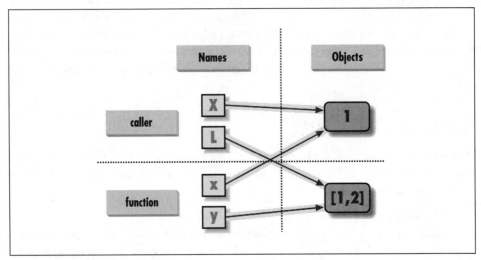

Figure 4-2. References: arguments share objects with the caller

If you recall some of the discussion about shared mutable objects in Chapter 2,
Types and Operators, you'll recognize that this is the exact same phenomenon at
work: changing a mutable object in place can impact other references to the
object. Here, its effect is to make one of the arguments an *output* of the function.
(To avoid this, type y = y[:] to make a copy.)

Python's pass-by-assignment scheme isn't the same as C++'s reference parameters,
but it turns out to be very similar to C's in practice:

Immutable arguments act like C's "by value" mode
   Objects such as integers and strings are passed by object reference (assignment), but since you can't change immutable objects in place anyhow, the
   effect is much like making a copy.

Mutable arguments act like C's "by pointer" mode
   Objects such as lists and dictionaries are passed by object reference too, which
   is similar to the way C passes arrays as pointers—mutable objects can be
   changed in place in the function, much like C arrays.

Of course, if you've never used C, Python's argument-passing mode will be simpler still; it's just an assignment of objects to names, which works the same
whether the objects are mutable or not.

More on return

We've already discussed the **return** statement, and used it in a few examples. But here's a trick we haven't shown yet: because **return** sends back any sort of object, it can return *multiple* values, by packaging them in a tuple. In fact, although Python doesn't have call *by reference*, we can simulate it by returning tuples and assigning back to the original argument names in the caller:

```
>>> def multiple(x, y):
...     x = 2                 # changes local names only
...     y = [3, 4]
...     return x, y           # return new values in a tuple
...
>>> X = 1
>>> L = [1, 2]
>>> X, L = multiple(X, L)     # assign results to caller's names
>>> X, L
(2, [3, 4])
```

It looks like we're returning two values here, but it's just one—a two-item tuple, with the surrounding parentheses omitted. If you've forgotten why, flip back to the discussion of tuples in Chapter 2.

Special Argument-Matching Modes

Although arguments are always passed by assignment, Python provides additional tools that alter the way the argument objects in the call are paired with argument names in the header. By default, they are matched by position, from left to right, and you must pass exactly as many arguments as there are argument names in the function header. But you can also specify a match by name, default values, and collectors for extra arguments.

Some of this section gets complicated, and before we get into syntactic details, we'd like to stress that these special modes are optional and only have to do with *matching* objects to names; the underlying passing mechanism is still *assignment*, after the matching takes place. But as an introduction, here's a synopsis of the available matching modes:

Positionals: matched left to right
    The normal case which we've used so far is to match arguments by position.

Keywords: matched by argument name
    Callers can specify which argument in the function is to receive a value by using the argument's name in the call.

varargs: catch unmatched positional or keyword arguments

Functions can use special arguments to collect arbitrarily many extra arguments (much as the **varargs** feature in C, which supports variable-length argument lists).

Defaults: specify values for arguments that aren't passed

Functions may also specify default values for arguments to receive if the call passes too few values

Table 4-2 summarizes the syntax that specify the special matching modes.

Table 4-2. Function Argument-Matching Forms

Syntax	Location	Interpretation
func(value)	Caller	Normal argument: matched by position
func(name=value)	Caller	Keyword argument: matched by name
def func(name)	Function	Normal argument: matches any by position or name
def func(name=value)	Function	Default argument value, if not passed in the call
def func(*name)	Function	Matches remaining positional args (in a tuple)
def func(**name)	Function	Matches remaining keyword args (in a dictionary)

In the caller (the first two rows of the table), simple names are matched by position, but using the **name=value** form tells Python to match by name instead; these are called keyword arguments.

In the function header, a simple name is matched by position or name (depending on how the caller passes it), but the **name=value** form specifies a default value, the ***name** collects any extra positional arguments in a tuple, and the ****name** form collects extra keyword arguments in a dictionary.

As a result, special matching modes let you be fairly liberal about how many arguments must be passed to a function. If a function specifies defaults, they are used if you pass too few arguments. If a function uses the **varargs** forms, you can pass too many arguments; the **varargs** names collect the extra arguments in a data structure.

A first example

Let's look at an example that demonstrates keywords and defaults in action. In the following, the caller must always pass at least two arguments (to match **spam** and **eggs**), but the other two are optional; if omitted, Python assigns **toast** and **ham** to the defaults specified in the header:

```
def func(spam, eggs, toast=0, ham=0):    # first 2 required
    print (spam, eggs, toast, ham)
```

```
func(1, 2)                          # output: (1, 2, 0, 0)
func(1, ham=1, eggs=0)              # output: (1, 0, 0, 1)
func(spam=1, eggs=0)                # output: (1, 0, 0, 0)
func(toast=1, eggs=2, spam=3)       # output: (3, 2, 1, 0)
func(1, 2, 3, 4)                    # output: (1, 2, 3, 4)
```

Notice that when keyword arguments are used in the call, the order in which arguments are listed doesn't matter; Python matches by name, not position. The caller must supply values for spam and eggs, but they can be matched by position or name. Also notice that the form name=value means different things in the call and def: a keyword in the call, and a default in the header.

A second example: Arbitrary-argument set functions

Here's a more useful example of special argument-matching modes at work. Earlier in the chapter, we wrote a function that returned the intersection of two sequences (it picked out items that appeared in both). Here is a version that intersects an arbitrary number of sequences (1 or more), by using the varargs matching form *args to collect all arguments passed. Because the arguments come in as a tuple, we can process them in a simple for loop. Just for fun, we've also coded an arbitrary-number-arguments union function too; it collects items which appear in *any* of the operands:

```
def intersect(*args):
    res = []
    for x in args[0]:            # scan first sequence
        for other in args[1:]:   # for all other args
            if x not in other: break   # item in each one?
        else:                    # no:  break out of loop
            res.append(x)        # yes: add items to end
    return res

def union(*args):
    res = []
    for seq in args:             # for all args
        for x in seq:            # for all nodes
            if not x in res:
                res.append(x)    # add new items to result
    return res
```

Since these are tools worth reusing (and are way too big to retype interactively), we've stored our functions in a module file called *inter2.py* here (more on modules in Chapter 5, *Modules*). In both functions, the arguments passed in at the call come in as the args tuple. As in the original intersect, both work on any kind of sequence. Here they are processing strings, mixed types, and more than two sequences:

```
% python
>>> from inter2 import intersect, union
>>> s1, s2, s3 = "SPAM", "SCAM", "SLAM"
```

```
>>> intersect(s1, s2), union(s1, s2)            # 2 operands
(['S', 'A', 'M'], ['S', 'P', 'A', 'M', 'C'])

>>> intersect([1,2,3], (1,4))                   # mixed types
[1]

>>> intersect(s1, s2, s3)                       # 3 operands
['S', 'A', 'M']

>>> union(s1, s2, s3)
['S', 'P', 'A', 'M', 'C', 'L']
```

The gritty details

If you choose to use and combine the special matching modes, Python has two ordering rules:

- In the call, keyword arguments must appear after all nonkeyword arguments.

- In a function header, the *name must be after normal arguments and defaults, and **name must be last.

Moreover, Python internally carries out the following steps to match arguments before assignment:

1. Assign nonkeyword arguments by position

2. Assign keyword arguments by matching names

3. Assign extra nonkeyword arguments to *name tuple

4. Assign extra keyword arguments to **name dictionary

5. Assign default values to unassigned arguments in header

This is as complicated as it looks, but tracing Python's matching algorithm helps to understand some cases, especially when modes are mixed. We'll postpone additional examples of these special matching modes until we do the exercises at the end of this chapter.

As you can see, advanced argument matching modes can be complex. They are also entirely optional; you can get by with just simple positional matching, and it's probably a good idea to do so if you're just starting out. However, some Python tools make use of them, so they're important to know.

Odds and Ends

So far, we've seen what it takes to write our own functions in Python. There are a handful of additional function-related ideas we'd like to introduce in this section:

- lambda creates anonymous functions.

Why You Will Care: Keyword Arguments

Keyword arguments play an important role in Tkinter, the de facto standard GUI API for Python. We meet Tkinter in Chapter 10, *Frameworks and Applications*, but as a preview, keyword arguments set configuration options when GUI components are built. For instance, a call of the form:

```
from Tkinter import *
widget = Button(text="Press me", command=someFunction)
```

creates a new button and specifies its text and callback function, using the `text` and `command` keyword arguments. Since the number of configuration options for a widget can be large, keyword arguments let you pick and choose. Without them, you might have to either list all possible options by position or hope for a judicious positional argument defaults protocol that handles every possible option arrangement.

- `apply` calls functions with argument tuples.

- `map` runs a function over a sequence and collects results.

- Functions return `None` if they don't use a `return` statement.

- Functions present design choices.

- Functions are objects, just like numbers and strings.

lambda Expressions

Besides the `def` statement, Python also provides an expression form that generates function objects. Because of its similarity to a tool in the LISP language, it's called `lambda`. Its general form is the keyword `lambda`, followed by one or more arguments, followed by an expression after a colon:

```
lambda argument1, argument2,... argumentN : Expression using arguments
```

Function objects returned by `lambda` expressions are exactly the same as those created and assigned by `def`. But the `lambda` has a few differences that make it useful in specialized roles:

lambda is an expression, not a statement

Because of this, a `lambda` can appear in places a `def` can't—inside a list constant, for example. As an expression, the `lambda` returns a value (a new function), which can be assigned a name optionally; the `def` statement always assigns the new function to the name in the header, instead of returning it as a result.

lambda bodies are a single expression, not a block of statements

The `lambda`'s body is similar to what you'd put in a `def` body's `return` statement; simply type the result as a naked expression, instead of explicitly returning it. Because it's limited to an expression, `lambda` is less general than a `def`; you can only squeeze so much logic into a `lambda` body without using statements such as `if`.

Apart from those distinctions, the `def` and `lambda` do the same sort of work. For instance, we've seen how to make functions with `def` statements:

```
>>> def func(x, y, z): return x + y + z
...
>>> func(2, 3, 4)
9
```

But you can achieve the same effect with a `lambda` expression, by explicitly assigning its result to a name:

```
>>> f = lambda x, y, z: x + y + z
>>> f(2, 3, 4)
9
```

Here, `f` is assigned the function object the `lambda` expression creates (this is how `def` works, but the assignment is automatic). Defaults work on `lambda` arguments too, just like the `def`:

```
>>> x = (lambda a="fee", b="fie", c="foe": a + b + c)
>>> x("wee")
'weefiefoe'
```

`lambda`s come in handy as a shorthand for functions. For instance, we'll see later that callback handlers are frequently coded as `lambda` expressions embedded directly in a registration call, instead of being defined elsewhere in a file and referenced by name.

The apply Built-in

Some programs need to call arbitrary functions in a generic fashion, without knowing their names or arguments ahead of time. We'll see examples of where this can be useful later, but by way of introduction, the `apply` built-in function does the job. For instance, after running the code in the prior section, you can call the generated functions by passing them as arguments to `apply`, along with a tuple of arguments:

```
>>> apply(func, (2, 3, 4))
9
>>> apply(f, (2, 3, 4))
9
```

Why You Will Care: lambdas

The `lambda` expression is most handy as a shorthand for `def`, when you need to stuff small pieces of executable code in places where statements are illegal syntactically. For example, you can build up a list of functions by embedding `lambda` expressions in a list constant:

```
L = [lambda x: x**2, lambda x: x**3, lambda x: x**4]

for f in L:
    print f(2)       # prints 4, 8, 16

print L[0](3)        # prints 9
```

Without `lambda`, you'd need to instead code three `def` statements outside the list in which the functions that they define are to be used. `lambdas` also come in handy in function argument lists; one very common application of this is to define in-line callback functions for the Tkinter GUI API (more on Tkinter in Chapter 10). The following creates a button that prints a message on the console when pressed:

```
import sys
widget = Button(text    ="Press me",
                command = lambda: sys.stdout.write("Hello world\n"))
```

`apply` simply calls the passed-in function, matching the passed-in arguments list with the function's expected arguments. Since the arguments list is passed in as a tuple (a data structure), it can be computed at runtime by a program. The real power of `apply` is that it doesn't need to know how many arguments a function is being called with; for example, you can use `if` logic to select from a set of functions and argument lists, and use `apply` to call any:

```
if <test>:
    action, args = func1, (1,)
else:
    action, args = func2, (1, 2, 3)
. . .
apply(action, args)
```

The map Built-in

One of the more common things programs do with lists is to apply an operation to each node and collect the results. For instance, updating all the counters in a list can be done easily with a `for` loop:

```
>>> counters = [1, 2, 3, 4]
>>>
>>> updated = []
```

```
>>> for x in counters:
...     updated.append(x + 10)            # add 10 to each item
...
>>> updated
[11, 12, 13, 14]
```

Because this is such a common operation, Python provides a built-in that does
most of the work for you: the map function applies a passed-in function to each
item in a sequence object and returns a list containing all the function call results.
For example:

```
>>> def inc(x): return x + 10            # function to be run
...
>>> map(inc, counters)                   # collect results
[11, 12, 13, 14]
```

Since map expects a function, it also happens to be one of the places where
lambdas commonly appear:

```
>>> map((lambda x: x + 3), counters)     # function expression
[4, 5, 6, 7]
```

map is the simplest representative of a class of Python built-ins used for *functional programming* (which mostly just means tools that apply functions to
sequences). Its relatives filter out items based on a test (filter) and apply operations to pairs of items (reduce). We say more about these built-in tools in
Chapter 8, *Built-in Tools.*

Python "Procedures"

In Python functions, return statements are optional. When a function doesn't
return a value explicitly, the function exits when control falls off the end. Technically, all functions return a value; if you don't provide a return, your function
returns the None object automatically:

```
>>> def proc(x):
...     print x            # no return is a None return
...
>>> x = proc('testing 123...')
testing 123...
>>> print x
None
```

Functions such as this without a return are Python's equivalent of what are called
procedures in some languages (such as Pascal). They're usually called as a statement (and the None result is ignored), since they do their business without computing a useful result. This is worth knowing, because Python won't tell you if you
try to use the result of a function that doesn't return one. For instance, assigning
the result of a list append method won't raise an error, but you'll really get back
None, not the modified list:

```
>>> list = [1, 2, 3]
>>> list = list.append(4)      # append is a 'procedure'
>>> print list                 # append changes list in-place
None
```

Function Design Concepts

When you start using functions, you're faced with choices about how to glue components together—for instance, how to decompose a task into functions, how functions should communicate, and so on. Some of this falls into the category of structured analysis and design, which is too broad a topic to discuss in this book. But here are a few general hints for Python beginners:

Use arguments for inputs and return for outputs
Generally speaking, you should strive to make a function independent of things outside of it. Arguments and **return** statements are often the best way to isolate dependencies.

Use global variables only when absolutely necessary
Global variables (i.e., names in the enclosing module) are usually a poor way to communicate with a function. They can create dependencies that make programs difficult to change.

Don't change mutable arguments unless the caller expects it
Functions can also change parts of mutable objects passed in. But as with global variables, this implies lots of coupling between the caller and callee, which can make a function too specific and brittle.

Table 4-3 summarizes the ways functions can talk to the outside world; inputs may come from items in the left column, and results may be sent out in any of the forms on the right. Politically correct function designers usually only use arguments for inputs and **return** statements for outputs. But there are plenty of exceptions, including Python's OOP support—as we'll see in Chapter 6, Python classes depend on changing a passed-in mutable object. Class functions set attributes of an automatically passed-in **self** object, to change per-object state information (e.g., **self.name = 'bob'**); side effects aren't dangerous if they're expected.

Table 4-3. Common Function Inputs and Outputs

Function Inputs	Function Outputs
Arguments	Return statement
Global (module) variables	Mutable arguments
Files, streams	Global (module) variables

Functions Are Objects: Indirect Calls

Because Python functions are objects at runtime, you can write programs that process them generically. Function objects can be assigned, passed to other functions, stored in data structures, and so on, as if they were simple numbers or strings. Function objects happen to export a special operation; they can be called by listing arguments in parentheses after a function expression. But functions belong to the same general category as other objects.

For instance, as we've seen, there's really nothing special about the name we use in a def statement: it's just a variable assigned in the current scope, as if it had appeared on the left of an = sign. After a def runs, the function name is a reference to an object; you can *reassign* that object to other names and call it through any reference—not just the original name:

```
>>> def echo(message):          # echo assigned to a function object
...     print message
...
>>> x = echo                    # now x references it too
>>> x('Hello world!')           # call the object by adding ()
Hello world!
```

Since arguments are passed by assigning objects, it's just as easy to pass functions to other functions, as arguments; the callee may then call the passed-in function just by adding arguments in parentheses:

```
>>> def indirect(func, arg):
...     func(arg)                          # call object by adding ()
...
>>> indirect(echo, 'Hello jello!')         # pass function to a function
Hello jello!
```

You can even stuff function objects into data structures, as though they were integers or strings. Since Python compound types can contain any sort of object, there's no special case here either:

```
>>> schedule = [ (echo, 'Spam!'), (echo, 'Ham!') ]
>>> for (func, arg) in schedule:
...     apply(func, (arg,))
...
Spam!
Ham!
```

This code simply steps through the schedule list, calling the echo function with one argument each time through. As we hope you're starting to notice by now, Python's lack of type declarations makes for an incredibly flexible programming language. Notice the use of apply to run functions generically, the single-item tuple in the second argument to apply, and the tuple unpacking assignment in the for loop header (all ideas introduced earlier).

Function Gotchas

Here are some of the more jagged edges of functions you might not expect. They're all obscure, but most have been known to trip up a new user.

Local Names Are Detected Statically

As we've seen, Python classifies names assigned in a function as locals by default; they live in the function's scope and exist only while the function is running. What we didn't tell you is that Python detects locals statically, when it compiles the code, rather than by noticing assignments as they happen at runtime. Usually, we don't care, but this leads to one of the most common oddities posted on the Python newsgroup by beginners.

Normally, a name that isn't assigned in a function is looked up in the enclosing module:

```
>>> X = 99
>>> def selector():        # X used but not assigned
...     print X            # X found in global scope
...
>>> selector()
99
```

Here, the X in the function resolves to the X in the module outside. But watch what happens if you add an assignment to X after the reference:

```
>>> def selector():
...     print X            # does not yet exist!
...     X = 88             # X classified as a local name (everywhere)
...                        # can also happen if "import X", "def X",...
>>> selector()
Traceback (innermost last):
  File "<stdin>", line 1, in ?
  File "<stdin>", line 2, in selector
NameError: X
```

You get an undefined name error, but the reason is subtle. Python reads and compiles this code when it's typed interactively or imported from a module. While compiling, Python sees the assignment to X and decides that X will be a local name everywhere in the function. But later, when the function is actually run, the assignment hasn't yet happened when the print executes, so Python says you're using an undefined name. According to its name rules, it should; local X is used before being assigned.[*]

---

[*] In fact, *any* assignment in a function body makes a name local: import, =, nested defs, nested classes, and so on.

Solution

The problem occurs because assigned names are treated as locals everywhere in a function, not just after statements where they are assigned. Really, the code above is ambiguous at best: did you mean to print the global X and then create a local X, or is this a genuine programming error? Since Python treats X as a local everywhere, it is an error; but if you really mean to print global X, you need to declare it in a global statement:

```
>>> def selector():
...     global X              # force X to be global (everywhere)
...     print X
...     X = 88
...
>>> selector()
99
```

Remember, though, that this means the assignment also changes the global X, not a local X. Within a function, you can't use both local and global versions of the same simple name. If you really meant to print the global and then set a local of the same name, import the enclosing module and qualify to get to the global version:

```
>>> X = 99
>>> def selector():
...     import __main__        # import enclosing module
...     print __main__.X       # qualify to get to global version of name
...     X = 88                 # unqualified X classified as local
...     print X                # prints local version of name
...
>>> selector()
99
88
```

Qualification (the .X part) fetches a value from a namespace object. The interactive namespace is a module called __main__, so __main__.X reaches the global version of X. If that isn't clear, check out Chapter 5.

Nested Functions Aren't Nested Scopes

As we've seen, the Python def is an executable statement: when it runs, it assigns a new function object to a name. Because it's a statement, it can appear anywhere a statement can—even nested in other statements. For instance, it's completely legal to nest a function def inside an if statement, to select between alternative definitions:

```
if test:
    def func():          # define func this way
        ...
else:
    def func():          # or else this way instead
```

```
       . . .
    . . .
    func()
```

One way to understand this code is to realize that the **def** is much like an = statement: it assigns a name at runtime. Unlike C, Python functions don't need to be fully defined before the program runs. Since **def** is an executable statement, it can also show up nested inside another **def**. But unlike languages such as Pascal, nested **defs** don't imply nested scopes in Python. For instance, consider this example that defines a function (**outer**), which in turn defines and calls another function (**inner**) that calls itself recursively:[*]

```
>>> def outer(x):
...     def inner(i):        # assign in outer's local
...         print i,         # i is in inner's local
...         if i: inner(i-1) # not in my local or global!
...     inner(x)
...
>>> outer(3)
3
Traceback (innermost last):
  File "<stdin>", line 1, in ?
  File "<stdin>", line 5, in outer
  File "<stdin>", line 4, in inner
NameError: inner
```

This won't work. A nested **def** really only assigns a new function object to a name in the enclosing function's scope (namespace). Within the nested function, the LGB three-scope rule still applies for all names. The nested function has access only to its own local scope, the global scope in the enclosing module, and the built-in names scope. It does *not* have access to names in the enclosing function's scope; no matter how deeply functions nest, each sees only three scopes.

For instance, in the example above, the nested **def** creates the name **inner** in the **outer** function's local scope (like any other assignment in **outer** would). But inside the **inner** function, the name **inner** isn't visible; it doesn't live in **inner**'s local scope, doesn't live in the enclosing module's scope, and certainly isn't a built-in. Because **inner** has no access to names in **outer**'s scope, the call to **inner** from **inner** fails and raises an exception.

---

[*] By "recursively," we mean that the function is called again, before a prior call exits. In this example, the function calls itself, but it could also call another function that calls it, and so on. Recursion could be replaced with a simple while or for loop here (all we're doing is counting down to zero), but we're trying to make a point about self-recursive function names and nesting. Recursion tends to be more useful for processing data structures whose shape can't be predicted when you're writing a program.

Solution

Don't expect scopes to nest in Python. This is really more a matter of understanding than anomaly: the def statement is just an *object constructor*, not a scope nester. However, if you really need access to the nested function name from inside the nested function, simply force the nested function's name out to the enclosing module's scope with a global declaration in the outer function. Since the nested function shares the global scope with the enclosing function, it finds it there according to the LGB rule:

```
>>> def outer(x):
...     global inner
...     def inner(i):         # assign in enclosing module
...         print i,
...         if i: inner(i-1)  # found in my global scope now
...     inner(x)
...
>>> outer(3)
3 2 1 0
```

Using Defaults to Save References

Really, nested functions have no access to any names in an enclosing function, so this is actually a more general gotcha than the example above implies. To get access to names assigned prior to the nested function's def statement, you can also assign their values to the nested function's arguments as defaults. Because default arguments save their values when the def runs (not when the function is actually called), they can squirrel away objects from the enclosing function's scope:

```
>>> def outer(x, y):
...     def inner(a=x, b=y):  # save outer's x,y bindings/objects
...         return a**b        # can't use x and y directly here
...     return inner
...
>>> x = outer(2, 4)
>>> x()
16
```

Here, a call to outer returns the new function created by the nested def. When the nested def statement runs, inner's arguments a and b are assigned the values of x and y from the outer function's local scope. In effect, inner's a and b remembers the values of outer's x and y. When a and b are used later in inner's body, they still refer to the values x and y had when outer ran (even though outer has already returned to its caller).* This scheme works in lambdas too, since lambdas are really just shorthand for defs:

```
>>> def outer(x, y):
...     return lambda a=x, b=y: a**b
...
>>> y = outer(2, 5)
>>> y()
32
```

Note that defaults won't quite do the trick in the last section's example, because the name inner isn't assigned until the inner def has completed. Global declarations may be the best workaround for nested functions that call themselves:

```
>>> def outer(x):
...     def inner(i, self=inner):     # name not defined yet
...         print i,
...         if i: self(i-1)
...     inner(x)
...
>>> outer(3)
Traceback (innermost last):
  File "<stdin>", line 1, in ?
  File "<stdin>", line 2, in outer
NameError: inner
```

But if you're interested in exploring the *Twilight Zone* of Python hackerage, you can instead save a mutable object as a default and plug in a reference to inner after the fact, in the enclosing function's body:

```
>>> def outer(x):
...     fillin = [None]
...     def inner(i, self=fillin):    # save mutable
...         print i,
...         if i: self[0](i-1)        # assume it's set
...     fillin[0] = inner             # plug value now
...     inner(x)
...
>>> outer(3)
3 2 1 0
```

Although this code illustrates Python properties (and just might amaze your friends, coworkers, and grandmother), we don't recommend it. In this example, it makes much more sense to avoid function nesting altogether:

```
>>> def inner(i):            # define module level name
...     print i,
...     if i: inner(i-1)     # no worries: it's a global
...
```

---

* In computer-science lingo, this sort of behavior is usually called a *closure*—an object that remembers values in enclosing scopes, even though those scopes may not be around any more. In Python, you need to explicitly list which values are to be remembered, using argument defaults (or class object attributes, as we'll see in Chapter 6).

```
>>> def outer(x):
...     inner(x)
...
>>> outer(3)
3 2 1 0
```

As a rule of thumb, the easy way out is usually the right way out.

Defaults and Mutable Objects

Default argument values are evaluated and saved when the def statement is run, not when the resulting function is called. That's what you want, since it lets you save values from the enclosing scope, as we've just seen. But since defaults retain an object between calls, you have to be careful about changing mutable defaults. For instance, the following function uses an empty list as a default value and then changes it in place each time the function is called:

```
>>> def saver(x=[]):        # saves away a list object
...     x.append(1)         # changes same object each time!
...     print x
...
>>> saver([2])              # default not used
[2, 1]
>>> saver()                 # default used
[1]
>>> saver()                 # grows on each call
[1, 1]
>>> saver()
[1, 1, 1]
```

The problem is that there's just one list object here—the one created when the def was executed. You don't get a new list every time the function is called, so the list grows with each new append.

Solution

If that's not the behavior you wish, simply move the default value into the function body; as long as the value resides in code that's actually executed each time the function runs, you'll get a new object each time through:

```
>>> def saver(x=None):
...     if x is None:       # no argument passed?
...         x = []          # run code to make a new list
...     x.append(1)         # changes new list object
...     print x
...
>>> saver([2])
[2, 1]
>>> saver()                 # doesn't grow here
[1]
>>> saver()
[1]
```

By the way, the `if` statement above could *almost* be replaced by the assignment `x = x or []`, which takes advantage of the fact that Python's `or` returns one of its operand objects: if no argument was passed, `x` defaults to `None`, so the `or` returns the new empty list on the right. This isn't exactly the same, though: when an empty list is passed in, the function extends and returns a newly created list, rather than extending and returning the passed-in list like the previous version (the expression becomes `[] or []`, which evaluates to the new empty list on the right; see the discussion of truth tests in Chapter 3 if you don't recall why). Since real program requirements may call for either behavior, we won't pick a winner here.

Summary

In this chapter, you've learned how to write and call functions of your own. We've explored scope and namespace issues, talked about argument passing, saw a number of functional tools such as `lambda` and `map`, and studied new function-related statements—`def`, `return`, and `global`. We've also talked a little about how to go about gluing functions together, and looked at common function cases that can trip up new users. In Chapter 5 we'll learn about modules, which, among other things, lets you group functions into packages of related tools.

Exercises

We're going to start coding more sophisticated programs in this session. Be sure to check Appendix C if you get stuck, and be sure to start writing your code in module files. You won't want to retype some of these exercises from scratch if you make a mistake.

1. *Basics.* At the Python interactive prompt, write a function that prints its single argument to the screen and call it interactively, passing a variety of object types: string, integer, list, dictionary. Then try calling it without passing any argument: what happens? What happens when you pass two arguments?

2. *Arguments.* Write a function called `adder` in a Python module file. `adder` should accept two arguments and return the sum (or concatenation) of its two arguments. Then add code at the bottom of the file to call the function with a variety of object types (two strings, two lists, two floating points), and run this file as a script from the system command line. Do you have to print the call statement results to see results on the screen?

3. *varargs.* Generalize the `adder` function you wrote in the last exercise to compute the sum of an arbitrary number of arguments, and change the calls to pass more or less than two. What type is the return value sum? (Hints: a slice such as `S[:0]` returns an empty sequence of the same type as `S`, and the

type built-in function can test types.) What happens if you pass in arguments of different types? What about passing in dictionaries?

4. *Keywords.* Change the adder function from Exercise 2 to accept and add three arguments: def adder(good, bad, ugly). Now, provide default values for each argument and experiment with calling the function interactively. Try passing one, two, three, and four arguments. Then, try passing keyword arguments. Does the call adder(ugly=1, good=2) work? Why? Finally, generalize the new adder to accept and add an arbitrary number of keyword arguments, much like Exercise 3, but you'll need to iterate over a dictionary, not a tuple. (Hint: the dictionary.keys() method returns a list you can step through with a for or while.)

5. Write a function called copyDict(dict) that copies its dictionary argument. It should return a new dictionary with all the items in its argument. Use the dictionary keys method to iterate. Copying sequences is easy (X[:] makes a top-level copy); does this work for dictionaries too?

6. Write a function called addDict(dict1, dict2) that computes the union of two dictionaries. It should return a new dictionary, with all the items in both its arguments (assumed to be dictionaries). If the same key appears in both arguments, feel free to pick a value from either. Test your function by writing it in a file and running the file as a script. What happens if you pass lists instead of dictionaries? How could you generalize your function to handle this case too? (Hint: see the type built-in function used earlier.) Does the order of arguments passed matter?

7. *More argument matching examples.* First, define the following six functions (either interactively, or in an importable module file):

```
def f1(a, b): print a, b           # normal args

def f2(a, *b): print a, b          # positional varargs

def f3(a, **b): print a, b         # keyword varargs

def f4(a, *b, **c): print a, b, c  # mixed modes

def f5(a, b=2, c=3): print a, b, c # defaults

def f6(a, b=2, *c): print a, b, c  # defaults + positional varargs
```

Now, test the following calls interactively and try to explain each result; in some cases, you'll probably need to fall back on the matching algorithm shown earlier in this chapter. Do you think mixing matching modes is a good idea in general? Can you think of cases where it would be useful anyhow?

```
>>> f1(1, 2)
>>> f1(b=2, a=1)

>>> f2(1, 2, 3)
```

```
>>> f3(1, x=2, y=3)
>>> f4(1, 2, 3, x=2, y=3)

>>> f5(1)
>>> f5(1, 4)

>>> f6(1)
>>> f6(1, 3, 4)
```

5

Modules

This chapter presents the Python module—the highest-level program organization unit, which packages program code and data for reuse. In concrete terms, modules take the form of Python program files (and C extensions); clients import modules to use the names they define. Modules are processed with two new statements and one important built-in function we explore here:

`import`
> Lets a client fetch a module as a whole

`from`
> Allows clients to fetch particular names from a module

`reload`
> Provides a way to reload a module's code without stopping Python

We introduced module basics in Chapter 1, *Getting Started*, and you may have been using module files in the exercises, so some of this chapter may be a review. But we also flesh out module details we've omitted so far: reloads, module compilation semantics, and so on. Because modules and classes are really just glorified *namespaces*, we explore namespace basics here as well, so be sure to read most of this chapter before tackling the next.

Why Use Modules?

Let's start with the obvious first question: why should we care about modules? The short answer is that they provide an easy way to organize components into a system. But from an abstract perspective, modules have at least three roles:

Code reuse

As we saw in Chapter 1, modules let us save code in files permanently.* Unlike code you type at the Python interactive prompt (which goes away when you exit Python), code in module files is persistent—it can be reloaded and rerun as many times as needed. More to the point, modules are a place to define names (called *attributes*) that may be referenced by external clients.

System namespace partitioning

Modules are also the highest-level program organization unit in Python. As we'll see, everything "lives" in a module; code you execute and some objects you create are always implicitly enclosed by a module. Because of that, modules are a natural tool for grouping system components.

Implementing shared services or data

From a functional perspective, modules also come in handy for implementing components shared across a system, and hence only require a single copy. For instance, if you need to provide a global data structure that's used by more than one function, you can code it in a module that's imported by many clients.

Module Basics

Python modules are easy to create; they're just files of Python program code, created with your favorite text editor. You don't need to write special syntax to tell Python you're making a module; almost any text file will do. Because Python handles all the details of finding and loading modules, modules are also easy to use; clients simply import a module or specific names a module defines and use the objects they reference. Here's an overview of the basics:

Creating modules: Python files, C extensions

Modules can actually be coded as either Python files or C extensions. We won't be studying C extensions in this book, but we'll use a few along the way. Many of Python's built-in tools are really imported C extension modules; to their clients, they look identical to Python file modules.

Using modules: import, from, reload()

As we'll see in a moment, clients can *load* modules with either `import` or `from` statements. By calling the `reload` built-in function, they may also reload a module's code without stopping programs that use it. Module files can also be *run* as top-level programs from the system prompt, as we saw in Chapter 1.

---

* Until you delete the module file, at least.

Module search path: PYTHONPATH

As we also saw in Chapter 1, Python searches for imported module files by inspecting all directories listed on the `PYTHONPATH` environment variable. You can store modules anywhere, so long as you add all your source directories to this variable.

Definition

Let's look at a simple example of module basics in action. To define a module, use your text editor to type Python code into a text file. Names assigned at the top level of the module become its attributes (names associated with the module object), and are exported for clients to use. For instance, if we type the `def` below into a file called *module1.py*, we create a module with one attribute—the name `printer`, which happens to be a reference to a function object:

```
def printer(x):          # module attribute
    print x
```

A word on filenames: you can call modules just about anything you like, but module filenames should end in a *.py* suffix if you plan to import them. Since their names become variables inside a Python program without the *.py,* they should also follow the variable naming rules in Chapter 3, *Basic Statements*. For instance, a module named *if.py* won't work, because *if* is a reserved word (you'll get a syntax error). When modules are imported, Python maps the internal module name to an external filename, by adding directory paths in the `PYTHONPATH` variable to the front and a *.py* at the end: a module name `M` maps to the external file *<directory-path>/M.py* which stores our code.[*]

Usage

Clients can use the module file we just wrote by running `import` or `from` statements. Both load the module file's code; the chief difference is that `import` fetches the module as a whole (so you must qualify to fetch its names out), but `from` fetches specific names out of the module. Here are three clients of the module at work:

```
% python
>>> import module1                  # get module
>>> module1.printer('Hello world!') # qualify to get names (module.name)
Hello world!

>>> from module1 import printer     # get an export
```

---

[*] It can also map to *<directory-path>/M.pyc* if there's already a compiled version of the module lying around; more on this later. Dynamically loaded C extension modules are found on `PYTHONPATH` too, but that's outside this book's scope.

```
>>> printer('Hello world!')        # no need to qualify name
Hello world!

>>> from module1 import *          # get all exports
>>> printer('Hello world!')
Hello world!
```

The last example uses a special form of from: when we use a *, we get copies of
all the names assigned at the top-level of the referenced module. In each of the
three cases, we wind up calling the `printer` function defined in the external
module file. And that's it; modules really are simple to use. But to give you a better understanding of what really happens when you define and use modules, let's
look at some of their properties in more detail.

Module Files Are Namespaces

Modules are probably best understood as places to define names you want visible
to the rest of a system. In Python-speak, modules are a namespace—a place
where names are created. And names that live in a module are called its attributes.
Technically, modules correspond to files, and Python creates a module object to
contain all the names defined in the file; but in simple terms, modules are just
namespaces.

So how do files become namespaces? Every name that is assigned a value at the
top level of a module file (i.e., not in a function body) becomes an attribute of that
module. For instance, given an assignment statement such as *X=1* at the top level
of a module file *M.py*, the name *X* becomes an attribute of *M*, which we can refer
to from outside the module as *M.X*. The name *X* also becomes a global variable to
other code inside *M.py*, but we need to explain the notion of module loading and
scopes a bit more formally to understand why:

Module statements run on the first import
> The first time a module is imported anywhere in a system, Python creates an
> empty module object and executes the statements in the module file one after
> another, from the top of the file to the bottom.

Top-level assignments create module attributes
> During an import, statements at the top-level of the file that assign names (e.g.,
> =, def) create attributes of the module object; assigned names are stored in the
> module's namespace.

Module namespace: attribute __dict__, or dir()
> Module namespaces created by imports are *dictionaries*; they may be accessed
> through the built-in __dict__ attribute associated with module objects and
> may be inspected with the dir function we met in Chapter 1.

Modules are a single scope (local is global)

As we saw in Chapter 4, *Functions*, names at the top level of a module follow the same reference/assignment rules as names in a function, but the local and global scopes are the same (or, if you prefer, the LGB rule, without the G). But in modules, the local scope becomes an attribute dictionary of a module object, after the module has been loaded. Unlike functions (where the local namespace exists only while the function runs), a module file's scope becomes a module object's attribute namespace and may be used after the import.

Let's look at an example of these ideas. Suppose we create the following module file with our favorite text editor and call it *module2.py*:

```
print 'starting to load...'

import sys
name = 42

def func(): pass

class klass: pass

print 'done loading.'
```

The first time this module is imported (or run as a program), Python executes its statements from top to bottom. Some statements create names in the module's namespace as a side effect, but others may do actual work while the import is going on. For instance, the two `print` statements in this file execute at import time:

```
>>> import module2
starting to load...
done loading.
```

But once the module is loaded, its scope becomes an attribute namespace in the module object we get back from `import`; we access attributes in the namespace by qualifying them with the name of the enclosing module:

```
>>> module2.sys
<module 'sys'>
>>> module2.name
42
>>> module2.func, module2.klass
(<function func at 765f20>, <class klass at 76df60>)
```

Here, `sys`, `name`, `func`, and `klass` were all assigned while the module's statements were being run, so they're attributes after the import. We'll talk about classes in Chapter 6, *Classes*, but notice the `sys` attribute; `import` statements really assign module objects to names (more on this later). Internally, module namespaces are stored as dictionary objects. In fact, we can access the namespace dictionary through the module's `__dict__` attribute; it's just a normal dictionary object, with the usual methods:

```
>>> module2.__dict__.keys()
['__file__', 'name', '__name__', 'sys', '__doc__', '__builtins__', 'klass',
'func']
```

The names we assigned in the module file become dictionary keys internally. As you can see, some of the names in the module's namespace are things Python adds for us; for instance, `__file__` gives the name of the file the module was loaded from, and `__name__` gives its name as known to importers (without the *.py* extension and directory path).

Name Qualification

Now that you're becoming familiar with modules, we should clarify the notion of name qualification. In Python, you can access attributes in any object that has attributes, using the qualification syntax `object.attribute`. Qualification is really an expression that returns the value assigned to an attribute name associated with an object. For example, the expression `module2.sys` in the next-to-last example fetches the value assigned to `sys` in `module2`. Similarly, if we have a built-in list object L, `L.append` returns the method associated with the list.

So what does qualification do to the scope rules we saw in Chapter 4? Nothing, really: it's an independent concept. When you use qualification to access names, you give Python an explicit object to fetch from. The LGB rule applies only to bare, unqualified names. Here are the rules:

Simple variables
> "X" means search for name X in the current scopes (LGB rule)

Qualification
> "X.Y" means search for attribute Y in the object X (not in scopes)

Qualification paths
> "X.Y.Z" means look up name Y in object X, then look up Z in object X.Y

Generality
> Qualification works on all objects with attributes: modules, classes, C types, etc.

In Chapter 6, we'll see that qualification means a bit more for classes (it's also the place where inheritance happens), but in general, the rules here apply to all names in Python.

Import Model

As we've seen, qualification is needed only when you use `import` to fetch a module as a whole. When you use the `from` statement, you copy names from the module to the importer, so the imported names are used without qualifying. Here are a few more details on the import process.

Imports Happen Only Once

One of the most common questions beginners seem to ask when using modules is: why won't my imports keep working? The first import works fine, but later imports during an interactive session (or in a program) seem to have no effect. They're not supposed to, and here's why:

- Modules are loaded and run on the first `import` or `from`.
- Running a module's code creates its top-level names.
- Later `import` and `from` operations fetch an already loaded module.

Python loads, compiles, and runs code in a module file only on the *first* import, on purpose; since this is an expensive operation, Python does it just once per process by default. Moreover, since code in a module is usually executed once, you can use it to initialize variables. For example:

```
% cat simple.py
print 'hello'
spam = 1                        # initialize variable

% python
>>> import simple               # first import: loads and runs file's code
hello
>>> simple.spam                 # assignment makes an attribute
1
>>> simple.spam = 2             # change attribute in module
>>>
>>> import simple               # just fetches already-loaded module
>>> simple.spam                 # code wasn't rerun: attribute unchanged
2
```

In this example, the `print` and `=` statements run only the first time the module is imported. The second import doesn't rerun the module's code, but just fetches the already created module object in Python's internal modules table. Of course, sometimes you really want a module's code to be rerun; we'll see how to do it with `reload` in a moment.

import and from Are Assignments

Just like `def`, `import` and `from` are executable statements, not compile-time declarations. They can be nested in `if` tests, appear in function `def`s, and so on.

Imported modules and names aren't available until importing statements run. Moreover, **import** and **from** are also implicit assignments, just like the **def**:

- **import** assigns an entire module object to a name.

- **from** assigns one or more names to objects of the same name in another module.

All the things we've already said about assignment apply to module access too. For instance, names copied with a **from** become references to possibly shared objects; like function arguments, reassigning a fetched name has no effect on the module it was copied from, but changing a fetched mutable object can change it in the module it was imported from:[*]

```
% cat small.py
x = 1
y = [1, 2]

% python
>>> from small import x, y     # copy two names out
>>> x = 42                     # changes local x only
>>> y[0] = 42                  # changes shared mutable in-place
>>>
>>> import small               # get module name (from doesn't)
>>> small.x                    # small's x is not my x
1
>>> small.y                    # but we share a changed mutable
[42, 2]
```

Here, we change a shared mutable object we got with the **from** assignment: name y in the importer and importee reference the same list object, so changing it from one place changes it in the other. Incidentally, notice that we have to execute an **import** statement after the **from**, in order to gain access to the module name to qualify it; **from** copies names only in the module and doesn't assign the module name itself. At least symbolically, **from** is equivalent to this sequence:

```
import module              # fetch the module object
name1 = module.name1       # copy names out by assignment
name2 = module.name2
...
del module                 # get rid of the module name
```

Reloading Modules

At the start of the last section, we noted that a module's code is run only once per process by default. To force a module's code to be reloaded and rerun, you need to ask Python explicitly to do so, by calling the **reload** built-in function. In this

---

[*] In fact, for a graphical picture of what **from** does, flip back to Figure 4-2 (function argument passing). Just replace *caller* and *function* with *imported* and *importer*, to see what **from** assignments do with references; it's the exact same effect, except that here we're dealing with names in modules, not functions.

section, we'll explore how to use `reload` to make your systems more dynamic. In a nutshell:

- Imports load and run a module's code only the first time.
- Later imports use the already loaded module object without rerunning code.
- The `reload` function forces an already loaded module's code to be reloaded and rerun.

Why all the fuss about reloading modules? The `reload` function allows parts of programs to be changed without stopping the whole program. With `reload`, the effects of changes in components can be observed immediately. Reloading doesn't help in every situation, but where it does, it makes for a much shorter development cycle. For instance, imagine a database program that must connect to a server on startup; since program changes can be tested immediately after reloads, you need to connect only once while debugging.[*]

General Form

Unlike `import` and `from`:

- `reload` is a built-in function in Python, not a statement.
- `reload` is passed an existing module object, not a name.

Because `reload` expects an object, a module must have been previously imported successfully before you can reload it. (In fact, if the import was unsuccessful due to a syntax or other error, you may need to repeat an import before you can reload). Reloading looks like this:

```
import module              # initial import
Use module.attributes
...                        # now, go change the module file
...
reload(module)             # get updated exports
Use module.attributes
```

You typically import a module, then change its source code in a text editor and reload. When you call `reload`, Python rereads the module file's source code and reruns its top-level statements. But perhaps the most important thing to know about `reload` is that it changes a module object *in-place*; because of that, every reference to a module object is automatically effected by a `reload`. The details:

---

[*] We should note that because Python is interpreted (more or less), it already gets rid of the compile/link steps you need to go through to get a C program to run: modules are loaded dynamically, when imported by a running program. Reloading adds to this, by allowing you to also change parts of running programs without stopping. We should also note that `reload` currently only works on modules written in Python; C extension modules can be dynamically loaded at runtime too, but they can't be reloaded. We should finally note that since this book isn't about C modules, we've probably already noted too much.

reload runs a module file's new code in the module's current namespace
> Rerunning a module file's code overwrites its existing namespace, rather than deleting and recreating it.

Top-level assignments in the file replace names with new values
> For instance, rerunning a def statement replaces the prior version of the function in the module's namespace.

Reloads impact all clients that use import to fetch modules
> Because clients that use import qualify to fetch attributes, they'll find new values in the module after a reload.

Reloads impacts future from clients only
> Clients that use from to fetch attributes in the past won't be effected by a reload; they'll still have references to the old objects fetched before the reload (we'll say more about this later).

Example

Here's a more concrete example of reload in action. In the following session, we change and reload a module file without stopping the interactive Python session. Reloads are used in many other scenarios too (see the next sidebar), but we'll keep things simple for illustration here. First, let's write a module file with the text editor of our choice:

```
% cat changer.py
message = "First version"

def printer():
    print message
```

This module creates and exports two names—one bound to a string, and another to a function. Now, start the Python interpreter, import the module, and call the function it exports; as you should know by now, the function prints the value of the global variable message:

```
% python
>>> import changer
>>> changer.printer()
First version
>>>
```

Next, let's keep the interpreter active and edit the module file in another window; here, we change the global message variable, as well as the printer function body:

Modify changer.py without stopping Python

```
% vi changer.py
% cat changer.py
```

```
message = "After editing"

def printer():
    print 'reloaded:', message
```

Finally, we come back to the Python window and reload the module to fetch the new code we just changed. Notice that importing the module again has no effect; we get the original message even though the file's been changed. We have to call `reload` in order to get the new version:

Back to the Python interpreter/program

```
>>> import changer
>>> changer.printer()        # no effect: uses loaded module
First version

>>> reload(changer)          # forces new code to load/run
<module 'changer'>
>>> changer.printer()        # runs the new version now
reloaded: After editing
```

Notice that `reload` actually returns the module object for us; its result is usually ignored, but since expression results are printed at the interactive prompt, Python shows us a default <module name> representation.

Why You Will Care: Module Reloads

Besides allowing you to reload (and hence rerun) modules at the interactive prompt, module reloads are also useful in larger systems, especially when the cost of restarting the entire application is prohibitive. For instance, systems that must connect to servers over a network on startup are prime candidates for dynamic reloads.

They're also useful in GUI work (a widget's callback action can be changed while the GUI remains active) and when Python is used as an embedded language in a C or C++ program (the enclosing program can request a reload of the Python code it runs, without having to stop). See *Programming Python* for more on reloading GUI callbacks and embedded Python code.

Odds and Ends

In this section, we introduce a few module-related ideas that seem important enough to stand on their own (or obscure enough to defy our organizational skills).

Module Compilation Model

As currently implemented, the Python system is often called an interpreter, but it's really somewhere between a classic interpreter and compiler. As in Java, Python programs are compiled to an intermediate form called bytecode, which is then executed on something called a virtual machine. Since the Python virtual machine interprets the bytecode form, we can get away with saying that Python is interpreted, but it still goes through a compile phase first.

Luckily, the compile step is completely automated and hidden in Python. Python programmers simply import modules and use the names they define; Python takes care to automatically compile modules to bytecode when they are first imported. Moreover, Python tries to save a module's bytecode in a file, so it can avoid recompiling in the future if the source code hasn't been changed. In effect, Python comes with an automatic *make* system to manage recompiles.*

Here's how this works. You may have noticed *.pyc* files in your module directories after running programs; these are the files Python generates to save a module's bytecode (provided you have write access to source directories). When a module *M* is imported, Python loads a *M.pyc* bytecode file instead of the corresponding *M.py* source file, as long as the *M.py* file hasn't been changed since the *M.pyc* bytecode was saved. If you change the source code file (or delete the *.pyc*), Python is smart enough to recompile the module when imported; if not, the saved bytecode files make your program start quicker by avoiding recompiles at runtime.

Data Hiding Is a Convention

As we've seen, Python modules export all names assigned at the top level of their file. There is no notion of declaring which names should and shouldn't be visible outside the module. In fact, there's no way to prevent a client from changing names inside a module if they want to.

In Python, data hiding in modules is a convention, not a syntactical constraint. If you want to break a module by trashing its names, you can (though we have yet to meet a programmer who would want to). Some purists object to this liberal attitude towards data hiding and claim that it means Python can't implement encapsulation. We disagree (and doubt we could convince purists of anything in any event). Encapsulation in Python is more about packaging, than restricting.†

---

* For readers who have never used C or C++, a *make* system is a way to automate compiling and linking programs. *make* systems typically use file modification dates to know when a file must be recompiled (just like Python).

† Purists would probably also be horrified by the rogue C++ programmer who types `#define private public` to break C++'s hiding mechanism in a single blow. But then those are rogue programmers for you.

Why You Will Care: Shipping Options

Incidentally, compiled *.pyc* bytecode files also happen to be one way to ship a system without source code. Python happily loads a *.pyc* file if it can't find a *.py* source file for a module on its module search path, so all you really need to ship to customers are the *.pyc* files. Moreover, since Python bytecode is portable, you can usually run a *.pyc* file on multiple platforms. To force pre-compilation into *.pyc* files, simply import your modules (also see the `compileall` utility module).

It's also possible to "freeze" Python programs into a C executable; the standard `freeze` tool packages your program's compiled byte code, any Python utilities it uses, and as much of the C code of the Python interpreter as needed to run your program. It produces a C program, which you compile with a generated *makefile* to produce a standalone executable program. The executable works the same as the Python files of your program. Frozen executables don't require a Python interpreter to be installed on the target machine and may start up faster; on the other hand, since the bulk of the interpreter is included, they aren't small. A similar tool, `squeeze`, packages Python bytecode in a Python program; search Python's web site for details.

As a special case, prefixing names with an underscore (e.g., _X) prevents them from being copied out when a client imports with a `from*` statement. This really is intended only to minimize *namespace pollution*; since `from*` copies out all names, you may get more than you bargained for (including names which overwrite names in the importer). But underscores aren't "private" declarations: you can still see and change such names with other `import` forms.

Mixed Modes: __name__ and __main__

Here's a special module-related trick that lets you both import a module from clients and run it as a standalone program. Each module has a built-in attribute called `__name__`, which Python sets as follows:

- If the file is being run as a program, `__name__` is set to the string `__main__` when it starts

- If the file is being imported, `__name__` is set to the module's name as known by its clients

The upshot is that a module can test its own `__name__` to determine whether it's being run or imported. For example, suppose we create the module file below, to export a single function called `tester`:

```
def tester():
    print "It's Christmas in Heaven..."
```

```
if __name__ == '__main__':         # only when run
    tester()                       # not when imported
```

This module defines a function for clients to import and use as usual:

```
% python
>>> import runme
>>> runme.tester()
It's Christmas in Heaven...
```

But the module also includes code at the bottom that is set up to call the function when this file is run as a program:

```
% python runme.py
It's Christmas in Heaven...
```

Perhaps the most common place you'll see the __main__ test applied is for *self-test code*: you can package code that tests a module's exports in the module itself by wrapping it in a __main__ test at the bottom. This way, you can use the file in clients and test its logic by running it from the system shell.

Changing the Module Search Path

We've mentioned that the module search path is a list of directories in environment variable PYTHONPATH. What we haven't told you is that a Python program can actually change the search path, by assigning to a built-in list called sys.path (the path attribute in the built-in sys module). sys.path is initialized from PYTHONPATH (plus compiled-in defaults) on startup, but thereafter, you can delete, append, and reset its components however you like:

```
>>> import sys
>>> sys.path
['.', 'c:\\python\\lib', 'c:\\python\\lib\\tkinter']

>>> sys.path = ['.']                          # change module search path
>>> sys.path.append('c:\\book\\examples')     # escape backlashes as "\\"
>>> sys.path
['.', 'c:\\book\\examples']

>>> import string
Traceback (innermost last):
  File "<stdin>", line 1, in ?
ImportError: No module named string
```

You can use this to dynamically configure a search path inside a Python program. Be careful, though; if you delete a critical directory from the path, you may lose access to critical utilities. In the last command above, for example, we no longer have access to the string module, since we deleted the Python source library's directory from the path.

Module Packages (New in 1.5)

Packages are an advanced tool, and we debated whether to cover them in this book. But since you may run across them in other people's code, here's a quick overview of their machinery.

In short, Python packages allow you to import modules using directory paths; qualified names in `import` statements reflect the directory structure on your machine. For instance, if some module C lives in a directory B, which is in turn a subdirectory of directory A, you can say `import A.B.C` to load the module. Only directory A needs to be found in a directory listed in the PYTHONPATH variable, since the path from A to C is given by qualification.

Packages come in handy when integrating systems written by independent developers; by storing each system's set of modules in its own subdirectory, we can reduce the risk of name clashes. For instance, if each developer writes a module called *spam.py*, there's no telling which will be found on PYTHONPATH first if package qualifier paths aren't used. If another subsystem's directory appears on PYTHONPATH first, a subsystem may see the wrong one.

Again, if you're new to Python, make sure that you've mastered simple modules before stepping up to packages. Packages are more complex than we've described here; for instance, each directory used as a package must include a `__init__.py` module to identify itself as such. See Python's reference manuals for the whole story.

Why You Will Care: Module Packages

Now that packages are a standard part of Python, you're likely to start seeing third-party extensions shipped as a set of package directories, rather than a flat list of modules. The PythonWin port of Python for MS-Windows was one of the first to jump on the package bandwagon. Many of its utility modules reside in packages, which you import with qualification paths; for instance, to load client-side COM tools, we say:

```
from win32com.client import constants, Dispatch
```

which fetches names from the `client` module of the PythonWin `win32com` package (an install directory). We'll see more about COM in Chapter 10, *Frameworks and Applications*.

Module Design Concepts

Like functions, modules present design tradeoffs: deciding which functions go in which module, module communication mechanisms, and so on. Here too, it's a bigger topic than this book allows, so we'll just touch on a few general ideas that will become clearer when you start writing bigger Python systems:

You're always in a module in Python
> There's no way to write code that doesn't live in some module. In fact, code typed at the interactive prompt really goes in a built-in module called __main__.

Minimize module coupling: global variables
> Like functions, modules work best if they're written to be closed boxes. As a rule of thumb, they should be as independent of global names in other modules as possible.

Maximize module cohesion: unified purpose
> You can minimize a module's couplings by maximizing its cohesion; if all the components of a module share its general purpose, you're less likely to depend on external names.

Modules should rarely change other modules' variables
> It's perfectly okay to use globals defined in another module (that's how clients import services, after all), but changing globals in another module is usually a symptom of a design problem. There are exceptions of course, but you should try to communicate results through devices such as function return values, not cross-module changes.

Modules Are Objects: Metaprograms

Finally, because modules expose most of their interesting properties as built-in attributes, it's easy to write programs that manage other programs. We usually call such manager programs *metaprograms*, because they work on top of other systems. This is also referred to as *introspection*, because programs can see and process object internals.

For instance, to get to an attribute called **name** in a module called **M**, we can either use qualification, or index the module's attribute dictionary exposed in the built-in __dict__ attribute. Further, Python also exports the list of all loaded modules as the **sys.modules** dictionary (that is, the **modules** attribute of the **sys** module), and provides a built-in called **getattr** that lets us fetch attributes from their string names. Because of that, all the following expressions reach the same attribute and object:

```
M.name                  # qualify object
M.__dict__['name']      # index namespace dictionary manually
sys.modules['M'].name   # index loaded-modules table manually
getattr(M, 'name')      # call built-in fetch function
```

By exposing module internals like this, Python helps you build programs about programs.* For example, here is a module that puts these ideas to work, to implement a customized version of the built-in dir function. It defines and exports a function called listing, which takes a module object as an argument and prints a formatted listing of the module's namespace:

```
# a module that lists the namespaces of other modules

verbose = 1

def listing(module):
    if verbose:
        print "-"*30
        print "name:", module.__name__, "file:", module.__file__
        print "-"*30

    count = 0
    for attr in module.__dict__.keys():        # scan namespace
        print "%02d) %s" % (count, attr),
        if attr[0:2] == "__":
            print "<built-in name>"            # skip __file__, etc.
        else:
            print getattr(module, attr)        # same as .__dict__[attr]
        count = count+1

    if verbose:
        print "-"*30
        print module.__name__, "has %d names" % count
        print "-"*30

if __name__ == "__main__":
    import mydir
    listing(mydir)         # self-test code: list myself
```

We've also provided self-test logic at the bottom of this module, which narcissistically imports and lists itself. Here's the sort of output produced:

```
C:\python> python mydir.py
------------------------------
name: mydir file: mydir.py
------------------------------
00) __file__ <built-in name>
01) __name__ <built-in name>
02) listing <function listing at 885450>
03) __doc__ <built-in name>
04) __builtins__ <built-in name>
```

---

* Notice that because a function can access its enclosing module by going through the sys.modules table like this, it's possible to emulate the effect of the global statement we met in Chapter 4. For instance, the effect of global X; X=0 can be simulated by saying, inside a function: import sys; glob=sys.modules[__name__]; glob.X=0 (albeit with much more typing). Remember, each module gets a __name__ attribute for free; it's visible as a global name inside functions within a module. This trick provides a way to change both local and global variables of the same name, inside a function.

```
05) verbose 1
-----------------------------
mydir has 6 names
-----------------------------
```

We'll meet `getattr` and its relatives again. The point to notice here is that `mydir` is a program that lets you browse other programs. Because Python exposes its internals, you can process objects generically.[*]

Module Gotchas

Finally, here is the usual collection of boundary cases, which make life interesting for beginners. Some are so obscure it was hard to come up with examples, but most illustrate something important about Python.

Importing Modules by Name String

As we've seen, the module name in an `import` or `from` statement is a hardcoded variable name; you can't use these statements directly to load a module given its name as a Python string. For instance:

```
>>> import "string"
  File "<stdin>", line 1
    import "string"
                  ^
SyntaxError: invalid syntax
```

Solution

You need to use special tools to load modules dynamically, from a string that exists at runtime. The most general approach is to construct an `import` statement as a string of Python code and pass it to the `exec` statement to run:

```
>>> modname = "string"
>>> exec "import " + modname        # run a string of code
>>> string                          # imported in this namespace
<module 'string'>
```

The `exec` statement (and its cousin, the `eval` function) compiles a string of code, and passes it to the Python interpreter to be executed. In Python, the bytecode compiler is available at runtime, so you can write programs that construct and run other programs like this. By default, `exec` runs the code in the current scope, but

---

[*] By the way, tools such as `mydir.listing` can be preloaded into the interactive namespace, by importing them in the file referenced by the PYTHONSTARTUP environment variable. Since code in the startup file runs in the interactive namespace (module `__main__`), imports of common tools in the startup file can save you some typing. See Chapter 1 for more details.

you can get more specific by passing in optional namespace dictionaries. We'll say more about these tools later in this book.

The only real drawback to **exec** is that it must compile the **import** statement each time it runs; if it runs many times, you might be better off using the built-in **__import__** function to load from a name string instead. The effect is similar, but **__import__** returns the module object, so we assign it to a name here:

```
>>> modname = "string"
>>> string = __import__(modname)
>>> string
<module 'string'>
```

from Copies Names but Doesn't Link

Earlier, we mentioned that the **from** statement is really an *assignment* to names in the importer's scope—a name-copy operation, not a name aliasing. The implications of this are the same as for all assignments in Python, but subtle, especially given that the code that shares objects lives in different files. For instance, suppose we define a module **nested1** as follows:

```
X = 99
def printer(): print X
```

Now, if we import its two names using **from** in another module, we get copies of those names, not links to them. Changing a name in the importer resets only the binding of the local version of that name, not the name in **nested1**:

```
from nested1 import X, printer    # copy names out
X = 88                            # changes my "X" only!
printer()                         # nested1's X is still 99

% python nested2.py
99
```

Solution

On the other hand, if you use **import** to get the whole module and assign to a *qualified* name, you change the name in **nested1**. Qualification directs Python to a name in the module object, rather than a name in the importer:

```
import nested1                    # get module as a whole
nested1.X = 88                    # okay: change nested1's X
nested1.printer()

% python nested3.py
88
```

Statement Order Matters in Top-Level Code

As we also saw earlier, when a module is first imported (or reloaded), Python executes its statements one by one, from the top of file to the bottom. This has a few subtle implications regarding forward references that are worth underscoring here:

- Code at the top level of a module file (not nested in a function) runs as soon as Python reaches it during an import; because of that, it can't reference names assigned lower in the file.

- Code inside a function body doesn't run until the function is called; because names in a function aren't resolved until the function actually runs, they can usually reference names anywhere in the file.

In general, forward references are only a concern in top-level module code that executes immediately; functions can reference names arbitrarily. Here's an example that illustrates forward reference dos and don'ts:

```
func1()              # error: "func1" not yet assigned

def func1():
    print func2()    # okay:  "func2" looked up later

func1()              # error: "func2" not yet assigned

def func2():
    return "Hello"

func1()              # okay:  "func1" and "func2" assigned
```

When this file is imported (or run as a standalone program), Python executes its statements from top to bottom. The first call to `func1` fails because the `func1 def` hasn't run yet. The call to `func2` inside `func1` works as long as `func2`'s `def` has been reached by the time `func1` is called (it hasn't when the second top-level `func1` call is run). The last call to `func1` at the bottom of the file works, because `func1` and `func2` have both been assigned.

Solution

Don't do that. Mixing `defs` with top-level code is not only hard to read, it's dependent on statement ordering. As a rule of thumb, if you need to mix immediate code with `defs`, put your `defs` at the top of the file and top-level code at the bottom. That way, your functions are defined and assigned by the time code that uses them runs.

Recursive "from" Imports May Not Work

Because imports execute a file's statements from top to bottom, we sometimes need to be careful when using modules that import each other (something called *recursive imports*). Since the statements in a module have not all been run when it imports another module, some of its names may not yet exist. If you use import to fetch a module as a whole, this may or may not matter; the module's names won't be accessed until you later use qualification to fetch their values. But if you use from to fetch specific names, you only have access to names already assigned.

For instance, take the following modules recur1 and recur2. recur1 assigns a name X, and then imports recur2, *before* assigning name Y. At this point, recur2 can fetch recur1 as a whole with an import (it already exists in Python's internal modules table), but it can see only name X if it uses from; the name Y below the import in recur1 doesn't yet exist, so you get an error:

module recur1.py

```
X = 1
import recur2            # run recur2 now if doesn't exist
Y = 2
```

module recur2.py

```
from recur1 import X     # okay: "X" already assigned
from recur1 import Y     # error: "Y" not yet assigned
```

```
>>> import recur1
Traceback (innermost last):
  File "<stdin>", line 1, in ?
  File "recur1.py", line 2, in ?
    import recur2
  File "recur2.py", line 2, in ?
    from recur1 import Y   # error: "Y" not yet assigned
ImportError: cannot import name Y
```

Python is smart enough to avoid rerunning recur1's statements when they are imported recursively from recur2 (or else the imports would send the script into an infinite loop), but recur1's namespace is incomplete when imported by recur2.

Solutions

Don't do that....really! Python won't get stuck in a cycle, but your programs will once again be dependent on the order of statements in modules. There are two ways out of this gotcha:

- You can usually eliminate import cycles like this by careful design; maximizing cohesion and minimizing coupling are good first steps.

- If you can't break the cycles completely, postpone module name access by using `import` and qualification (instead of `from`), or running your `from`s inside functions (instead of at the top level of the module).

reload May Not Impact from Imports

The `from` statement is the source of all sorts of gotchas in Python. Here's another: because `from` copies (assigns) names when run, there's no link back to the module where the names came from. Names imported with `from` simply become references to objects, which happen to have been referenced by the same names in the importee when the `from` ran. Because of this behavior, reloading the importee has no effect on clients that use `from`; the client's names still reference the objects fetched with `from`, even though names in the original module have been reset:

```
from module import X      # X may not reflect any module reloads!
. . .
reload(module)            # changes module, not my names
X                         # still references old object
```

Solution

Don't do it that way. To make reloads more effective, use `import` and name qualification, instead of `from`. Because qualifications always go back to the module, they will find the new bindings of module names after calling `reload`:

```
import module             # get module, not names
. . .
reload(module)            # changes module in-place
module.X                  # get current X: reflects module reloads
```

reload Isn't Applied Transitively

When you reload a module, Python only reloads that particular module's file; it doesn't automatically reload modules that the file being reloaded happens to import. For example, if we reload some module A, and A imports modules B and C, the reload only applies to A, not B and C. The statements inside A that import B and C are rerun during the reload, but they'll just fetch the already loaded B and C module objects (assuming they've been imported before):

```
% cat A.py
import B                  # not reloaded when A is
import C                  # just an import of an already loaded module

% python
>>> . . .
>>> reload(A)
```

Solution

Don't depend on that. Use multiple `reload` calls to update subcomponents independently. If desired, you can design your systems to reload their subcomponents automatically by adding `reload` calls in parent modules like A.*

Summary

We've learned all about modules in this chapter—how to write them and how to use them. Along the way we explored namespaces and qualification, saw how to reload modules to change running programs, peeked at a few module design issues, and studied the module-related statements and functions listed in Table 5-1. In the next chapter, we're going to move on to study Python classes. As we'll see, classes are cousins to modules; they define namespaces too, but add support for making multiple copies, specialization by inheritance, and more.

Table 5-1. Module Operations

Operation	Interpretation
`import mod`	Fetch a module as a whole
`from mod import name`	Fetch a specific name from a module
`from mod import*`	Fetch all top-level names from a module
`reload(mod)`	Force a reload of a loaded module's code

Exercises

1. *Basics, import.* With your favorite text editor, write a Python module called *mymod.py*, which exports three top-level names:

    — A `countLines(name)` function that reads an input file and counts the number of lines in it (hint: `file.readlines()` does most of the work for you)

    — A `countChars(name)` function that reads an input file and counts the number of characters in it (hint: `file.read()` returns a single string)

    — A `test(name)` function that calls both counting functions with a given input filename

    A filename string should be passed into all three `mymod` functions. Now, test your module interactively, using `import` and name qualification to fetch your exports. Does your `PYTHONPATH` include the directory where you created *mymod.py*? Try running your module on itself: e.g., `test("mymod.py")`. Note

---

* You could also write a general tool to do transitive reloads automatically, by scanning module `__dict__`s (see the section "Modules Are Objects: Metaprograms"), and checking each item's `type()` to find nested modules to reload recursively. This is an advanced exercise for the ambitious.

that `test` opens the file twice; if you're feeling ambitious, you might be able to improve this by passing an open file object into the two count functions.

2. *from/from*. Test your `mymod` module from Exercise 1 *interactively*, by using `from` to load the exports directly, first by name, then using the `from*` variant to fetch everything.

3. *__main__*. Now, add a line in your `mymod` module that calls the `test` function automatically only when the module is run as a *script*. Try running your module from the system command line; then import the module and test its functions interactively. Does it still work in both modes?

4. *Nested imports*. Finally, write a second module, *myclient.py*, which imports `mymod` and tests its functions; run *myclient* from the system command line. If *myclient* uses `from` to fetch from `mymod`, will `mymod`'s functions be accessible from the top level of *myclient?* What if it imports with `import` instead? Try coding both variations in *myclient* and test interactively, by importing *myclient* and inspecting its `__dict__`.

5. *Reload*. Experiment with module reloads: perform the tests in the *changer.py* example, changing the called function's message and/or behavior repeatedly, without stopping the Python interpreter. Depending on your system, you might be able to edit `changer` in another window, or suspend the Python interpreter and edit in the same window (on Unix, a Ctrl-Z key combination usually suspends the current process, and a `fg` command later resumes it).

6. *Circular imports* (and other acts of cruelty).[*] In the section on recursive import gotchas, importing `recur1` raised an error. But if we restart Python and import `recur2` interactively, the error doesn't occur: test and see this for yourself. Why do you think it works to import `recur2`, but not `recur1`? (Hint: Python stores new modules in the built-in `sys.modules` table (a dictionary) before running their code; later imports fetch the module from this table first, whether the module is "complete" yet or not.) Now try running `recur1` as a script: `% python recur1.py`. Do you get the same error that occurs when `recur1` is imported interactively? Why? (Hint: when modules are run as programs they aren't imported, so this case has the same effect as importing `recur2` interactively; `recur2` is the first module imported.) What happens when you run `recur2` as a script?

---

[*] We should note that circular imports are extremely rare in practice. In fact, we have never coded or come across a circular import in six years of Python coding—except on the Internet (where such things receive an inordinate amount of attention), and when writing books like this. On the other hand, if you can understand why it's a potential problem, you know a lot about Python's import semantics.

6

Classes

This chapter explores the Python class—a device used to implement new kinds of objects in Python. Classes are Python's main object-oriented programming (OOP) tool, so we'll also look at OOP basics along the way in this chapter. In Python, classes are created with a new statement we'll meet here too: the `class` statement. As we'll see, objects defined with classes can look a lot like the built-in types we saw earlier in the book.

One note up front: Python OOP is entirely optional, and you don't need to use classes just to get started. In fact, you can get plenty of work done with simpler constructs such as functions. But classes turn out to be one of the most useful tools Python provides, and we hope to show you why here. They're also employed in popular Python tools like the Tkinter GUI API, so most Python programmers will usually find at least a working knowledge of class basics helpful.

Why Use Classes?

Remember when we told you that programs do things with stuff? In simple terms, classes are just a way to define new sorts of stuff, which reflect real objects in your program's domain. For instance, suppose we've decided to implement that hypothetical pizza-making robot we used as an example in Chapter 4, *Functions*. If we implement it using classes, we can model more of its real-world structure and relationships:

Inheritance

Pizza-making robots are a kind of robot, and so posses the usual robot-y properties. In OOP terms, we say they inherit properties from the general category of all robots. These common properties need be implemented only once for the general case and reused by all types of robots we may build in the future.

Composition

Pizza-making robots are really collections of components that work together as a team. For instance, for our robot to be successful, it might need arms to roll dough, motors to maneuver to the oven, and so on. In OOP parlance, our robot is an example of composition; it contains other objects it activates to do its bidding. Each component might be coded as a class, which defines its own behavior and relationships.

Of course, most of us aren't getting paid to build pizza-making robots yet, but general OOP ideas like inheritance and composition apply to any application that can be decomposed into a set of objects. For example, in typical GUI systems, interfaces are written as collections of widgets (buttons, labels, and so on), which are all drawn when their container is (composition). Moreover, we may be able to write our own custom widgets, which are specialized versions of more general interface devices (inheritance).

From a more concrete programming perspective, classes are a Python program unit, just like functions and modules. They are another compartment for packaging logic and data. In fact, classes also define a new namespace much like modules. But compared to other program units we've already seen, classes have three critical distinctions that make them more useful when it comes to building new objects:

Multiple instances

Classes are roughly templates for generating one or more objects. Every time we call a class, we generate a new object, with a distinct namespace. As we'll see, each object generated from a class has access to the class's attributes and gets a namespace of its own for data that varies per object.

Customization via inheritance

Classes also support the OOP notion of inheritance; they are extended by overriding their attributes outside the class itself. More generally, classes can build up namespace hierarchies, which define names to be used by objects created from classes in the hierarchy.

Operator overloading

By providing special protocol methods, classes can define objects that respond to the sorts of operations we saw work on built-in types. For instance, objects made with classes can be sliced, concatenated, indexed, and so on. As we'll see, Python provides hooks classes can use to intercept any built-in type operation.

Class Basics

If you've never been exposed to OOP in the past, classes can be somewhat complicated if taken in a single dose. To make classes easier to absorb, let's start off by taking a quick first look at classes in action here, to illustrate the three distinctions described previously. We'll expand on the details in a moment; but in their basic form, Python classes are easy to understand.

Classes Generate Multiple Instance Objects

As we mentioned at the end of Chapter 5, *Modules*, classes are mostly just a namespace, much like modules. But unlike modules, classes also have support for multiple copies, namespace inheritance, and operator overloading. Let's look at the first of these extensions here.

To understand how the multiple copies idea works, you have to first understand that there are two kinds of objects in Python's OOP model—class objects and instance objects. Class objects provide default behavior and serve as generators for instance objects. Instance objects are the real objects your programs process; each is a namespace in its own right, but inherits (i.e., has access to) names in the class it was created from. Class objects come from statements and instances from calls; each time you call a class, you get a new instance. Now, pay attention, because we're about to summarize the bare essentials of Python OOP.

Class objects provide default behavior

The class statement creates a class object and assigns it a name

Like `def`, the Python `class` statement is an executable statement; when run, it generates a new class object and assigns it the name in the `class` header.

Assignments inside class statements make class attributes

Like modules, assignments in a `class` statement generate attributes in a class object; class attributes are accessed by name qualification (`object.name`).

Class attributes export object state and behavior

Attributes of a class object record state information and behavior, to be shared by all instances created from the class; function `def` statements inside a `class` generate *methods*, which process instances.

Instance objects are generated from classes

Calling a class object like a function makes a new instance object

Each time a class is called, it generates and returns a new instance object.

Each instance object inherits class attributes and gets its own namespace

Instance objects generated from classes are new namespaces; they start out empty, but inherit attributes that live in the class object they were generated from.

Assignments to self in methods make per-instance attributes

Inside class method functions, the first argument (called `self` by convention) references the instance object being processed; assignments to attributes of `self` create or change data in the instance, not the class.

An example

Apart from a few details, that's all there is to OOP in Python. Let's turn to a real example to show how these ideas work in practice. First, let's define a class called `FirstClass`, using the Python `class` statement:

```
>>> class FirstClass:          # define a class object
...     def setdata(self, value):   # define class methods
...         self.data = value       # self is the instance
...     def display(self):
...         print self.data         # self.data: per instance
```

Like all compound statements, `class` starts with a *header* line that lists the class name, followed by a *body* of one or more nested and indented statements. Here, the nested statements are `defs`; they define functions that implement the behavior the class means to export. As we've seen, `def` is an assignment; here, it assigns to names in the `class` statement's scope and so generates attributes of the class. Functions inside a class are usually called *method* functions; they're normal `defs`, but the first argument automatically receives an implied instance object when called. We need a couple of instances to see how:

```
>>> x = FirstClass()          # make two instances
>>> y = FirstClass()          # each is a new namespace
```

By calling the class as we do, we generate instance objects, which are just namespaces that get the class's attributes for free. Properly speaking, at this point we have three objects—two instances and a class; but really, we have three linked *namespaces*, as sketched in Figure 6-1. In OOP terms, we say that x is a `FirstClass`, as is y. The instances start empty, but have links back to the class; if we qualify an instance with the name of an attribute in the class object, Python fetches the name from the class (unless it also lives in the instance):

```
>>> x.setdata("King Arthur")    # call methods: self is x or y
>>> y.setdata(3.14159)          # runs: FirstClass.setdata(y, 3.14159)
```

Neither x nor y has a `setdata` of its own; instead, Python follows the link from instance to class if an attribute doesn't exist in an instance. And that's about all there is to *inheritance* in Python: it happens at attribute qualification time, and just involves looking up names in linked objects (by following the `is-a` links in Figure 6-1).

In the `setdata` function in `FirstClass`, the value passed in is assigned to `self.data`; within a method, `self` automatically refers to the instance being processed (x or y), so the assignments store values in the instances' namespaces, not the class (that's how the `data` names in Figure 6-1 get created). Since classes generate multiple instances, methods must go through the `self` argument to get to the instance to be processed. When we call the class's `display` method to print `self.data`, we see that it's different in each instance; on the other hand, `display` is the same in x and y, since it comes (is *inherited*) from the class:

```
>>> x.display()                    # self.data differs in each
King Arthur
>>> y.display()
3.14159
```

Notice that we stored different object types in the `data` member (a string and a float). Like everything else in Python, there are no declarations for instance attributes (sometimes called *members*); they spring into existence the first time they are assigned a value, just like simple variables. In fact, we can change instance attributes either in the class itself by assigning to `self` in methods, or outside the class by assigning to an explicit instance object:

```
>>> x.data = "New value"           # can get/set attributes
>>> x.display()                    # outside the class too
New value
```

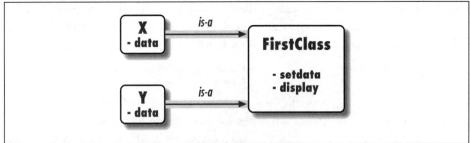

Figure 6-1. Classes and instances are linked namespace objects

Classes Are Specialized by Inheritance

Unlike modules, classes also allow us to make changes by introducing new components (*subclasses*), instead of changing existing components in place. We've already seen that instance objects generated from a class inherit its attributes.

Python also allows classes to inherit from other classes, and this opens the door to what are usually called *frameworks*—hierarchies of classes that specialize behavior by overriding attributes lower in the hierarchy. The key ideas behind this machinery are:

Superclasses are listed in parentheses in a class header
> To inherit attributes from another class, just list the class in parentheses in a class statement's header. The class that inherits is called a *subclass*, and the class that is inherited from is its *superclass*.

Classes inherit attributes from their superclasses
> Just like instances, a class gets all the names defined in its superclasses for free; they're found by Python automatically when qualified, if they don't exist in the subclass.

Instances inherit attributes from all accessible classes
> Instances get names from the class they are generated from, as well as all of the class's superclasses; when looking for a name, Python checks the instance, then its class, then all superclasses above.

Logic changes are made by subclassing, not by changing superclasses
> By redefining superclass names in subclasses, subclasses *override* inherited behavior.

An example

Our next example builds on the one before. Let's define a new class, `SecondClass`, which inherits all of `FirstClass`'s names and provides one of its own:

```
>>> class SecondClass(FirstClass):          # inherits setdata
...     def display(self):                   # changes display
...         print 'Current value = "%s"' % self.data
```

`SecondClass` redefines the `display` method to print with a different format. But because `SecondClass` defines an attribute of the same name, it replaces the `display` attribute in `FirstClass`. Inheritance works by searching up from instances, to subclasses, to superclasses, and stops at the first appearance of an attribute name it finds. Since it finds the `display` name in `SecondClass` before the one in `FirstClass`, we say that `SecondClass` overrides `FirstClass`'s `display`. In other words, `SecondClass` specializes `FirstClass`, by changing the behavior of the `display` method. On the other hand, `SecondClass` (and instances created from it) still inherits the `setdata` method in `FirstClass` verbatim. Figure 6-2 sketches the namespaces involved; let's make an instance to demonstrate:

```
>>> z = SecondClass()
>>> z.setdata(42)            # setdata found in FirstClass
>>> z.display()              # finds overridden method in SecondClass
Current value = "42"
```

As before, we make a SecondClass instance object by calling it. The setdata call still runs the version in FirstClass, but this time the display attribute comes from SecondClass and prints a different message. Now here's a very important thing to notice about OOP: the specialization introduced in SecondClass is completely external to FirstClass; it doesn't effect existing or future FirstClass objects, like x from the prior example:

```
>>> x.display()              # x is still a FirstClass instance (old message)
New value
```

Naturally, this is an artificial example, but as a rule, because changes can be made in external components (subclasses), classes often support extension and reuse better than functions or modules do.

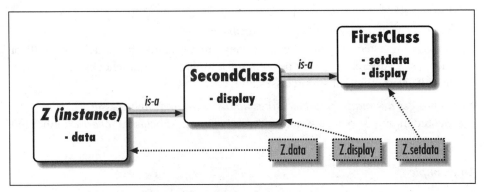

Figure 6-2. Specialization by overriding inherited names

Classes Can Intercept Python Operators

Finally, let's take a quick look at the third major property of classes: operator overloading in action. In simple terms, operator overloading lets objects we implement with classes respond to operations we've already seen work on built-in types: addition, slicing, printing, qualification, and so on. Although we could implement all our objects' behavior as method functions, operator overloading lets our objects be more tightly integrated with Python's object model. Moreover, because operator overloading makes our own objects act like built-ins, it tends to foster object interfaces that are more consistent and easy to learn. The main ideas are:

Methods with names such as __ X __ are special hooks

Python operator overloading is implemented by providing specially named methods to intercept operations.

Such methods are called automatically when Python evaluates operators

For instance, if an object inherits an __add__ method, it is called when the object appears in a + expression.

Classes may override most built-in type operations

There are dozens of special operator method names for catching nearly every built-in type operation.

Operators allow classes to integrate with Python's object model

By overloading type operations, user-defined objects implemented with classes act just like built-ins.

An example

On to another example. This time, we define a subclass of SecondClass, which implements three special attributes: __init__ is called when a new instance object is being constructed (self is the new ThirdClass object), and __add__ and __mul__ are called when a ThirdClass instance appears in + and * expressions, respectively:

```
>>> class ThirdClass(SecondClass):              # is-a SecondClass
...       def __init__(self, value):            # on "ThirdClass(value)"
...           self.data = value
...       def __add__(self, other):             # on "self + other"
...           return ThirdClass(self.data + other)
...       def __mul__(self, other):
...           self.data = self.data * other      # on "self * other"
...
>>> a = ThirdClass("abc")        # new __init__ called
>>> a.display()                  # inherited method
Current value = "abc"

>>> b = a + 'xyz'                # new __add__ called: makes a new instance
>>> b.display()
Current value = "abcxyz"

>>> a * 3                        # new __mul__ called: changes instance in-place
>>> a.display()
Current value = "abcabcabc"
```

ThirdClass is a SecondClass, so its instances inherit display from SecondClass. But ThirdClass generation calls pass an argument now ("abc"); it's passed to the value argument in the __init__ constructor and assigned to self.data there. Further, ThirdClass objects can show up in + and * expressions; Python passes the instance object on the left to the self argument and the value on the right to other, as illustrated in Figure 6-3.

Special methods such as __init__ and __add__ are inherited by subclasses and instances, just like any other name assigned in a class statement. Notice that the __add__ method makes a *new* object (by calling ThirdClass with the result

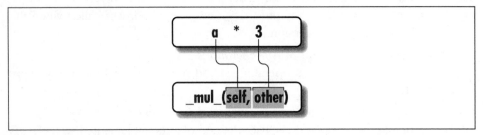

Figure 6-3. Operators map to special methods

value), but `__mul__` changes the current instance object in place (by reassigning a `self` attribute). The `*` operator makes a new object when applied to built-in types such as numbers and lists, but you can interpret it any way you like in class objects.[*]

Using the Class Statement

Did all of the above make sense? If not, don't worry; now that we've had a quick tour, we're going to dig a bit deeper and study the concepts we've introduced in more detail. We met the `class` statement in our first examples, but let's formalize some of the ideas we introduced. As in C++, the `class` statement is Python's main OOP tool. Unlike in C++, `class` isn't really a declaration; like `def`, `class` is an object builder, and an implicit assignment—when run, it generates a class object, and stores a reference to it in the name used in the header.

General Form

As we saw on our quick tour, `class` is a compound statement with a body of indented statements under it. In the header, superclasses are listed in parentheses after the class name, separated by commas. Listing more than one superclass leads to multiple inheritance (which we'll say more about later in this chapter):

```
class <name>(superclass,...):      # assign to name
    data = value                   # shared class data
    def method(self,...):          # methods
        self.member = value        # per-instance data
```

---

[*] But you probably shouldn't (one reviewer went so far as to call this example "evil!"). Common practice dictates that overloaded operators should work the same way built-in operator implementations do. In this case, that means our `__mul__` method should return a *new* object as its result, rather than changing the instance (`self`) in place; a `mul` method may be better style than a `*` overload here (e.g., `a.mul(3)` instead of `a * 3`). On the other hand, one person's common practice may be another person's arbitrary constraint.

Within the class statement, specially-named methods overload operators; for instance, a function called __init__ is called at instance object construction time, if defined.

Example

At the start of this chapter, we mentioned that classes are mostly just *namespaces*—a tool for defining names (called attributes) that export data and logic to clients. So how do you get from the statement to a namespace?

Here's how. Just as with modules, the statements nested in a **class** statement body create its attributes. When Python executes a **class** statement (not a call to a class), it runs all the statements in its body from top to bottom. Assignments that happen during this process create names in the class's local scope, which become attributes in the associated class object. Because of this, classes resemble both modules and functions:

- Like functions, **class** statements are a local scope where names created by nested assignments live.

- Like modules, names assigned in a **class** statement become attributes in a class object.

The main distinction for classes is that their namespaces are also the basis of inheritance in Python; attributes are fetched from other classes if not found in a class or instance object. Because **class** is a compound statement, any sort of statement can be nested inside its body—for instance, **print**, **=**, **if**, and **def**. As we've seen, nested **defs** make class methods, but other assignments make attributes too. For example, suppose we run the following class:

```
class Subclass(aSuperclass):          # define subclass
    data = 'spam'                     # assign class attr
    def __init__(self, value):        # assign class attr
        self.data = value             # assign instance attr
    def display(self):
        print self.data, Subclass.data   # instance, class
```

This class contains two **defs**, which bind class attributes to method functions. It also contains a = assignment statement; since the name **data** is assigned inside the **class**, it lives in the class's local scope and becomes an attribute of the class object. Like all class attributes, **data** is inherited and *shared* by all instances of the class:[*]

---

[*] If you've used C++, you may recognize this as similar to the notion of C++'s static class data—members that are stored in the class, independent of instances. In Python, it's nothing special: all class attributes are just names assigned in the **class** statement, whether they happen to reference functions (C++'s *methods*) or something else (C++'s *members*).

```
>>> x = Subclass(1)            # make two instance objects
>>> y = Subclass(2)            # each has its own "data"
>>> x.display(); y.display()   # "self.data" differs, "Subclass.data" same
1 spam
2 spam
```

When we run this code, the name data lives in two places—in instance objects (created in the __init__ constructor) and in the class they inherit names from (created by the = assignment). The class's display method prints both versions, by first qualifying the self instance, and then the class itself. Since classes are objects with attributes, we can get to their names by qualifying, even if there's no instance involved.

Using Class Methods

Since you already know about functions, you already know class methods. Methods are just function objects created by def statements nested in a class statement's body. From an abstract perspective, methods provide behavior for instance objects to inherit. From a programming perspective, methods work in exactly the same way as simple functions, with one crucial exception: their first argument always receives the instance object that is the implied subject of a method call. In other words, Python automatically maps instance method calls to class method functions like so:

```
instance.method(args...)  => becomes => class.method(instance, args...)
```

where the class is determined by Python's inheritance search procedure. The special first argument in a class method is usually called self by convention; it's similar to C++'s this pointer, but Python methods must always explicitly qualify self to fetch or change attributes of the instance being processed by the current method call.

Example

Let's turn to an example; suppose we define the following class:

```
class NextClass:              # define class
    def printer(self, text):  # define method
        print text
```

The name printer references a function object; because it's assigned in the class statement's scope, it becomes a class attribute and is inherited by every instance made from the class. The printer function may be called in one of two ways—through an instance, or through the class itself:

```
>>> x = NextClass()            # make instance
>>> x.printer('Hello world!')  # call its method
Hello world!
```

When called by qualifying an *instance* like this, `printer`'s `self` argument is automatically assigned the instance object (`x`), and `text` gets the string passed at the call (`"Hello world!"`). Inside `printer`, `self` can access or set per-instance data, since it refers to the instance currently being processed. We can also call `printer` by going through the class, provided we pass an instance to the `self` argument explicitly:

```
>>> NextClass.printer(x, 'Hello world!')    # class method
Hello world!
```

Calls routed through the instance and class have the exact same effect, provided we pass the same instance object in the class form. In a moment, we'll see that calls through a class are the basis of extending (instead of replacing) inherited behavior.

Inheritance Searches Namespace Trees

The whole point of a namespace tool like the `class` statement is to support name inheritance. In Python, inheritance happens when an object is qualified, and involves searching an attribute definition tree (one or more namespaces). Every time you use an expression of the form `object.attr` where object is an instance or class object, Python searches the namespace tree at and above `object`, for the first `attr` it can find. Because lower definitions in the tree override higher ones, inheritance forms the basis of specialization.

Attribute Tree Construction

Figure 6-4 sketches the way namespace trees are constructed. In general:

- *Instance* attributes are generated by assignments to `self` attributes in methods.
- *Class* attributes are created by statements (assignments) in `class` statements.
- *Superclass* links are made by listing classes in parentheses in a `class` statement header.

The net result is a tree of attribute namespaces, which grows from an instance, to the class it was generated from, to all the superclasses listed in the class headers. Python searches upward in this tree from instances to superclasses, each time you use qualification to fetch an attribute name from an instance object.[*]

---

[*] This description isn't 100% complete, because instance and class attributes can also be created by assigning to objects outside `class` statements. But that's less common and sometimes more error prone (changes aren't isolated to `class` statements). In Python all attributes are always accessible by default; we talk about privacy later in this chapter.

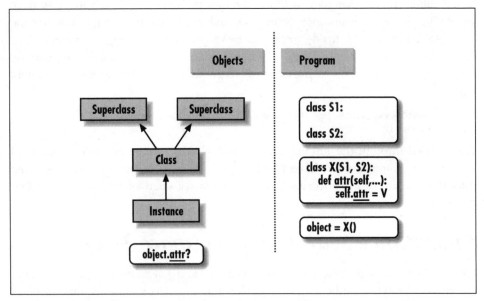

Figure 6-4. Namespaces tree construction and inheritance

Specializing Inherited Methods

The tree-searching model of inheritance we just described turns out to be a great way to specialize systems. Because inheritance finds names in subclasses before it checks superclasses, subclasses can *replace* default behavior by redefining the superclass's attributes. In fact, you can build entire systems as hierarchies of classes, which are extended by adding new external subclasses rather than changing existing logic in place.

The idea of overloading inherited names leads to a variety of specialization techniques. For instance, subclasses may replace inherited names completely, provide names a superclass expects to find, and extend superclass methods by calling back to the superclass from an overridden method. We've already seen replacement in action; here's an example that shows how extension works:

```
>>> class Super:
...     def method(self):
...         print 'in Super.method'
...
>>> class Sub(Super):
...     def method(self):                    # override method
...         print 'starting Sub.method'      # add actions here
...         Super.method(self)               # run default action
...         print 'ending Sub.method'
...
```

Direct superclass method calls are the crux of the matter here. The Sub class replaces Super's method function with its own specialized version. But within the replacement, Sub calls back to the version exported by Super to carry out the default behavior. In other words, Sub.method just extends Super.method's behavior, rather than replace it completely:

```
>>> x = Super()          # make a Super instance
>>> x.method()           # runs Super.method
in Super.method

>>> x = Sub()            # make a Sub instance
>>> x.method()           # runs Sub.method, which calls Super.method
starting Sub.method
in Super.method
ending Sub.method
```

Extension is commonly used with constructors; since the specially named __init__ method is an inherited name, only *one* is found and run when an instance is created. To run superclass constructors, subclass __init__ methods should call superclass __init__ methods, by qualifying classes (e.g., Class.__init__(self, ...)).

Extension is only one way to interface with a superclass; the following shows subclasses that illustrate these common schemes:

- Super defines a method function and a delegate that expects an action in a subclass.

- Inheritor doesn't provide any new names, so it gets everything defined in Super.

- Replacer overrides Super's method with a version of its own.

- Extender customizes Super's method by overriding and calling back to run the default.

- Provider implements the action method expected by Super's delegate method.

```
class Super:
    def method(self):
        print 'in Super.method'     # default
    def delegate(self):
        self.action()               # expected

class Inheritor(Super):
    pass

class Replacer(Super):
    def method(self):
        print 'in Replacer.method'

class Extender(Super):
    def method(self):
```

```
            print 'starting Extender.method'
            Super.method(self)
            print 'ending Extender.method'

    class Provider(Super):
        def action(self):
            print 'in Provider.action'

    if __name__ == '__main__':
        for klass in (Inheritor, Replacer, Extender):
            print '\n' + klass.__name__ + '...'
            klass().method()
        print '\nProvider...'
        Provider().delegate()
```

A few things are worth pointing out here: the self-test code at the end of this
example creates instances of three different classes; because classes are objects,
you can put them in a tuple and create instances generically (more on this idea
later). Classes also have the special `__name__` attribute as modules; it's just preset
to a string containing the name in the class header. When you call the `delegate`
method though a `Provider` instance, Python finds the `action` method in
`Provider` by the usual tree search: inside the `Super delegate` method, `self` references a `Provider` instance.

```
% python specialize.py

Inheritor...
in Super.method

Replacer...
in Replacer.method

Extender...
starting Extender.method
in Super.method
ending Extender.method

Provider...
in Provider.action
```

Operator Overloading in Classes

We introduced operator overloading at the start of this chapter; let's fill in a few
blanks here and look at a handful of commonly used overloading methods. Here's
a review of the key ideas behind overloading:

- Operator overloading lets classes intercept normal Python operations.

- Classes can overload all Python expression operators.

- Classes can also overload object operations: printing, calls, qualification, etc.

- Overloading makes class instances act more like built-in types.

- Overloading is implemented by providing specially named class methods.

Here's a simple example of overloading at work. When we provide specially named methods in a class, Python automatically calls them when instances of the class appear in the associated operation. For instance, the **Number** class below provides a method to intercept instance construction (__init__), as well as one for catching subtraction expressions (__sub__). Special methods are the hook that lets you tie into built-in operations:

```
class Number:
    def __init__(self, start):          # on Number(start)
        self.data = start
    def __sub__(self, other):           # on instance - other
        return Number(self.data - other)   # result is a new instance

>>> from number import Number           # fetch class from module
>>> X = Number(5)                        # calls Number.__init__(X, 5)
>>> Y = X - 2                            # calls Number.__sub__(X, 2)
>>> Y.data
3
```

Common Operator Overloading Methods

Just about everything you can do to built-in objects such as integers and lists has a corresponding specially named method for overloading in classes. Table 6-1 lists a handful of the most common; there are many more than we have time to cover in this book. See other Python books or the Python *Library Reference Manual* for an exhaustive list of special method names available. All overload methods have names that start and end with two underscores, to keep them distinct from other names you define in your classes.

Table 6-1. A Sampling of Operator Overloading Methods

Method	Overloads	Called for
__init__	Constructor	Object creation: `Class()`
__del__	Destructor	Object reclamation
__add__	Operator '+'	X + Y
__or__	Operator '|' (bitwise or)	X	Y
__repr__	Printing, conversions	print X, `X`
__call__	Function calls	X()
__getattr__	Qualification	X.undefined
__getitem__	Indexing	X[key], for loops, in tests
__setitem__	Index assignment	X[key] = value
__getslice__	Slicing	X[low:high]

Table 6-1. A Sampling of Operator Overloading Methods (continued)

Method	Overloads	Called for
__len__	Length	len(X), truth tests
__cmp__	Comparison	X == Y, X < Y
__radd__	Right-side operator '+'	Noninstance + X

Examples

Let's illustrate a few of the methods in Table 6-1 by example.

__getitem__ intercepts all index references

The __getitem__ method intercepts instance indexing operations: When an instance X appears in an indexing expression like X[i], Python calls a __getitem__ method inherited by the instance (if any), passing X to the first argument and the index in brackets to the second argument. For instance, the following class returns the square of index values:

```
>>> class indexer:
...     def __getitem__(self, index):
...         return index ** 2
...
>>> X = indexer()
>>> for i in range(5):
...     print X[i],              # X[i] calls __getitem__(X, i)
...
0 1 4 9 16
```

Now, here's a special trick that isn't always obvious to beginners, but turns out to be incredibly useful: when we introduced the for statement back in Chapter 3, *Basic Statements*, we mentioned that it works by repeatedly indexing a sequence from zero to higher indexes, until an out-of-bounds exception is detected. Because of that, __getitem__ also turns out to be the way to overload iteration and membership tests in Python. It's a case of "buy one, get two free": any built-in or user-defined object that responds to indexing also responds to iteration and membership automatically:

```
>>> class stepper:
...     def __getitem__(self, i):
...         return self.data[i]
...
>>> X = stepper()               # X is a stepper object
>>> X.data = "Spam"
>>>
>>> for item in X:              # for loops call __getitem__
...     print item,             # for indexes items 0..N
...
S p a m
>>>
```

```
>>> 'p' in X                    # 'in' operator calls __getitem__ too
1
```

__getattr__ *catches undefined attribute references*

The `__getattr__` method intercepts attribute qualifications. More specifically, it's called with the attribute name as a string, whenever you try to qualify an instance on an undefined (nonexistent) attribute name. It's not called if Python can find the attribute using its inheritance tree-search procedure. Because of this behavior, `__getattr__` is useful as a hook for responding to attribute requests in a generic fashion. For example:

```
>>> class empty:
...     def __getattr__(self, attrname):
...         if attrname == "age":
...             return 36
...         else:
...             raise AttributeError, attrname
...
>>> X = empty()
>>> X.age
36
>>> X.name
Traceback (innermost last):
  File "<stdin>", line 1, in ?
  File "<stdin>", line 6, in __getattr__
AttributeError: name
```

Here, the `empty` class and its instance X have no real attributes of their own, so the access to `X.age` gets routed to the `__getattr__` method; `self` is assigned the instance (X), and `attrname` is assigned the undefined attribute name string (`"age"`). Our class makes `age` look like a real attribute by returning a real value as the result of the `X.age` qualification expression (36).

For other attributes the class doesn't know how to handle, it raises the built-in `AttributeError` exception, to tell Python that this is a bona fide undefined name; asking for `X.name` triggers the error. We'll see `__getattr__` again when we show delegation at work, and we will say more about exceptions in Chapter 7, *Exceptions*.

__repr__ *returns a string representation*

Here's an example that exercises the `__init__` constructor and the `__add__` + overload methods we've already seen, but also defines a `__repr__` that returns a string representation of instances. Backquotes are used to convert the managed `self.data` object to a string. If defined, `__repr__` is called automatically when class objects are printed or converted to strings.

```
>>> class adder:
...     def __init__(self, value=0):
```

```
...        self.data = value                # initialize data
...    def __add__(self, other):
...        self.data = self.data + other    # add other in-place
...    def __repr__(self):
...        return `self.data`                # convert to string
...
>>> X = adder(1)          # __init__
>>> X + 2; X + 2          # __add__
>>> X                     # __repr__
5
```

That's as many overloading examples as we have space for here. Most work similarly to ones we've already seen, and all are just hooks for intercepting built-in type operations we've already studied; but some overload methods have unique argument lists or return values. We'll see a few others in action later in the text, but for a complete coverage, we'll defer to other documentation sources.

Namespace Rules: The Whole Story

Now that we've seen class and instance objects, the Python namespace story is complete; for reference, let's quickly summarize all the rules used to resolve names. The first things you need to remember are that qualified and unqualified names are treated differently, and that some scopes serve to initialize object namespaces:

- Unqualified names (X) deal with scopes.
- Qualified names (object.X) use object namespaces.
- Scopes initialize object namespaces (in modules and classes).

Unqualified Names: Global Unless Assigned

Unqualified names follow the LGB rules we outlined for functions in Chapter 4.

Assignment: X = value
   Makes names local: creates or changes name X in the current local scope, unless declared global

Reference: X
   Looks for name X in the current local scope, then the current global scope, then the built-in scope

Qualified Names: Object Namespaces

Qualified names refer to attributes of specific objects and obey the rules we met when discussing modules. For instance and class objects, the reference rules are augmented to include the inheritance search procedure:

Assignment: `object.X = value`

> Creates or alters the attribute name `X` in the namespace of the object being qualified

Reference: `object.X`

> Searches for the attribute name `X` in the object, then in all accessible classes above it (but not for modules)

Namespace Dictionaries

Finally, in Chapter 5, we saw that module namespaces were actually implemented as dictionaries and exposed with the built-in `__dict__` attribute. The same holds for class and instance objects: qualification is really a dictionary indexing internally, and attribute inheritance is just a matter of searching linked dictionaries.

The following example traces the way namespace dictionaries grow when classes are involved. The main thing to notice is this: whenever an attribute of `self` is assigned in one of the two classes, it creates (or changes) an attribute in the instance's namespace dictionary, not the class's. Instance object namespaces record data that can vary from instance to instance; they also have links to class namespaces that are followed by inheritance lookups. For example, `X.hello` is ultimately found in the **super** class's namespace dictionary.

```
>>> class super:
...     def hello(self):
...         self.data1 = "spam"
...
>>> class sub(super):
...     def howdy(self):
...         self.data2 = "eggs"
...
>>> X = sub()           # make a new namespace (dictionary)
>>> X.__dict__
{}
>>> X.hello()           # changes instance namespace
>>> X.__dict__
{'data1': 'spam'}

>>> X.howdy()           # changes instance namespace
>>> X.__dict__
{'data2': 'eggs', 'data1': 'spam'}

>>> super.__dict__
{'hello': <function hello at 88d9b0>, '__doc__': None}

>>> sub.__dict__
{'__doc__': None, 'howdy': <function howdy at 88ea20>}

>>> X.data3 = "toast"
>>> X.__dict__
{'data3': 'toast', 'data2': 'eggs', 'data1': 'spam'}
```

Note that the `dir` function we met in Chapters 1 and 2 works on class and instance objects too. In fact, it works on anything with attributes. `dir(object)` returns the same list as a `object.__dict__.keys()` call.

Designing with Classes

So far, we've concentrated on the OOP tool in Python—the class. But OOP is also about design issues—how to use classes to model useful objects. In this section, we're going to touch on a few OOP core ideas and look at some examples that are more realistic than the ones we've seen so far. Most of the design terms we throw out here require more explanation than we can provide; if this section sparks your curiosity, we suggest exploring a text on OOP design or design patterns as a next step.

Python and OOP

Python's implementation of OOP can be summarized by three ideas:

Inheritance
> Is based on attribute lookup in Python (in `X.name` expressions).

Polymorphism
> In `X.method`, the meaning of `method` depends on the type (class) of `X`.

Encapsulation
> Methods and operators implement behavior; data hiding is a convention by default.

By now, you should have a good feel for what inheritance is all about in Python. Python's flavor of polymorphism flows from its lack of type declarations. Because attributes are always resolved at runtime, objects that implement the same interfaces are interchangeable; clients don't need to know what sort of object is implementing a method they call.* Encapsulation means packaging in Python, not privacy; privacy is an option, as we'll see later in this chapter.

OOP and Inheritance: "is-a"

We've talked about the mechanics of inheritance in depth already, but we'd like to show you an example of how it can be used to model real-world relationships.

---

* Some OOP languages also define polymorphism to mean overloading functions based on the type signatures of their arguments. Since there is no type declaration in Python, the concept doesn't really apply, but type-base selections can be always be coded using `if` tests and `type(X)` built-in functions (e.g., `if type(X) is type(0): doIntegerCase()`).

From a programmer's point of view, inheritance is kicked off by attribute qualifications and searches for a name in an instance, its class, and then its superclasses. From a designer's point of view, inheritance is a way to specify set membership. A class defines a set of properties that may be inherited by more specific sets (i.e., subclasses).

To illustrate, let's put that pizza-making robot we talked about at the start of the chapter to work. Suppose we've decided to explore alternative career paths and open a pizza restaurant. One of the first things we'll need to do is hire employees to service customers, make the pizza, and so on. Being engineers at heart, we've also decided to build a robot to make the pizzas; but being politically and cybernetically correct, we've also decided to make our robot a full-fledged employee, with a salary.

Our pizza shop team can be defined by the following classes in the example file *employees.py*. It defines four classes and some self-test code. The most general class, Employee, provides common behavior such as bumping up salaries (giveRaise) and printing (__repr__). There are two kinds of employees, and so two subclasses of Employee—Chef and Server. Both override the inherited work method to print more specific messages. Finally, our pizza robot is modeled by an even more specific class: PizzaRobot is a kind of Chef, which is a kind of Employee. In OOP terms, we call these relationships "is-a" links: a robot is a chef, which is a(n) employee.

```
class Employee:
    def __init__(self, name, salary=0):
        self.name   = name
        self.salary = salary
    def giveRaise(self, percent):
        self.salary = self.salary + (self.salary * percent)
    def work(self):
        print self.name, "does stuff"
    def __repr__(self):
        return "<Employee: name=%s, salary=%s>" % (self.name, self.salary)

class Chef(Employee):
    def __init__(self, name):
        Employee.__init__(self, name, 50000)
    def work(self):
        print self.name, "makes food"

class Server(Employee):
    def __init__(self, name):
        Employee.__init__(self, name, 40000)
    def work(self):
        print self.name, "interfaces with customer"

class PizzaRobot(Chef):
    def __init__(self, name):
```

```
            Chef.__init__(self, name)
        def work(self):
            print self.name, "makes pizza"

    if __name__ == "__main__":
        bob = PizzaRobot('bob')        # make a robot named bob
        print bob                      # runs inherited __repr__
        bob.giveRaise(0.20)            # give bob a 20% raise
        print bob; print

        for klass in Employee, Chef, Server, PizzaRobot:
            obj = klass(klass.__name__)
            obj.work()
```

When we run this module's self-test code, we create a pizza-making robot named bob, which inherits names from three classes: `PizzaRobot`, `Chef`, and `Employee`. For instance, printing bob runs the `Employee.__repr__` method, and giving bob a raise invokes `Employee.giveRaise`, because that's where inheritance finds it.

```
C:\python\examples> python employees.py
<Employee: name=bob, salary=50000>
<Employee: name=bob, salary=60000.0>

Employee does stuff
Chef makes food
Server interfaces with customer
PizzaRobot makes pizza
```

In a class hierarchy like this, you can usually make instances of any of the classes, not just the ones at the bottom. For instance, the `for` loop in this module's self-test code creates instances of all four classes; each responds differently when asked to work, because the `work` method is different in each. Really, these classes just simulate real world objects; `work` prints a message for the time being, but could be expanded to really work later.

OOP and Composition: "has-a"

We introduced the notion of composition at the start of this chapter. From a programmer's point of view, composition involves embedding other objects in a container object and activating them to implement container methods. To a designer, composition is another way to represent relationships in a problem domain. But rather than set membership, composition has to do with components—parts of a whole. Composition also reflects the relationships between parts; it's usually called a "has-a" relationship, when OOP people speak of such things.

Now that we've implemented our employees, let's throw them in the pizza shop and let them get busy. Our pizza shop is a composite object; it has an oven, and employees like servers and chefs. When a customer enters and places an order, the components of the shop spring into action—the server takes an order, the chef makes the pizza, and so on. The following example simulates all the objects and relationships in this scenario:

```
from employees import PizzaRobot, Server

class Customer:
    def __init__(self, name):
        self.name = name
    def order(self, server):
        print self.name, "orders from", server
    def pay(self, server):
        print self.name, "pays for item to", server

class Oven:
    def bake(self):
        print "oven bakes"

class PizzaShop:
    def __init__(self):
        self.server = Server('Pat')          # embed other objects
        self.chef   = PizzaRobot('Bob')      # a robot named bob
        self.oven   = Oven()

    def order(self, name):
        customer = Customer(name)            # activate other objects
        customer.order(self.server)          # customer orders from server
        self.chef.work()
        self.oven.bake()
        customer.pay(self.server)

if __name__ == "__main__":
    scene = PizzaShop()                      # make the composite
    scene.order('Homer')                     # simulate Homer's order
    print '...'
    scene.order('Shaggy')                    # simulate Shaggy's order
```

The `PizzaShop` class is a container and controller; its constructor makes and embeds instances of the employee classes we wrote in the last section, as well as an `Oven` class defined here. When this module's self-test code calls the `PizzaShop` order method, the embedded objects are asked to carry out their actions in turn. Notice that we make a new `Customer` object for each order, and pass on the embedded `Server` object to `Customer` methods; customers come and go, but the server is part of the pizza shop composite. Also notice that employees are still involved in an inheritance relationship; composition and inheritance are complementary tools:

```
C:\python\examples> python pizzashop.py
Homer orders from <Employee: name=Pat, salary=40000>
Bob makes pizza
oven bakes
Homer pays for item to <Employee: name=Pat, salary=40000>
...
```

```
Shaggy orders from <Employee: name=Pat, salary=40000>
Bob makes pizza
oven bakes
Shaggy pays for item to <Employee: name=Pat, salary=40000>
```

When we run this module, our pizza shop handles two orders—one from Homer, and then one from Shaggy. Again, this is mostly just a toy simulation; a real pizza shop would have more parts, and there's no real pizza to be had here. But the objects and interactions are representative of composites at work. As a rule of thumb, classes can represent just about any objects and relationships you can express in a sentence; just replace nouns with classes and verbs with methods, and you have a first cut at a design.

Why You Will Care: Classes and Persistence

Besides allowing us to simulate real-world interactions, the pizza shop classes could also be used as the basis of a persistent restaurant database. As we'll see in Chapter 10, *Frameworks and Applications*, instances of classes can be stored away on disk in a single step using Python's `pickle` or `shelve` modules. The object pickling interface is remarkably easy to use:

```
import pickle
object = someClass()
file   = open(filename, 'w')          # create external file
pickle.dump(object, file)             # save object in file

file   = open(filename, 'r')
object = pickle.load(file)            # fetch it back later
```

Shelves are similar, but they automatically pickle objects to an access-by-key database:

```
import shelve
object = someClass()
dbase  = shelve.open('filename')
dbase['key'] = object                 # save under key
object = dbase['key']                 # fetch it back later
```

(Pickling converts objects to serialized byte streams, which may be stored in files, sent across a network, and so on.) In our example, using classes to model employees means we can get a simple database of employees and shops for free: pickling such instance objects to a file makes them persistent across Python program executions. See Chapter 10 for more details on pickling.

OOP and Delegation

Object-oriented programmers often talk about something called delegation too, which usually implies controller objects that embed other objects, to which they pass off operation requests. The controllers can take care of administrative activities such as keeping track of accesses and so on. In Python, delegation is often implemented with the __getattr__ method hook; because it intercepts accesses to nonexistent attributes, a wrapper class can use __getattr__ to route arbitrary accesses to a wrapped object. For instance:

```
class wrapper:
    def __init__(self, object):
        self.wrapped = object                    # save object
    def __getattr__(self, attrname):
        print 'Trace:', attrname                 # trace fetch
        return getattr(self.wrapped, attrname)   # delegate fetch
```

You can use this module's **wrapper** class to control any object with attributes—lists, dictionaries, and even classes and instances. Here, the class simply prints a trace message on each attribute access:

```
>>> from trace import wrapper
>>> x = wrapper([1,2,3])         # wrap a list
>>> x.append(4)                  # delegate to list method
Trace: append
>>> x.wrapped                    # print my member
[1, 2, 3, 4]

>>> x = wrapper({"a": 1, "b": 2})   # wrap a dictionary
>>> x.keys()                        # delegate to dictionary method
Trace: keys
['a', 'b']
```

Extending Built-in Object Types

Classes are also commonly used to extend the functionality of Python's built-in types, to support more exotic data structures. For instance, to add queue insert and delete methods to lists, you can code classes that *wrap* (embed) a list object, and export insert and delete methods that process the list.

Remember those set functions we wrote in Chapter 4? Here's what they look like brought back to life as a Python class. The following example implements a new set *object* type, by moving some of the set functions we saw earlier in the book to methods, and adding some basic operator overloading. For the most part, this class just wraps a Python list with extra set operations, but because it's a class, it also supports multiple instances and customization by inheritance in subclasses.

```
class Set:
    def __init__(self, value = []):    # constructor
        self.data = []                 # manages a list
        self.concat(value)

    def intersect(self, other):        # other is any sequence
        res = []                       # self is the subject
```

```
        for x in self.data:
            if x in other:                  # pick common items
                res.append(x)
        return Set(res)                     # return a new Set

    def union(self, other):                 # other is any sequence
        res = self.data[:]                  # copy of my list
        for x in other:                     # add items in other
            if not x in res:
                res.append(x)
        return Set(res)

    def concat(self, value):                # value: list, Set...
        for x in value:                     # removes duplicates
            if not x in self.data:
                self.data.append(x)

    def __len__(self):         return len(self.data)          # on len(self)
    def __getitem__(self, key): return self.data[key]         # on self[i]
    def __and__(self, other):  return self.intersect(other)   # on self & other
    def __or__(self, other):   return self.union(other)       # on self | other
    def __repr__(self):        return 'Set:' + `self.data`     # on print
```

By overloading indexing, our set class can often masquerade as a real list. Since we're going to ask you to interact with and extend this class in an exercise at the end of this chapter, we won't say much more about this code until Appendix C, *Solutions to Exercises.*

Multiple Inheritance

When we discussed details of the **class** statement, we mentioned that more than one superclass can be listed in parentheses in the header line. When you do this, you use something called *multiple inheritance;* the class and its instances inherit names from all listed superclasses. When searching for an attribute, Python searches superclasses in the class header from left to right until a match is found. Technically, the search proceeds depth-first, and then left to right, since any of the superclasses may have superclasses of its own.

In theory, multiple inheritance is good for modeling objects which belong to more than one set. For instance, a person may be an engineer, a writer, a musician, and so on, and inherit properties from all such sets. In practice, though, multiple inheritance is an advanced tool and can become complicated if used too much; we'll revisit this as a gotcha at the end of the chapter. But like everything else in programming, it's a useful tool when applied well.

One of the most common ways multiple inheritance is used is to "mix in" general-purpose methods from superclasses. Such superclasses are usually called *mixin* classes; they provide methods you add to application classes by inheritance. For instance, Python's default way to print a class instance object isn't incredibly useful:

```
>>> class Spam:
...     def __init__(self):            # no __repr__
...         self.data1 = "food"
...
>>> X = Spam()
>>> print X                            # default format: class, address
<Spam instance at 87f1b0>
```

As seen in the previous section on operator overloading, you can provide a __repr__ method to implement a custom string representation of your own. But rather than code a __repr__ in each and every class you wish to print, why not code it once in a general-purpose tool class, and inherit it in all classes?

That's what mixins are for. The following code defines a mixin class called Lister that overloads the __repr__ method for each class that includes Lister in its header line. It simply scans the instance's attribute dictionary (remember, it's exported in __dict__) to build up a string showing the names and values of all instance attributes. Since classes are objects, Lister's formatting logic can be used for instances of any subclass; it's a generic tool.

Lister uses two special tricks to extract the instance's classname and address. Instances have a built-in __class__ attribute that references the class the instance was created from, and classes have a __name__ that is the name in the header, so self.__class__.__name__ fetches the name of an instance's class. You get the instance's memory address by calling the built-in id function, which returns any object's address:

```
# Lister can be mixed-in to any class, to
# provide a formatted print of instances
# via inheritance of __repr__ coded here;
# self is the instance of the lowest class;

class Lister:
    def __repr__(self):
        return ("<Instance of %s, address %s:\n%s>" %
                        (self.__class__.__name__,    # my class's name
                         id(self),                   # my address
                         self.attrnames()) )         # name=value list
    def attrnames(self):
        result = ''
        for attr in self.__dict__.keys():      # scan instance namespace dict
            if attr[:2] == '__':
                result = result + "\tname %s=<built-in>\n" % attr
            else:
                result = result + "\tname %s=%s\n" % (attr, self.__dict__[attr])
        return result
```

Now, the Lister class is useful for any class you write—even classes that already have a superclass. This is where multiple inheritance comes in handy: by adding

Lister to the list of superclasses in a class header, you get its `__repr__` for free, while still inheriting from the existing superclass:

```
from mytools import Lister              # get tool class

class Super:
    def __init__(self):                 # superclass __init__
        self.data1 = "spam"

class Sub(Super, Lister):               # mix-in a __repr__
    def __init__(self):                 # Lister has access to self
        Super.__init__(self)
        self.data2 = "eggs"             # more instance attrs
        self.data3 = 42

if __name__ == "__main__":
    X = Sub()
    print X                             # mixed-in repr
```

Here, Sub inherits names from both Super and Lister; it's a composite of its own names and names in both its superclasses. When you make a Sub instance and print it, you get the custom representation mixed in from Lister:

```
C:\python\examples> python testmixin.py
<Instance of Sub, address 7833392:
        name data3=42
        name data2=eggs
        name data1=spam
>
```

Lister works in any class it's mixed into, because self refers to an instance of the subclass that pulls Lister in, whatever that may be. If you later decide to extend Lister's `__repr__` to also print class attributes an instance inherits, you're safe; because it's an inherited method, changing Lister's `__repr__` updates each subclass that mixes it in.* In some sense, mixin classes are the class equivalent of modules. Here is Lister working in single-inheritance mode, on a different class's instances; like we said, OOP is about code reuse:

```
>>> from mytools import Lister
>>> class x(Lister):
...     pass
...
>>> t = x()
>>> t.a = 1; t.b = 2; t.c = 3
>>> t
<Instance of x, address 7797696:
        name b=2
```

---

* For the curious reader, classes also have a built-in attribute called `__bases__`, which is a tuple of the class's superclass objects. A general-purpose class hierarchy lister or browser can traverse from an instance's `__class__` to its class, and then from the class's `__bases__` to all superclasses recursively. We'll revisit this idea in an exercise, but see other books or Python's manuals for more details on special object attributes.

```
name a=1
name c=3
>
```

Classes Are Objects: Generic Object Factories

Because classes are objects, it's easy to pass them around a program, store them in data structures, and so on. You can also pass classes to functions that generate arbitrary kinds of objects; such functions are sometimes called *factories* in OOP design circles. They are a major undertaking in a strongly typed language such as C++, but almost trivial in Python: the `apply` function we met in Chapter 4 can call any class with any argument in one step, to generate any sort of instance:[*]

```
def factory(aClass, *args):                # varargs tuple
    return apply(aClass, args)             # call aClass

class Spam:
    def doit(self, message):
        print message

class Person:
    def __init__(self, name, job):
        self.name = name
        self.job  = job

object1 = factory(Spam)                    # make a Spam
object2 = factory(Person, "Guido", "guru") # make a Person
```

In this code, we define an object generator function, called `factory`. It expects to be passed a class object (any class will do), along with one or more arguments for the class's constructor. The function uses `apply` to call the function and return an instance. The rest of the example simply defines two classes and generates instances of both by passing them to the `factory` function. And that's the only `factory` function you ever need write in Python; it works for any class and any constructor arguments. The only possible improvement worth noting: to support keyword arguments in constructor calls, the factory can collect them with a `**args` argument and pass them as a third argument to `apply`:

```
def factory(aClass, *args, **kwargs):      # +kwargs dict
    return apply(aClass, args, kwargs)     # call aClass
```

By now, you should know that everything is an "object" in Python; even things like classes, which are just compiler input in languages like C++. However, only objects derived from classes are OOP objects in Python; you can't do inheritance with nonclass-based objects such as lists and numbers, unless you wrap them in classes.

---

[*] Actually, `apply` can call *any* callable object; that includes functions, classes, and methods. The `factory` function here can run any callable, not just a class (despite the argument name).

Methods Are Objects: Bound or Unbound

Speaking of objects, it turns out that methods are a kind of object too, much like functions. Because class methods can be accessed from either an instance or a class, they actually come in two flavors in Python:

Unbound class methods: no self
> Accessing a class's function attribute by qualifying a class returns an *unbound method object*. To call it, you must provide an instance object explicitly as its first argument.

Bound instance methods: self + function pairs
> Accessing a class's function attribute by qualifying an instance returns a *bound method object*. Python automatically packages the instance with the function in the bound method object, so we don't need to pass an instance to call the method.

Both kinds of methods are full-fledged objects; they can be passed around, stored in lists, and so on. Both also require an instance in their first argument when run (i.e., a value for `self`), but Python provides one for you automatically when calling a bound method through an instance. For example, suppose we define the following class:

```
class Spam:
    def doit(self, message):
        print message
```

Now, we can make an instance, and fetch a bound method without actually calling it. An `object.name` qualification is an object expression; here, it returns a bound method object that packages the instance (`object1`) with the method function (`Spam.doit`). We can assign the bound method to another name and call it as though it were a simple function:

```
object1 = Spam()
x = object1.doit          # bound method object
x('hello world')          # instance is implied
```

On the other hand, if we qualify the class to get to `doit`, we get back an unbound method object, which is simply a reference to the function object. To call this type of method, pass in an instance in the leftmost argument:

```
t = Spam.doit             # unbound method object
t(object1, 'howdy')       # pass in instance
```

Most of the time, you call methods immediately after fetching them with qualification (e.g., `self.attr(args)`), so you don't always notice the method object along the way. But if you start writing code that calls objects generically, you need to be careful to treat unbound methods specially; they require an explicit object.

Odds and Ends

Private Attributes (New in 1.5)

In the last chapter, we noted that every name assigned at the top level of a file is exported by a module. By default, the same holds for classes; data hiding is a convention, and clients may fetch or change any class or instance attribute they like. In fact, attributes are all `public` and `virtual` in C++ terms; they're all accessible everywhere and all looked up dynamically at runtime.

At least until Python 1.5. In 1.5, Guido introduced the notion of *name mangling* to localize some names in classes. Private names are an advanced feature, entirely optional, and probably won't be very useful until you start writing large class hierarchies. But here's an overview for the curious.

In Python 1.5, names inside a `class` statement that start with two underscores (and don't end with two underscores) are automatically changed to include the name of the enclosing class. For instance, a name like `__X` in a class `Class` is changed to `_Class__X` automatically. Because the modified name includes the name of the enclosing class, it's somewhat unusual; it won't clash with similar names in other classes in a hierarchy.

Python mangles names wherever they appear in the class. For example, an instance attribute called `self.__X` is transformed to `self._Class__X`, thereby mangling an attribute name for *instance* objects too. Since more than one class may add attributes to an instance, name mangling helps avoid clashes automatically.

Name mangling happens only in `class` statements and only for names you write with two leading underscores. Because of that, it can make code somewhat unreadable. It also isn't quite the same as `private` declarations in C++ (if you know the name of the enclosing class, you can still get to mangled attributes!), but it can avoid accidental name clashes when an attribute name is used by more than one class of a hierarchy.

Documentation Strings

Now that we know about classes, we can tell what those `__doc__` attributes we've seen are all about. So far we've been using comments that start with a `#` to describe our code. Comments are useful for humans reading our programs, but they aren't available when the program runs. Python also lets us associate *strings* of documentation with program-unit objects and provides a special syntax for it. If a module file, `def` statement, or `class` statement begins with a string constant instead of a statement, Python stuffs the string into the `__doc__` attribute of the generated object. For instance, the following program defines documentation strings for multiple objects:

```
"I am: docstr.__doc__"

class spam:
    "I am: spam.__doc__ or docstr.spam.__doc__"

    def method(self, arg):
        "I am: spam.method.__doc__ or self.method.__doc__"
        pass

def func(args):
    "I am: docstr.func.__doc__"
    pass
```

The main advantage of documentation strings is that they stick around at runtime; if it's been coded as a documentation string, you can qualify an object to fetch its documentation.

```
>>> import docstr
>>> docstr.__doc__
'I am: docstr.__doc__'
>>> docstr.spam.__doc__
'I am: spam.__doc__ or docstr.spam.__doc__'
>>> docstr.spam.method.__doc__
'I am: spam.method.__doc__ or self.method.__doc__'
>>> docstr.func.__doc__
'I am: docstr.func.__doc__'
```

This can be especially useful during development. For instance, you can look up components' documentation at the interactive command line as done above, without having to go to the source file to see # comments. Similarly, a Python object browser can take advantage of documentation strings to display descriptions along with objects.

On the other hand, documentation strings are not universally used by Python programmers. To get the most benefit from them, programmers need to follow some sort of conventions in their documentation styles, and it's our experience that these sorts of conventions are rarely implemented or followed in practice. Further, documentation strings are available at runtime, but they are also less flexible than # comments (which can appear anywhere in a program). Both forms are useful tools, and *any* program documentation is a good thing, as long as it's accurate.

Classes Versus Modules

Finally, let's step back for a moment and compare the topics of the last two chapters—modules and classes. Since they're both about namespaces, the distinction can sometimes be confusing. In short:

Modules

- Are data/logic packages
- Are created by writing Python files or C extensions
- Are used by being imported

Classes

- Implement new objects
- Are created by class statements
- Are used by being called
- Always live in a module

Classes also support extra features modules don't, such as operator overloading, multiple instances, and inheritance. Although both are namespaces, we hope you can tell by now that they're very different animals.

Class Gotchas

Most class issues can usually be boiled down to namespace issues (which makes sense, given that classes are just namespaces with a few extra tricks up their sleeves).

Changing Class Attributes Can Have Side Effects

Theoretically speaking, classes (and class instances) are all mutable objects. Just as with built-in lists and dictionaries, they can be changed in place, by assigning to their attributes. As with lists and dictionaries, this also means that changing a class or instance object may impact multiple references to it.

That's usually what we want (and is how objects change their state in general), but this becomes especially critical to know when changing class attributes. Because all instances generated from a class share the class's namespace, any changes at the class level are reflected in all instances, unless they have their own versions of changed class attributes.

Since classes, modules, and instances are all just objects with attribute namespaces, you can normally change their attributes at runtime by assignments. Consider the following class; inside the class body, the assignment to name a generates an attribute X.a, which lives in the class object at runtime and will be inherited by all of X's instances:

```
>>> class X:
...     a = 1          # class attribute
...
```

```
>>> I = X()
>>> I.a                  # inherited by instance
1
>>> X.a
1
```

So far so good. But notice what happens when we change the class attribute
dynamically: it also changes it in every object which inherits from the class. Moreover, new instances created from the class get the dynamically set value, regardless of what the class's source code says:

```
>>> X.a = 2          # may change more than X
>>> I.a              # I changes too
2
>>> J = X()          # J inherits from X's runtime values
>>> J.a              # (but assigning to J.a changes a in J, not X or I)
2
```

Solution

Useful feature or dangerous trap? You be the judge, but you can actually get work
done by changing class attributes, without ever making a single instance. In fact,
this technique can simulate "records" or "structs" in other languages. For example,
consider the following unusual but legal Python program:

```
class X: pass                    # make a few attribute namespaces
class Y: pass

X.a = 1                          # use class attributes as variables
X.b = 2                          # no instances anywhere to be found
X.c = 3
Y.a = X.a + X.b + X.c

for X.i in range(Y.a): print X.i       # prints 0..5
```

Here, classes X and Y work like file-less modules—namespaces for storing variables we don't want to clash. This is a perfectly legal Python programming trick,
but is less appropriate when applied to classes written by others; you can't always
be sure that class attributes you change aren't critical to the class's internal behavior. If you're out to simulate a C struct, you may be better off changing instances
than classes, since only one object is affected:

```
>>> class Record: pass
...
>>> X = Record()
>>> X.name = 'bob'
>>> X.job  = 'Pizza maker'
```

Multiple Inheritance: Order Matters

This may be obvious, but is worth underscoring: if you use multiple inheritance, the order in which superclasses are listed in a `class` statement header can be critical. For instance, in the example we saw earlier, suppose that the `Super` implemented a `__repr__` method too; would we then want to inherit `Lister`'s or `Super`'s? We would get it from whichever class is listed first in `Sub`'s class header, since inheritance searches left to right. But now suppose `Super` and `Lister` have their own versions of other names too; if we want one name from `Super` and one from `Lister`, we have to override inheritance by manually assigning to the attribute name in the `Sub` class:

```
class Lister:
    def __repr__(self): ...
    def other(self): ...

class Super:
    def __repr__(self): ...
    def other(self): ...

class Sub(Super, Lister):    # pick up Super's __repr__, by listing it first
    other = Lister.other     # but explicitly pick up Lister's version of other
    def __init__(self):
        ...
```

Solution

Multiple inheritance is an advanced tool; even if you understood the last paragraph, it's still a good idea to use it sparingly and carefully. Otherwise, the meaning of a name may depend on the order in which classes are mixed in an arbitrarily far removed subclass.

Class Function Attributes Are Special

This one is simple if you understand Python's underlying object model, but it tends to trip up new users with backgrounds in other OOP languages (especially Smalltalk). In Python, class method functions can never be called without an instance. Earlier in the chapter, we talked about unbound methods: when we fetch a method function by qualifying a class (instead of an instance), we get an unbound method. Even though they are defined with a `def` statement, unbound method objects are not simple functions; they cannot be called without an instance.

For example, suppose we want to use class attributes to count how many instances are generated from a class. Remember, class attributes are shared by all instances, so we can store the counter in the class object itself:

```
class Spam:
    numInstances = 0
```

```
    def __init__(self):
        Spam.numInstances = Spam.numInstances + 1
    def printNumInstances():
        print "Number of instances created: ", Spam.numInstances
```

This won't work: the `printNumInstances` method still expects an instance to be passed in when called, because the function is associated with a class (even though there are no arguments in the `def` header):

```
>>> from spam import *
>>> a = Spam()
>>> b = Spam()
>>> c = Spam()
>>> Spam.printNumInstances()
Traceback (innermost last):
  File "<stdin>", line 1, in ?
TypeError: unbound method must be called with class instance 1st argument
```

Solution

Don't expect this: unbound methods aren't exactly the same as simple functions. This is really a knowledge issue, but if you want to call functions that access class members without an instance, just make them simple functions, not class methods. This way, an instance isn't expected in the call:

```
def printNumInstances():
    print "Number of instances created: ", Spam.numInstances

class Spam:
    numInstances = 0
    def __init__(self):
        Spam.numInstances = Spam.numInstances + 1
```

```
>>> import spam
>>> a = spam.Spam()
>>> b = spam.Spam()
>>> c = spam.Spam()
>>> spam.printNumInstances()
Number of instances created:  3
```

We can also make this work by calling through an instance, as usual:

```
class Spam:
    numInstances = 0
    def __init__(self):
        Spam.numInstances = Spam.numInstances + 1
    def printNumInstances(self):
        print "Number of instances created: ", Spam.numInstances
```

```
>>> from spam import Spam
>>> a, b, c = Spam(), Spam(), Spam()
>>> a.printNumInstances()
Number of instances created:  3
>>> b.printNumInstances()
```

```
Number of instances created:  3
>>> Spam().printNumInstances()
Number of instances created:  4
```

Some language theorists claim that this means Python doesn't have class methods, only instance methods. We suspect they really mean Python classes don't work the same as in some other language. Python really has bound and unbound method objects, with well-defined semantics; qualifying a class gets you an unbound method, which is a special kind of function. Python really does have class attributes, but functions in classes expect an instance argument.

Moreover, since Python already provides *modules* as a namespace partitioning tool, there's usually no need to package functions in classes unless they implement object behavior. Simple functions in modules usually do most of what instance-less class methods could. For example, in the first example in this section, `printNumInstances` is already associated with the class, because it lives in the same module.

Methods, Classes, and Nested Scopes

Classes introduce a local scope just as functions do, so the same sorts of scope gotchas can happen in a `class` statement body. Moreover, methods are further nested functions, so the same issues apply. Confusion seems to be especially common when classes are nested. For instance, in the following example, the `generate` function is supposed to return an instance of the nested `Spam` class. Within its code, the class name `Spam` is assigned in the `generate` function's local scope. But within the class's `method` function, the class name `Spam` is not visible; `method` has access only to its own local scope, the module surrounding `generate`, and built-in names:

```
def generate():
    class Spam:
        count = 1
        def method(self):        # name Spam not visible:
            print Spam.count     # not local (def), global (module), built-in
    return Spam()

generate().method()

C:\python\examples> python nester.py
Traceback (innermost last):
  File "nester.py", line 8, in ?
    generate().method()
  File "nester.py", line 5, in method
    print Spam.count                # not local (def), global (module), built-in
NameError: Spam
```

Solution

The most general piece of advice we can pass along here is to remember the LGB rule; it works in classes and method functions just as it does in simple functions. For instance, inside a method function, code has unqualified access only to local names (in the method `def`), global names (in the enclosing module), and built-ins. Notably missing is the enclosing `class` statement; to get to class attributes, methods need to qualify `self`, the instance. To call one method from another, the caller must route the call through `self` (e.g., `self.method()`).

There are a variety of ways to get the example above to work. One of the simplest is to move the name `Spam` out to the enclosing module's scope with global declarations; since `method` sees names in the enclosing module by the LGB rule, `Spam` references work:

```
def generate():
    global Spam                     # force Spam to module scope
    class Spam:
        count = 1
        def method(self):
            print Spam.count    # works: in global (enclosing module)
    return Spam()

generate().method()             # prints 1
```

Perhaps better, we can also restructure the example such that class `Spam` is defined at the top level of the module by virtue of its nesting level, rather than `global` declarations. Both the nested `method` function and the top-level `generate` find `Spam` in their global scopes:

```
def generate():
    return Spam()

class Spam:                      # define at module top-level
    count = 1
    def method(self):
        print Spam.count        # works: in global (enclosing module)

generate().method()
```

We can also get rid of the `Spam` reference in `method` altogether, by using the special `__class__` attribute, which, as we've seen, returns an instance's class object:

```
def generate():
    class Spam:
        count = 1
        def method(self):
            print self.__class__.count      # works: qualify to get class
    return Spam()

generate().method()
```

Finally, we could use the *mutable default* argument trick we saw in Chapter 4 to make this work, but it's so complicated we're almost embarrassed to show you; the prior solutions usually make more sense:

```
def generate():
    class Spam:
        count = 1
        fillin = [None]
        def method(self, klass=fillin):      # save from enclosing scope
            print klass[0].count             # works: default plugged-in
    Spam.fillin[0] = Spam
    return Spam()

generate().method()
```

Notice that we can't say klass=Spam in method's def header, because the name Spam isn't visible in Spam's body either; it's not local (in the class body), global (the enclosing module), or built-in. Spam only exists in the generate function's local scope, which neither the nested class nor its method can see. The LGB rule works the same for both.

Summary

This chapter has been about two special objects in Python—classes and instances—and the language tools that create and process them. Class objects are created with **class** statements, provide default behavior, and serve as generators for multiple instance objects. Together, these two objects support full-blown object-oriented development and code reuse. In short, classes allow us to implement new objects, which export both data and behavior.

In terms of their main distinctions, classes support multiple copies, specialization by inheritance, and operator overloading, and we explored each of these features in this chapter. Since classes are all about namespaces, we also studied the ways they extend module and function namespace notions. And finally, we explored a few object-oriented design ideas such as composition and delegation, by seeing how to implement them in Python.

The next chapter concludes our core language tour, with a quick look at exception handling—a simple tool used to process events, rather than build program components. As a summary and reference of what we learned in this chapter, here's a synopsis of the terms we've used to talk about classes in Python:

Class

    An object (and statement) that defines inherited attributes

Instance

    Objects created from a class, which inherit its attributes, and get their own namespace

Method
> An attribute of a class object that's bound to a function object

self
> By convention, the name given to the implied instance object in methods

Inheritance
> When an instance or class accesses a class's attributes by qualification

Superclass
> A class another class inherits attributes from

Subclass
> A class that inherits attribute names from another class

Exercises

This laboratory session asks you to write a few classes and experiment with some existing code. Of course, the problem with existing code is that it must be existing. To work with the set class in Exercise 5, either pull down the class source code off the Internet (see the Preface) or type it up by hand (it's fairly small). These programs are starting to get more sophisticated, so be sure to check the solutions at the end of the book for pointers. If you're pressed for time, we suspect that the last exercise dealing with composition will probably be the most fun of the bunch (of course, we already know the answers).

1. *The basics.* Write a class called `Adder` that exports a method `add(self, x, y)` that prints a "Not Implemented" message. Then define two subclasses of `Adder` that implement the `add` method:

   — `ListAdder`, with an `add` method that returns the concatenation of its two list arguments

   — `DictAdder`, with an `add` method that returns a new dictionary with the items in both its two dictionary arguments (any definition of addition will do)

   Experiment by making instances of all three of your classes interactively and calling their `add` methods. Finally, extend your classes to save an object in a constructor (a list or a dictionary) and overload the + operator to replace the `add` method. Where is the best place to put the constructors and operator overload methods (i.e., in which classes)? What sorts of objects can you add to your class instances?

2. *Operator overloading.* Write a class called `Mylist` that "wraps" a Python list: it should overload most list operators and operations—+, indexing, iteration, slicing, and list methods such as `append` and `sort`. See the Python reference manual for a list of all possible methods to overload. Also provide a construc-

tor for your class that takes an existing list (or a `Mylist` instance) and copies its components into an instance member. Experiment with your class interactively. Things to explore:

— Why is copying the initial value important here?

— Can you use an empty slice (e.g., `start[:]`) to copy the initial value if it's a `Mylist` instance?

— Is there a general way to route list method calls to the wrapped list?

— Can you add a `Mylist` and a regular list? How about a list and a `Mylist` instance?

— What type of object should operations like + and slicing return; how about indexing?

3. *Subclassing.* Now, make a subclass of `Mylist` from Exercise 2 called `MylistSub`, which extends `Mylist` to print a message to `stdout` before each overloaded operation is called and counts the number of calls. `MylistSub` should inherit basic method behavior from `Mylist`. For instance, adding a sequence to a `MylistSub` should print a message, increment the counter for + calls, and perform the superclass's method. Also introduce a new method that displays the operation counters to `stdout` and experiment with your class interactively. Do your counters count calls per instance, or per class (for all instances of the class)? How would you program both of these? (Hint: it depends on which object the count members are assigned to: class members are shared by instances, `self` members are per-instance data.)

4. *Metaclass methods.* Write a class called `Meta` with methods that intercept every attribute qualification (both fetches and assignments) and prints a message with their arguments to `stdout`. Create a `Meta` instance and experiment with qualifying it interactively. What happens when you try to use the instance in expressions? Try adding, indexing, and slicing the instance of your class.

5. *Set objects.* Experiment with the set class described in this chapter (from the section "Extending Built-in Object Types"). Run commands to do the following sorts of operations:

   a. Create two sets of integers, and compute their intersection and union by using & and | operator expressions.

   b. Create a set from a string, and experiment with indexing your set; which methods in the class are called?

   c. Try iterating through the items in your string set using a `for` loop; which methods run this time?

   d. Try computing the intersection and union of your string set and a simple Python string; does it work?

e. Now, extend your set by subclassing to handle arbitrarily many operands using a `*args` argument form (hint: see the function versions of these algorithms in Chapter 4). Compute intersections and unions of multiple operands with your set subclass. How can you intersect three or more sets, given that & has only two sides?

f. How would you go about emulating other list operations in the set class? (Hints: `__add__` can catch concatenation, and `__getattr__` can pass most list method calls off to the wrapped list.)

6. *Class tree links.* In a footnote in the section on multiple inheritance, we mentioned that classes have a `__bases__` attribute that returns a tuple of the class's superclass objects (the ones in parentheses in the class header). Use `__bases__` to extend the `Lister` mixin class, so that it prints the names of the immediate superclasses of the instance's class too. When you're done, the first line of the string representation should look like this:

```
<Instance of Sub(Super, Lister), address 7841200:.
```

How would you go about listing class attributes too?

7. *Composition.* Simulate a fast-food ordering scenario by defining four classes:

— `Lunch`: a container and controller class

— `Customer`: the actor that buys food

— `Employee`: the actor that a customer orders from

— `Food`: what the customer buys

To get you started, here are the classes and methods you'll be defining:

```
class Lunch:
    def __init__(self)          # make/embed Customer and Employee
    def order(self, foodName)   # start a Customer order simulation
    def result(self)            # ask the Customer what kind of Food it has

class Customer:
    def __init__(self)                          # initialize my food to None
    def placeOrder(self, foodName, employee)    # place order with an Employee
    def printFood(self)                         # print the name of my food

class Employee:
    def takeOrder(self, foodName)     # return a Food, with requested name

class Food:
    def __init__(self, name)          # store food name
```

The order simulation works as follows:

— The `Lunch` class's constructor should make and embed an instance of `Customer` and `Employee`, and export a method called `order`. When called, this `order` method should ask the `Customer` to place an order, by calling its `placeOrder` method. The `Customer`'s `placeOrder` method should in turn ask the `Employee` object for a new `Food` object, by calling the `Employee`'s `takeOrder` method.

— `Food` objects should store a food name string (e.g., `"burritos"`), passed down from `Lunch.order` to `Customer.placeOrder`, to `Employee.takeOrder`, and finally to `Food`'s constructor. The top-level `Lunch` class should also export a method called `result`, which asks the customer to print the name of the food it received from the `Employee` (this can be used to test your simulation).

— Note that `Lunch` needs to either pass the `Employee` to the `Customer`, or pass itself to the `Customer`, in order to allow the `Customer` to call `Employee` methods.

8. Experiment with your classes interactively by importing the `Lunch` class, calling its `order` method to run an interaction, and then calling its `result` method to verify that the `Customer` got what he or she ordered. In this simulation, the `Customer` is the active agent; how would your classes change if `Employee` were the object that initiated customer/employee interaction instead?

7

Exceptions

Our last chapter in this part of the book has to do with exceptions—events that can modify the flow of control through a program. In Python, exceptions can be both intercepted and triggered by our programs. They are processed by two new statements we'll study in this chapter:

`try`

> Catches exceptions raised by Python or a program

`raise`

> Triggers an exception manually

With a few exceptions (pun intended), we'll find that exception handling is simple in Python, because it's integrated into the language itself as another high-level tool.

Why Use Exceptions?

In a nutshell, exceptions let us jump around arbitrarily large chunks of a program. Remember that pizza-making robot we talked about in the last chapter? Suppose we took the idea seriously and actually built such a machine (there are worse hobbies, after all). To make a pizza, our culinary automaton would need to execute a plan, which we implement as a Python program. It would take an order, prepare the dough, add toppings, bake the pie, and so on.

Now, suppose that something goes very wrong during the "bake the pie" step. Perhaps the oven is broken. Or perhaps our robot miscalculates its reach and spontaneously bursts into flames. Clearly, we want to be able to jump to code that handles such states quickly (especially if our robot is melting all over the kitchen floor!). Since we have no hope of finishing the pizza task in such unusual cases, we might as well abandon the entire plan.

That's exactly what exceptions let you do; you can jump to an exception handler in a single step, past all suspended function calls. They're a sort of "super-goto."* An exception handler (`try` statement) leaves a *marker* and executes some code. Somewhere further ahead in the program, an exception is raised that makes Python jump back to the marker immediately, without resuming any active functions that were called since the marker was left. Code in the exception handler can respond to the raised exception as appropriate (calling the fire department, for instance). Moreover, because Python jumps to the handler statement immediately, there is usually no need to check status codes after every call to a function that could possibly fail.

In typical Python programs, exceptions may be used for a variety of things:

Error handling

Python raises exceptions when it detects errors in programs at runtime; you can either catch and respond to the errors internally in your programs or ignore the exception. If ignored, Python's default exception-handling behavior kicks in; it kills the program and prints an error message showing where the error occurred.

Event notification

Exceptions can also signal a valid condition, without having to pass result flags around a program or test them explicitly. For instance, a search routine might raise an exception on success, rather than return an integer 1.

Special-case handling

Sometimes a condition may happen so rarely that it's hard to justify convoluting code to handle it. You can often eliminate special-case code by handling unusual cases in exception handlers instead.

Unusual control-flows

And finally, because exceptions are a type of high-level goto, you can use them as the basis for implementing exotic control flows. For instance, although backtracking is not part of the language itself, it can be implemented in Python with exceptions and a bit of support logic to unwind assignments.†

We'll see some of these typical uses in action later in this chapter. First, let's get started with a closer look at Python's exception-processing tools.

---

* In fact, if you've used C, you may be interested to know that Python exceptions are roughly equivalent to C's `setjmp`/`longjmp` standard function pair. The `try` statement acts much like a `setjmp`, and `raise` works like a `longjmp`. But in Python, exceptions are based on objects and are a standard part of the execution model.

† Backtracking isn't part of the Python language, so we won't say more about it here. See a book on artificial intelligence or the Prolog or icon programming languages if you're curious.

Exception Basics

Python exceptions are a high-level control flow device. They may be raised either by Python or by our programs; in both cases, they may be caught by **try** statements. Python **try** statements come in two flavors—one that handles exceptions and one that executes finalization code whether exceptions occur or not.

try/except/else

The **try** is another compound statement; its most complete form is sketched below. It starts with a **try** header line followed by a block of indented statements, then one or more optional **except** clauses that name exceptions to be caught, and an optional **else** clause at the end:

```
try:
    <statements>          # run/call actions
except <name>:
    <statements>          # if 'name' raised during try block
except <name>, <data>:
    <statements>          # if 'name' raised; get extra data
else:
    <statements>          # if no exception was raised
```

Here's how **try** statements work. When a **try** statement is started, Python marks the current program context, so it can come back if an exception occurs. The statements nested under the **try** header are run first; what happens next depends on whether exceptions are raised while the **try** block's statements are running or not:

- If an exception occurs while the **try** block's statements are running, Python jumps back to the **try** and runs the statements under the first **except** clause that matches the raised exception. Control continues past the entire **try** statement after the **except** block runs (unless the **except** block raises another exception).

- If an exception happens in the **try** block and no **except** clause matches, the exception is propagated up to a **try** that was entered earlier in the program, or to the top level of the process (which makes Python kill the program and print a default error message).

- If no exception occurs while the statements under the **try** header run, Python runs the statements under the **else** line (if present), and control then resumes past the entire **try** statement.

In other words, **except** clauses catch exceptions that happen while the **try** block is running, and the **else** clause is run only if no exceptions happen while the **try** block runs. The **except** clauses are very focused exception handlers; they catch exceptions that occur only within the statements in the associated **try** block.

However, since the `try` block's statements can call functions elsewhere in a program, the source of an exception may be outside the `try`.

try/finally

The other flavor of the `try` statement is a specialization and has to do with finalization actions. If a `finally` clause is used in a `try`, its block of statements are always run by Python "on the way out," whether an exception occurred while the `try` block was running or not:

- If no exception occurs, Python runs the `try` block, then the `finally` block, and then continues execution past the entire `try` statement.

- If an exception does occur during the `try` block's run, Python comes back and runs the `finally` block, but then propagates the exception to a higher `try` (or the top level); control doesn't continue past the `try` statement.

The `try/finally` form is useful when you want to be completely sure that an action happens after some code runs, regardless of the exception behavior of the program; we'll see an example in a moment. The `finally` clause can't be used in the same `try` statement as `except` and `else`, so they are best thought of as two different statements:

```
try:
    <statements>
finally:
    <statements>        # always run "on the way out"
```

raise

To trigger exceptions, you need to code `raise` statements. Their general form is simple: the word `raise` followed by the name of the exception to be raised. You can also pass an extra data item (an object) along with the exception, by listing it after the exception name. If extra data is passed, it can be caught in a `try` by listing an assignment target to receive it: `except name, data`:

```
raise <name>            # manually trigger an exception
raise <name>, <data>    # pass extra data to catcher too
```

So what's an exception name? It might be the name of a built-in exception from the built-in scope (e.g., `IndexError`), or the name of an arbitrary string object you've assigned in your program. It can also reference a class or class instance; this form generalizes `raise` statements, but we'll postpone this topic till later in this chapter. Exceptions are identified by objects, and at most one is active at any given time. Once caught by an `except` clause, an exception dies (won't propagate to another `try`), unless reraised by a `raise` or error.

First Examples

Exceptions are simpler than they seem. Since control flow through a program is easier to capture in Python than in English, let's look at some simple examples that illustrate exception basics.

Default behavior: Error messages

As mentioned, exceptions not caught by `try` statements reach the top level of a Python process and run Python's default exception-handling logic. By default, Python terminates the running program and prints an error message describing the exception, showing where the program was when the exception occurred. For example, running the following module generates a divide-by-zero exception; since the program ignores it, Python kills the program and prints:

```
% cat bad.py
def gobad(x, y):
    return x / y

def gosouth(x):
    print gobad(x, 0)

gosouth(1)

% python bad.py
Traceback (innermost last):
  File "bad.py", line 7, in ?
    gosouth(1)
  File "bad.py", line 5, in gosouth
    print gobad(x, 0)
  File "bad.py", line 2, in gobad
    return x / y
ZeroDivisionError: integer division or modulo
```

When an uncaught exception occurs, Python ends the program, and prints a stack trace and the name and extra data of the exception that was raised. The *stack trace* shows the filename, line number, and source code, for each function active when the exception occurred, from oldest to newest. For example, you can see that the bad divide happens at the lowest entry in the trace—line 2 of file *bad.py*, a `return` statement.

Because Python reports almost all errors at runtime by raising exceptions, exceptions are intimately bound up with the idea of error handling in general. For instance, if you've worked through the examples, you've almost certainly seen an exception or two along the way (even typos usually generate a `SyntaxError` exception). By default, you get a useful error display like the one above, which helps track down the problem. For more heavy-duty debugging jobs, you can catch exceptions with try statements.*

Catching built-in exceptions

If you don't want your program terminated when an exception is raised by Python, simply catch it by wrapping program logic in a **try**. For example, the following code catches the **IndexError** Python raises when the list is indexed out of bounds (remember that list indexes are zero-based offsets; 3 is past the end):

```
def kaboom(list, n):
    print list[n]              # trigger IndexError

try:
    kaboom([0, 1, 2], 3)
except IndexError:             # catch exception here
    print 'Hello world!'
```

When the exception occurs in function **kaboom**, control jumps to the **try** statement's **except** clause, which prints a message. Since an exception is "dead" after it's been caught, the program continues past the whole **try**, rather than being terminated by Python. In effect, you process and ignore the error.

Raising and catching user-defined exceptions

Python programs can raise exceptions of their own too, using the **raise** statement. In their simplest form, user-defined exceptions are usually string objects, like the one **MyError** is assigned to in the following:

```
MyError = "my error"

def stuff(file):
    raise MyError

file = open('data', 'r')       # open an existing file
try:
    stuff(file)                # raises exception
finally:
    file.close()               # always close file
```

User-defined exceptions are caught with **try** statements just like built-in exceptions. Here, we've wrapped a call to a file-processing function in a **try** with a **finally** clause, to make sure that the file is always closed, whether the function triggers an exception or not. This particular function isn't all that useful (it just raises an exception!), but wrapping calls in **try/finally** statements is a good way to ensure that your closing-time activities always run.

---

* You can also use Python's standard debugger, pdb, to isolate problems. Like C debuggers such as dbx and gdb, pdb lets you step through Python programs line by line, inspect variable values, set breakpoints, and so on. pdb is shipped with Python as a standard module and is written in Python. See Python's library manual or other Python texts for information on pdb usage.

Exception Idioms

We've seen the mechanics behind exceptions; now, let's take look at some of the
ways they're typically used.

Exceptions Aren't Always a Bad Thing

Python raises exceptions on errors, but not all exceptions are errors. For instance, we
saw in Chapter 2, *Types and Operators*, that file object **read** methods return empty
strings at the end of a file. Python also provides a built-in function called **raw_input**
for reading from the standard input stream; unlike file methods, **raw_input** raises
the built-in **EOFError** at end of file, instead of returning an empty string (an empty
string means an empty line when **raw_input** is used). Because of that, **raw_input**
often appears wrapped in a **try** handler and nested in a loop, as in the following
code

```
while 1:
    try:
        line = raw_input()      # read line from stdin
    except EOFError:
        break                   # exit loop at end of file
    else:
      Process next 'line' here
```

Searches Sometimes Signal Success by raise

User-defined exceptions can signal nonerror conditions also. For instance, a search
routine can be coded to raise an exception when a match is found, instead of
returning a status flag that must be interpreted by the caller. In the following, the
try/except/else exception handler does the work of an **if/else** return value
tester:

```
Found = "Item found"

def searcher():
  raise Found or return

try:
    searcher()
except Found:              # exception if item was found
  Success
else:                      # else returned: not found
  Failure
```

Outer try Statements Can Debug Code

You can also make use of exception handlers to replace Python's default top-level
exception-handling behavior seen previously. By wrapping an entire program (or
a call to it) in an outer **try**, you can catch any exception that may occur while

your program runs, thereby subverting the default program termination. In the following, the empty except clause catches any uncaught exception raised while the program runs. To get hold of the actual exception that occurred, fetch the exc_type and exc_value attributes from the built-in **sys** module; they're automatically set to the current exception's name and extra data:[*]

```
try:
    Run program
except:              # all uncaught exceptions come here
    import sys
    print 'uncaught!', sys.exc_type, sys.exc_value
```

Exception Catching Modes

Now that we've taken a first look, let's fill in a few details behind Python's exception model.

try Statement Clauses

When you write **try** statements, a variety of clauses can appear after the **try** statement block; Table 7-1 summarizes all the possible forms. We've already seen most of these in the previous examples—empty except clauses catch any exception, finally runs on the way out, and so on. There may be any number of excepts, but finally must appear by itself (without an else or except), and there should be only one else in a try.

Table 7-1. try Statement Clause Forms

Clause Form	Interpretation
except:	Catch all (other) exception types
except name:	Catch a specific exception only
except name, value:	Catch exception and its extra data
except (name1, name2):	Catch any of the listed exceptions
else:	Run block if no exceptions raised
finally:	Always perform block

---

[*] By the way, the built-in traceback module allows the current exception to be processed in a generic fashion, and as of Python 1.5.1, a new sys.exc_info() function returns a tuple containing the current exception's type, data, and traceback. sys.exc_type and sys.exc_value still work, but manage a single, global exception; exc_info() keeps track of each thread's exception information and so is thread-specific. This distinction matters only when using multiple threads in Python programs (a subject beyond this book's scope). See the Python library manual for more details.

Catching 1-of-N Exceptions

The fourth entry in Table 7-1 is new. except clauses can also provide a set of exceptions to be caught, in parentheses; Python runs such a clause's statement block if any of the listed exceptions occur. Since Python looks for a match within a given try by inspecting except clauses from top to bottom, the parenthesized version is like listing each exception in its own except clause, except that the statement body needs to be coded only once.

Here's an example of multiple except clauses at work. In the following, when an exception is raised while the call to the action function is running, Python returns to the try and searches for the first except that catches the exception raised. It inspects except clauses from top to bottom and left to right, and runs the statements under the first that matches. If none match, the exception is propagated past this try; the else runs only when no exception occurred. If you really want a catch-all clause, an empty except does the trick:

```
try:
    action()
except NameError:
    ...
except IndexError
    ...
except KeyError:
    ...
except (AttributeError, TypeError, SyntaxError):
    ...
else:
    ...
```

Exceptions Nest at Runtime

So far, our examples have used only a single try to catch exceptions, but what happens if one try is physically nested inside another? For that matter, what does it mean if a try calls a function that runs another try? Both these cases can be understood if you realize that Python stacks try statements at runtime. When an exception is raised, Python returns to the most recently entered try statement with a matching except clause. Since each try statement leaves a marker, Python can jump back to earlier trys by inspecting the markers stack.

An example will help make this clear. The following module defines two functions; action2 is coded to trigger an exception (you can't add numbers and sequences), and action1 wraps a call to action2 in a try handler, to catch the exception. However, the top-level module code at the bottom wraps a call to action1 in a try handler too. When action2 triggers the TypeError exception, there will be two active try statements—the one in action1, and the one at the top level of the module. Python picks the most recent (youngest) with a matching

except, which in this case is the `try` inside `action1`. In general, the place where an exception winds up jumping to depends on the control flow through a program at runtime:

```
def action2():
    print 1 + []             # generate TypeError

def action1():
    try:
        action2()
    except TypeError:        # most recent matching try
        print 'inner try'

try:
    action1()
except TypeError:            # here only if action1 reraises
    print 'outer try'

% python nestexc.py
inner try
```

finally Clauses Run "On the Way Out"

We've already talked about the `finally` clause, but here's a more sophisticated example. As we've seen, the `finally` clause doesn't really catch specific exceptions; rather, it taps into the exception propagation process. When used, a `finally` block is always executed on the way out of a `try` statement, whether the exit is caused by an exception or normal completion of the statements in the `try` block. This makes `finally` blocks a good place to code clean-up actions (like closing files, as in the previous example).

The next code snippet shows `finally` in action with and without exceptions. It defines two functions: `divide`, which may or may not trigger a divide-by-zero error, and `tester`, which wraps a call to `divide` in a `try`/`finally` statement:

```
def divide(x, y):
    return x / y             # divide-by-zero error?

def tester(y):
    try:
        print divide(8, y)
    finally:
        print 'on the way out...'

print '\nTest 1:'; tester(2)
print '\nTest 2:'; tester(0)     # trigger error

% python finally.py

Test 1:
4
on the way out...
```

```
Test 2:
on the way out...
Traceback (innermost last):
  File "finally.py", line 11, in ?
    print 'Test 2:'; tester(0)
  File "finally.py", line 6, in tester
    print divide(8, y)
  File "finally.py", line 2, in divide
    return x / y                       # divide-by-zero error?
ZeroDivisionError: integer division or modulo
```

Now, the module's top-level code at the bottom calls `tester` twice:

- The first call doesn't generate an exception (8/2 works fine), and the result (4) is printed. But the `finally` clause's block is run anyhow, so you get the **on the way out** message.

- The second call does generate an exception (8/0 is a very bad thing to say). Control immediately jumps from the `divide` function to the `finally` block, and the message prints again. However, Python continues propagating the exception, which reaches the top level and runs the default exception action (a stack trace).

Odds and Ends

Passing Optional Data

As we've seen, `raise` statements can pass an extra data item along with the exception for use in a handler. In general, the extra data allows you to send context information to a handler. In fact, every exception has the extra data; much like function results, it's the special `None` object if nothing was passed explicitly. The following code illustrates:

```
myException = 'Error'           # string object

def raiser1():
    raise myException, "hello"    # raise, pass data

def raiser2():
    raise myException             # raise, None implied

def tryer(func):
    try:
        func()
    except myException, extraInfo:  # run func, catch exception + data
        print 'got this:', extraInfo

% python
>>> from helloexc import *
>>> tryer(raiser1)                    # gets explicitly passed extra data
```

Why You Will Care: Lazy Programs

One way to see why exceptions are useful is to compare coding styles in Python and languages without exceptions. For instance, if you want to write robust programs in the C language, you have to test return values or status codes after every operation that could possibly go astray:

```
doStuff()
{                                   // C program:
    if (doFirstThing() == ERROR)    // must detect errors everywhere
        return ERROR;               // even if not processed here
    if (doNextThing() == ERROR)
        return ERROR;
    ...
    return doLastThing();
}

main()
{
    if (doStuff() == ERROR)
        badEnding();
    else
        goodEnding();
}
```

In fact, realistic C programs have as much code devoted to error detection as to doing actual work. But, in Python, you don't have to be so methodical; instead you can wrap arbitrarily vast pieces of a program in exception handlers and write the parts that do the actual work to assume all is well:

```
def doStuff():
    doFirstThing()        # we don't care about exceptions here
    doNextThing()         # so we don't need to detect them here
    ...
    doLastThing()

if_ _name_ _ == '_ _main_ _':
    try:
        doStuff()         # this is where we care about the result
    except:               # so it's the only place we need to check
        badEnding()
    else:
        goodEnding()
```

Because control jumps immediately and automatically to a handler when an exception occurs, there's no need to instrument all your code to guard for errors. The upshot is that exceptions let you largely ignore the unusual cases and avoid much error-checking code.

```
    got this: hello
    >>> tryer(raiser2)                    # gets None by default
    got this: None
```

The assert Statement

As a special case, Python 1.5 introduced an **assert** statement, which is mostly syntactic shorthand for a **raise**. A statement of the form:

```
    assert <test>, <data>          # the <data> part is optional
```

works like the following code:

```
    if __debug__:
        if not <test>:
            raise AssertionError, <data>
```

but **assert** statements may be removed from the compiled program's byte code if the –O command-line flag is used, thereby optimizing the program. **Assertion-Error** is a built-in exception, and the **__debug__** flag is a built-in name which is automatically set to 1 unless the –O flag is used. Assertions are typically used to verify program conditions during development; when displayed, their message text includes source-code line information automatically.

Class Exceptions

Recently, Python generalized the notion of exceptions. They may now also be identified by classes and class instances. Like module packages and private class attributes, class exceptions are an advanced topic you can choose to use or not. If you're just getting started, you may want to mark this section as optional reading.

So far we've used strings to identify our own exceptions; when raised, Python matches the exception to **except** clauses based on object identity (i.e., using the is test we saw in Chapter 2). But when a class exception is raised, an **except** clause matches the current exception if it names the raised class or a superclass of it. The upshot is that class exceptions support the construction of exception hierarchies: by naming a general exception superclass, an **except** clause can catch an entire category of exceptions; any more specific subclass will match.

In general, user-defined exceptions may be identified by string or class objects. Beginning with Python 1.5, all built-in exceptions Python may raise are pre-defined class objects, instead of strings. You normally won't need to care, unless you assume some built-in exception is a string and try to concatenate it without converting (e.g., KeyError + "spam", versus str(KeyError) + "spam").

General raise forms

With the addition of class-based exceptions, the `raise` statement can take the following five forms: the first two raise string exceptions, the next two raise class exceptions, and the last is an addition in Python Version 1.5, which simply reraises the current exception (it's useful if you need to propagate an arbitrary exception you've caught in a `except` block). Raising an instance really raises the instance's class; the instance is passed along with the class as the extra data item (it's a good place to store information for the handler).

```
raise string          # matches except with same string object
raise string, data    # optional extra data (default=None)

raise class, instance # matches except with this class, or a superclass of it
raise instance        # same as: raise instance.__class__, instance

raise                 # re-raise the current exception (new in 1.5)
```

For backward compatibility with Python versions in which built-in exceptions were strings, you can also use these forms of the `raise` statement:

```
raise class                  # same as: raise class()
raise class, arg             # all are really: raise instance
raise class, (arg, arg,...)
```

These are all the same as saying `raise class(arg...)`, and therefore the same as the `raise instance` form above (Python calls the class to create and raise an instance of it). For example, you may raise an instance of the built-in `KeyError` exception by saying simply `raise KeyError`, even though `KeyError` is now a class.

If that sounds confusing, just remember that exceptions may be identified by string, class, or class instance objects, and you may pass extra data with the exception or not. If the extra data you pass with a class isn't an instance object, Python makes an instance for you.

Example

Let's look at an example to see how class exceptions work. In the following, we define a superclass `General` and one subclass of it called `Specific`. We're trying to illustrate the notion of exception categories here; handlers that catch `General` will also catch a subclass of it like `Specific`. We then create functions that raise instances of both classes as exceptions and a top-level `try` that catches `General`; the same `try` catches `General` and `Specific` exceptions, because `Specific` is a subclass of `General`:

```
class General:        pass
class Specific(General): pass
```

```
def raiser1():
    X = General()          # raise listed class instance
    raise X

def raiser2():
    X = Specific()         # raise instance of subclass
    raise X

for func in (raiser1, raiser2):
    try:
        func()
    except General:                    # match General or any subclass of it
        import sys
        print 'caught:', sys.exc_type
```

```
% python classexc.py
caught: <class General at 881ee0>
caught: <class Specific at 881100>
```

Since there are only two possible exceptions here, this doesn't really do justice to the utility of class exceptions; we can achieve the same effects by coding a list of string exception names in the except (e.g., except (a, b, c):), and passing along an instance object as the extra data item. But for large or high exception hierarchies, it may be easier to catch categories using classes than to list every member of a category in a single except clause. Moreover, exception hierarchies can be extended by adding new subclasses, without breaking existing code.

For example, the built-in exception ArithmeticError is a superclass to more specific exceptions such as OverflowError and ZeroDivisionError, but catching just ArithmeticError in a try, you catch any more specific kind of numeric error subclass raised. Furthermore, if you add new kinds of numeric error subclasses in the future, existing code that catches the ArithmeticError superclass (category) also catches the new specific subclasses without modification; there's no need to explicitly extend a list of exception names.

Besides supporting hierarchies, class exceptions also provide storage for extra state information (as instance attributes), but this isn't much more convenient than passing compound objects as extra data with string exceptions (e.g., raise string, object). As usual in Python, the choice to use OOP or not is mostly yours to make.

Exception Gotchas

There isn't much to trip over here, but here are a few general pointers on exception use.

Exceptions Match by Identity, Not Equality

As we've seen, when an exception is raised (by you or by Python itself), Python searches for the most recently entered **try** statement with a *matching* **except** clause, where matching means the same string object, the same class object, or a superclass of the raised class object. It's important to notice that matching is performed by identity, not equality. For instance, suppose we define two string objects we want to raise as exceptions:

```
>>> ex1 = "spam"
>>> ex2 = "spam"
>>>
>>> ex1 == ex2, ex1 is ex2
(1, 0)
```

Applying the == test returns true (1) because they have equal values, but **is** returns false (0) since they are two distinct string objects in memory. Now, an **except** clause that names the same string object will always match:

```
>>> try:
...     raise ex1
... except ex1:
...     print 'got it'
...
got it
```

But one that lists an equal but not identical object will fail:

```
>>> try:
...     raise ex1
... except ex2:
...     print 'Got it'
...
Traceback (innermost last):
  File "<stdin>", line 2, in ?
spam
```

Here, the exception isn't caught, so Python climbs to the top level of the process and prints a stack trace and the exception automatically (the string **"spam"**). For class exceptions, the behavior is similar, but Python generalizes the notion of exception matching to include superclass relationships.

Catching Too Much?

Because Python lets you pick and choose which exceptions to catch, you sometimes have to be careful to not be too inclusive. For example, you've seen that an empty **except** clause catches every exception that might be raised while the code in the **try** block runs. Sometimes that's wanted, but you may also wind up intercepting an error that's expected by a **try** handler higher up in a system. An exception handler such as the following catches and stops every exception that reaches it, whether or not another handler is waiting for it:

```
try:
    ...
except:
    ...                                    # everything comes here!
```

The problem here is that you might not expect all the kinds of exceptions that could occur during an operation:

```
try:
    x = myditctionary[spam]      # oops: misspelled
except:
    x = None                     # assume we got KeyError or IndexError
```

Solution

In this case, you're assuming the only sort of error that can happen when indexing a dictionary is an indexing error. But because the name **myditctionary** is misspelled (you meant to say **mydictionary**), Python raises a **NameError** instead (since it's an undefined name reference), which will be silently caught and ignored by your handler. You should say: **except (KeyError, IndexError):** to make your intentions explicit.

Catching Too Little?

Conversely, you sometimes need to not be so exclusive. When listing specific exceptions in a **try**, you catch only what you actually list. This isn't necessarily a bad thing either, but if a system evolves to raise other exceptions in the future, you may need to go back and add them to exception lists elsewhere in the code. For instance, the following handler is written to treat **myerror1** and **myerror2** as normal cases and treat everything else as an error. If a **myerror3** is added in the future, it is processed as an error unless you update the exception list:

```
try:
    ...
except (myerror1, myerror2):     # what if I add a myerror3?
    ...                          # nonerrors
else:
    ...                          # assumed to be an error
```

Solution

Careful use of class exceptions can make this gotcha go away completely. As we saw earlier in this chapter, if you catch a general superclass, you can add and raise more specific subclasses in the future without having to extend **except** clause lists manually.

Whether you use classes here or not, a little design goes a long way. The moral of the story is that you have to be careful not to be too general or too specific in exception handlers. Especially in larger systems, exception policies should be a part of the overall design.

Summary

In this chapter, we've learned about exceptions—both how to catch them with `try` statements and how to trigger them with `raise` statements. Exceptions are identified by string objects or class objects; built-in exceptions are predefined class objects in Python 1.5, but user-defined exceptions may be strings or classes. Either way, exceptions let us jump around programs arbitrarily, and provide a coherent way of dealing with errors and other unusual events. Along the way, we studied common exception idioms, touched on error handling in general, and saw a variety of ways to catch and match raised exceptions.

This chapter concludes our look at the core Python programming language. If you've gotten this far, you can consider yourself an official Python programmer; you've already seen just about everything there is to see in regards to the language itself. In this part of the book, we studied built-in types, statements, and exceptions, as well as tools used to build-up larger program units—functions, modules, and classes. In general, Python provides a *hierarchy* of tool sets:

Built-ins
    Built-in types like strings, lists, and dictionaries make it easy to write simple programs fast.

Python extensions
    For more demanding tasks, we can extend Python in Python, by writing our own functions, modules, and classes.

C extensions
    Although we don't cover them in this book, Python can also be extended with modules written in C or C++.

Because Python layers its tool sets, we can decide how complicated we need to get for a given task. We've covered the first two of the categories above in this book already, and that's plenty to do substantial programming in Python.

The next part of this book takes you on a tour of standard modules and common tasks in Python. Table 7-2 summarizes some of the sources of built-in or existing functionality available to Python programmers, and topics we'll explore in the remainder of this book. Up until now, most of our examples have been very small and self-contained. We wrote them that way on purpose, to help you master the basics. But now that you know all about the core language, it's time to start learning how to use Python's built-in interfaces to do real work. We'll find that with a simple language like Python, common tasks are often much easier than you might expect.

Table 7-2. Python's Built-in Toolbox

Category	Examples
Object types	`lists, dictionaries, files, strings`
Functions	`len, range, apply, open`
Modules	`string, os, Tkinter, pickle`
Exceptions	`IndexError, KeyError`
Attributes	`__dict__, __name__`
Peripheral tools	`NumPy, SWIG, JPython, PythonWin`

Exercises

Since we're at the end of Part I, we'll just work on a few short exception exercises to give you a chance to play with the basics. Exceptions really are a simple tool, so if you get these, you've got exceptions mastered.

1. *try/except*. Write a function called **oops** that explicitly raises a **IndexError** exception when called. Then write another function that calls **oops** inside a **try/except** statement to catch the error. What happens if you change **oops** to raise **KeyError** instead of **IndexError**? Where do the names **KeyError** and **IndexError** come from? (Hint: recall that all unqualified names come from one of three scopes, by the LGB rule.)

2. *Exception lists*. Change the **oops** function you just wrote to raise an exception you define yourself, called **MyError**, and pass an extra data item along with the exception. Then, extend the **try** statement in the catcher function to catch this exception and its data in addition to **IndexError**, and print the extra data item.

3. *Error handling*. Write a function called **safe(func, *args)** that runs any function using **apply**, catches any exception raised while the function runs, and prints the exception using the **exc_type** and **exc_value** attributes in the **sys** module. Then, use your **safe** function to run the **oops** function you wrote in Exercises 1 and/or 2. Put **safe** in a module file called *tools.py*, and pass it the **oops** function interactively. What sort of error messages do you get? Finally, expand **safe** to also print a Python stack trace when an error occurs by calling the built-in **print_exc()** function in the standard **traceback** module (see the Python library reference manual or other Python books for details).

II

The Outer Layers

In Part I we covered the core of the Python language. With this knowledge, you should be able to read almost all Python code written, with few language-related surprises. However, as anyone who's ever looked at existing programs knows, understanding the syntax of a language doesn't guarantee a clear and easy understanding of a program, even if it is well written. Indeed, knowing which tools are being used, be they simple functions, coherent packages, or even complex frameworks, is the important step between a theoretical understanding of a language and a practical, effective mastery of a system.

How can you make this transition? No amount of reading of woodworking magazines is going to turn a novice into a master woodworker. For that to happen, you have to have talent, of course, but also spend years examining furniture, taking furniture apart, building new pieces, learning from your mistakes and others' successes. The same is true in programming. The role of textbooks is to give a bird's eye view of the kinds of problems and appropriate solutions, to show some of the basic tricks of the trade, and, finally, to motivate the frustrated beginner by showing some of the nicer pieces of work others have built. This section presents a different view of the Python landscape in each chapter and each gives plentiful pointers to other sources of information.

8

Built-in Tools

This chapter presents a selection of the essential tools that make up the Python standard library—built-in functions, library modules, and their most useful functions and classes. These are the sine qua non; while you most likely won't use all of these in any one program, no useful program we've ever seen avoids all of these. Just as Python provides a list data structure object type because sequence manipulations occur in all programming contexts, the library provides a set of modules that will come in handy over and over again. Before designing and writing any piece of generally useful code, check to see if a similar module already exists. If it's part of the standard Python library, you can be assured that it's been heavily tested; even better, others are committed to fixing any remaining bugs—for free.

Note that this chapter gives only a brief look at the best of the standard library. As of current writing, the *Python Library Reference* is over 200 pages long. More details on the reference are available in Appendix A, *Python Resources*, but you should know that it's the ideal companion to this book; it provides the completeness we don't have the room for, and, being available online, is the most up-to-date description of the standard Python toolset. Also, O'Reilly's *Python Pocket Reference*, written by coauthor Mark Lutz, covers the most important modules in the standard library, along with the syntax and built-in functions.

This chapter includes descriptions of two kinds of tools—built-in functions and standard modules. Before we get to those sections, however, we'll say a brief word about built-in objects. When introducing lists, for example, we've presented their behavior as well as their most important methods (`append`, `insert`, `sort`, `reverse`, `index`, etc.). We have not been exhaustive in this coverage in order to focus on the most important aspects of the objects. If you're curious about what we've left out, you can look it up in the *Library Reference*, or you can poke around in the Python interactive interpreter. Starting with Python 1.5, the `dir` built-in function returns a list of all of the important attributes of objects, and, along with the `type` built-in, provides a great way to learn about the objects you're manipulating. For example:

```
>>> dir([])                         # what are the attributes of lists?
['append', 'count', 'index', 'insert', 'remove', 'reverse', 'sort']
>>> dir(())                         # what are the attributes of tuples?
[]                                  # tuples have no attributes!
>>> dir(sys.stdin)                  # what are the attributes of files?
['close', 'closed', 'fileno', 'flush', 'isatty', 'mode', 'name', 'read',
'readinto', 'readline', 'readlines', 'seek', 'softspace', 'tell', 'truncate',
'write', 'writelines']
>>> dir(sys)                        # modules are objects too
['__doc__', '__name__', 'argv', 'builtin_module_names', 'copyright', 'dllhandle'
'exc_info', 'exc_type', 'exec_prefix', 'executable', 'exit',
'getrefcount','maxint', 'modules', 'path', 'platform', 'prefix', 'ps1',
'ps2','setcheckinterval', 'setprofile', 'settrace', 'stderr', 'stdin',
'stdout','version', 'winver']
>>> type(sys.version)               # what kind of thing is 'version'?
<type 'string'>
>>> print sys.version               # what is the value of this string?
1.5 (#0, Dec 30 1997, 23:24:20) [MSC 32 bit (Intel)]
```

Aside: The sys Module

The `sys` module contains several functions and attributes internal to Python; `sys` in this case means Python system, not operating system. Some of the most useful attributes are:

`sys.path`
> A list containing the directories Python looks into when doing imports.

`sys.modules`
> A dictionary of the modules that have been loaded in the current session.

`sys.platform`
> A string referring to the current platform. Its possible values include `'win32'`, `'mac'`, `'osf1'`, `'linux-i386'`, `'sunos4'`, etc. It's sometimes useful to check the value of `sys.platform` when doing platform-specific things (such as starting a window manager).

`sys.ps1` and `sys.ps2`
> Two printable objects, used by Python in the interactive interpreter as the primary and secondary prompts. Their default values are `...` and `>>>` . You can set them to strings or to instances of classes that define a `__repr__` method.

One of the most frequently used attributes of the `sys` module is `sys.argv`, a list of the words input on the command line, excluding the reference to Python itself if it exists. In other words, if you type at the shell:

```
csh> python run.py a x=3 foo
```

then when `run.py` starts, the value of the `sys.argv` attribute is `['run.py', 'a', 'x=3', 'foo']`. The `sys.argv` attribute is mutable (after all, it's just a list). Common usage involves iterating over the arguments of the Python program, that is, `sys.argv[1:]`; slicing from index 1 till the end gives all of the arguments to the program itself, but doesn't include the name of the program (module) stored in `sys.argv[0]`.

Finally, there are three file attributes in the `sys` module: `sys.stdin`, `sys.stdout`, and `sys.stderr`. They are references to the standard input, output, and error streams respectively. Standard input is generally associated by the operating system with the user's keyboard; standard output and standard error are usually associated with the console. The `print` statement in Python outputs to standard output (`sys.stdout`), while error messages such as exceptions are output on the standard error stream (`sys.stderr`). Finally, as we'll see in an example, these are mutable attributes: you can redirect output of a Python program to a file simply by assigning to `sys.stdout`:

```
sys.stdout = open('log.out', 'w')
```

Built-in Functions

The `dir` function is a built-in function: it lives in the built-in namespace. Applying the LGB rule means that the function is always available, and that no `import` statement is needed to access it.* You've already encountered many of the built-in functions, such as `len`, `open`, `type`, `list`, `map`, `range`, `reload`. You can find them listed with the standard exceptions in the `__builtins__` namespace:

```
>>> dir(__builtins__)
['ArithmeticError', 'AssertionError', 'AttributeError', 'EOFError',
'Ellipsis','Exception', 'FloatingPointError', 'IOError', 'ImportError',
'IndexError','KeyError', 'KeyboardInterrupt', 'LookupError', 'MemoryError',
'NameError','None', 'OverflowError', 'RuntimeError', 'StandardError',
'SyntaxError','SystemError', 'SystemExit', 'TypeError', 'ValueError',
'ZeroDivisionError','__debug__', '__doc__', '__import__', '__name__', 'abs',
'apply', 'callable','chr', 'cmp', 'coerce', 'compile', 'complex', 'delattr',
'dir', 'divmod', 'eval','execfile', 'filter', 'float', 'getattr', 'globals',
'hasattr', 'hash', 'hex','id', 'input', 'int', 'intern', 'isinstance',
'issubclass', 'len', 'list','locals', 'long', 'map', 'max', 'min', 'oct',
'open', 'ord', 'pow', 'range', 'raw_input', 'reduce', 'reload', 'repr',
'round', 'setattr', 'slice', 'str','tuple', 'type', 'vars', 'xrange']
```

---

* It also means that if you define a local or module-global reference with the same name, subsequent uses of `dir` will use your new variable instead of the built-in version. This feature is the source of some subtle bugs; one of us recently wrote a program that used a variable called o and a list of such variables called os (as in the plural of o). Surprise surprise, the (supposedly unrelated) previously bugfree code that used `os.system` now complained of AttributeErrors! Another frequent bug of the same kind is doing `type = type(myObject)`, which works only the first time around, since it results in assigning to a new local variable (called `type`) a reference to the type of whatever `myObject` was. This local variable is what Python tries (and fails) to call the second time around.

Conversions, Numbers, and Comparisons

A few functions are used for converting between object types. We've already seen
str, which takes anything and returns a string representation of it, and list and
tuple, which take sequences and return list and tuple versions of them, respectively. int, complex, float, and long take numbers and convert them to their
respective types. hex and oct take integers (int or long) as arguments and
return string representations of them in hexadecimal or octal format, respectively.

int, long, and float have additional features that can be confusing. First, int
and long truncate their numeric arguments if necessary to perform the operation,
thereby losing information and performing a conversion that may not be what you
want (the round built-in rounds numbers the standard way and returns a float).
Second, int, long, and float convert strings to their respective types, provided
the strings are valid integer (or long, or float) literals:*

```
>>> int(1.0), int(1.4), int(1.9), round(1.9), int(round(1.9))
(1, 1, 1, 2.0, 2)
>>> int("1")
1
>>> int("1.2")                          # this doesn't work
Traceback (innermost last):
  File "<stdin>", line 1, in ?
ValueError: invalid literal for int(): 1.2
>>> int("1.0")                          #neither does this
Traceback (innermost last):             # since 1.0 is also not a valid
  File "<stdin>", line 1, in ?          # integer literal
ValueError: invalid literal for int(): 1.0
>>> hex(1000), oct(1000), complex(1000), long(1000)
('0x3e8', '01750', (1000+0j), 1000L)
```

Given the behavior of int, it may make sense in some cases to use a custom variant that does only conversion, refusing to truncate:

```
>>> def safeint(candidate):
...     import math
...     truncated = math.floor(float(candidate))
...     rounded = round(float(candidate))
...     if truncated == rounded:
...             return int(truncated)
...     else:
...             raise ValueError, "argument would lose precision when cast to
integer"
...
>>> safeint(3.0)
3
>>> safeint("3.0")
```

---

* Literals are the text strings that are converted to numbers early in the Python compilation process. So,
the string "1244" in your Python program file (which is necessarily a string) is a valid integer literal, but
"def foo():" isn't.

```
3
>>> safeint(3.1)
Traceback (innermost last):
  File "<stdin>", line 1, in ?
  File "<stdin>", line 6, in safeint
ValueError: argument would lose precision when cast to integer
```

The **abs** built-in returns the absolute value of scalars (integers, longs, floats) and the magnitude of complex numbers (the square root of the sum of the squared real and imaginary parts):

```
>>> abs(-1), abs(-1.2), abs(-3+4j)
(1, 1.2, 5.0)                           # 5 is sqrt(3*3 + 4*4)
```

The **ord** and **chr** functions return the ASCII value of single characters and vice versa, respectively:

```
>>> map(ord, "test")    # remember that strings are sequences
[116, 101, 115, 116]    # of characters, so map can be used
>>> chr(64)
'@'
>>> ord('@')
64
# map returns a list of single characters, so it
# needs to be 'join'ed into a str
>>> map(chr, (83, 112, 97, 109, 33))
['S', 'p', 'a', 'm', '! ']
>>> import string
>>> string.join(map(chr, (83, 112, 97, 109, 33)), '')
'Spam!'
```

The **cmp** built-in returns a negative integer, 0, or a positive integer, depending on whether its first argument is less than, equal to, or greater than its second one. It's worth emphasizing that **cmp** works with more than just numbers; it compares characters using their ASCII values, and sequences are compared by comparing their elements. Comparisons can raise exceptions, so the comparison function is not guaranteed to work on all objects, but all reasonable comparisons will work. The comparison process used by **cmp** is the same as that used by the **sort** method of lists. It's also used by the built-ins **min** and **max**, which return the smallest and largest elements of the objects they are called with, dealing reasonably with sequences:

```
>>> min("pif", "paf", "pof")    # when called with multiple
'paf' arguments                 # return appropriate one
>>> min("ZELDA!"), max("ZELDA!")  # when called with a sequence,
'!', 'Z'                        # return the min/max element of it
```

Table 8-1 summarizes the built-in functions dealing with type conversions.

Table 8-1. Type Conversion Built-in Functions

Function Name	Behavior

str(*string*)	Returns the string representation of any object:
	```>>> str(dir())```
	```"['__builtins__', '__doc__', '__name__']"```

list(*seq*)	Returns the list version of a sequence:
	```>>> list("tomato")```
	```['t', 'o', 'm', 'a', 't', 'o']```
	```>>> list((1,2,3))```
	```[1, 2, 3]```

tuple(*seq*)	Returns the tuple version of a sequence:
	```>>> tuple("tomato")```
	```('t', 'o', 'm', 'a', 't', 'o')```
	```>>> tuple([0])```
	```(0,)```

int(*x*)	Converts a string or number to a plain integer; truncates floating point values:
	```>>> int("3")```
	```3```

long(*x*)	Converts a string or number to a long integer; truncates floating point values:
	```>>> long("3")```
	```3L```

float(*x*)	Converts a string or a number to floating point:
	```>>> float("3")```
	```3.0```

complex(*real*, *imag*)	Creates a complex number with the value *real* + *imag**j:
	```>>> complex(3,5)```
	```(3+5j)```

hex(*i*)	Converts an integer number (of any size) to a hexadecimal string:
	```>>> hex(10000)```
	```'0x2710'```

oct(*i*)	Converts an integer number (of any size) to an octal string:
	```>>> oct(10000)```
	```'023420'```

ord(*c*)	Returns the ASCII value of a string of one character:
	```>>> ord('A')```
	```65```

chr(*i*)	Returns a string of one character whose ASCII code is the integer *i*:
	```>>> chr(65)```
	```'A'```

min(*i* [, *i*]*)	Returns the smallest item of a nonempty sequence:
	```>>> min([5,1,2,3,4])```
	```1```
	```>>> min(5,1,2,3,4)```
	```1```

Table 8-1. Type Conversion Built-in Functions (continued)

Function Name	Behavior

max(i [, i]*)	Returns the largest item of a nonempty sequence:
	```>>> max([5,1,2,3,4])```
	5
	```>>> max(5,1,2,3,4)```
	5

Attribute Manipulation

The four built-in functions hasattr, getattr, setattr, and delattr test attribute existence, get, set, and delete attributes of namespaces, respectively, given the attribute's name as the second argument. They are useful when manipulating objects and attributes whose names aren't available beforehand. They can be used with modules, classes, and instances, and are summarized in Table 8-2.

Table 8-2. Built-ins that Manipulate Attributes of Objects

Function Name	Behavior
hasattr(object, attributename)	Returns 1 if *object* has an attribute *attributename*, 0 otherwise
getattr(object, attributename [, default])	Returns the attribute *attributename* of *object*; if it doesn't exist, returns *default* if it's specified or raises an AttributeError if not
delattr(object, attributename)	Deletes the attribute *attributename* of *object* or raises an AttributeError exception if it doesn't exist
setattr(object, attributename, value)	Assigns *value* to attribute *attributename* of object; raises TypeError if not supported; creates of changes attribute

We saw these built-ins put to good use in the examples in Chapter 6, *Classes*, but for now, consider a toy example that creates a specified attribute in a given namespace (in this case, a class object), or increments it if it's already there:

```
>>> def increment_attribute(object, attrname):
...     if not hasattr(object, attrname):
...         setattr(object, attrname, 1)
...     else:
...         setattr(object, attrname, getattr(object, attrname) + 1)
...
>>> class Test: pass
...
>>> aname = 'foo'
>>> increment_attribute(Test, aname)       # create Test.foo and set it to 1
>>> increment_attribute(Test, aname)       # increment Test.foo
>>> Test.foo
2
```

In Python 1.5.2, an optional third argument to `getattr` has been added that specifies what value to use if the object doesn't have the specified argument. Thus the code above can now be simplified:

```
def increment_attribute(object, attrname):
    setattr(object, attrname, getattr(object, attrname, 0) + 1)
```

Executing Programs

The last set of built-in functions in this section have to do with creating, manipulating, and calling Python code. See Table 8-3 for a summary.

Table 8-3. Ways to Execute Python Code

Name	Behavior
`import`	Executes the code in a module as part of the importing and returns the module object
`exec` *code* [in *globaldict* [, *localdict*]]	Executes the specified code (string, file, or compiled code object) in the optionally specified global and local namespaces
`compile(`*string*, *filename*, *kind*)	Compiles the *string* into a code object (see following Note)
`execfile(`*filename* [, *globaldict* [, *localdict*]])	Executes the program in the specified filename, using the optionally specified global and local namespaces
`eval(`*code*[, *globaldict* [, *localdict*]])	Evaluates the specified expression (string or compiled code object) in the optionally specified global and local namespaces

It's a simple matter to write programs that run other programs. Shortly, we'll talk about ways to call any program from within a Python program. And we've seen the `import` statement that executes code existing in files on the Python path. There are several mechanisms that let you execute arbitrary Python code. The first uses **exec**, which is a statement, not a function. Here is the **exec** syntax:

```
exec code [ in globaldict [, localdict]]
```

As you can see, **exec** takes between one and three arguments. The first argument must contain Python code—either in a string, as in the following example; in an open file object; or in a compiled code object (more on this later). For example:

```
>>> code = "x = 'Something'"
>>> x = "Nothing"                        # sets the value of x
>>> exec code                            # modifies the value of x!
>>> print x
'Something'
```

exec can take optional arguments. If a single dictionary argument is provided (after the then-mandatory `in` word), it's used as both the local and global namespaces for the execution of the specified code. If two dictionary arguments are provided, they are used as the global and local namespaces, respectively. If both arguments are omitted, as in the previous example, the current global and local namespaces are used.

When **exec** is called, Python needs to parse the code that is being executed. This can be a computationally expensive process, especially if a large piece of code needs to be executed thousands of times. If this is the case, it's worth compiling the code first (once), and executing it as many times as needed. The **compile** function takes a string containing the Python code and returns a compiled code object, which can then be processed efficiently by the **exec** statement.

compile takes three arguments. The first is the code string. The second is the filename corresponding to the Python source file (or '*<string>*' if it wasn't read from a file); it's used in the traceback in case an exception is generated when executing the code. The third argument is one of '**single**', '**exec**', or '**eval**', depending on whether the code is a single statement whose result would be printed (just as in the interactive interpreter), a set of statements, or an expression (creating a compiled code object for use by the **eval** function).

A related function to the **exec** statement is the **execfile** built-in function, which works similarly to **exec**, but its first argument must be the filename of a Python script instead of a file object or string (remember that file objects are the things the **open** built-in returns when it's passed a filename). Thus, if you want your Python script to start by running its arguments as Python scripts, you can do something like:

```
import sys
for argument in sys.argv[1:]:          # we'll skip ourselves, or it'll loop!
    execfile(argument)                 # do whatever
```

Two more functions can execute Python code. The first is the **eval** function, which takes a code string (and the by now usual optional pair of dictionaries) or a compiled code object and returns the evaluation of that expression. For example:

```
>>> z = eval("'xo'*10")
>>> print z
'xoxoxoxoxoxoxoxoxoxo'
```

The **eval** function can't work with statements, as shown in the following example, because expressions and statements are different syntactic beasts:

```
>>> z = eval("x = 3")
Traceback (innermost last):
  File "<stdin>", line 1, in ?
  File "<string>", line 1
    x = 3
      ^
SyntaxError: invalid syntax
```

The last function that executes code is **apply**. It's called with a callable object, an optional tuple of the positional arguments, and an optional dictionary of the key-words arguments. A callable object is any function (standard functions, methods, etc.), any class object (that creates an instance when called), or any instance of a class that defines a __call__ method. If you're not sure what's callable (e.g., if it's an argument to a function), test it using the **callable** built-in, which returns true if the object it's called with is callable.*

```
>>> callable(sys.exit), type(sys.exit)
(1, <type 'builtin_function_or_method'>)
>>> callable(sys.version), type(sys.version)
(0, <type 'string'>)
```

There are other built-in functions we haven't covered; if you're curious, check a reference source such as the *Library Reference* (Section 2.3).

Library Modules

Currently, there are more than 200 modules in the standard distribution, covering topics such as string and text processing, networking and web tools, system inter-faces, database interfaces, serialization, data structures and algorithms, user inter-faces, numerical computing, and others. We touch on only the most widely used here and mention some of the more powerful and specialized ones in Chapter 9, *Common Tasks in Python*, and Chapter 10, *Frameworks and Applications*.

Basic String Operations: The string Module

The **string** module is somewhat of a historical anomaly. If Python were being designed today, chances are many functions currently in the **string** module would be implemented instead as methods of string objects.† The **string** module operates on strings. Table 8-4 lists the most useful functions defined in the **string** module, along with brief descriptions, just to give you an idea as to the module's purpose. The descriptions given here are not complete; for an exhaustive listing, check the *Library Reference* or the *Python Pocket Reference*. Except when other-wise noted, each function returns a string.

---

* You can find many things about callable objects, such as how many arguments they expect and what the names and default values of their arguments are by checking the *Language Reference* for details, especially Section 3.2, which describes all attributes for each type.

† For a more detailed discussion of this and of many other commonly asked questions about Python, check out the FAQ list at *http://www.python.org/doc/FAQ.html*. For the question of string methods ver-sus string functions, see Question 6.4 in that document.

Table 8-4. String Module Functions

Function Name	Behavior

atof(*string*)	Converts a string to a floating point number (see the float built-in):
	`>>> string.atof("1.4")`
	`1.4`

atoi(*string* [, *base*])	Converts a string to an integer, using the base specified (base 10 by default (see the int built-in):
	`>>> string.atoi("365")`
	`365`

atol(*string* [, *base*])	Same as atoi, except converts to a long integer (see the long built-in):
	`>>> string.atol("987654321")`
	`987654321L`

capitalize(*word*)	Capitalizes the first letter of *word*:
	`>>> string.capitalize("tomato")`
	`'Tomato'`

capwords(*string*)	Capitalizes each word in the *string*:
	`>>> string.capwords("now is the time")`
	`'Now Is The Time'`

expandtabs(*string, tabsize*)	Expands the tab characters in *string*, using the specified tab size (no default)

find(*s, sub* [, *start* [, *end*]])	Returns the index of the string *s* corresponding to the first occurrence of the substring *sub* in *s*, or –1 if *sub* isn't in *s*:
	`>>> string.find("now is the time", 'is')`
	`4`

rfind(*s, sub* [, *start* [, *end*]])	Same as find, but gives the index of the last occurrence of *sub* in *s*
index(*s, sub* [, *start* [, *end*]])	Same as find, but raises a ValueError exception if *sub* isn't found in *s*
rindex(*s, sub* [, *start* [, *end*]])	Same as rfind, but raises a ValueError exception if *sub* is not found in *s*

count(*s, sub* [, *start* [, *end*]])	Returns the number of occurrences of *sub* in *s*:
	`>>> string.count("now is the time", 'i')`
	`2`

replace(*str, old,* new[, *maxsplit*])	Returns a string like *str* except that all (or some) occurrences of *old* have been replaced with *new*:
	`>>> string.replace("now is the time", ' ', '_')`
	`'now_is_the_time'`

lower(*string*), upper(*string*)	Returns a lowercase (or uppercase) version of *string*

split(*s* [, *sep* [, *maxsplit*]])	Splits the string *s* at the specified separator string *sep* (whitespace by default), and returns a list of the "split" substrings:
	`>>> string.split("now is the time")`
	`['now', 'is', 'the', 'time']`

Table 8-4. String Module Functions (continued)

Function Name	Behavior

`join(wordlist`
`[, sep`
`[, maxsplit]])`
	Joins a sequence of strings, inserting copies of *sep* between each (a single space by default):
	`>>> string.join(["now","is","the","time", '*'])`
	`'now*is*the*time'`
	`>>> string.join("now is the time", '*')`
	`'n*o*w* *i*s* *t*h*e* *t*i*m*e'`
	Remember that a string is itself a sequence of one-character strings!

`lstrip(s),`
`rstrip(s),`
`strip(s)`
	Strips whitespace occurring at the left, right, or both ends of *s*:
	`>>> string.strip("  before  and  after    ")`
	`'before and after'`

`swapcase(s)`	Returns a version of *s* with the lowercase letters replaced with their uppercase equivalent and vice versa

`ljust(s, width),`
`rjust(s, width),`
`center(s, width)`
	Left-pads, right-pads, or centers the string *s* with spaces so that the returned string has *width* characters

The string module also defines a few useful constants, as shown in Table 8-5.

Table 8-5. String Module Constants

Constant Name	Value
`digits`	`'0123456789'`
`octdigits`	`'01234567'`
`hexdigits`	`'0123456789abcdefABCDEF'`
`lowercase`	`'abcdefghijklmnopqrstuvwxyz'`[a]
`uppercase`	`'ABCDEFGHIJKLMNOPQRSTUVWXYZ'`
`letters`	`lowercase + uppercase`
`whitespace`	`' \t\n\r\v'` (all whitespace characters)

[a] On most systems, the `string.lowercase`, `string.uppercase`, and `string.letters` have the values listed above. If one uses the `locale` module to specify a different cultural locale, they are updated. Thus for example, after doing `locale.setlocale(locale.LC_ALL, 'fr')`, the `string.letters` attribute will also include accented letters and other valid French letters.

The constants in Table 8-5 generally test whether specific characters fit a criterion—for example, `x in string.whitespace` returns true only if `x` is one of the whitespace characters.

A typical use of the **string** module is to clean up user input. The following line removes all "extra" whitespace, meaning it replaces sequences of whitespace with single space characters, and it deletes leading and trailing spaces:

```
thestring = string.strip(string.join(string.split(thestring)))
```

Advanced String Operations: The re Module

The `string` module defines basic operations on strings. It shows up in almost all programs that interact with files or users. Because Python strings can contain null bytes, they can also process binary data—more on this when we get to the `struct` module.

In addition, Python provides a specialized string-processing tool to use with regular expressions. For a long time, Python's regular expressions (available in the `regex` and `regsub` modules), while adequate for some tasks, were not up to par with those offered by competing languages, such as Perl. As of Python 1.5, a new module called `re` provides a completely overhauled regular expression package, which significantly enhances Python's string-processing abilities.

Regular expressions

Regular expressions are strings that let you define complicated pattern matching and replacement rules for strings. These strings are made up of symbols that emphasize compact notation over mnemonic value. For example, the single character . means "match any single character." The character + means "one or more of what just preceded me." Table 8-6 lists some of the most commonly used regular expression symbols and their meanings in English.

Table 8-6. Common Elements of Regular Expression Syntax

Special Character	Meaning
.	Matches any character except newline by default
^	Matches the start of the string
$	Matches the end of the string
*	"Any number of occurrences of what just preceded me"
+	"One or more occurrences of what just preceded me"
|	"Either the thing before me or the thing after me"
\w	Matches any alphanumeric character
\d	Matches any decimal digit
tomato	Matches the string `tomato`

A real regular expression problem

Suppose you need to write a program to replace the strings "green pepper" and "red pepper" with "bell pepper" if and only if they occur together in a paragraph before the word "salad" and not if they are followed (with no space) by the string "corn." These kinds of requirements are surprisingly common in computing. Assume that the file you need to process is called *pepper.txt*. Here's a silly example of such a file:

```
This is a paragraph that mentions bell peppers multiple times. For
one, here is a red pepper and dried tomato salad recipe. I don't like
to use green peppers in my salads as much because they have a harsher
flavor.

This second paragraph mentions red peppers and green peppers but not
the "s" word (s-a-l-a-d), so no bells should show up.

This third paragraph mentions red peppercorns and green peppercorns,
which aren't vegetables but spices (by the way, bell peppers really
aren't peppers, they're chilies, but would you rather have a good cook
or a good botanist prepare your salad?).
```

The first task is to open it and read in the text:

```
file = open('pepper.txt')
text = file.read()
```

We read the entire text at once and avoid splitting it into lines, since we will
assume that paragraphs are defined by two consecutive newline characters. This is
easy to do using the **split** function of the **string** module:

```
import string
paragraphs = string.split(text, '\n\n')
```

At this point we've split the text into a list of paragraph strings, and all there is left
is to do is perform the actual replacement operation. Here's where regular expressions come in:

```
import re
matchstr = re.compile(
    r"""\b(red|green)      # 'red' or 'green' starting new words
        (\s+                # followed by whitespace
        pepper              # the word 'pepper'
        (?!corn)            # if not followed immediately by 'corn'
        (?=.*salad))""",    # and if followed at some point by 'salad',
    re.IGNORECASE |         # allow pepper, Pepper, PEPPER, etc.
    re.DOTALL |             # allow to match newlines as well
    re.VERBOSE)             # this allows the comments and the newlines above
for paragraph in paragraphs:
    fixed_paragraph = matchstr.sub(r'bell\2', paragraph)
    print fixed_paragraph+'\n'
```

The bold line is the hardest one; it creates a compiled regular expression pattern,
which is like a program. Such a pattern specifies two things: which parts of the strings
we're interested in and how they should be grouped. Let's go over these in turn.

Defining which parts of the string we're interested in is done by specifying a pattern of characters that defines a match. This is done by concatenating smaller patterns, each of which specifies a simple matching criterion (e.g., "match the string
'pepper'," "match one or more whitespace characters," "don't match **'corn'**,"
etc.). As mentioned, we're looking for the words **red** or **green**, if they're followed by the word **pepper**, that is itself followed by the word **salad**, as long as

`pepper` isn't followed immediately by `'corn'`. Let's take each line of the `re.compile(...)` expression in turn.

The first thing to notice about the string in the `re.compile()` is that it's a "raw" string (the quotation marks are preceded by an `r`). Prepending such an `r` to a string (single- or triple-quoted) turns off the interpretation of the backslash characters within the string.* We could have used a regular string instead and used `\\b` instead of `\b` and `\\s` instead of `\s`. In this case, it makes little difference; for complicated regular expressions, raw strings allow much more clear syntax than escaped backslashes.

The first line in the pattern is `\b(red|green)`. `\b` stands for "the empty string, but only at the beginning or end of a word"; using it here prevents matches that have `red` or `green` as the final part of a word (as in "tired pepper"). The `(red|green)` pattern specifies an alternation: either `'red'` or `'green'`. Ignore the left parenthesis that follows for now. `\s` is a special symbol that means "any whitespace character," and `+` means "one or more occurrence of whatever comes before me," so, put together, `\s+` means "one or more whitespace characters." Then, `pepper` just means the string `'pepper'`. `(?!corn)` prevents matches of "patterns that have `'corn'` at this point," so we prevent the match on `'peppercorn'`. Finally, `(?=.*salad)` says that for the pattern to match, it must be followed by any number of characters (that's what `.*` means), followed by the word `salad`. The `?=` bit specifies that while the pattern should determine whether the match occurs, it shouldn't be "used up" by the match process; it's a subtle point, which we'll ignore for now. At this point we've defined the pattern corresponding to the substring.

Now, note that there are two parentheses we haven't explained yet—the one before `\s+` and the last one. What these two do is define a "group," which starts after the red or green and go to the end of the pattern. We'll use that group in the next operation, the actual replacement. First, we need to mention the three flags that are joined by the logical operation "or". These specify kinds of pattern matches. The first, `re.IGNORECASE`, says that the text comparisons should ignore whether the text and the match have similar or different cases. The second, `re.DOTALL`, specifies that the `.` character should match any character, including the newline character (that's not the default behavior). Finally, the third, `re.VERBOSE`, allows us to insert extra newlines and `#` comments in the regular expression, making it easier to read and understand. We could have written the statement more compactly as:

```
matchstr = re.compile(r"\b(red|green)(\s+pepper(?!corn)(?=.*salad))", re.I | re.S)
```

The actual replacement operation is done with the line:

```
fixed_paragraph = matchstr.sub(r'bell\2', paragraph)
```

---

* Raw strings can't end with an odd number of backslash characters. That's unlikely to be a problem when using raw strings for regular expressions, however, since regular expressions can't end with backslashes.

First, it should be fairly clear that we're calling the `sub` method of the `matchstr` object. That object is a *compiled regular expression object*, meaning that some of the processing of the expression has already been done (in this case, outside the loop), thus speeding up the total program execution. We use a raw string again to write the first argument to the method. The `\2` is a reference to group 2 in the regular expression—the second group of parentheses in the regular expression—in our case, everything starting with `pepper` and up to and including the word `'salad'`. This line therefore means, "Replace the matched string with the string that is `'bell'` followed by whatever starts with `'pepper'` and goes up to the end of the matched string, in the `paragraph` string."

So, does it work? The *pepper.txt* file we saw earlier had three paragraphs: the first satisfied the requirements of the match twice, the second didn't because it didn't mention the word "salad," and the third didn't because the `red` and `green` words are before `peppercorn`, not `pepper`. As it was supposed to, our program (saved in a file called *pepper.py*) modifies only the first paragraph:

```
/home/David/book$ python pepper.py
This is a paragraph that mentions bell peppers multiple times. For
one, here is a bell pepper and dried tomato salad recipe. I don't like
to use bell peppers in my salads as much because they have a harsher
flavor.

This second paragraph mentions red peppers and green peppers but not
the "s" word (s-a-l-a-d), so no bells should show up.

This third paragraph mentions red peppercorns and green peppercorns,
which aren't vegetables but spices (by the way, bell peppers really
aren't peppers, they're chilies, but would you rather have a good cook
or a good botanist prepare your salad?).
```

This example, while artificial, shows how regular expressions can compactly express complicated matching rules. If this kind of problem occurs often in your line of work, mastering regular expressions is a worthwhile investment of time and effort.

A thorough coverage of regular expressions is beyond the scope of this book. Jeffrey Friedl gives an excellent coverage of regular expressions in his book *Mastering Regular Expressions* (O'Reilly & Associates). His description of Python regular expressions (at least in the First Edition) uses the old-style syntax, which is no longer the recommended one, so those specifics should mostly be ignored; the regular expressions currently used in Python are much more similar to those of Perl. Still, his book is a must-have for anyone doing serious text processing. For the casual user (such as these authors), the descriptions in the *Library Reference* do the job most of the time. Use the `re` module, not the `regexp`, `regex`, and `regsub` modules, which are deprecated.

Generic Operating-System Interfaces: The os Module

The operating-system interface defines the mechanism by which programs are expected to manipulate things like files, processes, users, and threads.

The os and os.path modules

The os module provides a generic interface to the operating system's most basic set of tools. The specific set of calls it defines depend on which platform you use. (For example, the permission-related calls are available only on platforms that support them, such as Unix and Windows.) Nevertheless, it's recommended that you always use the os module, instead of the platform-specific versions of the module (called posix, nt, and mac). Table 8-7 lists some of the most often-used functions in the os module. When referring to files in the context of the os module, one is referring to filenames, not file objects.

Table 8-7. Most Frequently Used Functions From the os Module

Function Name	Behavior

getcwd()	Returns a string referring to the current working directory (cwd):
	 `>>> print os.getcwd()`
	 `h:\David\book`

listdir(path)	Returns a list of all of the files in the specified directory:
	 `>>> os.listdir(os.getcwd())`
	 `['preface.doc', 'part1.doc', 'part2.doc']`

chown(path, uid, gid)	Changes the owner ID and group ID of specified file
chmod(path, mode)	Changes the permissions of specified file with numeric mode *mode* (e.g., 0644 means read/write for owner, read for everyone else)
rename(src, dest)	Renames file named *src* with name *dest*
remove(path) or unlink(path)	Deletes specified file (see rmdir to remove directories)
mkdir(path [, mode])	Creates a directory named *path* with numeric mode *mode* (see os.chmod): `>>> os.mkdir('newdir')`
rmdir(path)	Removes directory named *path*
system(command)	Executes the shell *command* in a subshell; the return value is the return code of the command
symlink(src, dest)	Creates soft link from file *src* to file *dest*
link(src, dest)	Creates hard link from file *src* to file *dest*

There are many other functions in the os module; in fact, any function that's part of the POSIX standard and widely available on most Unix platforms is supported by Python on Unix. The interfaces to these routines follow the POSIX conventions. You can retrieve and set UIDs, PIDs, and process groups; control nice levels; create pipes; manipulate file descriptors; fork processes; wait for child processes; send signals to processes; use the **execv** variants; etc.

The os module also defines some important attributes that aren't functions:

- The os.name attribute defines the current version of the platform-specific operating-system interface. Registered values for os.name are 'posix', 'nt', 'dos', and 'mac'. It's different from sys.platform, which we discussed earlier in this chapter.

- os.error defines a class used when calls in the os module raise errors. When this exception is raised, the value of the exception contains two variables. The first is the number corresponding to the error (known as **errno**), and the second is a string message explaining it (known as **strerror**):

```
>>> os.rmdir('nonexistent_directory')       # how it usually shows up
Traceback (innermost last):
  File "<stdin>", line 1, in ?
os.error: (2, 'No such file or directory')
>>> try:                                     # we can catch the error and take
...     os.rmdir('nonexistent directory')    # it apart
... except os.error, value:
...     print value[0], value[1]
...
2 No such file or directory
```

- The os.environ dictionary contains key/value pairs corresponding to the environment variables of the shell from which Python was started. Because this environment is inherited by the commands that are invoked using the os.system call, modifying the os.environ dictionary modifies the environment:

```
>>> print os.environ['SHELL']
/bin/sh
>>> os.environ['STARTDIR'] = 'MyStartDir'
>>> os.system('echo $STARTDIR')             # 'echo %STARTDIR%' on DOS/Win
MyStartDir                                  # printed by the shell
0                                           # return code from echo
```

The os module also includes a set of strings that define portable ways to refer to directory-related operations, as shown in Table 8-8.

Table 8-8. String Attributes of the os Module

Attribute Name	Meaning and Value
curdir	A string that denotes the current directory: '.' on Unix, DOS, and Windows; ':' on the Mac
pardir	A string that denotes the parent directory: '..' on Unix, DOS, and Windows; '::' on the Mac
sep	The character that separates pathname components: '/' on Unix; '\' on DOS, Windows; ':' on the Mac

Table 8-8. String Attributes of the os Module (continued)

Attribute Name	Meaning and Value
altsep	An alternate character to sep when available; set to None on all systems except DOS and Windows, where it's '/'
pathsep	The character that separates path components: ':' on Unix; ';' on DOS and Windows

These strings are especially useful when combined with the functionality in the os.path module, which provides many functions that manipulate file paths (see Table 8-9). Note that the os.path module is an attribute of the os module; it's imported automatically when the os module is loaded, so you don't need to import it explicitly. The outputs of the examples in Table 8-9 correspond to code run on a Windows or DOS machine. On another platform, the appropriate path separators would be used instead.

Table 8-9. Most Frequently Used Functions from the os.path Module

Function Name	Behavior

split(*path*) is equivalent to the tuple: (dirname(*path*), basename(*path*))	Splits the given path into a pair consisting of a head and a tail; the head is the path up to the directory, and the tail is the filename:
	 `>>> os.path.split("h:/David/book/part2.doc"`
	 `('h:/David/book', 'part2.doc')`

join(*path*, ...)	Joins path components intelligently:
	 `>>> print os.path.join(os.getcwd(),`
	 `... os.pardir, 'backup', 'part2.doc')`
	 `h:\David\book\..\backup\part2.doc`

exists(*path*)	Returns true if *path* corresponds to an existing path

expanduser(*path*)	Expands the argument with an initial argument of ~ followed optionally by a username:
	 `>>> print os.path.expanduser('~/mydir')`
	 `h:\David\mydir`

expandvars(*path*)	Expands the *path* argument with the variables specified in the environment:
	 `>>> print os.path.expandvars('$TMP')`
	 `C:\TEMP`

isfile(*path*), isdir(*path*), islink(*path*), ismount(*path*)	Returns true if the specified *path* is a file, directory, link, or mount point, respectively

normpath(*path*)	Normalizes the given path, collapsing redundant separators and uplevel references:
	 `>>> print os.path.normpath("/foo/bar\\../tmp")`
	 `\foo\tmp`

samefile(*p*, *q*)	Returns true if both arguments refer to the same file

Table 8-9. Most Frequently Used Functions from the os.path Module (continued)

Function Name	Behavior

`walk(p, visit, arg)`	Calls the function `visit` with arguments (`arg`, `dirname`, `names`) for each directory in the directory tree rooted at `p` (including `p` itself, if it's a directory); the argument `dirname` specifies the visited directory; the argument `names` lists the files in the directory:
	
	`>>> def test_walk(arg, dirname, names):`
	`... print arg, dirname, names`
	`...`
	`>>> os.path.walk('..', test_walk, 'show')`
	`show ..\logs ['errors.log', 'access.log']`
	`show ..\cgi-bin ['test.cgi']`
	`...`

Copying Files and Directories: The shutil Module

The keen-eyed reader might have noticed that the os module, while it provides lots of file-related functions, doesn't include a copy function. On DOS, copying a file is basically the same thing as opening one file in read/binary modes, reading all its data, opening a second file in write/binary mode, and writing the data to the second file. On Unix and Windows, making that kind of copy fails to copy the so-called *stat bits* (permissions, modification times, etc.) associated with the file. On the Mac, that operation won't copy the resource fork, which contains data such as icons and dialog boxes. In other words, copying is just not so simple. Nevertheless, often you can get away with a fairly simple function that works on Windows, DOS, Unix, and Macs as long as you're manipulating just data files with no resource forks. That function, called copyfile, lives in the shutil module. It includes a few generally useful functions, shown in Table 8-10.

Table 8-10. Functions of the shutil Module

Function Name	Behavior
`copyfile(src, dest)`	Makes a copy of the file *src* and calls it *dest* (straight binary copy).
`copymode(src, dest)`	Copies mode information (permissions) from *src* to *dest*.
`copystat(src, dest)`	Copies all stat information (mode, utime) from *src* to *dest*.
`copy(src, dest)`	Copies data and mode information from *src* to *dest* (doesn't include the resource fork on Macs).
`copy2(src, dest)`	Copies data and stat information from *src* to *dest* (doesn't include the resource fork on Macs).
`copytree(src, dest, symlinks=0)`	Copies a directory recursively using copy2. The `symlinks` flag specifies whether symbolic links in the source tree must result in symbolic links in the destination tree, or whether the files being linked to must be copied. The destination directory must not already exist.

Table 8-10. Functions of the shutil Module (continued)

Function Name	Behavior
rmtree(*path*, *ignore_errors=0*, *onerror=None*)	Recursively deletes the directory indicated by *path*. If *ignore_error* is set to 0 (the default behavior), errors are ignored. Otherwise, if *onerror* is set, it's called to handle the error; if not, an exception is raised on error.

Internet-Related Modules

The Common Gateway Interface: The cgi module

Python programs often process forms from web pages. To make this task easy, the standard Python distribution includes a module called `cgi`. Chapter 10 includes an example of a Python script that uses the CGI.

Manipulating URLs: the urllib and urlparse modules

Universal resource locators are strings such as *http://www.python.org/* that are now ubiquitous.* Two modules, `urllib` and `urlparse`, provide tools for processing URLs.

`urllib` defines a few functions for writing programs that must be active users of the Web (robots, agents, etc.). These are listed in Table 8-11.

Table 8-11. Functions of the urllib Module

Function Name	Behavior

urlopen (*url* [, *data*])	Opens a network object denoted by a URL for reading; it can also open local files:
	`>>> page = urlopen('http://www.python.org')`
	`>>> page.readline()`
	`'<HTML>\012'`
	`>>> page.readline()`
	`'<!-- THIS PAGE IS AUTOMATICALLY GENERATED.`
	`DO NOT EDIT. -->\012'`

urlretrieve (*url* [, *filename*] [, *hook*])	Copies a network object denoted by a URL to a local file (uses a cache):
	`>>> urllib.urlretrieve('http://www.python.org/',`
	`'wwwpython.html')`

urlcleanup()	Cleans up the cache used by urlretrieve

quote(*string* [, *safe*])	Replaces special characters in string using the %xx escape; the optional safe parameter specifies additional characters that shouldn't be quoted: its default value is:
	`>>> quote('this & that @ home')`
	`'this%20%26%20that%20%40%20home'`

---

* The syntax for URLs was designed in the early days of the Web with the expectation that users would rarely see them and would instead click on hyperlinks tagged with the URLs, which would then be processed by computer programs. Had their future in advertising been predicted, a syntax making them more easily pronounced would probably have been chosen!

Table 8-11. Functions of the urllib Module (continued)

Function Name	Behavior
quote_plus (*string* [, *safe*])	Like quote(), but also replaces spaces by plus signs

unquote
(*string*)
	Replaces %xx escapes by their single-character equivalent:
	`>>> unquote('this%20%26%20that%20%40%20home')`
	`'this & that @ home'`

urlencode
(*dict*)
	Converts a dictionary to a URL-encoded string, suitable to pass to
	urlopen() as the optional data argument:
	`>>> locals()`
	`{'urllib': <module 'urllib'>, '__doc__': None, 'x':`
	`3, '__name__': '__main__', '__builtins__': <module`
	`'__builtin__'>}`
	`>>> urllib.urlencode(locals())`
	`'urllib=%3cmodule+%27urllib%27%3e&__doc__=None&x=3&`
	`__name__=__main__&__builtins__=%3cmodule+%27`
	`__builtin__%27%3e'`

urlparse defines a few functions that simplify taking URLs apart and putting new URLs together. These are listed in Table 8-12.

Table 8-12. Functions of the urlparse Module

Function Name	Behavior

urlparse(*urlstring*
[, *default_scheme*
[,*allow fragments*]])
	Parses a URL into six components, returning a six tuple:
	(addressing scheme, network location, path, parameters, query,
	fragment identifier):
	`>>> urlparse('http://www.python.org/FAQ.html')`
	`('http', 'www.python.org', '/FAQ.html', '', '', '')`

urlunparse(*tuple*)	Constructs a URL string from a tuple as returned by urlparse()

urljoin(*base*,
url
[,*allow fragments*])
	Constructs a full (absolute) URL by combining a base URL
	(*base*) with a relative URL (*url*):
	`>>> urljoin('http://www.python.org', 'doc/lib')`
	`'http://www.python.org/doc/lib'`

Specific Internet protocols

The most commonly used protocols built on top of TCP/IP are supported with modules named after them. These are the httplib module (for processing web pages with the HTTP protocol); the ftplib module (for transferring files using the FTP protocol); the gopherlib module (for browsing Gopher servers); the poplib and imaplib modules for reading mail files on POP3 and IMAP servers, respectively; the nntplib module for reading Usenet news from NNTP servers; the smtplib protocol for communicating with standard mail servers. We'll use some of these in Chapter 9. There are also modules that can build Internet servers, specifically a generic socket-based IP server (`socketserver`), a simple web server (`SimpleHTTPServer`), and a CGI-compliant HTTP server (`CGIHTTPSserver`).

Processing Internet data

Once you use an Internet protocol to obtain files from the Internet (or before you serve them to the Internet), you must process these files. They come in many different formats. Table 8-13 lists each module in the standard library that processes a specific kind of Internet-related file format (there are others for sound and image format processing: see the *Library Reference*).

Table 8-13. Modules Dedicated to Internet File Processing

Module Name	File Format
sgmllib	A simple parser for SGML files
htmllib	A parser for HTML documents
xmllib	A parser for XML documents
formatter	Generic output formatter and device interface
rfc822	Parse RFC-822 mail headers (i.e., `"Subject: hi there!"`)
mimetools	Tools for parsing MIME-style message bodies (a.k.a. file attachments)
multifile	Support for reading files that contain distinct parts
binhex	Encode and decode files in binhex4 format
uu	Encode and decode files in uuencode format
binascii	Convert between binary and various ASCII-encoded representations
xdrlib	Encode and decode XDR data
mailcap	Mailcap file handling
mimetypes	Mapping of filename extensions to MIME types
base64	Encode and decode MIME base64 encoding
quopri	Encode and decode MIME quoted-printable encoding
mailbox	Read various mailbox formats
mimify	Convert mail messages to and from MIME format

Dealing with Binary Data: The struct Module

A frequent question about file manipulation is "How do I process binary files in Python?" The answer to that question usually involves the `struct` module. It has a simple interface, since it exports just three functions: `pack`, `unpack`, and `calcsize`.

Let's start with the task of decoding a binary file. Imagine a binary file *bindat.dat* that contains data in a specific format: first there's a float corresponding to a version number, then a long integer corresponding to the size of the data, and then the number of unsigned bytes corresponding to the actual data. The key to using the `struct` module is to define a "format" string, which corresponds to the format of the data you wish to read, and find out which subset of the file corresponds to that data. For our example, we could use:

```
import struct

data = open('bindat.dat').read()
start, stop = 0, struct.calcsize('fl')
version_number, num_bytes = struct.unpack('fl', data[start:stop])
start, stop = stop, start + struct.calcsize('B'*num_bytes)
bytes = struct.unpack('B'*num_bytes, data[start:stop])
```

`'f'` is a format string for a single floating point number (a C float, to be precise), `'l'` is for a long integer, and `'B'` is a format string for an unsigned char. The available unpack format strings are listed in Table 8-14. Consult the *Library Reference* for usage details.

Table 8-14. Format Codes Used by the struct Module

Format	C Type	Python
x	pad byte	No value
c	char	String of length 1
b	signed char	Integer
B	unsigned char	Integer
h	short	Integer
H	unsigned short	Integer
i	int	Integer
I	unsigned int	Integer
l	long	Integer
L	unsigned long	Integer
f	float	Float
d	double	Float
s	char[]	String
p	char[]	String
P	void *	Integer

At this point, bytes is a tuple of **num_bytes** Python integers. If we know that the data is in fact storing characters, we could either use `chars = map(chr, bytes)`. To be more efficient, we could change the last unpack to use `'c'` instead of `'B'`, which would do the conversion for us and return a tuple of **num_bytes** single-character strings. More efficiently still, we could use a format string that specifies a string of characters of a specified length, such as:

```
chars = struct.unpack(str(num_bytes)+'s', data[start:stop])
```

The packing operation is the exact converse; instead of taking a format string and a data string, and returning a tuple of unpacked values, it takes a format string and a variable number of arguments and packs those arguments using that format string into a new "packed" string.

Note that the **struct** module can process data that's encoded with either kind of byte-ordering,* thus allowing you to write platform-independent binary file manipulation code. For large files, consider using the **array** module.

Debugging, Timing, Profiling

These last few modules will help debug, time, and optimize your Python programs.

The first task is, not surprisingly, debugging. Python's standard distribution includes a debugger called pdb. Using pdb is fairly straightforward. You import the pdb module and call its run method with the Python code the debugger should execute. For example, if you're debugging the program in *spam.py* from Chapter 6, do this:

```
>>> import spam                          # import the module we wish to debug
>>> import pdb                           # import pdb
>>> pdb.run('instance = spam.Spam()')   # start pdb with a statement to run
> <string>(0)?()
(Pdb) break spam.Spam.__init__                    # we can set break points
(Pdb) next
> <string>(1)?()
(Pdb) n                                           # 'n' is short for 'next'
> spam.py(3)__init__()
-> def __init__(self):
(Pdb) n
> spam.py(4)__init__()
-> Spam.numInstances = Spam.numInstances + 1
(Pdb) list                                        # show the source code listing
  1     class Spam:
  2         numInstances = 0
  3 B       def __init__(self):              # note the B for Breakpoint
  4 ->          Spam.numInstances = Spam.numInstances + 1  # where we are
  5         def printNumInstances(self):
  6             print "Number of instances created: ", Spam.numInstances
  7
[EOF]
(Pdb) where                                       # show the calling stack
  <string>(1)?()
> spam.py(4)__init__()
```

---

* The order with which computers list multibyte words depends on the chip used (so much for standards). Intel and DEC systems use so-called little-endian ordering, while Motorola and Sun-based systems use big-endian ordering. Network transmissions also use big-endian ordering, so the struct module comes in handy when doing network I/O on PCs.

```
-> Spam.numInstances = Spam.numInstances + 1
(Pdb) Spam.numInstances = 10          # note that we can modify variables
(Pdb) print Spam.numInstances         # while the program is being debugged
10
(Pdb) continue                        # this continues until the next break-
--Return--                            # point, but there is none, so we're
> <string>(1)?()->None                # done
(Pdb) c                               # this ends up quitting Pdb
<spam.Spam instance at 80ee60>        # this is the returned instance
>>> instance.numInstances             # note that the change to numInstance
11                                    # was *before* the increment op
```

As the session above shows, with **pdb** you can list the current code being
debugged (with an arrow pointing to the line about to be executed), examine variables, modify variables, and set breakpoints. The *Library Reference*'s Chapter 9
covers the debugger in detail.

Even when a program is working, it can sometimes be too slow. If you know what
the bottleneck in your program is, and you know of alternative ways to code the
same algorithm, then you might time the various alternative methods to find out
which is fastest. The `time` module, which is part of the standard distribution, provides many time-manipulation routines. We'll use just one, which returns the time
since a fixed "epoch" with the highest precision available on your machine. As
we'll use just relative times to compare algorithms, the precision isn't all that
important. Here's two different ways to create a list of 10,000 zeros:

```
def lots_of_appends():
  zeros = []
  for i in range(10000):
    zeros.append(0)

def one_multiply():
  zeros = [0] * 10000
```

How can we time these two solutions? Here's a simple way:

```
import time, makezeros

def do_timing(num_times, funcs):
    totals = {}
    for func in funcs: totals[func] = 0.0
    for x in range(num_times):
        for func in funcs:
            starttime = time.time()        # record starting time
            apply(func)
            stoptime = time.time()         # record ending time
            elapsed = stoptime-starttime   # difference yields time elapsed
            totals[func] = totals[func] + elapsed
    for func in funcs:
        print "Running %s %d times took %.3f seconds" % (func.__name__,
                                                         num_times,
                                                         totals[func])
do_timing(100, (makezeros.lots_of_appends, makezeros.one_multiply))
```

And running this program yields:

```
csh> python timings.py
Running lots_of_appends 100 times took 7.891 seconds
Running one_multiply 100 times took 0.120 seconds
```

As you might have suspected, a single list multiplication is much faster than lots of appends. Note that in timings, it's always a good idea to compare lots of runs of functions instead of just one. Otherwise the timings are likely to be heavily influenced by things that have nothing to do with the algorithm, such as network traffic on the computer or GUI events.

What if you've written a complex program, and it's running slower than you'd like, but you're not sure what the problem spot is? In those cases, what you need to do is *profile* the program: determine which parts of the program are the time-sinks and see if they can be optimized, or if the program structure can be modified to even out the bottlenecks. The Python distribution includes just the right tool for that, the `profile` module, documented in the *Library Reference*. Assuming that you want to profile a given function in the current namespace, do this:

```
>>> from timings import *
>>> from makezeros import *
>>> profile.run('do_timing(100, (lots_of_appends, one_multiply))')
Running lots_of_appends 100 times took 8.773 seconds
Running one_multiply 100 times took 0.090 seconds
         203 function calls in 8.823 CPU seconds

   Ordered by: standard name

   ncalls  tottime  percall  cumtime  percall filename:lineno(function)
      100    8.574    0.086    8.574    0.086 makezeros.py:1(lots_of_appends)
      100    0.101    0.001    0.101    0.001 makezeros.py:6(one_multiply)
        1    0.001    0.001    8.823    8.823 profile:0(do_timing(100,
                                                      (lots_of_appends, one_multiply)))
        0    0.000             0.000           profile:0(profiler)
        1    0.000    0.000    8.821    8.821 python:0(194.C.2)
        1    0.147    0.147    8.821    8.821 timings.py:2(do_timing)
```

As you can see, this gives a fairly complicated listing, which includes such things as per-call time spent in each function and the number of calls made to each function. In complex programs, the profiler can help find surprising inefficiencies. Optimizing Python programs is beyond the scope of this book; if you're interested, however, check the Python newsgroup: periodically, a user asks for help speeding up a program and a spontaneous contest starts up, with interesting advice from expert users.

Exercises

1. *Describing a directory.* Write a function that takes a directory name and describes the contents of the directory, recursively (in other words, for each file, print the name and size, and proceed down any eventual directories).

2. *Modifying the prompt.* Modify your interpreter so that the prompt is, instead of the >>> string, a string describing the current directory and the count of the number of lines entered in the current Python session.

3. *Avoiding regular expressions.* Write a program that obeys the same requirements as *pepper.py* but doesn't use regular expressions to do the job. This is somewhat difficult, but a useful exercise in building program logic.

4. *Wrapping a text file with a class.* Write a class that takes a filename and reads the data in the corresponding file as text. Make it so that this class has three methods: `paragraph`, `line`, `word`, each of which take an integer argument, so that if `mywrapper` is an instance of this class, printing `mywrapper.paragraph[0]` prints the first paragraph of the file, `mywrapper.line[-2]` prints the next-to-last line in the file, and `mywrapper.word[3]` prints the fourth word in the file.

5. *Common tasks.* These exercises don't have solutions in Appendix C, but instead are selected from the examples shown in Chapter 9. Try them now before you read Chapter 9 if you wish to be challenged!

   — How would you make a copy of a list object? How about a dictionary?

   — How would you sort a list? How about randomizing the order of its elements?

   — If you've heard of a stack data structure before, how would you code it?

   — Write a program to count the number of lines in a file.

   — Write a program that prints all the lines in a file starting with a # character.

   — Write a program that prints the fourth word in each line of a file.

   — Write a program that counts the number of times a given word exists in a file.

   — Write a program that looks for every occurrence of a string in all the files in a directory.

9

Common Tasks in Python

In this chapter:
- *Data Structure Manipulations*
- *Manipulating Files*
- *Manipulating Programs*
- *Internet-Related Activities*
- *Bigger Examples*
- *Exercises*

At this point, we have covered the syntax of Python, its basic data types, and many of our favorite functions in the Python library. This chapter assumes that all the basic components of the language are at least understood and presents some ways in which Python is, in addition to being elegant and "cool," just plain useful. We present a variety of tasks common to Python programmers. These tasks are grouped by categories—data structure manipulations, file manipulations, etc.

Data Structure Manipulations

One of Python's greatest features is that it provides the list, tuple, and dictionary built-in types. They are so flexible and easy to use that once you've grown used to them, you'll find yourself reaching for them automatically.

Making Copies Inline

Due to Python's reference management scheme, the statement a = b doesn't make a copy of the object referenced by b; instead, it makes a new reference to that object. Sometimes a new copy of an object, not just a shared reference, is needed. How to do this depends on the type of the object in question. The simplest way to make copies of lists and tuples is somewhat odd. If myList is a list, then to make a copy of it, you can do:

```
newList = myList[:]
```

which you can read as "slice from beginning to end," since you'll remember from Chapter 2, *Types and Operators*, that the default index for the start of a slice is the beginning of the sequence (0), and the default index for the end of a slice is the end of sequence. Since tuples support the same slicing operation as lists, this same technique can also copy tuples. Dictionaries, on the other hand, don't support slicing. To make a copy of a dictionary myDict, you can use:

```
newDict = {}
for key in myDict.keys():
    newDict[key] = myDict[key]
```

This is such a common task that a new method was added to the dictionary object in Python 1.5, the copy() method, which performs this task. So the preceding code can be replaced with the single statement:

```
newDict = myDict.copy()
```

Another common dictionary operation is also now a standard dictionary feature. If you have a dictionary oneDict, and want to update it with the contents of a different dictionary otherDict, simply type oneDict.update(otherDict). This is the equivalent of:

```
for key in otherDict.keys():
    oneDict[key] = otherDict[key]
```

If oneDict shared some keys with otherDict before the update() operation, the old values associated with the keys in oneDict are obliterated by the update. This may be what you want to do (it usually is, which is why this behavior was chosen and why it was called "update"). If it isn't, the right thing to do might be to complain (raise an exception), as in:

```
def mergeWithoutOverlap(oneDict, otherDict):
    newDict = oneDict.copy()
    for key in otherDict.keys():
        if key in oneDict.keys():
            raise ValueError, "the two dictionaries are sharing keys!"
        newDict[key] = otherDict[key]
    return newDict
```

or, alternatively, combine the values of the two dictionaries, with a tuple, for example:

```
def mergeWithOverlap(oneDict, otherDict):
    newDict = oneDict.copy()
    for key in otherDict.keys():
        if key in oneDict.keys():
            newDict[key] = oneDict[key], otherDict[key]
        else:
            newDict[key] = otherDict[key]
    return newDict
```

To illustrate the differences between the preceding three algorithms, consider the following two dictionaries:

```
phoneBook1 = {'michael': '555-1212', 'mark': '554-1121', 'emily': '556-0091'}
phoneBook2 = {'latoya': '555-1255', 'emily': '667-1234'}
```

If phoneBook1 is possibly out of date, and phoneBook2 is more up to date but less complete, the right usage is probably phoneBook1.update(phoneBook2). If the two phoneBooks are supposed to have nonoverlapping sets of keys, using newBook = mergeWithoutOverlap(phoneBook1, phoneBook2) lets you know if that assumption is wrong. Finally, if one is a set of home phone numbers and the other a set of office phone numbers, chances are newBook = mergeWithOverlap(phoneBook1, phoneBook2) is what you want, as long as the subsequent code that uses newBook can deal with the fact that newBook['emily'] is the tuple ('556-0091', '667-1234').

Making Copies: The copy Module

Back to making copies: the [:] and .copy() trickswill get you copies in 90% of the cases. If you are writing functions that, in true Python spirit, can deal with arguments of any type, it's sometimes necessary to make copies of X, regardless of what X is. In comes the copy module. It provides two functions, copy and deepcopy. The first is just like the [:] sequence slice operation or the copy method of dictionaries. The second is more subtle and has to do with deeply nested structures (hence the term *deepcopy*). Take the example of copying a list listOne by slicing it from beginning to end using the [:] construct. This technique makes a new list that contains references to the same objects contained in the original list. If the contents of that original list are immutable objects, such as numbers or strings, the copy is as good as a "true" copy. However, suppose that the first element in listOne is itself a dictionary (or any other mutable object). The first element of the copy of listOne is a new reference to the *same* dictionary. So if you then modify that dictionary, the modification is evident in both listOne and the copy of listOne. An example makes it much clearer:

```
>>> import copy
>>> listOne = [{"name": "Willie", "city": "Providence, RI"}, 1, "tomato", 3.0]
>>> listTwo = listOne[:]
>>> listThree = copy.deepcopy(listOne)          # or listTwo=copy.copy(listOne)
>>> listOne.append("kid")
>>> listOne[0]["city"] = "San Francisco, CA"
>>> print listOne, listTwo, listThree
[{'name': 'Willie', 'city': 'San Francisco, CA'}, 1, 'tomato', 3.0, 'kid']
[{'name': 'Willie', 'city': 'San Francisco, CA'}, 1, 'tomato', 3.0]
[{'name': 'Willie', 'city': 'Providence, RI'}, 1, 'tomato', 3.0]
```

As you can see, modifying listOne directly modified only listOne. Modifying the first entry of the list *referenced by* listOne led to changes in listTwo, but not in listThree; that's the difference between a shallow copy ([:]) and a deepcopy. The `copy` module functions know how to copy all the built-in types that are reasonably copyable,* including classes and instances.

Sorting and Randomizing

In Chapter 2, you saw that lists have a sort method that does an in-place sort. Sometimes you want to iterate over the sorted contents of a list, without disturbing the contents of this list. Or you may want to list the sorted contents of a tuple. Because tuples are immutable, an operation such as `sort`, which modifies it in place, is not allowed. The only solution is to make a list copy of the elements, sort the list copy, and work with the sorted copy, as in:

```
listCopy = list(myTuple)
listCopy.sort()
for item in listCopy:
    print item                          # or whatever needs doing
```

This solution is also the way to deal with data structures that have no inherent order, such as dictionaries. One of the reasons that dictionaries are so fast is that the implementation reserves the right to change the order of the keys in the dictionary. It's really not a problem, however, given that you can iterate over the keys of a dictionary using an intermediate copy of the keys of the dictionary:

```
keys = myDict.keys()                    # returns an unsorted list of
                                        # the keys in the dict
keys.sort()
for key in keys:                        # print key, value pairs
    print key, myDict[key]              # sorted by key
```

The `sort` method on lists uses the standard Python comparison scheme. Sometimes, however, that scheme isn't what's needed, and you need to sort according to some other procedure. For example, when sorting a list of words, case (lower versus UPPER) may not be significant. The standard comparison of text strings, however, says that all uppercase letters "come before" all lowercase letters, so `'Baby'` is "less than" `'apple'` but `'baby'` is "greater than" `'apple'`. In order to do a case-independent sort, you need to define a comparison function that takes two arguments, and returns −1, 0, or 1 depending on whether the first argument is smaller than, equal to, or greater than the second argument. So, for our case-independent sorting, you can use:

```
>>> def caseIndependentSort(something, other):
...     something, other  = string.lower(something), string.lower(other)
...     return cmp(something, other)
...
>>> testList = ['this', 'is', 'A', 'sorted', 'List']
>>> testList.sort()
```

---

* Some objects don't qualify as "reasonably copyable," such as modules, file objects, and sockets. Remember that file objects are different from files on disk.

```
>>> print testList
['A', 'List', 'is', 'sorted', 'this']
>>> testList.sort(caseIndependentSort)
>>> print testList
['A', 'is', 'List', 'sorted', 'this']
```

We're using the built-in function cmp, which does the hard part of figuring out that 'a' comes before 'b', 'b' before 'c', etc. Our sort function simply lowercases both items and sorts the lowercased versions, which is one way of making the comparison case-independent. Also note that the lowercasing conversion is local to the comparison function, so the elements in the list aren't modified by the sort.

Randomizing: The random Module

What about randomizing a sequence, such as a list of lines? The easiest way to randomize a sequence is to repeatedly use the choice function in the random module, which returns a random element from the sequence it receives as an argument.[*] In order to avoid getting the same line multiple times, remember to remove the chosen item. When manipulating a list object, use the remove method:

```
while myList:                          # will stop looping when myList is empty
    element = random.choice(myList)
    myList.remove(element)
    print element,
```

If you need to randomize a nonlist object, it's usually easiest to convert that object to a list and randomize the list version of the same data, rather than come up with a new strategy for each data type. This might seem a wasteful strategy, given that it involves building intermediate lists that might be quite large. In general, however, what seems large to you probably won't seem so to the computer, thanks to the reference system. Also, consider the time saved by not having to come up with a different strategy for each data type! Python is designed to save time; if that means running a slightly slower or bigger program, so be it. If you're handling enormous amounts of data, it may be worthwhile to optimize. But never optimize until the need for optimization is clear; *that* would be a waste of time.

Making New Data Structures

The last point about not reinventing the wheel is especially true when it comes to data structures. For example, Python lists and dictionaries might not be the lists and dictionaries or mappings you're used to, but you should avoid designing your own data structure if these structures will suffice. The algorithms they use have been tested under wide ranges of conditions, and they're fast and stable. Sometimes, however, the interface to these algorithms isn't convenient for a particular task.

---

[*] The random module provides many other useful functions, such as the random function, which returns a random floating-point number between 0 and 1. Check a reference source for details.

For example, computer-science textbooks often describe algorithms in terms of other data structures such as queues and stacks. To use these algorithms, it may make sense to come up with a data structure that has the same methods as these data structures (such as `pop` and `push` for stacks or `enqueue`/`dequeue` for queues). However, it also makes sense to reuse the built-in list type in the implementation of a stack. In other words, you need something that acts like a stack but is based on a list. The easiest solution is to use a class wrapper around a list. For a minimal stack implementation, you can do this:

```
class Stack:
    def __init__(self, data):
        self._data = list(data)
    def push(self, item):
        self._data.append(item)
    def pop(self):
        item = self._data[-1]
        del self._data[-1]
        return item
```

The following is simple to write, to understand, to read, and to use:

```
>>> thingsToDo = Stack(['write to mom', 'invite friend over', 'wash the
kid'])
>>> thingsToDo.push('do the dishes')
>>> print thingsToDo.pop()
do the dishes
>>> print thingsToDo.pop()
wash the kid
```

Two standard Python naming conventions are used in the `Stack` class above. The first is that class names start with an uppercase letter, to distinguish them from functions. The other is that the `_data` attribute starts with an underscore. This is a half-way point between public attributes (which don't start with an underscore), private attributes (which start with two underscores; see Chapter 6, *Classes*), and Python-reserved identifiers (which both start and end with two underscores). What it means is that `_data` is an attribute of the class that shouldn't be needed by clients of the class. The class designer expects such "pseudo-private" attributes to be used only by the class methods and by the methods of any eventual subclass.

Making New Lists and Dictionaries: The UserList and UserDict Modules

The `Stack` class presented earlier does its minimal job just fine. It assumes a fairly minimal definition of what a stack is, specifically, something that supports just two operations, a `push` and a `pop`. Quickly, however, you find that some of the features of lists are really nice, such as the ability to iterate over all the elements using the `for...in...` construct. This can be done by reusing existing code. In this case, you should use the `UserList` class defined in the `UserList` module as a class from which the `Stack` can be derived. The library also includes a `UserDict` module that is a class wrapper around a dictionary. In general, they are there to be specialized by subclassing. In our case:

```
# import the UserList class from the UserList module
from UserList import UserList

# subclass the UserList class
class Stack(UserList):
    push = UserList.append
    def pop(self):
        item = self[-1]                     # uses __getitem__
        del self[-1]
        return item
```

This `Stack` is a subclass of the `UserList` class. The `UserList` class implements the behavior of the [] brackets by defining the special __getitem__ and __delitem__ methods among others, which is why the code in `pop` works. You don't need to define your own __init__ method because `UserList` defines a perfectly good default. Finally, the `push` method is defined just by saying that it's the same as `UserList`'s `append` method. Now we can do list-like things as well as stack-like things:

```
>>> thingsToDo = Stack(['write to mom', 'invite friend over', 'wash the
kid'])
>>> print thingsToDo                # inherited from UserList
['write to mom', 'invite friend over', 'wash the kid']
>>> thingsToDo.pop()
'wash the kid'
>>> thingsToDo.push('change the oil')
>>> for chore in thingsToDo:        # we can also iterate over the contents
...     print chore                 # as "for .. in .." uses __getitem__
...
write to mom
invite friend over
change the oil
```

 As this book was being written, Guido van Rossum announced that in Python 1.5.2 (and subsequent versions), list objects now have an additional method called **pop**, which behaves just like the one here. It also has an optional argument that specifies what index to use to do the pop (with the default being the last element in the list).

Manipulating Files

Scripting languages were designed in part in order to help people do repetitive tasks quickly and simply. One of the common things webmasters, system administrators, and programmers need to do is to take a set of files, select a subset of those files, do some sort of manipulation on this subset, and write the output to one or a set of output files. (For example, in each file in a directory, find the last word of every other line that starts with something other than the # character, and print it along with the name of the file.) This is a task for which special-purpose tools have been developed, such as *sed* and *awk*. We find that Python does the job just fine using very simple tools.

Doing Something to Each Line in a File

The `sys` module is most helpful when it comes to dealing with an input file, parsing the text it contains and processing it. Among its attributes are three file objects, called `sys.stdin`, `sys.stdout`, and `sys.stderr`. The names come from the notion of the three *streams*, called standard in, standard out, and standard error, which are used to connect command line tools. Standard output (`stdout`) is used by every `print` statement. It's a file object with all the output methods of file objects opened in write mode, such as `write` and `writelines`. The other often-used stream is standard in (`stdin`), which is also a file object, but with the input methods, such as `read`, `readline`, and `readlines`. For example, the following script counts all the lines in the file that is "piped in":

```
import sys
data = sys.stdin.readlines()
print "Counted", len(data), "lines."
```

On Unix, you could test it by doing something like:

```
% cat countlines.py | python countlines.py
Counted 3 lines.
```

On Windows or DOS, you'd do:

```
C:\> type countlines.py | python countlines.py
Counted 3 lines.
```

The `readlines` function is useful when implementing simple filter operations. Here are a few examples of such filter operations:

Finding all lines that start with a #
```
import sys
for line in sys.stdin.readlines():
    if line[0] == '#':
        print line,
```

Note that a final comma is needed after the `print` statement because the `line` string already includes a newline character as its last character.

Extracting the fourth column of a file (where columns are defined by whitespace)
```
import sys, string
for line in sys.stdin.readlines():
```

```
words = string.split(line)
if len(words) >= 4:
    print words[3]
```

We look at the length of the words list to find if there are indeed at least four words. The last two lines could also be replaced by the try/except idiom, which is quite common in Python:

```
try:
    print words[3]
except IndexError:                      # there aren't enough words
    pass
```

Extracting the fourth column of a file, where columns are separated by colons, and lowercasing it

```
import sys, string
for line in sys.stdin.readlines():
    words = string.split(line, ':')
    if len(words) >= 4:
        print string.lower(words[3])
```

Printing the first 10 lines, the last 10 lines, and every other line

```
import sys, string
lines = sys.stdin.readlines()
sys.stdout.writelines(lines[:10])       # first ten lines
sys.stdout.writelines(lines[-10:])      # last ten lines
for lineIndex in range(0, len(lines), 2):  # get 0, 2, 4, ...
    sys.stdout.write(lines[lineIndex])  # get the indexed line
```

Counting the number of times the word "Python" occurs in a file

```
import string
text = open(fname).read()
print string.count(text, 'Python')
```

Changing a list of columns into a list of rows

In this more complicated example, the task is to "transpose" a file; imagine you have a file that looks like:

```
Name:   Willie   Mark   Guido   Mary   Rachel   Ahmed
Level:    5        4       3      1       6        4
Tag#:    1234     4451    5515   5124    1881     5132
```

And you really want it to look like the following instead:

```
Name:  Level:  Tag#:
Willie 5       1234
Mark   4       4451
...
```

You could use code like the following:

```
import sys, string
lines = sys.stdin.readlines()
wordlists = []
for line in lines:
    words = string.split(line)
    wordlists.append(words)
```

```
for row in range(len(wordlists[0])):
    for col in range(len(wordlists)):
        print wordlists[col][row] + '\t',
    print
```

Of course, you should really use much more defensive programming techniques to deal with the possibility that not all lines have the same number of
words in them, that there may be missing data, etc. Those techniques are task-
specific and are left as an exercise to the reader.

Choosing chunk sizes

All the preceding examples assume you can read the entire file at once (that's
what the `readlines` call expects). In some cases, however, that's not possible, for
example when processing really huge files on computers with little memory, or
when dealing with files that are constantly being appended to (such as log files).
In such cases, you can use a `while`/`readline` combination, where some of the
file is read a bit at a time, until the end of file is reached. In dealing with files that
aren't line-oriented, you must read the file a character at a time:

```
# read character by character
while 1:
    next = sys.stdin.read(1)            # read a one-character string
    if not next:                        # or an empty string at EOF
        break
    Process character 'next'
```

Notice that the `read()` method on file objects returns an empty string at end of
file, which breaks out of the `while` loop. Most often, however, the files you'll deal
with consist of line-based data and are processed a line at a time:

```
# read line by line
while 1:
    next = sys.stdin.readline()         # read a one-line string
    if not next:                        # or an empty string at EOF
        break
    Process line 'next'
```

Doing Something to a Set of Files Specified on the Command Line

Being able to read `stdin` is a great feature; it's the foundation of the Unix toolset.
However, one input is not always enough: many tasks need to be performed on
sets of files. This is usually done by having the Python program parse the list of
arguments sent to the script as command-line options. For example, if you type:

```
% python myScript.py input1.txt input2.txt input3.txt output.txt
```

you might think that *myScript.py* wants to do something with the first three input files and write a new file, called *output.txt*. Let's see what the beginning of such a program could look like:

```
import sys
inputfilenames, outputfilename = sys.argv[1:-1], sys.argv[-1]
for inputfilename in inputfilenames:
    inputfile = open(inputfilename, "r")
    do_something_with_input(inputfile)
outputfile = open(outputfilename, "w")
write_results(outputfile)
```

The second line extracts parts of the **argv** attribute of the **sys** module. Recall that it's a list of the words on the command line that called the current program. It starts with the name of the script. So, in the example above, the value of **sys.argv** is:

```
['myScript.py', 'input1.txt', 'input2.txt', 'input3.txt', 'output.txt'].
```

The script assumes that the command line consists of one or more input files and one output file. So the slicing of the input file names starts at 1 (to skip the name of the script, which isn't an input to the script in most cases), and stops before the last word on the command line, which is the name of the output file. The rest of the script should be pretty easy to understand (but won't work until you provide the **do_something_with_input()** and **write_results()** functions).

Note that the preceding script doesn't actually read in the data from the files, but passes the file object down to a function to do the real work. Such a function often uses the **readlines()** method on file objects, which returns a list of the lines in that file. A generic version of **do_something_with_input()** is:

```
def do_something_with_input(inputfile):
    for line in inputfile.readlines()
        process(line)
```

Processing Each Line of One or More Files: The fileinput Module

The combination of this idiom with the preceding one regarding opening each file in the **sys.argv[1:]** list is so common that Python 1.5 introduced a new module that's designed to help do just this task. It's called **fileinput** and works like this:

```
import fileinput
for line in fileinput.input():
    process(line)
```

The **fileinput.input()** call parses the arguments on the command line, and if there are no arguments to the script, uses **sys.stdin** instead. It also provides a bunch of useful functions that let you know which file and line number you're currently manipulating:

```
import fileinput, sys, string
# take the first argument out of sys.argv and assign it to searchterm
searchterm, sys.argv[1:] = sys.argv[1], sys.argv[2:]
for line in fileinput.input():
    num_matches = string.count(line, searchterm)
    if num_matches:                          # a nonzero count means there was a match
        print "found '%s' %d times in %s on line %d." % (searchterm, num_matches,
            fileinput.filename(), fileinput.filelineno())
```

If this script were called *mygrep.py*, it could be used as follows:

```
% python mygrep.py in *.py
found 'in' 2 times in countlines.py on line 2.
found 'in' 2 times in countlines.py on line 3.
found 'in' 2 times in mygrep.py on line 1.
found 'in' 4 times in mygrep.py on line 4.
found 'in' 2 times in mygrep.py on line 5.
found 'in' 2 times in mygrep.py on line 7.
found 'in' 3 times in mygrep.py on line 8.
found 'in' 3 times in mygrep.py on line 12.
```

Filenames and Directories

We have now covered reading existing files, and if you remember the discussion on the open built-in function in Chapter 2, you know how to create new files. There are a lot of tasks, however, that need different kinds of file manipulations, such as directory and path management and removing files. Your two best friends in such cases are the os and os.path modules described in Chapter 8, *Built-in Tools*.

Let's take a typical example: you have lots of files, all of which have a space in their name, and you'd like to replace the spaces with underscores. All you really need is the os.curdir attribute (which returns an operating-system specific string that corresponds to the current directory), the os.listdir function (which returns the list of filenames in a specified directory), and the os.rename function:

```
import os, string
if len(sys.argv) == 1:                  # if no filenames are specified,
    filenames = os.listdir(os.curdir)   #   use current dir
else:                                   # otherwise, use files specified
    filenames = sys.argv[1:]            #   on the command line
for filename in filenames:
    if ' ' in filename:
        newfilename = string.replace(filename, ' ', '_')
        print "Renaming", filename, "to", newfilename, "..."
        os.rename(filename, newfilename)
```

This program works fine, but it reveals a certain Unix-centrism. That is, if you call it with wildcards, such as:

```
python despacify.py *.txt
```

you find that on Unix machines, it renames all the files with names with spaces in them and that end with *.txt.* In a DOS-style shell, however, this won't work because the shell normally used in DOS and Windows doesn't convert from **.txt* to the list of filenames; it expects the program to do it. This is called *globbing,* because the * is said to match a glob of characters.

Matching Sets of Files: The glob Module

The `glob` module exports a single function, also called `glob`, which takes a file-name pattern and returns a list of all the filenames that match that pattern (in the current working directory):

```
import sys, glob, operator
print sys.argv[1:]
sys.argv = reduce(operator.add, map(glob.glob, sys.argv))
print sys.argv[1:]
```

Running this on Unix and DOS shows that on Unix, the Python `glob` didn't do anything because the globbing was done by the Unix shell before Python was invoked, and on DOS, Python's globbing came up with the same answer:

```
/usr/python/book$ python showglob.py *.py
['countlines.py', 'mygrep.py', 'retest.py', 'showglob.py', 'testglob.py']
['countlines.py', 'mygrep.py', 'retest.py', 'showglob.py', 'testglob.py']

C:\python\book> python showglob.py *.py
['*.py']
['countlines.py', 'mygrep.py', 'retest.py', 'showglob.py', 'testglob.py']
```

This script isn't trivial, though, because it uses two conceptually difficult operations; a `map` followed by a `reduce`. `map` was mentioned in Chapter 4, *Functions*, but `reduce` is new to you at this point (unless you have background in LISP-type languages). `map` is a function that takes a callable object (usually a function) and a sequence, calls the callable object with each element of the sequence in turn, and returns a list containing the values returned by the function. For an graphical representation of what `map` does, see Figure 9-1.*

`map` is needed here (or something equivalent) because you don't know how many arguments were entered on the command line (e.g., it could have been `*.py *.txt *.doc`). So the `glob.glob` function is called with each argument in turn. Each `glob.glob` call returns a list of filenames that match the pattern. The `map` operation then returns a list of lists, which you need to convert to a single list—the combination of all the lists in this list of lists. That means doing `list1 + list2 + ... +`

---

* It turns out that `map` can do more; for example, if None is the first argument, `map` converts the sequence that is its second argument to a list. It can also operate on more than one sequence at a time. Check a reference source for details.

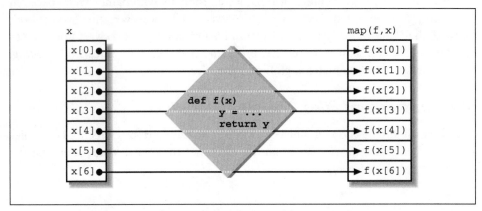

Figure 9-1. Graphical representation of the behavior of the map built-in

listN. That's exactly the kind of situation where the **reduce** function comes in handy.

Just as with **map**, **reduce** takes a function as its first argument and applies it to the first two elements of the sequence it receives as its second argument. It then takes the result of that call and calls the function again with that result and the next element in the sequence, etc. (See Figure 9-2 for an illustration of **reduce**.) But wait: you need + applied to a set of things, and + doesn't look like a function (it isn't). So a function is needed that works the same as +. Here's one:

```
define myAdd(something, other):
    return something + other
```

You would then use **reduce(myAdd, map(...))**. This works fine, but better yet, you can use the **add** function defined in the **operator** module, which does the same thing. The **operator** module defines functions for every syntactic operation in Python (including attribute-getting and slicing), and you should use those instead of homemade ones for two reasons. First, they've been coded, debugged, and tested by Guido, who has a pretty good track record at writing bugfree code. Second, they're actually C functions, and applying **reduce** (or **map**, or **filter**) to C functions results in much faster performance than applying it to Python functions. This clearly doesn't matter when all you're doing is going through a few hundred files once. If you do thousands of globs all the time, however, speed can become an issue, and now you know how to do it quickly.

The **filter** built-in function, like **map** and **reduce**, takes a function and a sequence as arguments. It returns the subset of the elements in the sequence for which the specified function returns something that's true. To find all of the even numbers in a set, type this:

```
>>> numbers = range(30)
>>> def even(x):
...     return x % 2 == 0
...
```

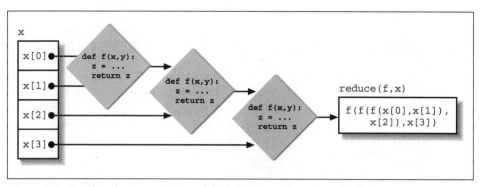

Figure 9-2. Graphical representation of the behavior of the reduce built-in

```
>>> print numbers
[0, 1, 2, 3, 4, 5, 6, 7, 8, 9, 10, 11, 12, 13, 14, 15, 16, 17, 18, 19, 20, 21, 22,
23, 24, 25, 26, 27, 28, 29]
>>> print filter(even, numbers)
[0, 2, 4, 6, 8, 10, 12, 14, 16, 18, 20, 22, 24, 26, 28]
```

Or, if you wanted to find all the words in a file that are at least 10 characters long, you could use:

```
import string
words = string.split(open('myfile.txt').read())        # get all the words

def at_least_ten(word):
    return len(word) >= 10

longwords = filter(at_least_ten, words)
```

For a graphical representation of what **filter** does, see Figure 9-3. One nice special feature of **filter** is that if one passes **None** as the first argument, it filters out all false entries in the sequence. So, to find all the nonempty lines in a file called *myfile.txt*, do this:

```
lines = open('myfile.txt').readlines()
lines = filter(None, lines)              # remember, the empty string is false
```

map, **filter**, and **reduce** are three powerful constructs, and they're worth knowing about; however, they are never necessary. It's fairly simple to write a Python function that does the same thing as any of them. The built-in versions are probably faster, especially when operating on built-in functions written in C, such as the functions in the **operator** module.

Using Temporary Files

If you've ever written a shell script and needed to use intermediary files for storing the results of some intermediate stages of processing, you probably suffered from directory litter. You started out with 20 files called *log_001.txt*, *log_002.txt*

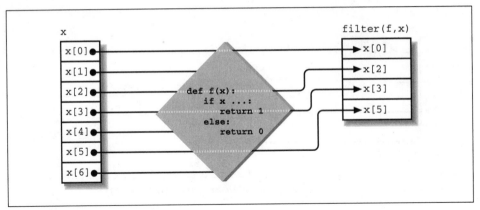

Figure 9-3. Graphical representation of the behavior of the filter built-in

etc., and all you wanted was one summary file called *log_sum.txt*. In addition, you had a whole bunch of *log_001.tmp*, *log_001.tm2*, etc. files that, while they were labeled temporary, stuck around. At least that's what we've seen happen in our own lives. To put order back into your directories, use temporary files in specific directories and clean them up afterwards.

To help in this temporary file-management problem, Python provides a nice little module called `tempfile` that publishes two functions: `mktemp()` and `TemporaryFile()`. The former returns the name of a file not currently in use in a directory on your computer reserved for temporary files (such as */tmp* on Unix or *C:\TMP* on Windows). The latter returns a new file object directly. For example:

```
# read input file
inputFile = open('input.txt', 'r')

import tempfile
# create temporary file
tempFile = tempfile.TemporaryFile()          # we don't even need to
first_process(input = inputFile, output = tempFile)   # know the filename...

# create final output file
outputFile = open('output.txt', 'w')
second_process(input = tempFile, output = outputFile)
```

Using `tempfile.TemporaryFile()` works well in cases where the intermediate steps manipulate file objects. One of its nice features is that when it's deleted, it automatically deletes the file it created on disk, thus cleaning up after itself. One important use of temporary files, however, is in conjunction with the `os.system` call, which means using a shell, hence using filenames, not file objects. For example, let's look at a program that creates form letters and mails them to a list of email addresses (on Unix only):

```
formletter = """Dear %s,\nI'm writing to you to suggest that ..."""    # etc.
myDatabase = [('Bill Clinton', 'bill@whitehouse.gov.us'),
              ('Bill Gates', 'bill@microsoft.com'),
              ('Bob', 'bob@subgenius.org')]
for name, email in myDatabase:
    specificLetter = formletter % name
    tempfilename = tempfile.mktemp()
    tempfile = open(tempfilename, 'w')
    tempfile.write(specificLetter)
    tempfile.close()
    os.system('/usr/bin/mail %(email)s -s "Urgent!" < %(tempfilename)s' % vars())
    os.remove(tempfilename)
```

The first line in the `for` loop returns a customized version of the form letter based on the name it's given. That text is then written to a temporary file that's emailed to the appropriate email address using the `os.system` call (which we'll cover later in this chapter). Finally, to clean up, the temporary file is removed. If you forgot how the `%` bit works, go back to Chapter 2 and review it; it's worth knowing. The `vars()` function is a built-in function that returns a dictionary corresponding to the variables defined in the current local namespace. The keys of the dictionary are the variable names, and the values of the dictionary are the variable values. `vars()` comes in quite handy for exploring namespaces. It can also be called with an object as an argument (such as a module, a class, or an instance), and it will return the namespace of that object. Two other built-ins, `locals()` and `globals()`, return the local and global namespaces, respectively. In all three cases, modifying the returned dictionaries doesn't guarantee any effect on the namespace in question, so view these as read-only and you won't be surprised. You can see that the `vars()` call creates a dictionary that is used by the string interpolation mechanism; it's thus important that the names inside the `%(...)s` bits in the string match the variable names in the program.

More on Scanning Text Files

Suppose you've run a program that stores its output in a text file, which you need to load. The program creates a file that's composed of a series of lines that each contain a value and a key separated by whitespace:

```
value key
value key
value key
```
and so on...

A key can appear on more than one line in the file, and you'd probably like to collect all the values that appear for each given key as you scan the file. Here's one way to solve this problem:

```
#!/usr/bin/env python
import sys, string
```

```
entries = {}
for line in open(sys.argv[1], 'r').readlines():
    left, right = string.split(line)
    try:
        entries[right].append(left)        # extend list
    except KeyError:
        entries[right] = [left]            # first time seen

for (right, lefts) in entries.items():
  print "%04d '%s'\titems => %s" % (len(lefts), right, lefts)
```

This script uses the **readlines** method to scan the text file line by line, and calls the built-in **string.split** function to chop the line into a list of substrings—a list containing the value and key strings separated by blanks or tabs in the file. To store all occurrences of a key, the script uses a dictionary called **entries**. The **try** statement in the loop tries to add new values to an existing entry for a key; if no entry exists for the key, it creates one. Notice that the **try** could be replaced with an **if** here:

```
if entries.has_key(right):        # is it already in the dictionary?
    entries[right].append(left)   # add to the list of current values for key
else:
    entries[right] = [left]       # initialize key's values list
```

Testing whether a dictionary contains a key is sometimes faster than catching an exception with the **try** technique; it depends on how many times the test is true. Here's an example of this script in action. The input filename is passed in as a command-line argument (**sys.argv[1]**):

```
% cat data.txt
1         one
2         one
3         two
7         three
8         two
10        one
14        three
19        three
20        three
30        three

% python collector1.py data.txt
0003 'one'      items => ['1', '2', '10']
0005 'three'    items => ['7', '14', '19', '20', '30']
0002 'two'      items => ['3', '8']
```

You can make this code more useful by packaging the scanner logic in a function that returns the **entries** dictionary as a result and wrapping the printing loop logic at the bottom in an **if** test:

```
#!/usr/bin/env python
import sys, string
```

```
    def collect(file):
        entries = {}
        for line in file.readlines():
            left, right = string.split(line)
            try:
                entries[right].append(left)          # extend list
            except KeyError:
                entries[right] = [left]              # first time seen
        return entries

    if __name__ == "__main__":                       # when run as a script
        if len(sys.argv) == 1:
            result = collect(sys.stdin)              # read from stdin stream
        else:
            result = collect(open(sys.argv[1], 'r')) # read from passed filename
        for (right, lefts) in result.items():
            print "%04d '%s'\titems => %s" % (len(lefts), right, lefts)
```

This way, the program becomes a bit more flexible. By using the `if __name__ ==` `"__main__"` trick, you can still run it as a top-level script (and get a display of the `results`), or import the function it defines and process the resulting dictionary explicitly:

```
# run as a script file
% collector2.py < data.txt
result displayed here...

# use in some other component (or interactively)
from collector2 import collect
result = collect(open("spam.txt", "r"))
process result here...
```

Since the `collect` function accepts an open file object, it also works on any object that provides the methods (i.e., interface) built-in files do. For example, if you want to read text from a simple string, wrap it in a class that implements the required interface and pass an instance of the class to the `collect` function:

```
>>> from collector2 import collect
>>> from StringIO import StringIO
>>>
>>> str = StringIO("1 one\n2 one\n3 two")
>>> result = collect(str)                   # scans the wrapped string
>>> print result                            # {'one':['1','2'],'two':['3']}
```

This code uses the `StringIO` class in the standard Python library to wrap the string into an instance that has all the methods file objects have; see the *Library Reference* for more details on `StringIO`. You could also write a different class or subclass from `StringIO` if you need to modify its behavior. Regardless, the `collect` function happily reads text from the `StringIO` object `str`, which happens to be an in-memory object, not a file.

The main reason all this works is that the `collect` function was designed to avoid making assumptions about the type of object its `file` parameter references. As long as the object exports a `readlines` method that returns a list of strings, `collect` doesn't care what type of object it processes. The interface is all that matters. This runtime binding[*] is an important feature of Python's object system, and allows you to easily write component programs that communicate with other components. For instance, consider a program that reads and writes satellite telemetry data using the standard file interface. By plugging in an object with the right sort of interface, you can redirect its streams to live sockets, GUI boxes, web interfaces, or databases without changing the program itself or even recompiling it.

Manipulating Programs

Calling Other Programs

Python can be used like a shell scripting language, to steer other tools by calling them with arguments the Python program determines at runtime. So, if you have to run a specific program (call it **analyzeData**) with various data files and various parameters specified on the command line, you can use the `os.system()` call, which takes a string specifying a command to run in a subshell. Specifically:

```
for datafname in ['data.001', 'data.002', 'data.003']:
    for parameter1 in range(1, 10):
        os.system("analyzeData -in %(datafname)s -param1 %(paramter1)d" % vars())
```

If **analyzeData** is a Python program, you're better off doing it without invoking a subshell; simply use the `import` statement up front and a function call in the loop. Not every useful program out there is a Python program, though.

In the preceding example, the output of **analyzeData** is most likely either a file or standard out. If it's standard out, it would be nice to be able to capture its output. The `popen()` function call is an almost standard way to do this. We'll show it off in a real-world task.

When we were writing this book, we were asked to avoid using tabs in source-code listings and use spaces instead. Tabs can wreak havoc with typesetting, and since indentation matters in Python, incorrect typesetting has the potential to break examples. But since old habits die hard (at least one of us uses tabs to indent his own Python code), we wanted a tool to find any tabs that may have crept into our

---

[*] Runtime binding means that Python doesn't know which sort of object implements an interface until the program is running. This behavior stems from the lack of type declarations in Python and leads to the notion of polymorphism; in Python, the meaning of a object operation (such as indexing, slicing, etc.) depends on the object being operated on.

code before it was shipped off for publication. The following script, *findtabs.py*, does the trick:

```
#!/usr/bin/env python
# find files, search for tabs

import string, os
cmd = 'find . -name "*.py" -print'        # find is a standard Unix tool

for file in os.popen(cmd).readlines():    # run find command
    num  = 1
    name = file[:-1]                       # strip '\n'
    for line in open(name).readlines():   # scan the file
        pos = string.find(line, "\t")
        if  pos >= 0:
            print name, num, pos          # report tab found
            print '....', line[:-1]       # [:-1] strips final \n
            print '....', ' '*pos + '*', '\n'
        num = num+1
```

This script uses two nested **for** loops. The outer loop uses **os.popen** to run a **find** shell command, which returns a list of all the Python source filenames accessible in the current directory and its subdirectories. The inner loop reads each line in the current file, using **string.find** to look for tabs. But the real magic in this script is in the built-in tools it employs:

os.popen

Takes a shell command passed in as a string (called **cmd** in the example) and returns a file-like object connected to the command's standard input or output streams. Output is the default if you don't pass an explicit **"r"** or **"w"** mode argument. By reading the file-like object, you can intercept the command's output as we did here—the result of the **find**. It turns out that there's a module in the standard library called **find.py** that provides a function that does a very similar thing to our use of **popen** with the **find** Unix command. As an exercise, you could rewrite *findtabs.py* to use it instead.

string.find

Returns the index of the first occurrence of one string in another, searching from left to right. In the script, we use it to look for a tab, passed in as an (escaped) one-character string (**'\t'**).

When a tab is found, the script prints the matching line, along with a pointer to where the tab occurs. Notice the use of string repetition: the expression **' '*pos** moves the print cursor to the right, up to the index of the first tab. Use double quotes inside a single-quoted string without backslash escapes in **cmd**. Here is the script at work, catching illegal tabs in the unfortunately named file *happyfingers.py*:

```
C:\python\book-examples> python findtabs.py
./happyfingers.py 2 0
```

```
....    for i in range(10):
.... *

./happyfingers.py 3 0
....             print "oops..."
.... *

./happyfingers.py 5 5
.... print        "bad style"
....        *
```

A note on portability: the `find` shell command used in the *findtabs* script is a
Unix command, which may or may not be available on other platforms (it ran
under Windows in the listing above because a `find` utility program was installed).
`os.popen` functionality is available as `win32pipe.popen` in the `win32` extensions
to Python for Windows.[*] If you want to write code that catches shell command
output portably, use something like the following code early in your script:

```
import sys
if sys.platform == "win32":                  # on a Windows port
    try:
        import win32pipe
        popen = win32pipe.popen
    except ImportError:
        raise ImportError, "The win32pipe module could not be found"
else:                                        # else on POSIX box
    import os
    popen = os.popen
...And use popen in blissful platform ignorance
```

The `sys.platform` attribute is always preset to a string that identifies the underlying
platform (and hence the Python port you're using). Although the Python language
isn't platform-dependent, some of its libraries may be; checking `sys.platform` is the
standard way to handle cases where they are. Notice the nested `import` statements
here; as we've seen, `import` is just an executable statement that assigns a variable
name.

Internet-Related Activities

The Internet is a treasure trove of information, but its exponential growth can
make it hard to manage. Furthermore, most tools currently available for "surfing
the Web" are not programmable. Many web-related tasks can be automated quite
simply with the tools in the standard Python distribution.

---

[*] Two important compatibility comments: the `win32pipe` module also has a `popen2` call, which is like
the `popen2` call on Unix, except that it returns the read and write pipes in swapped order (see the documentation for `popen2` in the `posix` module for details on its interface). There is no equivalent of `popen`
on Macs, since pipes don't exist on that operating system.

Downloading a Web Page Programmatically

If you're interested in finding out what the weather in a given location is over a period of months, it's much easier to set up an automated program to get the information and collect it in a file than to have to remember to do it by hand.

Here is a program that finds the weather in a couple of cities and states using the pages of the *weather.com* web site:

```
import urllib, urlparse, string, time

def get_temperature(country, state, city):
    url = urlparse.urljoin('http://www.weather.com/weather/cities/',
                           string.lower(country)+'_' + \
                           string.lower(state) + '_' + \
                           string.replace(string.lower(city), ' ',
                                          '_') + '.html')
    data = urllib.urlopen(url).read()
    start = string.index(data, 'current temp: ') + len('current temp: ')
    stop = string.index(data, '&deg;F', start-1)
    temp = int(data[start:stop])
    localtime = time.asctime(time.localtime(time.time()))
    print ("On %(localtime)s, the temperature in %(city)s, " +\
           "%(state)s %(country)s is %(temp)s F.") % vars()

get_temperature('FR', '', 'Paris')
get_temperature('US', 'RI', 'Providence')
get_temperature('US', 'CA', 'San Francisco')
```

When run, it produces output like:

```
~/book:> python get_temperature.py
On Wed Nov 25 16:22:25 1998, the temperature in Paris,  FR is 39 F.
On Wed Nov 25 16:22:30 1998, the temperature in Providence, RI US is 39 F.
On Wed Nov 25 16:22:35 1998, the temperature in San Francisco, CA US is 58 F.
```

The code in *get_temperature.py* suffers from one flaw, which is that the logic of the URL creation and of the temperature extraction is dependent on the specific HTML produced by the web site you use. The day the site's graphic designer decides that "current temp:" should be spelled with capitalized words, this script won't work. This is a problem with programmatic parsing of web pages that will go away only when more structural formats (such as XML) are used to produce web pages.[*]

---

[*] XML (eXtensible Markup Language) is a language for marking up structured text files that emphasizes the structure of the document, not its graphical nature. XML processing is an entirely different area of Python text processing, with much ongoing work. See Appendix A, *Python Resources*, for some pointers to discussion groups and software.

Checking the Validity of Links and Mirroring Web Sites: *webchecker.py* and Friends

One of the big hassles of maintaining a web site is that as the number of links in the site increases, so does the chance that some of the links will no longer be valid. Good web-site maintenance therefore includes periodic checking for such stale links. The standard Python distribution includes a tool that does just this. It lives in the *Tools/webchecker* directory and is called *webchecker.py*.

A companion program called *websucker.py* located in the same directory uses similar logic to create a local copy of a remote web site. Be careful when trying it out, because if you're not careful, it will try to download the entire Web on your machine! The same directory includes two programs called *wsgui.py* and *webgui.py* that are Tkinter-based frontends to *websucker* and *webchecker*, respectively. We encourage you to look at the source code for these programs to see how one can build sophisticated web-management systems with Python's standard toolset.

In the *Tools/Scripts* directory, you'll find many other small to medium-sized scripts that might be of interest, such as an equivalent of *websucker.py* for FTP servers called *ftpmirror.py*.

Checking Mail

Electronic mail is probably the most important medium on the Internet today; it's certainly the protocol with which most information passes between individuals. Python includes several libraries for processing mail. The one you'll need to use depends on the kind of mail server you're using. Modules for interacting with POP3 servers (`poplib`) and IMAP servers (`imaplib`) are included. If you need to talk to a Microsoft Exchange server, you'll need some of the tools in the *win32* distribution (see Appendix B, *Platform-Specific Topics*, for pointers to the *win32* extensions web page).

Here's a simple test of the `poplib` module, which is used to talk to a mail server running the POP protocol:

```
>>> from poplib import *
>>> server = POP3('mailserver.spam.org')
>>> print server.getwelcome()
+OK QUALCOMM Pop server derived from UCB (version 2.1.4-R3) at spam starting.
>>> server.user('da')
'+OK Password required for da.'
>>> server.pass_('youllneverguess')
'+OK da has 153 message(s) (458167 octets).'
>>> header, msg, octets = server.retr(152)  # let's get the latest msgs
>>> import string
>>> print string.join(msg[:3], '\n')    # and look at the first three lines
Return-Path: <jim@bigbad.com>
```

```
Received: from gator.bigbad.com by mailserver.spam.org (4.1/SMI-4.1)
         id AA29605; Wed, 25 Nov 98 15:59:24 PST
```

In a real application, you'd use a specialized module such as **rfc822** to parse the header lines, and perhaps the **mimetools** and **mimify** modules to get the data out of the message body (e.g., to process attached files).

Bigger Examples

Compounding Your Interest

Someday, most of us hope to put a little money away in a savings account (assuming those student loans ever go away). Banks hope you do too, so much so that they'll pay you for the privilege of holding onto your money. In a typical savings account, your bank pays you interest on your principal. Moreover, they keep adding the percentage they pay you back to your total, so that your balance grows a little bit each year. The upshot is that you need to project on a year-by-year basis if you want to track the growth in your savings. This program, *interest.py*, is an easy way to do it in Python:

```
trace = 1  # print each year?

def calc(principal, interest, years):
    for y in range(years):
        principal = principal * (1.00 + (interest / 100.0))
        if trace: print y+1, '=> %.2f' % principal
    return principal
```

This function just loops through the number of years you pass in, accumulating the principal (your initial deposit plus all the interest added so far) for each year. It assumes that you'll avoid the temptation to withdraw money. Now, suppose we have $65,000 to invest in a 5.5% interest yield account, and want to track how the principal will grow over 10 years. We import and call our compounding function passing in a starting principal, an interest rate, and the number of years we want to project:

```
% python
>>> from interest import calc
>>> calc(65000, 5.5, 10)
1 => 68575.00
2 => 72346.63
3 => 76325.69
4 => 80523.60
5 => 84952.40
6 => 89624.78
7 => 94554.15
8 => 99754.62
9 => 105241.13
```

```
10 => 111029.39
111029.389793
```

and we wind up with $111,029. If we just want to see the final balance, we can set the `trace` global (module-level) variable in `interest` to 0 before we call the `calc` function:

```
>>> import interest
>>> interest.trace = 0
>>> calc(65000, 5.5, 10)
111029.389793
```

Naturally, there are many ways to calculate compound interest. For example, the variation of the interest calculator function below adds to the principal explicitly, and prints both the interest earned (`earnings`) and current balance (`principal`) as it steps through the years:

```
def calc(principal, interest, years):
    interest = interest / 100.0
    for y in range(years):
        earnings  = principal * interest
        principal = principal + earnings
        if trace: print y+1, '(+%d)' % earnings, '=> %.2f' % principal
    return principal
```

We get the same results with this version, but more information:

```
>>> interest.trace = 1
>>> calc(65000, 5.5, 10)
1 (+3575) => 68575.00
2 (+3771) => 72346.63
3 (+3979) => 76325.69
4 (+4197) => 80523.60
5 (+4428) => 84952.40
6 (+4672) => 89624.78
7 (+4929) => 94554.15
8 (+5200) => 99754.62
9 (+5486) => 105241.13
10 (+5788) => 111029.39
111029.389793
```

The last comment on this script is that it may not give you exactly the same numbers as your bank. Bank programs tend to round everything off to the cent on a regular basis. Our program rounds off the numbers to the cent when printing the results (that's what the `%.2f` does; see Chapter 2 for details), but keeps the full precision afforded by the computer in its intermediate computation (as shown in the last line).

An Automated Dial-Out Script

One upon a time, a certain book's coauthor worked at a company without an Internet feed. The system support staff did, however, install a dial-out modem on site, so anyone with a personal Internet account and a little Unix savvy could connect to a shell account and do all their Internet business at work. Dialing out meant using the Kermit file transfer utility.

One drawback with the modem setup was that people wanting to dial out had to keep trying each of 10 possible modems until one was free (dial on one; if it's busy, try another, and so on). Since modems were addressable under Unix using the filename pattern */dev/modem**, and modem locks via */var/spool/locks/ LCK*modem**, a simple Python script was enough to check for free modems automatically. The following program, *dokermit,* uses a list of integers to keep track of which modems are locked, `glob.glob` to do filename expansion, and `os.system` to run a kermit command when a free modem has been found:

```
#!/usr/bin/env python
# find a free modem to dial out on

import glob, os, string
LOCKS = "/var/spool/locks/"

locked = [0] * 10
for lockname in glob.glob(LOCKS + "LCK*modem*"):    # find locked modems
    print "Found lock:", lockname
    locked[string.atoi(lockname[-1])] = 1           # 0..9 at end of name

print 'free: ',
for i in range(10):                                 # report, dial-out
    if not locked[i]: print i,
print

for i in range(10):
    if not locked[i]:
        if raw_input("Try %d? " % i) == 'y':
            os.system("kermit -m hayes -l /dev/modem%d -b 19200 -S" % i)
            if raw_input("More? ") != 'y': break
```

By convention, modem lock files have the modem number at the end of their names; we use this hook to build a modem device name in the Kermit command. Notice that this script keeps a list of 10 integer flags to mark which modems are free (1 means locked). The program above works only if there are 10 or fewer modems; if there are more, you'd need to use larger lists and loops, and parse the lock filename, not just look at its last character.

An Interactive Rolodex

While most of the preceding examples use lists as the primary data structures, dictionaries are in many ways more powerful and fun to use. Their presence as a built-in data type is part of what makes Python high level, which basically means "easy to use for complex tasks." Complementing this rich set of built-in data types is an

extensive standard library. One powerful module in this library is the `cmd` module
that provides a class `Cmd` you can subclass to make simple command-line interpreter. The following example is fairly large, but it's really not that complicated, and
illustrates well the power of dictionaries and of reuse of standard modules.

The task at hand is to keep track of names and phone numbers and allow the user
to manipulate this list using an interactive interface, with error checking and user-
friendly features such as online help. The following example shows the kind of
interaction our program allows:

```
% python rolo.py
Monty's Friends: help

Documented commands (type help <topic>):
========================================
EOF             add             find            list            load
save

Undocumented commands:
======================
help
```

We can get help on specific commands:

```
Monty's Friends: help find        # compare with the help_find() method
Find an entry (specify a name)
```

We can manipulate the entries of the Rolodex easily enough:

```
Monty's Friends: add larry              # we can add entries
Enter Phone Number for larry: 555-1216
Monty's Friends: add                    # if the name is not specified...
Enter Name: tom                         # ...the program will ask for it
Enter Phone Number for tom: 555-1000
Monty's Friends: list
==========================================
          larry : 555-1216
            tom : 555-1000
==========================================
Monty's Friends: find larry
The number for larry is 555-1216.
Monty's Friends: save myNames           # save our work
Monty's Friends: ^D                     # quit the program  (^Z on Windows)
```

And the nice thing is, when we restart this program, we can recover the saved
data:

```
% python rolo.py                        # restart
Monty's Friends: list                   # by default, there is no one listed
Monty's Friends: load myNames           # it only takes this to reload the dir
Monty's Friends: list
==========================================
          larry : 555-1216
            tom : 555-1000
==========================================
```

Most of the interactive interpreter functionality is provided by the `Cmd` class in the
`cmd` module, which just needs customization to work. Specifically, you need to set
the `prompt` attribute and add some methods that start with `do_` and `help_`. The
`do_` methods must take a single argument, and the part after the `do_` is the name
of the command. Once you call the `cmdloop()` method, the `Cmd` class does the
rest. Read the following code, *rolo.py*, one method at a time and compare the
methods with the previous output:

```python
#!/usr/bin/env python
# An interactive rolodex

import string, sys, pickle, cmd

class Rolodex(cmd.Cmd):

    def __init__(self):
        cmd.Cmd.__init__(self)               # initialize the base class
        self.prompt = "Monty's Friends: "    # customize the prompt
        self.people = {}                     # at first, we know nobody

    def help_add(self):
        print "Adds an entry (specify a name)"
    def do_add(self, name):
        if name == "": name = raw_input("Enter Name: ")
        phone = raw_input("Enter Phone Number for "+ name+": ")
        self.people[name] = phone            # add phone number for name

    def help_find(self):
        print "Find an entry (specify a name)"
    def do_find(self, name):
        if name == "": name = raw_input("Enter Name: ")
        if self.people.has_key(name):
            print "The number for %s is %s." % (name, self.people[name])
        else:
            print "We have no record for %s." % (name,)

    def help_list(self):
        print "Prints the contents of the directory"
    def do_list(self, line):
        names = self.people.keys()           # the keys are the names
        if names == []: return               # if there are no names, exit
        names.sort()                         # we want them in alphabetic order
        print '='*41
        for name in names:
            print string.rjust(name, 20), ":", string.ljust(self.people[name],
20)
        print '='*41

    def help_EOF(self):
        print "Quits the program"
    def do_EOF(self, line):
        sys.exit()
```

```
    def help_save(self):
        print "save the current state of affairs"
    def do_save(self, filename):
        if filename == "": filename = raw_input("Enter filename: ")
        saveFile = open(filename, 'w')
        pickle.dump(self.people, saveFile)

    def help_load(self):
        print "load a directory"
    def do_load(self, filename):
        if filename == "": filename = raw_input("Enter filename: ")
        saveFile = open(filename, 'r')
        self.people = pickle.load(saveFile) # note that this will override
                                            # any existing people directory

if __name__ == '__main__':              # this way the module can be
    rolo = Rolodex()                    # imported by other programs as well
    rolo.cmdloop()
```

So, the **people** instance variable is a simple mapping between names and phone numbers that the **add** and **find** commands use. Commands are the methods which start with **do_**, and their help is given by the corresponding **help_** methods. Finally, the **load** and **save** commands use the **pickle** module, which is explained in more detail in Chapter 10, *Frameworks and Applications*.

This example demonstrates the power of Python that comes from extending existing modules. The **cmd** module takes care of the prompt, help facility, and parsing of the input. The **pickle** module does all the loading and saving that can be so difficult in lesser languages. All we had to write were the parts specific to the task at hand. The generic aspect, namely an interactive interpreter, came free.

Exercises

This chapter is full of programs we encourage you to type in and play with. However, if you really want exercises, here are a few more challenging ones:

1. *Redirecting stdout.* Modify the *mygrep.py* script to output to the last file specified on the command line instead of to the console.

2. *Writing a shell.* Using the **Cmd** class in the **cmd** module and the functions listed in Chapter 8 for manipulating files and directories, write a little shell that accepts the standard Unix commands (or DOS commands if you'd rather): **ls** (**dir**) for listing the current directory, **cd** for changing directory, **mv** (or **ren**) for moving/renaming a file, and **cp** (**copy**) for copying a file.

3. *Understanding map, reduce, and filter.* The **map**, **reduce**, and **filter** functions are somewhat difficult to understand if it's the first time you've encountered this type of function, partly because they involve passing functions as arguments, and partly because they do a lot even with such small names. One good way to ensure you know how they work is to rewrite them; in this exer-

How Does the Cmd Class Work, Anyway?

To understand how the Cmd class works, read the cmd module in the standard Python library you've already installed on your computer.

The Cmd interpreter does most of the work we're interested in its onecmd() method, which is called whenever a line is entered by the user. This method figures out the first word of the line that corresponds to a command (e.g., help, find, save, load, etc.). It then looks to see if the instance of the Cmd subclass has an attribute with the right name (if the command was "find tom", it looks for an attribute called do_find). If it finds this attribute, it calls it with the arguments to the command (in this case 'tom'), and returns the result. Similar magic is done by the do_help() method, which is invoked by this same mechanism, which is why it's called do_help()! The code for the onecmd() method once looked like this (the version you have may have had features added):

```
# onecmd method of Cmd class, see Lib/cmd.py
def onecmd(self, line):        # line is something like "find tom"
    line = string.strip(line)  # get rid of extra whitespace
    if not line:               # if there is nothing left,
        line = self.lastcmd    # redo the last command
    else:
        self.lastcmd = line    # save for next time
    i, n = 0, len(line)
                               # next line finds end of first word
    while i < n and line[i] in self.identchars: i = i+1
                               # split line into command + arguments
    cmd, arg = line[:i], string.strip(line[i:])
    if cmd == '':              # happens if line doesn't start with A-z
        return self.default(line)
    else:                      # cmd is 'find', line is 'tom'
        try:
            func = getattr(self, 'do_' + cmd)  # look for method
        except AttributeError:
            return self.default(line)
        return func(arg)       # call method with the rest of the line
```

cise, write three functions (map2, reduce2, filter2), that do the same thing as map, filter, and reduce, respectively, at least as far as we've described how they work:

— map2 takes two arguments. The first should be a function accepting two arguments, or None. The second should be a sequence. If the first argument is a function, that function is called with each element of the sequence, and the resulting values are returned in a list. If the first argument is None, the sequence is converted to a list, and that list is returned.

— `reduce2` takes two arguments. The first must be a function accepting two arguments, and the second must be a sequence. The first two arguments of the sequence are used as arguments to the function, and the result of that call is sent as the first argument to the function again, with the third element to the sequence as the second argument, and so on, until all elements of the sequence have been used as arguments to the function. The last returned value from the function is then the return value for the `reduce2` call.

— `filter2` takes two arguments. The first can be None or a function accepting two arguments. The second must be a sequence. If the first argument is None, `filter2` returns the subset of the elements in the sequence that tests true. If the first argument is a function, `filter2` is called with every element in the sequence in turn, and only those elements for which the return value of the function applied to them is true are returned by `filter2`.

10

Frameworks and Applications

All the examples in this book so far have been quite small, and they may seem toys compared to real-world applications. This chapter shows some of the frameworks that are available to Python programmers who wish to build such applications in some specific domains. A framework can be thought of as a domain-specific set of classes and expected patterns of interactions between these classes. We mention just three here: the COM framework for interacting with Microsoft's Common Object Model, the Tkinter graphical user interface (GUI), and the Swing Java GUI toolkit. Along the way we also use a few of the web-related modules in the standard library.

We illustrate the power of frameworks using a hypothetical, real-world scenario, that of a small company's web site, and the need to collect, maintain, and respond to customer input about the product through a web form. We describe three programs in this scenario. The first program is a web-based data entry form that asks the user to enter some information in their web browser, and then saves that information on disk. The second program uses the same data and automatically uses Microsoft Word to print out a customized form letter based on that information. The final example is a simple browser for the saved data built with the Tkinter module, which uses the Tk GUI, a powerful, portable toolkit for managing windows, buttons, menus, etc. Hopefully, these examples will make you realize how these kinds of toolkits, when combined with the rapid development power of Python, can truly let you build "real" applications fast. Each program builds on the previous one, so we strongly recommend that you read through each program, even if you can't (or don't wish to) get them up and running on your computer.

The last section of this chapter covers JPython, the Java port of Python. The chapter closes with a medium-sized JPython program that allows users to manipulate mathematical functions graphically using the Swing toolkit.

An Automated Complaint System

The scenario we use for this example is that of a startup company, Joe's Toothpaste, Inc., which sells the latest in 100% organic, cruelty-free tofu-based toothpaste. Since there is only one employee, and that employee is quite busy shopping for the best tofu he can find, the tube doesn't say "For customer complaints or comments, call 1-800-TOFTOOT," but instead, says "If you have a complaint or wish to make a comment, visit our web site at *www.toftoot.com*." The web site has all the usual glossy pictures and an area where the customer can enter a complaint or comment. This page looks like that in Figure 10-1.

The key parts of the HTML that generated this page are displayed in the sidebar "Excerpt From the HTML File." As this is not a book about CGI, HTML, or any of that,* we just assume that you know enough about these technologies to follow this discussion. The important parts of the HTML code in the sidebar are in bold; here's a brief description:

- The FORM line specifies what CGI program should be invoked when the form is submitted; specifically, the URL points to a script called *feedback.py*, which we'll cover in detail.

- The INPUT tags indicate the names of the fields in the form (name, address, email, and text, as well as type). The values of those fields are whatever the user enters, except for the case of type, which takes either the value 'comment' or 'complaint', depending on which radio button the user checked.

- Finally, the INPUT TYPE=SUBMIT tag is for the submission button, which actually calls the CGI script.

We now get to the interesting part as far as Python is concerned: the processing of the request. Here is the entire *feedback.py* program:

```
import cgi, os, sys, string

def gush(data):
```

---

* If you've never heard of these acronyms: CGI stands for the Common Gateway Interface and is a protocol for having web browsers call programs on web servers; HTML stands for HyperText Markup Language, which is the format that encodes web pages.

Figure 10-1. What the customer finds at http://www.toftoot.com/comment.html

```
print "Content-type: text/html\n"
print "<h3>Thanks, %(name)s!</h3>" % vars(data)
print "Our customer's comments are always appreciated."
print "They drive our business directions, as well as"
print "help us with our karma."
print "<p>Thanks again for the feedback!<p>"
print "And feel free to enter more comments if you wish."
print "<p>"+10*" "+"--Joe."

def whimper(data):
    print "Content-type: text/html\n"
    print "<h3>Sorry, %(name)s!</h3>" % vars(data)
    print "We're very sorry to read that you had a complaint"
    print "regarding our product__We'll read your comments"
    print "carefully and will be in touch with you."
    print "<p>Nevertheless, thanks for the feedback.<p>"
    print "<p>"+10*" "+"--Joe."
```

Excerpt From the HTML File

This is the important part of the code that generates the web page shown in
Figure 10-1:

```
<FORM METHOD=POST ACTION="http://toftoot.com/cgi-bin/feedback.py">
<UL><I>Please fill out the entire form:</I></UL>
<CENTER><TABLE WIDTH="100%" >
<TR><TD ALIGN=RIGHT WIDTH="20%">Name:</TD>
    <TD><INPUT TYPE=text NAME=name SIZE=50 VALUE=""></TD></TR>
<TR><TD ALIGN=RIGHT>Email Address:</TD>
    <TD><INPUT TYPE=text NAME=email SIZE=50 VALUE=""></TD></TR>
<TR><TD ALIGN=RIGHT>Mailing Address:</TD>
    <TD><INPUT TYPE=text NAME=address SIZE=50 VALUE=""></TD></TR>
<TR><TD ALIGN=RIGHT>Type of Message:</TD>
<TD><INPUT TYPE=radio NAME=type CHECKED VALUE=comment>comment 
    <INPUT TYPE=radio NAME=type VALUE=complaint>complaint</TD></TR>
<TR><TD ALIGN=RIGHT VALIGN=TOP>Enter the text in here:</TD>
    <TD><TEXTAREA NAME=text ROWS=5, COLS=50  VALUE="">
        </TEXTAREA></TD></TR>
<TR><TD></TD>
<TD><INPUT type=submit name=send value="Send the feedback!"></TD></TR>
</TABLE></CENTER>
</FORM>
```

```
def bail():
    print "<H3>Error filling out form</H3>"
    print "Please fill in all the fields in the form.<P>"
    print '<a href="http://localhost/comment.html">'
    print 'Go back to the form</a>'
    sys.exit()

class FormData:
    """ A repository for information gleaned from a CGI form """
    def __init__(self, form):
        for fieldname in self.fieldnames:
            if not form.has_key(fieldname) or form[fieldname].value == "":
                bail()
            else:
                setattr(self, fieldname, form[fieldname].value)

class FeedbackData(FormData):
    """ A FormData generated by the comment.html form. """
    fieldnames = ('name', 'address', 'email', 'type', 'text')
    def __repr__(self):
        return "%(type)s from %(name)s on %(time)s" % vars(self)

DIRECTORY = r'C:\complaintdir'

if __name__ == '__main__':
```

```
sys.stderr = sys.stdout
form = cgi.FieldStorage()
data = FeedbackData(form)
if data.type == 'comment':
    gush(data)
else:
    whimper(data)

# save the data to file
import tempfile, pickle, time
tempfile.tempdir = DIRECTORY
data.time = time.asctime(time.localtime(time.time()))
pickle.dump(data, open(tempfile.mktemp(), 'w'))
```

The output of this script clearly depends on the input, but the output with the form filled out with the parameters shown in Figure 10-1 is displayed in Figure 10-2.

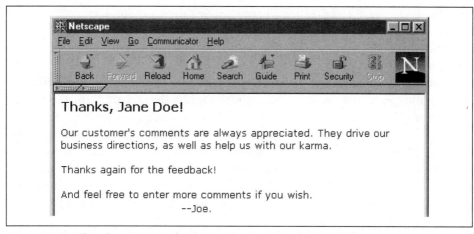

Figure 10-2. What the user sees after hitting the "send the feedback" button

How does the *feedback.py* script work? There are a few aspects of the script common to all CGI programs, and those are highlighted in bold. To start, the first line of the program needs to refer to the Python executable. This is a requirement of the web server we're using here, and it might not apply in your case; even if it does, the specific location of your Python program is likely to be different from this. The second line includes import cgi, which, appropriately enough, loads a module called cgi that deals with the hard part of CGI, such as parsing the environment variables and handling escaped characters. (If you've never had to do these things by hand, consider yourself lucky.) The documentation for the cgi module describes a very straightforward and easy way to use it. For this example, however, mostly because we're going to build on it, the script is somewhat more complicated than strictly necessary.

Let's just go through the code in the `if __name__ == '__main__'` block one statement at a time.* The first statement redirects the `sys.stderr` stream to whatever standard out is. This is done for debugging because the output of the `stdout` stream in a CGI program goes back to the web browser, and the `stderr` stream goes to the server's error log, which can be harder to read than simply looking at the web page. This way, if a runtime exception occurs, we can see it on the web page, as opposed to having to guess what it was. The second line is crucial and does all of the hard CGI work: it returns a dictionary-like object (called a `FieldStorage` object) whose keys are the names of the variables filled out in the form, and whose value can be obtained by asking for the `value` attribute of the entries in the `FieldStorage` object. Sounds complicated, but all it means is that for our form, the `form` object has keys `'name'`, `'type'`, `'email'`, `'address'`, and `'text'`, and that to find out what the user entered in the Name field of the web form, we need to look at `form['name'].value`.

The third line in the `if` block creates an instance of our user-defined class `FeedbackData`, passing it the `form` object as an argument. If you now look at the definition of the `FeedbackData` class, you'll see that it's a very simple subclass of `FormData`, which is also a user-defined class. All we've defined in the `FeedbackData` subclass is a class attribute `fieldnames` and a `__repr__` function used by the `print` statement, among others. Clearly, the `__init__` method of the `FormData` class must do something with the `FieldStorage` argument. Indeed, it looks at each of the field names defined in the `fieldnames` class attribute of the instance (that's what `self.fieldnames` refers to), and for each field name, checks to see that the `FieldStorage` object has a corresponding nonempty key. If it does, it sets an attribute with the same name as the field in the instance, giving it as value the text entered by the user. If it doesn't, it calls the `bail` function.

We'll get to what `bail` does in a minute, but first, let's walk through the usual case, when the user dutifully enters all of the required data. In those cases, `FieldStorage` has all of the keys (`'name'`, `'type'`, etc.) which the `FeedbackData` class says it needs. The `FormData` class `__init__` method in turn sets attributes for each field name in the instance. So, when the `data = FeedbackData(form)` call returns, `data` is guaranteed to be an instance of `FeedbackData`, which is a subclass of `FormData`, and `data` has the attributes `name`, `type`, `email`, etc., with the corresponding values the user entered.

A similar effect could have been gotten with code like:

```
form = cgi.FieldStorage()
form_ok = 1
if not form.has_key("name") or form["name"].value == "":
```

---

* You'll remember that this `if` statement is true only when the program is run as a script, not when it's imported. CGI programs qualify as scripts, so the code in the `if` block runs when this program is called by the web server. We use it later as an imported script, so keep your eyes peeled.

```
        form_ok = 0
    else:
        data_name = form["name"].value
    if not form.has_key("email") or form["email"].value == "":
        form_ok = 0
    else:
        data_email = form["email"].value
    ...
```

but it should be clear that this kind of programming can get very tedious, repetitive, and error-prone (thanks to the curse of cut and paste). With our scheme, when Joe changes the set of field names in the web page, all we need to change is the `fieldnames` attribute of the `FeedbackData` class. Also, we can use the same `FormData` class in any other CGI script, and thus reuse code.

What if the user didn't enter all of the required fields? Either the `FieldStorage` dictionary will be missing a key, or its value will be the empty string. The `FormData.__init__` method then calls the `bail` function, which displays a polite error message and exits the script. Control never returns back to the main program, so there is no need to test the validity of the `data` variable; if we got something back from `FeedbackData()`, it's a valid instance.

With the `data` instance, we check to see if the feedback type was a comment, in which case we thank the user for their input. If the feedback type was a complaint, we apologize profusely and promise to get back in touch with them.

We now have a basic CGI infrastructure in place. To save the data to file is remarkably easy. First, we define the `DIRECTORY` variable outside the `if` test because we'll use it from another script that will import this one, so we wish it to be defined even if this script is not run as a program.

Stepping through the last few lines of *feedback.py*:

- Import the `tempfile`, `pickle`, and `time` modules. The `tempfile` module, as we've seen in previous chapters, comes up with filenames currently not in use; that way we don't need to worry about "collisions" in any filename generation scheme. The `pickle` module allows the serialization, or saving, of any Python object. The `time` module lets us find the current time, which Joe judges to be an important aspect of the feedback.

- The next line sets the `tempdir` attribute of the `tempfile` module to the value of the `DIRECTORY` variable, which is where we want our data to be saved. This is an example of customizing an existing module by directly modifying its namespace, just as we modified the `stderr` attribute of the `sys` module earlier.

- The next line uses several functions in the `time` module to provide a string representation of the current date and time (something like `'Sat Jul 04`

`18:09:00 1998'`, which is precise enough for Joe's needs), and creates a new attribute called `time` in the `data` instance. It is therefore saved along with `data`.

- The last line does the actual saving; it opens the file with a name generated by the `tempfile` module in write mode and dumps the instance data into it. That's it! Now the specified file contains a so-called "pickled" instance.

Interfacing with COM: Cheap Public Relations

We use the data to do two things. First, we'll write a program that's run periodically (say, at 2 a.m., every night*) and looks through the saved data, finds out which saved pickled files correspond to complaints, and prints out a customized letter to the complainant. Sounds sophisticated, but you'll be surprised at how simple it is using the right tools. Joe's web site is on a Windows machine, so we'll assume that for this program, but other platforms work in similar ways.

Before we talk about how to write this program, a word about the technology it uses, namely Microsoft's Common Object Model (COM). COM is a standard for interaction between programs (an Object Request Broker service, to be technical), which allows any COM-compliant program to talk to, access the data in, and execute commands in other COM-compliant programs. Grossly, the program doing the calling is called a COM client, and the program doing the executing is called a COM server. Now, as one might suspect given the origin of COM, all major Microsoft products are COM-aware, and most can act as servers. Microsoft Word Version 8 is one of those, and the one we'll use here. Indeed, Microsoft Word is just fine for writing letters, which is what we're doing. Luckily for us, Python can be made COM-aware as well, at least on Windows 95, Windows 98, and Windows NT. Mark Hammond and Greg Stein have made available a set of extensions to Python for Windows called *win32com* that allow Python programs to do almost everything you can do with COM from any other language. You can write COM clients, servers, ActiveX scripting hosts, debuggers, and more, all in Python. We only need to do the first of these, which is also the simplest. Basically, our form letter program needs to do the following things:

---

* Setting up this kind of automatic regularly scheduled program is easily done on most platforms, using, for example, `cron` on Unix or the `AT` scheduler on Windows NT.

1. Open all of the pickled files in the appropriate directory and unpickle them.

2. For each unpickled instance file, test if the feedback is a complaint. If it is, find out the name and address of the person who filled out the form and go on to Step 3. If not, skip it.

3. Open a Word document containing a template of the letter we want to send, and fill in the appropriate pieces with the customized information.

4. Print the document and close it.

It's almost as simple in Python with *win32com*. Here's a little program called *form-letter.py*:

```python
from win32com.client import constants, Dispatch
WORD = 'Word.Application.8'
False, True = 0, -1
import string

class Word:
    def __init__(self):
        self.app = Dispatch(WORD)
    def open(self, doc):
        self.app.Documents.Open(FileName=doc)
    def replace(self, source, target):
        self.app.Selection.HomeKey(Unit=constants.wdLine)
        find = self.app.Selection.Find
        find.Text = "%"+source+"%"
        self.app.Selection.Find.Execute()
        self.app.Selection.TypeText(Text=target)
    def printdoc(self):
        self.app.Application.PrintOut()
    def close(self):
        self.app.ActiveDocument.Close(SaveChanges=False)

def print_formletter(data):
    word.open(r"h:\David\Book\tofutemplate.doc")
    word.replace("name", data.name)
    word.replace("address", data.address)
    word.replace("firstname", string.split(data.name)[0])
    word.printdoc()
    word.close()

if __name__ == '__main__':
    import os, pickle
    from feedback import DIRECTORY, FormData, FeedbackData
    word = Word()
    for filename in os.listdir(DIRECTORY):
        data = pickle.load(open(os.path.join(DIRECTORY, filename)))
        if data.type == 'complaint':
            print "Printing letter for %(name)s." % vars(data)
            print_formletter(data)
        else:
            print "Got comment from %(name)s, skipping printing." % vars(data)
```

The first few lines of the main program show the power of a well-designed framework. The first line is a standard import statement, except that it's worth noting that *win32com* is a package, not a module. It is, in fact, a collection of subpackages, modules, and functions. We need two things from the *win32com* package: the `Dispatch` function in the `client` module, a function that allows us to "dispatch" functions to other objects (in this case COM servers), and the `constants` submodule of the same module, which holds the constants defined by the COM objects we want to talk to.

The second line simply defines a variable that contains the name of the COM server we're interested in. It's called `Word.Application.8`, as you can find out from using a COM browser or reading Word's API (see the sidebar "Finding Out About COM Interfaces").

Let's focus now on the `if __name__ == '__main__'` block, which is the next statement after the class and function definitions.

The first task is to read the data. We import the `os` and `pickle` modules for fairly obvious reasons, and then three references from the `feedback` module we just wrote: the `DIRECTORY` where the data is stored (this way if we change it in *feedback.py*, this module reflects the change the next time it's run), and the `FormData` and `FeedbackData` classes. The next line creates an instance of the `Word` class; this opens a connection with the Word COM server, starting the server if needed.

The `for` loop is a simple iteration over the files in the directory with all the saved files. It's important that this directory contain only the pickled instances, since we're not doing any error checking. As usual we should make the code more robust, but we've ignored stability for simplicity.

The first line in the `for` loop does the unpickling. It uses the `load` function from the `pickle` module, which takes a single argument, the file which is being unpickled. It returns as many references as were stored in the file—in our case, just one. Now, the data that was stored was just the instance of the `FeedbackData` class. The definition of the class itself isn't stored in the pickled file, just the instance values and a reference to the class.[*]

---

[*] There are very good reasons for this behavior: first, it reduces the total size of pickled objects, and more importantly, it allows you to unpickle instances of previous versions of a class and automatically upgrade them to the newer class definitions.

At unpickling time, unpickling instances automatically causes an import of the module in which the class was defined. Why, then, did we need to import the classes specifically? In Chapter 5, *Modules*, we said the name of the currently running module is __main__. In other words, the name of the module in which the class is defined is __main__ (even though the name of the file is *feedback.py*), and alas, importing __main__ when we're unpickling imports the currently running module (which lives in *formletter.py*), which doesn't contain the definition of the classes of the pickled instances. This is why we need to import the class definitions explicitly from the feedback module. If they weren't made available to the code calling pickle.unload (in either the local or global namespaces), the unpickling would fail. Alternatively, we could save the source of the class in a file and import it first before any of the instances, or, even more simply, place the class definitions in a separate module that's imported explicitly by *feedback.py* and implicitly by the unpickling process in the *formletter.py*. The latter is the usual case, and as a result, in most circumstances, you don't need to explicitly import the class definitions; unpickling the instance does it all, "by magic."[*]

The if statement inside the loop is straightforward. All that remains is to explain is the print_formletter function, and, of course, the Word class.

The print_formletter function simply calls the various methods of the word instance of the Word class with the data extracted from the data instance. Note that we use the string.split function to extract the first name of the user, just to make the letter more friendly, but this risks strange behavior for nonstandard names.

In the Word class, the __init__ method appears simple yet hides a lot of work. It creates a connection with the COM server and stores a reference to that COM server in an instance variable app. Now, there are two ways in which the subsequent code might use this server: *dynamic dispatch* and *nondynamic dispatch*. In dynamic dispatch, Python doesn't "know" at the time the program is running what the interface to the COM server (in this case Microsoft Word) is. It doesn't matter, because COM allows Python to interrogate the server and determine the protocol, for example, the number and kinds of arguments each function expects. This approach can be slow, however. A way to speed it up is to run the *makepy.py* program, which does this once for each specified COM server and stores this information on disk. When a program using that specific server is executed, the dispatch routine uses the precomputed information rather than doing the dynamic

---

[*] This point about pickling of top-level classes is a subtle one; it's much beyond the level of this book. We mention it here because 1) we need to explain the code we used, and 2) this is about as complex as Python gets. In some ways this should be comforting—there is really no "magic" here. The apparently special-case behavior of pickle is in fact a natural consequence of understanding what the __main__ module is.

dispatch. The program as written works in both cases. If *makepy.py* was run on Word in the past, the fast dispatch method is used; if not, the dynamic dispatch method is used. For more information on these issues, see the information for the *win32* extensions at *http://www.python.org/windows/win32all/*.

To explain the Word class methods, let's start with a possible template document, so that we can see what needs to be done to it to customize it. It's shown in Figure 10-3.

J O E ' S T O O T H P A S T E , I N C .

February 18, 1999

%name%
%address%

Dear %firstname%,

  Thank you for filling out the feedback form at our website (www.toftoot.com). We're sorry to hear of your complaint, and we'll do our best to remedy it in the future. As a token of our deepest apologies, please accept a coupon for a free tube of our newest toothpaste, the "Firm Tofu Plus Toothpaste", enriched with Vitamin A, B and Z12.

                              Sincerely,

                              Joe Smith.

SUITE 101, 22 MAIN ST • TOFUTOWN, CA • 04122
PHONE: 415-555-1212 • FAX: 415-555-1211

Figure 10-3. Joe's template letter to complainants

As you can see, it's a pretty average document, with the exception of some text in between % signs. We've used this notation just to make it easy for a program to find the parts which need customization, but any other technique could work as well. To use this template, we need to open the document, customize it, print it, and close it. Opening it is done by the open method of the Word class. The printing and closing are done similarly. To customize, we replace the %name%, %firstname%, and %address% text with the appropriate strings. That's what the `replace` method of the `Word` class does (we won't cover how we figured out what the exact sequence of calls should be; see "Finding Out About COM Interfaces" for details).

Finding Out About COM Interfaces

How can you find out what the various methods and attributes of COM objects are? In general, COM objects are just like any other program; they should come with documentation. In the case of COM objects, however, it's quite possible to have the software without the documentation, simply because, as in the case of Word, it's possible to use Word without needing to program it. There are three strategies available to you if you want to explore a COM interface:

- Find or buy the documentation; some COM programs have their documentation available on the Web, or available in printed form.

- Use a COM browser to explore the objects. Pythonwin (part of the *win32all* extensions to Python on Windows, see Appendix B, *Platform-Specific Topics*), for example, comes with a COM browser tool that lets you explore the complex hierarchy of COM objects. It's not much more than a listing of available objects and functions, but sometimes that's all you need. Development tools such as Microsoft's Visual Studio also come with COM browsers.

- Use another tool to find what's available. For the example above, we simply used Microsoft Word's "macro recorder" facility to produce a VBA (Visual Basic for Applications) script, which is fairly straightforward to translate to Python. Macros tend to be fairly low-intelligence programs, meaning that the macro-recording facility can't pick up on the fact that you might want to do something 10 times, and so just records the same action multiple times. But they work fine for finding out that the equivalent of selecting the Print item of the File menu is to "say" `ActiveDocument.PrintOut()`.

Putting all of this at work, the program, when run, outputs text like:

```
C:\Programs> python formletter.py
Printing letter for John Doe.
Got comment from Your Mom, skipping printing.
Printing letter for Susan B. Anthony.
```

and prints two customized letters, ready to be sent in the mail. Note that the Word program doesn't show up on the desktop; by default, COM servers are invisible, so Word just acts behind the scenes. If Word is currently active on the desktop, each step is visible to the user (one more reason why it's good to run these things after hours).

A Tkinter-Based GUI Editor for Managing Form Data

Let's recap: we wrote a CGI program (*feedback.py*) that takes the input from a web form and stores the information on disk on our server. We then wrote a program (*formletter.py*) that takes some of those files and generates apologies to those deserving them. The next task is to construct a program to allow a human to look at the comments and complaints, using the Tkinter toolkit to build a GUI browser for these files.

The Tkinter toolkit is a Python-specific interface to a non-Python GUI library called Tk. Tk is the de facto choice for most Python users because it provides professional-looking GUIs within a fairly easy-to-use system. The interfaces it generates don't look exactly like Windows, the Mac, or any Unix toolkit, but they look very close to each of them, and the same Python program works on all those platforms, which is basically impossible with any platform-specific toolkit. Another portable toolkit worth considering is wxPython (*http://www.alldunn.com/wxPython*).

Tk, then, is what we'll use in this example. It's a toolkit developed by John Ousterhout, originally as a companion to Tcl, another scripting language. Since then, Tk has been adopted by many other scripting languages including Python and Perl. For more information on Perl and Tk, see O'Reilly's *Learning Perl/Tk* by Nancy Walsh.

The goals of this program are simple: to display in a window a listing of all of the feedback data items, allowing the user to select one to examine in greater detail (e.g., seeing the contents of the text widget). Furthermore, Joe wants to be able to discard items that are dealt with, to avoid having an always increasing list of items. A screenshot of the finished program in action is shown in Figure 10-4.

We'll work through one possible way of coding it. Our entire program, called *feedbackeditor.py*, is:

```
from FormEditor import FormEditor
from feedback import FeedbackData, FormData
from Tkinter import mainloop
FormEditor("Feedback Editor", FeedbackData, r"c:\Complaintdir")
mainloop()
```

This is cheating only if we don't tell you what's in *FormEditor*, but we will. The point of breaking these four lines out into a separate file is that we've broken out all that is specific to our form. As we'll see, the *FormEditor* program is completely

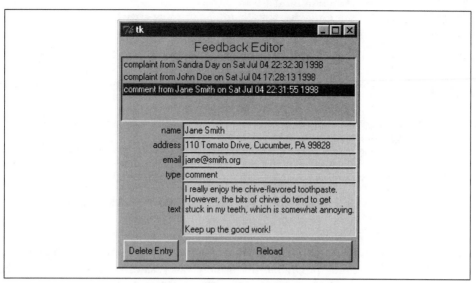

Figure 10-4. A sample screen dump of the feedbackeditor.py program

independent of the specific CGI form. A further point made explicit by this micro-program is that it shows how to interact with Tkinter; you create widgets and windows, and then call the *mainloop* function, which sets the GUI running. Every change in the program that follows happens as a result of GUI actions. As for *formletter.py*, this program imports the class objects from the `feedback` module, for the same reason (unpickling). Then, an instance of the `FormEditor` class is created, passing to its initialization function the name of the editor, the class of the objects being unpickled, and the location of the pickled instances.

The code for `FormEditor` is just a class definition, which we'll describe in parts, one method at a time. First, the import statements and the initialization method:

```
from Tkinter import *
import string, os, pickle

class FormEditor:
    def __init__(self, name, dataclass, storagedir):
        self.storagedir = storagedir     # stash away some references
        self.dataclass = dataclass
        self.row = 0
        self.current = None

        self.root = root = Tk()          # create window and size it
        root.minsize(300,200)

        root.rowconfigure(0, weight=1)     # define how columns and rows scale
        root.columnconfigure(0, weight=1)  # when the window is resized
        root.columnconfigure(1, weight=2)
```

```
            # create the title Label
            Label(root, text=name, font='bold').grid(columnspan=2)
            self.row = self.row + 1
            # create the main listbox and configure it
            self.listbox = Listbox(root, selectmode=SINGLE)
            self.listbox.grid(columnspan=2,sticky=E+W+N+S)
            self.listbox.bind('<ButtonRelease-1>', self.select)
            self.row = self.row + 1

        # call self.add_variable once per variable in the class's fieldnames var
            for fieldname in dataclass.fieldnames:
                setattr(self, fieldname, self.add_variable(root, fieldname))

        # create a couple of buttons, with assigned commands
            self.add_button(self.root, self.row, 0, 'Delete Entry', self.delentry)
            self.add_button(self.root, self.row, 1, 'Reload', self.load_data)

            self.load_data()
```

We use the sometimes dangerous `from ... import *` construct we warned you
about earlier. In Tkinter programs, it's usually fairly safe, because Tkinter only
exports variables that are fairly obviously GUI-related (`Label`, `Widget`, etc.), and
they all start with uppercase letters.

Understanding the `__init__` method is best done by comparing the structure of
the code to the structure of the window screen dump. As you move down the
`__init__` method lines, you should be able to match many statements with their
graphical consequences.

The first few lines simply stash away a few things in instance variables and assign
default values to variables. The next set of lines access a so-called `Toplevel` widget
(basically, a window; the `Tk()` call returns the currently defined top-level widget),
sets its minimum size, and sets a few properties. The row and column configuration
options allow the widgets inside the window to scale if the user enlarges the window and determines the relative width of the two columns of internal widgets.

The next call creates a `Label` widget, which is defined in the `Tkinter` module,
and which, as you can see in the screen dump, is just a text label. It spans both
columns of widgets, meaning that it extends from the leftmost edge of the window to the rightmost edge. Specifying the locations of graphical elements is
responsible for the majority of GUI calls, due to the wide array of possible
arrangements.

The `Listbox` widget is created next; it's a list of text lines, which can be selected
by the user using arrow keys and the mouse button. This specific listbox allows
only one line to be selected at a time (`selectmode=SINGLE`) and fills all the space
available to it (the `sticky` option).

The `for` loop block is the most interesting bit of code in the method; by iterating over the `fieldnames` attribute of the `dataclass` variable (in our example, the `fieldnames` class of the `FeedbackData` class), it finds out which variables are in the instance data, and for each, calls the `add_variable` method of the `FormEditor` class and takes the returned value and stuffs it in an instance variable. This is equivalent in our case to:

```
    ...
self.name = self.add_variable(root, 'name')
self.email = self.add_variable(root, 'email')
self.address = self.add_variable(root, 'address')
self.type = self.add_variable(root, 'type')
self.text = self.add_variable(root, 'text')
```

The version in the code sample, however, is better, because the list of field names is already available to the program and retyping anything is usually an indicator of bad design. Furthermore, there is nothing about `FormData` that is specific to our specific forms. It can be used to browse any instance of a class that defines a variable `fieldnames`. Making the program generic like this makes it more likely to be reused in other contexts for other tasks.

Finishing off with the `__init__` method, we see that two buttons finish the graphical layout of the window, each associated with a command that's executed when it's clicked. One is the `delentry` method, which deletes the current entry, and the other is a reloading function that rereads the data in the storage directory.

Finally, the data is loaded by a call to the `load_data` method. We'll describe it as soon as we're done with the calls that set up widgets, namely `add_variable` and `add_button`.

`add_variable` creates a `Label` widget, which displays the name of the field, and on the same row, places a `Label` widget, which will contain the value of the corresponding field in the entry selected in the listbox:

```
def add_variable(self, root, varname):
    Label(root, text=varname).grid(row=self.row, column=0, sticky=E)
    value = Label(root, text='', background='gray90',
                  relief=SUNKEN, anchor=W, justify=LEFT)
    value.grid(row=self.row, column=1, sticky=E+W)
    self.row = self.row + 1
    return value
```

`add_button` is simpler, as it needs to create only one widget:

```
def add_button(self, root, row, column, text, command):
    button = Button(root, text=text, command=command)
    button.grid(row=row, column=column, sticky=E+W, padx=5, pady=5)
```

The `load_data` function cleans up any contents in the listbox (the graphical list of items) and resets the `items` attribute (which is a Python list that will contain references to the actual data instances). The loop is quite similar to that used for *printcomplaints.py*, except that:

- The name of the file in which an instance is stored is attached as an attribute to that instance (we'll see why shortly)

- The instance is added to the items instance attribute

- The string representation of the item (note the use of the backtick `) is added to the listbox

- Finally, the first item in the listbox is selected:

```
def load_data(self):
    self.listbox.delete(0,END)
    self.items = []
    for filename in os.listdir(self.storagedir):
        item = pickle.load(open(os.path.join(self.storagedir, filename)))
        item._filename = filename
        self.items.append(item)
        self.listbox.insert('end', `item`)
    self.listbox.select_set(0)
    self.select(None)
```

We now get to the **select** method we mentioned previously. It's called in one of two circumstances. The first, as we just showed, is the last thing to happen when the data is loaded. The second is a consequence of the binding operation in the **__init__** method, which we reprint here:

```
self.listbox.bind('<ButtonRelease-1>', self.select)
```

This call binds the occurrence of a specific event (`'<ButtonRelease-1>'`) in a specific widget (**self.listbox**) to an action calling **self.select**. In other words, whenever you let go of the left mouse button on an item in the listbox, the **select** method of your editor is called. It's called with an argument of type **Event**, which can let us know such things as when the button click occurred, but since we don't need to know anything about the event except that it occurred, we'll ignore it. What must happen on selection? First, the instance corresponding to the item being selected in the GUI element must be identified, and then the fields corresponding to the values of that instance must be updated. This is performed by iterating over each field name (looking back to the **fieldnames** class variable again), finding the value of the field in the selected instance, and configuring the appropriate label widget to display the right text:[*]

```
def select(self, event):
    selection = self.listbox.curselection()
    self.selection = self.items[int(selection[0])]
    for fieldname in self.dataclass.fieldnames:
        label = getattr(self, fieldname)                # GUI field
```

---

[*] The replace operation is needed because Tk treats the \r\n sequence that occurs on Windows machines as two carriage returns instead of one.

```
        labelstr = getattr(self.selection, fieldname)   # instance attribute
        labelstr = string.replace(labelstr,'\r', '')
        label.config(text=labelstr)
```

The reload functionality we need is exactly that of the **load_data** method, which is why that's what was passed as the command to be called when the reload button is clicked. The deletion of an entry, however, is a tad more difficult. As we mentioned, the first thing to do when loading an instance from disk is to give it an attribute that corresponds to the filename whence it came. We use this information to delete the file before asking for a reload; the listbox is automatically updated:

```
    def delentry(self):
        os.remove(os.path.join(self.storagedir,self.selection._filename))
        self.load_data()
```

This program is probably the hardest to understand of any in this book, simply because it uses the complex and powerful Tkinter library extensively. There is documentation for Tkinter, as well as for Tk itself (see "Tkinter Documentation").

Tkinter Documentation

The documentation for Tkinter is as elusive as it is needed; it's getting better all the time, however. Tkinter was originally written by someone (Steen Lumholdt) who needed a GUI for his work with Python. He didn't write much documentation, alas. Tkinter has since been upgraded many times over, mostly by Guido van Rossum. The documentation for Tkinter is still incomplete; however, there are a few pieces of documentation currently available, and by the time you read this, much more may be available.

- The most complete documentation is Fredrik Lundh's documentation, available on the Web at *http://www.pythonware.com/library/tkinter/introduction/index.htm*.

- An older but still useful document called *Matt Conway's life preserver* is available at *http://www.python.org/doc/life-preserver/index.html*.

- *Programming Python* also has documentation on Tkinter, especially Chapters 11, 12, and 16.

- Possibly more: see the *python.org* web site section on Tkinter at *http://www.python.org/topics/tkinter/*.

Design Considerations

Think of the CGI script *feedback.py* and the GUI program *FormEditor.py* as two different ways of manipulating a common dataset (the pickled instances on disk). When should you use a web-based interface, and when should you use a GUI? The choice should be based on a couple of factors:

- How easy is it to implement the needed functionality in a given framework?

- What software can you require the user to install in order to access or modify the data?

The web frontend is therefore well suited to cases where the complexity of the data manipulation requirements is low and where it's more important that users be able to "work the program" than that the program be full-featured. Building a "real" program on top of a GUI toolkit, on the other hand, allows maximum flexibility, at the cost of having to teach the user how to use it and/or installing specific programs. One reason for Python's success among experienced programmers is that Python allows them to design programs based on such reasoned bases, as opposed to forcing them to use one type of programming framework just because it's what the language designer had in mind. It's also possible to develop full-featured applications that happen to use web browsers as their GUI. Zope is a framework for writing such applications, and is available free from Digital Creations under an Open Source license. If you're interested in developing full-fledged web-based applications, give Zope a look (see Appendix A, *Python Resources*, for more details).

JPython: The Felicitous Union of Python and Java

JPython is a recently released version of Python written entirely in Java by Jim Hugunin. JPython is a very exciting development for both the Python community and the Java community. Python users are happy that their current Python knowledge can transfer to Java-based development environments; Java programmers are happy that they can use the Python scripting language as a way to control their Java systems, test libraries, and learn about Java libraries from an interpreted environment.

JPython is available from *http://www.jpython.org*, with license and distribution terms similar to those of CPython (which is what the reference implementation of Python is called when contrasted with JPython).

The JPython installation includes several parts:

- jpython: The equivalent of the Python program used throughout the book.

- jpythonc: Takes a JPython program and compiles it to Java class files. The resulting Java class files can be used as any Java class file can, for example as applets, as servlets, or as beans.

- A set of modules that provide the JPython user with the vast majority of the modules in the standard Python library.

- A few programs demonstrating various aspects of JPython programming.

Using JPython is very similar to using Python:

```
~/book> jpython
JPython 1.0.3 on java1.2beta4
Copyright 1997-1998 Corporation for National Research Initiatives
>>> 2 + 3
5
```

In fact, JPython works almost identically to CPython. For an up-to-date listing of the differences between the two, see *http://www.jpython.org/docs/differences.html*. The most important differences are:

- JPython is currently slower than CPython. How much slower depends on the test code used and on the Java Virtual Machine JPython is using. JPython's author has, on the other hand, explored very promising optimizations, which could make future versions of JPython as fast or faster than CPython.

- Some of the built-ins or library modules aren't available for JPython. For example, the os.system() call is not implemented yet, as doing so is difficult given Java's interaction with the underlying operating system. Also, some of the largest extension modules such as the Tkinter GUI framework aren't available, because the underlying tools (the Tk/Tcl toolkit, in the case of Tkinter) aren't available in Java.

JPython Gives Python Programmers Access to Java Libraries

The most important difference between JPython and CPython, however, is that JPython offers the Python programmer seamless access to Java libraries. Consider the following program, *jpythondemo.py*, the output of which is shown in Figure 10-5.

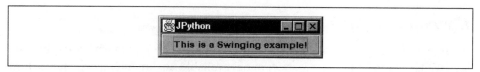

Figure 10-5. The output of jpythondemo.py

```
from pawt import swing
import java

def exit(e): java.lang.System.exit(0)

frame = swing.JFrame('Swing Example', visible=1)
button = swing.JButton('This is a Swinging button!', actionPerformed=exit)
frame.contentPane.add(button)
frame.pack()
```

This simple program demonstrates how easy it is to write a Python program that uses the Swing Java GUI framework.* The first line imports the **swing** Java package (the **pawt** module figures out the exact location of Swing, which can be in `java.awt.swing`, in `com.sun.java.swing`, or maybe in `javax.swing`). The second line imports the `java` package that we need for the `java.lang.System.exit()` call. The fourth line creates a **JFrame**, setting its bean property **visible** to true. The fifth line creates a **JButton** with a label and specifies what function should be called when the button is clicked. Finally, the last two lines put the **JButton** in the **JFrame** and make them both visible.

Experienced Java programmers might be a bit surprised at some of the code in *jpythondemo.py*, as it has some differences from the equivalent Java program. In order to make using Java libraries as easy as possible for Python users, JPython performs a lot of work behind the scenes. For example, when JPython imports a Java package, it actively tracks down the appropriate package, and then, using the Java Reflection API, finds the contents of packages, and the signatures of classes and methods. JPython also performs on-the-fly conversion between Python types and Java types. In *jpythondemo.py*, for example, the text of the button (`'This is a Swinging example!'`) is a Python string. Before the constructor for **JButton** is called, JPython finds which variant of the constructor can be used (e.g., by rejecting the version that accepts an **Icon** as a first argument), and automatically converts the Python string object to a Java string object. More sophisticated mechanisms allow the convenient `actionPerformed=exit` keyword argument to the **JButton** constructor. This idiom isn't possible in Java, since Java can't manipulate functions (or methods) as first-class objects. JPython makes it unnecessary to create an **ActionListener** class with a single `actionPerformed` method, although you can use the more verbose form if you wish.

JPython as a Java Scripting Language

JPython is gaining in popularity because it allows programmers to explore the myriad Java libraries that are becoming available in an interactive, rapid turn-

---

* Documentation for Swing and the Java Foundation Classes is available online at *http://java.sun.com/products/jfc/index.html*. Alternatively, Robert Eckstein, Marc Loy, and Dave Wood have published a thorough review of the Swing toolkit for Java, *Java Swing*, published by O'Reilly & Associates.

around environment. It also is proving useful to embed Python as a scripting language in Java frameworks, for customization, testing, and other programming tasks by end users (as opposed to systems developers). For an example of a Python interpreter embedded in a Java program, see the program in the *demo/embed* directory of the JPython distribution.

A Real JPython/Swing Application: grapher.py

The *grapher.py* program (output shown in Figure 10-6) allows users to graphically explore the behavior of mathematical functions. It's also based on the Swing GUI toolkit. There are two text-entry widgets in which Python code should be entered. The first is an arbitrary Python program that's invoked before the function is drawn; it imports the needed modules and defines any functions that might be needed in computing the value of the function. The second text area (labeled **Expression:**) should be a Python expression (as in `sin(x)`), not a statement. It's called for each data point, with the value of the variable **x** set to the horizontal coordinate.

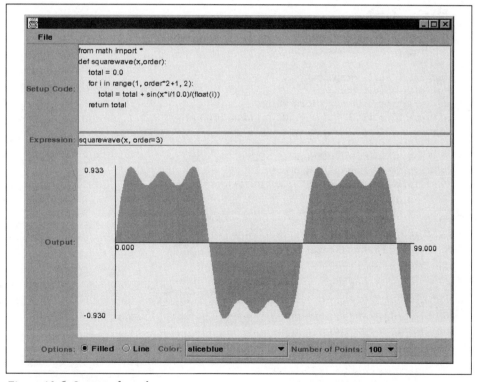

Figure 10-6. Output of grapher.py

The user can control whether to draw a line graph or a filled graph, the number of points to plot, and what color to plot the graph in. Finally, the user can save configurations to disk and reload them later (using the **pickle** module) Here is the *grapher.py* program:

```
from pawt import swing, awt, colors, GridBag
RIGHT = swing.JLabel.RIGHT
APPROVE_OPTION = swing.JFileChooser.APPROVE_OPTION
import java.io
import pickle, os

default_setup = """from math import *
def squarewave(x,order):
    total = 0.0
    for i in range(1, order*2+1, 2):
        total = total + sin(x*i/10.0)/(float(i))
    return total
"""
default_expression = "squarewave(x, order=3)"

class Chart(awt.Canvas):
    color = colors.darkturquoise
    style = 'Filled'

    def getPreferredSize(self):
        return awt.Dimension(600,300)

    def paint(self, graphics):
        clip = self.bounds
        graphics.color = colors.white
        graphics.fillRect(0, 0, clip.width, clip.height)

        width = int(clip.width * .8)
        height = int(clip.height * .8)
        x_offset = int(clip.width * .1)
        y_offset = clip.height - int(clip.height * .1)

        N = len(self.data); xs = [0]*N; ys = [0]*N

        xmin, xmax = 0, N-1
        ymax = max(self.data)
        ymin = min(self.data)

        zero_y = y_offset - int(-ymin/(ymax-ymin)*height)
        zero_x = x_offset + int(-xmin/(xmax-xmin)*width)

        for i in range(N):
            xs[i] = int(float(i)*width/N) + x_offset
            ys[i] = y_offset - int((self.data[i]-ymin)/(ymax-ymin)*height)
        graphics.color = self.color
        if self.style == "Line":
            graphics.drawPolyline(xs, ys, len(xs))
        else:
```

```
            xs.insert(0, xs[0]); ys.insert(0, zero_y)
            xs.append(xs[-1]); ys.append(zero_y)
            graphics.fillPolygon(xs, ys, len(xs))

        # draw axes
        graphics.color = colors.black
        graphics.drawLine(x_offset,zero_y, x_offset+width, zero_y)
        graphics.drawLine(zero_x, y_offset, zero_x, y_offset-height)

        # draw labels
        leading = graphics.font.size
        graphics.drawString("%.3f" % xmin, x_offset, zero_y+leading)
        graphics.drawString("%.3f" % xmax, x_offset+width, zero_y+leading)
        graphics.drawString("%.3f" % ymin, zero_x-50, y_offset)
        graphics.drawString("%.3f" % ymax, zero_x-50, y_offset-height+leading)

class GUI:
    def __init__(self):
        self.numelements = 100
        self.frame = swing.JFrame(windowClosing=self.do_quit)

        # build menu bar
        menubar = swing.JMenuBar()
        file = swing.JMenu("File")
        file.add(swing.JMenuItem("Load", actionPerformed = self.do_load))
        file.add(swing.JMenuItem("Save", actionPerformed = self.do_save))
        file.add(swing.JMenuItem("Quit", actionPerformed = self.do_quit))
        menubar.add(file)
        self.frame.JMenuBar = menubar

        # create widgets
        self.chart = Chart(visible=1)
        self.execentry = swing.JTextArea(default_setup, 8, 60)
        self.evalentry = swing.JTextField(default_expression,
                                    actionPerformed = self.update)

        # create options panel
        optionsPanel = swing.JPanel(awt.FlowLayout(
            alignment=awt.FlowLayout.LEFT))

        # whether the plot is a line graph or a filled graph
        self.filled = swing.JRadioButton("Filled",
                                    actionPerformed=self.set_filled)
        optionsPanel.add(self.filled)
        self.line = swing.JRadioButton("Line",
                                    actionPerformed=self.set_line)
        optionsPanel.add(self.line)
        styleGroup = swing.ButtonGroup()
        styleGroup.add(self.filled)
        styleGroup.add(self.line)

        # color selection
        optionsPanel.add(swing.JLabel("Color:", RIGHT))
        colorlist = filter(lambda x: x[0] != '_', dir(colors))
```

```
        self.colorname = swing.JComboBox(colorlist)
        self.colorname.itemStateChanged = self.set_color
        optionsPanel.add(self.colorname)

        # number of points
        optionsPanel.add(swing.JLabel("Number of Points:", RIGHT))
        self.sizes = [50, 100, 200, 500]
        self.numpoints = swing.JComboBox(self.sizes)
        self.numpoints.selectedIndex = self.sizes.index(self.numelements)
        self.numpoints.itemStateChanged = self.set_numpoints
        optionsPanel.add(self.numpoints)

        # do the rest of the layout in a GridBag
        self.do_layout(optionsPanel)

    def do_layout(self, optionsPanel):
        bag = GridBag(self.frame.contentPane, fill='BOTH',
                      weightx=1.0, weighty=1.0)
        bag.add(swing.JLabel("Setup Code: ", RIGHT))
        bag.addRow(swing.JScrollPane(self.execentry), weighty=10.0)
        bag.add(swing.JLabel("Expression: ", RIGHT))
        bag.addRow(self.evalentry, weighty=2.0)
        bag.add(swing.JLabel("Output: ", RIGHT))
        bag.addRow(self.chart, weighty=20.0)
        bag.add(swing.JLabel("Options: ", RIGHT))
        bag.addRow(optionsPanel, weighty=2.0)
        self.update(None)
        self.frame.visible = 1
        self.frame.size = self.frame.getPreferredSize()

        self.chooser = swing.JFileChooser()
        self.chooser.currentDirectory = java.io.File(os.getcwd())

    def do_save(self, event=None):
        self.chooser.rescanCurrentDirectory()
        returnVal = self.chooser.showSaveDialog(self.frame)
        if returnVal == APPROVE_OPTION:
            object = (self.execentry.text,  self.evalentry.text,
                      self.chart.style,
                      self.chart.color.RGB,
                      self.colorname.selectedIndex,
                      self.numelements)
            file = open(os.path.join(self.chooser.currentDirectory.path,
                        self.chooser.selectedFile.name), 'w')
            pickle.dump(object, file)
            file.close()

    def do_load(self, event=None):
        self.chooser.rescanCurrentDirectory()
        returnVal = self.chooser.showOpenDialog(self.frame)
        if returnVal == APPROVE_OPTION:
            file = open(os.path.join(self.chooser.currentDirectory.path,
                        self.chooser.selectedFile.name))
            (setup, each, style, color,
             colorname, self.numelements) = pickle.load(file)
```

```
            file.close()
            self.chart.color = java.awt.Color(color)
            self.colorname.selectedIndex = colorname
            self.chart.style = style
            self.execentry.text = setup
            self.numpoints.selectedIndex = self.sizes.index(self.numelements)
            self.evalentry.text = each
            self.update(None)

    def do_quit(self, event=None):
        import sys
        sys.exit(0)

    def set_color(self, event):
        self.chart.color = getattr(colors, event.item)
        self.chart.repaint()

    def set_numpoints(self, event):
        self.numelements = event.item
        self.update(None)

    def set_filled(self, event):
        self.chart.style = 'Filled'
        self.chart.repaint()

    def set_line(self, event):
        self.chart.style = 'Line'
        self.chart.repaint()

    def update(self, event):
        context = {}
        exec self.execentry.text in context
        each = compile(self.evalentry.text, '<input>', 'eval')
        numbers = [0]*self.numelements
        for x in xrange(self.numelements):
            context['x'] = float(x)
            numbers[x] = eval(each, context)
        self.chart.data = numbers
        if self.chart.style == 'Line':
            self.line.setSelected(1)
        else:
            self.filled.setSelected(1)
        self.chart.repaint()

GUI()
```

The logic of this program is fairly straightforward, and the class and method names make it easy to follow the flow of control. Most of this program could have been written in fairly analogous (but quite a bit longer) Java code. The parts in bold, however, show the power of having Python available: at the top of the module, default values for the **Setup** and **Expression** text widgets are defined. The former imports the functions in the **math** module and defines a function called **squarewave**. The latter specifies a call to this function, with a specific **order** parameter (as that parameter grows, the resulting graph looks more and more like a square wave, hence the name of the function). If you have Java, Swing, and JPython installed, feel free to play around with other possibilities for both the `Setup` and `Expression` text widgets.

The key asset of using JPython instead of Java in this example is in the `update` method: it simply calls the standard Python `exec` statement with the `Setup` code as an argument, and then calls `eval` with the compiled version of the `Expression` code for each coordinate. The user is free to use any part of Python in these text widgets!

JPython is still very much a work in progress; Jim Hugunin is constantly refining the interface between Python and Java and optimizing it. JPython, by being the second implementation of Python, is also forcing Guido van Rossum to decide what aspects of Python are core to the language and what aspects are features of his implementation. Luckily, Jim and Guido seem to be getting along and agreeing on most points.

Other Frameworks and Applications

With limited space, we could cover only a few of the most popular frameworks currently used with Python. There are several others, which are also deserving of mention and which might very well be what you need. We briefly describe some here.

Python Imaging Library (PIL)

The Python Imaging Library is an extensive framework written by Fredrik Lundh for creating, manipulating, converting, and saving bitmapped images in a variety of formats (such as GIF, JPEG, and PNG). It has interfaces to Tk and Pythonwin, so that one can use either Tk widgets or Pythonwin code to display PIL-generated images. Alternatively, the images can be saved to disk in a variety of formats. The home for PIL is at *http://www.pythonware.com*.

Numeric Python (NumPy)

Numeric Python is a set of extensions to Python designed to manipulate large arrays of numbers quickly and elegantly. It was written by Jim Hugunin (JPython's author), with the support of the subscribers to the Matrix-SIG (more on SIGs in Appendix A). Since Jim started work on JPython, the responsibility for Numeric Python has been taken over by folks at the Lawrence Livermore National Laboratory. NumPy is a remarkably powerful tool for scientists and engineers, and as such is close to the heart of one of these authors. More information on it is available at the main Python web site's topic guide for scientific computing (*http://www.python.org/topics/scicomp/*).

Here's an example of typical NumPy code, *numpytest.py*, and one representation of the data in generates:

```
from Numeric import *
coords = arange(-6, 6, .02)              # create a range of coordinates
xs = sin(coords)                         # take the sine of all of the x's
ys = cos(coords)*exp(-coords*coords/18.0) # take a complex function of the y's
zx = xs * ys[:,NewAxis]                  # multiply the x row with the y column
```

If you remember your math, you might figure out that **xs** is an array of the sines of the numbers between –6 and 6, and **ys** is an array of the cosines of those same numbers scaled by an exponential function centered at 0. **zs** is simply the outer product of those two arrays of numbers. If you're curious as to what that might look like, you could convert the array **zs** into an image (with the aforementioned PIL, for example) and obtain the image shown in Figure 10-7.

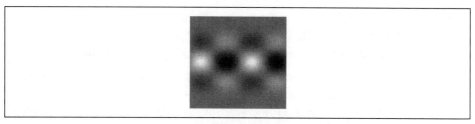

Figure 10-7. Graphical representation of the array zs in numpytest.py

NumPy lets you manipulate very large arrays of numbers very efficiently. The preceding code runs orders of magnitude faster than comparable code using large lists of numbers and uses a fraction of the memory. Many Python users never have to deal with these kinds of issues, but many scientists and engineers require such capabilities daily.

SWIG

Extension modules for Python can be written in C or C++. Such modules allow easy extension of Python with functions and new types. The guidelines for writing such extension modules are available as part of the standard Python library reference and described at some length in *Programming Python* as well. One common use of extension modules is to write interfaces between Python and existing libraries, which can contain hundreds or thousands of single functions. When this is the case, the use of automated tools is a lifesaver. David Beazley's SWIG, the Simple Wrapper Interface Generator, is the most popular such tool. It's available at *http://www.swig.org* and is very well documented. With SWIG, you write simple interface definitions, which SWIG then uses to generate the C programs that conform to the Python/C extension guidelines. One very nice feature of SWIG is that when it's used to wrap C++ class libraries, it automatically creates so-called *shadow classes* in Python that let the user manipulate C++ classes as if they were Python classes. SWIG can also create extensions for other languages, including Perl and Tcl.

Python MegaWidgets (Pmw)

Anyone doing serious GUI work with Tkinter should check out Pmw, a 100% Python framework built on top of Tkinter, designed to allow the creation of mega-widgets (compound widgets). Pmw, written by Greg McFarlane, is the next step beyond Tkinter, and learning it can pay off in the long run. Pmw's home page is at *http://www.dscpl.com.au/pmw/*.

ILU and Fnorb

If the notion of programs talking to programs is of interest to you, but you want a solution that works on platforms with no COM support, there are many other packages with similar functionality. Two favorites are ILU and Fnorb.

ILU stands for Xerox PARC's Inter Language Unification project. It's free, well-supported, stable, and efficient, and supports C, C++, Java, Common Lisp, Modula-3, and Perl 5, in addition to Python. It's available at *ftp://ftp.parc.xerox.com/pub/ilu/ilu.html*.

Unlike ILU, Fnorb is written in Python and supports only Python. It's especially helpful for learning more about CORBA systems, since it's easy to set up and play with once you know Python. Fnorb is available from *http://www.dstc.edu.au/Fnorb/*.

Exercises

Most of the topics of this chapter are not really good topics for exercises without first covering the frameworks they cover. A couple of things can be done with the knowledge you already have, however:

1. *Faking the Web.* You may not have a web server running, which makes using *formletter.py* and *FormEditor.py* difficult, since they use data generated by the CGI script. As an exercise, write a program that creates files with the same properties as those created by the CGI script.

2. *Cleaning up.* There's a serious problem with the *formletter.py* program: namely, if, as we mention, it's run nightly, any complaint is going to cause a

letter to be printed. That will happen every night, since there is no mechanism for indicating that a letter has been generated and that no more letters need be generated regarding that specific complaint. Fix this problem.

3. *Adding parametric plotting to grapher.py.* Modify *grapher.py* to allow the user to specify expressions that return both x and y values, instead of the current "just y" solution. For example, the user should be able to write in the **Expression** widget: `sin(x/3.1),cos(x/6.15)` (note the comma: this is a tuple!) and get a picture like that shown in Figure 10-8.

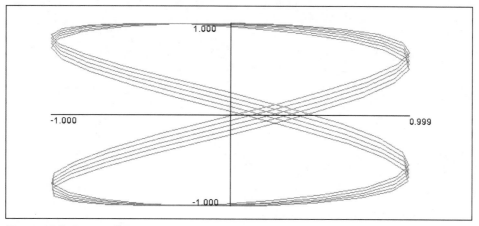

Figure 10-8. Output of Exercise 3

III

Appendixes

This last part of the book consists of three appendixes that are mostly pointers to other sources of information.

- Appendix A, *Python Resources*, presents general Python resources such as sources of documation, advice, and software.

- Appendix B, *Platform-Specific Topics*, covers resources that are specific to certain operating systems.

- Appendix C, *Solutions to Exercises*, lists the answers to all the exercises presented at the end of chapters in Parts I and II.

Python Resources

This appendix is a selection of the most useful resources for the Python programmer, including items that aren't part of the standard distribution. These include software (both Python modules and extension modules), documentation, discussion groups, and commercial sources of support.

The Python Language Web Site

The single most important source of information is *http://www.python.org*. This web site is the focal point of the Python community. All Python software, documentation, and other information is available either on that web site directly or from locations listed on the web site. We encourage you to spend a fair bit of time exploring it, as it's quite large and comprehensive. See Figure A-1 for a snapshot of the web site's home page .

Python Software

The Standard Python Distribution

The most essential piece of Python software is clearly the Python interpreter itself. It's available in many formats for a variety of platforms. We defer discussion of the platform-specific issues until Appendix B, *Platform-Specific Topics*. In general, the most reliable way to get an up-to-date distribution is to download it from the main Python web site (*http://www.python.org*). The Python web site is maintained by volunteers from the Python Software Association (see the next sidebar, "The Python Software Association (PSA) and the Python Consortium"), a group dedicated to the long-term success of Python. If you'd rather get Python binaries on a CD, Walnut Creek has a Python CD-ROM available that includes binaries for all common plat-

Figure A-1. A screenshot of the python.org web site

forms (Windows, Macs, many versions of Unix, BeOS, and VMS). The URL for the last distribution available at time of writing is *http://www.cdrom.com/titles/prog/python.htm*, but check the Walnut Creek catalog for eventual newer releases. As described in Appendix B, most Linux distributions include Python. Both *Programming Python* and *Internet Programming with Python* (see the section "Other Published Books") also come with CDs that include Python distributions.

The standard distribution comes with hundreds of modules, both in C and Python. These modules are all officially supported by Guido and his crew (unless otherwise noted; when replaced by newer tools, old modules are kept for a few years to give users time to upgrade their software, and support for them decreases gradually). The interpreter, the standard library, and the standard documentation constitute the minimum set of tools a Python user has access to.

In addition to the standard distribution, there are hundreds of packages and modules available on the Web, most of which are free. We'll mention a few specifically and where to get them.

The Python Software Association (PSA) and the Python Consortium

While Guido van Rossum is Python's primary creator, he has been getting some help in recent years, especially when it comes to the various public-relations aspect of the Python language. The Python Software Association is an association of companies and individuals who wish to help preserve Python's existence as a free, evolving, well-supported language. PSA volunteers help run the *python.org* web site, organize the Python conferences, and collect membership dues from PSA members to help underwrite the costs of the web site, conferences, and other Python-related events. If you or your company are interested in joining the PSA, visit the PSA's web site at: *http://www.python.org/psa/*.

One perk of a PSA membership is that it entitles you to a free account on the "Starship Python," a web site run by a grateful Python user, Christian Tismer, as a public service to the Python community. The starship's current URL is *http://starship.skyport.net*, but it will soon move to *http://starship.python.net*.

The Python Consortium is a recent development that holds promise for long-term support of Python's development. CNRI (Guido van Rossum's current employer) is proposing to host a consortium of companies that would support, through membership dues, the development of the Python and JPython development environments. More information about the Python Consortium is available at *http://www.python.org/consortium/*.

Gifts from Guido

As if Python and its standard libraries weren't enough, Guido ships a few other programs as part of the standard distribution. They are located in the Tools directory of the Python source tree (or the Python installation directory on Windows and Mac).

In this set, as of Python 1.5.2, there is a first cut at an integrated development environment for Python, called *idle*. As Figure A-2 shows, it's a GUI based on top of Tkinter, so it requires that you have Tk/Tcl installed. *idle* is still in its infancy, but already provides quite a few nice features that make it ideal for the Python novice uses to friendly development environments:

- A Python shell, smarter than the standard one we've been using all along.

- A Python-aware editor, which does automatic "colorization" of Python code: statements are drawn with one color, comments with another, etc. This is a feature of the Python mode for Emacs as well, and one that's easy to learn to love.

- A class browser that lets you explore a module's classes and jump directly to the method definitions in the source code.

- An interactive debugger.

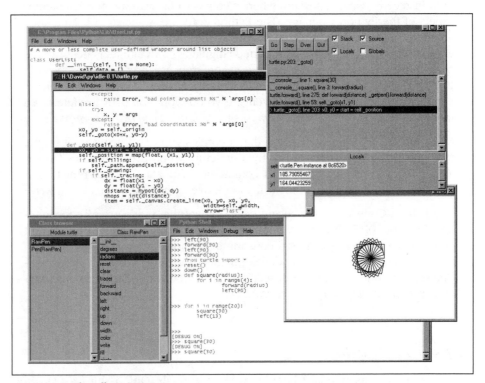

Figure A-2. The idle IDE in action

Offerings from Commercial Vendors

 We mention a few commercial software companies in this section. While this might seem at odds with a language that's usually "free," there is no contradiction in the Python community to having Python-based projects and "business models." Python's license is specifically crafted so that software vendors can use Python with no restrictions. Most Python users are glad to hear that companies are building successful companies based on Python. There are quite a few Python-related success stories that executives more or less freely disclose.* We mention only the companies that distribute code specifically aimed at Python programmers, not companies whose products include Python.

Scriptics Corporation's Tcl/Tk toolkits

The Tkinter GUI framework we've referred to throughout the text is built on top of the Tk GUI toolkit, which itself uses the Tcl language. These are available in binary and source form from the web site of the Scriptics Corporation: *http://www. scriptics.com/*. For information about Tkinter-related resources, consult the Tkinter topic guide at *http://www.python.org/topics/tkinter/*.

Digital Creation's free releases

Digital Creation is a software company that has recently shifted from selling Python-based software packages to distributing them for free under the Open Source license. They have made several significant contributions to the Python community, by contributing to the standard distribution (they are responsible for the `cPickle` and `cStringIO` modules, for example), by helping the Python Software Association grow in many ways, and by distributing at no cost two very powerful Python tools. These are:

ExtensionClass

A C extension module that allows the creation of extension types that can act as Python classes. In addition, ExtensionClasses allow you to modify the way these new types work, including support for Acquisition. Acquisition is a mechanism by which objects can get attributes from the objects that they are a part of, much like instances can get attributes from their class or from their class' base classes.

---

* Guido van Rossum is sometimes frustrated to hear companies say, off the record, that they use Python, but that they don't want it known publicly because they view their decision to use Python as a "strategic advantage."

Zope

A framework for publishing Python object hierarchies on the Web. With Zope, it's easy to set up a powerful interface to a database of Python objects. There are several extensions to Zope that allow scaling of web-based applications, by providing support for templates, interfaces to database engines, etc. If you're thinking about developing sophisticated web applications (as opposed to simple forms processing as we showed in Chapter 10, *Frameworks and Applications*), you should seriously investigate these tools.

Digital Creations' web site is at *http://www.digicool.com*; their free tools are available at *http://www.digicool.com/site/Free/*, and Zope is available at *http://www. zope.org*.

Pythonware

Pythonware is a Swedish Python toolsmith company, with several projects currently in development, including an Integrated Development Environment for Python, a lightweight replacement for Tk for Windows platforms, and an image processing framework. The reason we mention what is still "vaporware" is that the folks at Pythonware have already released other tools for free that have shown themselves to be quite useful, suggesting that these products will be worth the wait. Most important among their free releases is the Python Imaging Library (PIL), which we mentioned in Chapter 10, and the most comprehensive documentation for Tkinter anywhere. For PIL and other Pythonware tools, look at their web site, *http://www.pythonware.com*.

Other Modules and Packages

There are many other modules and packages available on the Web. These can be found in many locations:

- The Contributed Modules section on the main Python web site (*http://www. python.org/download/Contributed.html*) lists hundreds of modules, in a range of topics, including network tools, and graphic, database, and system interfaces.

- The PyModules FAQ is an always evolving list of modules, also organized by category. It's available at: *http://starship.skyport.net/crew/aaron_watters/faqwiz/ contrib.cgi*.

- The crew of the Starship make many of their tools available. The Starship project is a web site at which any member of the Python Software Association can get an account for free, including web pages. See the previous sidebar for details.

A few of the tools that can be found in these three directories deserve special mention, because they have been found remarkably useful. These are:

Gadfly

An SQL database engine written entirely in Python by Aaron Watters. While its speed is not that of a high-performance commercial software vendor's database engine, its speed compares well to Microsoft's Access. Gadfly is at *http://www.chordate.com/gadfly.html*.

Medusa

A high-performance Internet server framework also written entirely in Python, this time by Sam Rushing. By using a multiplexing I/O single-process server, it offers high-performance for HTTP, FTP, and other IP services. While only free for noncommercial use, commercial licenses are quite inexpensive. Medusa is at *http://www.nightmare.com/medusa/*.

If you're looking for tools to use to teach programming with Python, two tools to consider are:

turtle.py

A Python module written by Guido van Rossum, and part of the standard Python library as of Python 1.5.2. This module provides simple "turtle graphics" in a Tk window. Turtle graphics have been used extensively to teach programming to children using the Logo language.

Alice

A program designed to allow nonexperts to explore interactive 3-D graphics. It was developed originally by a group at the University of Virginia, but is now under the auspices of the computer science department at Carnegie-Mellon University. See *http://alice.cs.cmu.edu/*.

Emacs Support

While this is not truly Python software, there is very good support for editing Python code from within the Emacs editor (on all platforms for which Emacs is available). From within Emacs, you can edit syntax-colored Python code, browse the functions, classes, and methods within a buffer, and run a Python interpreter or the Pdb python debugger, all within one of the most popular and powerful editors available. Information on Python support in Emacs can be found at *http://www.python.org/emacs/*.

Python Documentation and Books

There are three kinds of sources of published information on Python: the standard Python documentation set, published books, and online material.

The Standard Python Documentation Set

The standard Python documentation set includes five separate documents. They are all available in various formats (HTML, PDF, and PostScript, among others) at *http://www.python.org/doc/*. They are:

The Tutorial

A fast-paced introduction to the language that most current Python programmers used to learn Python. It assumes a fair bit of previous programming knowledge, so novices tend to find it overwhelming in places, and it doesn't give Python's object-oriented features their due.

The Library Reference

The most important of the Python books. It lists all the built-in functions and what the built-in type methods and semantics are, and describes almost all the modules that make up the standard distribution. It's well worth keeping on your local hard disk and consulting when in doubt about a specific function's interface or semantics, or when you can't remember specific method names for the built-in objects.

The Language Reference

The most formal specification of the language itself. It gives the precise definition of syntactic operations, precedence rules, etc. Most users happily ignore it, but it does give the final word on intricate details of the language.

Extending and Embedding

A document describing the precise rules of interaction between Python and C extensions (and the simpler case of embedding, when Python is being called by an existing C or C++ program). If you wish to write an extension module for Python, this book defines just what to do. The section on keeping track of references is especially important for tracking bugs in such modules.

The Python/C API

A document describing the routines Python uses internally. You can also use these routines to manipulate Python objects from within C/C++ programs, usually in extension modules.

The FAQ

Like many other topics of interest on the Internet, Python has developed a list of Frequently Asked Questions. It's available at *http://www.python.org/doc/FAQ.html*, and covers everything from general information about Python (its name, origins, design choices, etc.) to issues arising when compiling or installing Python, programming questions, and more. The Python FAQ is maintained by the community at large. Any PSA member can log onto a web-driven program (a CGI program, like the one we saw in Chapter 10) and update existing entries or add new entries. As a result, the FAQ is both quite large and very current.

Other Published Books

There are three books besides the one you're holding that are available in book-stores. These are:

- *Programming Python*, by Mark Lutz, published by O'Reilly & Associates. This 860-page book is the logical next step after *Learning Python*. It covers in greater depth all the material covered here, and then some. Almost all aspects of Python are covered with progressively more sophisticated examples. *Programming Python* also discusses Python/C integration, and advanced applications such as Tkinter GUIs and persistence.

- *Internet Programming with Python,* by Aaron Watters, Guido van Rossum, and James Ahlstrom, published by M&T Books. This is a 477-page book that provides an introduction to most of the Python, with special emphasis on writing programs to publish web pages.

- *The Python Pocket Reference,* by Mark Lutz, published by O'Reilly & Associates. This is a short (75 pages) booklet listing the core aspect of the syntax, and the most commonly used modules and their function signatures. It covers Python 1.5.1.

Other Sources of Documentation

The number of web pages describing Python modules, howto's, guides for novices, common tasks, etc., makes it impossible to list them all here. Instead, we'll encourage you to browse the Web, starting at the main Python web site. The PSA volunteers (Ken Manheimer, Andrew Kuchling, Barry Warsaw, and Guido van Rossum, to be precise) spend considerable effort making sure the web site is both comprehensive and well organized, so you shouldn't have a problem finding what you need. Most significant packages and modules have associated web pages and documentation for them.

Newsgroups, Discussion Groups, and Email Help

Python owes a great deal of its growth to a worldwide community of users who exchange information about Python via the Internet. Most day-to-day exchanges about Python occur in various electronic forums, which each have specific aims and scopes.

comp.lang.python/python-list

The main "public space" for discussions of Python is the *comp.lang.python* Usenet newsgroup, which is bidirectionally gatewayed as the mailing list *python-list@cwi.nl* (although there are plans to move it to *python-list@python.org*). If you don't have access to a Usenet newsfeed already, you can read *comp.lang.python* using the Dejanews service (*www.dejanews.com*), or read the equivalent *python-list* mailing list via the eGroups service (*http://www.egroups.com/list/python-list/*). This mailing list/newsgroup is the appropriate forum to ask questions, discuss specific Python problems, post announcements of Python jobs, etc.

comp.lang.python.announce/python-list-announce

Recently, a new newsgroup was created, with the aim of being a low-traffic list just for significant announcements of Python-related news. The *comp.lang.python. announce* newsgroup (also gatewayed as *python-list-announce@cwi.nl*) is a moderated forum, so only postings deemed appropriate are allowed through.

python-help@python.org

One of the characteristics of the main Usenet newsgroup/mailing list is that it's automatically broadcast to tens of thousands of readers around the world. While this allows for rapid response time from someone almost always (no matter what time it is, someone is reading the Python newsgroup somewhere in the world), it also can be somewhat intimidating, especially to novices. A more private place to ask questions is the *python-help* address, which serves as a helpline. Email to *python-help@python.org* is broadcast to a set of about a dozen volunteers, who will try their best to promptly answer questions sent to *python-help*. When writing to this list, it helps to specify exactly what configuration you're using (Python version, operating system, etc.) and to describe your problem or question precisely. This helps the volunteers understand your problem, and hopefully help you solve it fast.

The SIGs

One more set of mailing lists should be mentioned here. The main Python newsgroup is remarkable by its generality. However, periodically, groups of concerned individuals decide to work together on as specific project, such as the development of a significant extension or the formalization of a standard interface for a tool or set of tools. These groups of volunteers are called *special interest groups*, or SIGs. These groups have their own mailing lists, which you should feel free to browse and join if you feel an affinity with the topic at hand. Successful SIGs have included the Matrix-SIG, which helped Jim Hugunin develop the Numeric Python extensions; the String-SIG, which has worked on the regular expression engine among other topics; and the XML-SIG, which is developing tools for parsing and processing of XML (eXtensible Markup Language). An up-to-date listing of the current SIGs (they die as their task is done, and are born as a need arises) can be found at *http://www.python.org/sigs/*. Each SIG has its own mailing list, archive page, and description.

JPython-interest

There is a mailing list for discussion of JPython-specific issues. It is worth reading if you're interested in JPython, as it's a forum Jim Hugunin and Barry Warsaw use to spread information about JPython and solicit feedback. Information on the list is available at *http://www.python.org/mailman/listinfo/jpython-interest*.

Conferences

While most Python communications happen electronically, the PSA also organizes periodic conferences. These conferences are the only forum where many folks get to meet their email colleagues.* They're also an important forum for presenting new work, learning about aspects of Python by attending tutorials and talks, and a place for discussions on the future directions of Python. Information about the conferences is regularly posted on the newsgroup as well as displayed on the main Python web site. Locations of past conferences have included Washington, DC; San Jose and Livermore, CA; and Houston, TX.

Support Companies, Consultants, Training

The last group of resources for Python users consists of support companies, consultants and trainers.

Python Professional Services, Inc., is a company that provides various types of technical support for Python and related modules. Their URL is *http://www. pythonpros.com*.

While there is at present no online listing of Python consultants, several experienced Python users are available for short- and long-term consulting work. Check *www.python.org* for information, and feel free to post a request for help on the Python newsgroup. If you want to keep your inquiries more private, email *python-help@python.org*.

---

* So far, your two authors have only met in person at Python conferences!

Finally, several training programs are available for companies who wish to have onsite classes for their employees. No global listing is available at present, but might be available by the time you read this. Again, check *http://www.python.org*, the newsgroup or *python-help@python.org*.

Tim Peters

He's not paid to do it, but a fellow by the name of Tim Peters is known to answer more questions about Python on the newsgroup than anyone in their right mind should. His comments are not only wise and helpful but quite often hilarious as well. Rumor has it that he is a living human being, although we have never met him in person, so there's always the possibility that he's just a nicely crafted Python program. Come to think of it, only one person we have talked to claims to have *met* Tim in person, and that's Guido. Makes you wonder...

B

Platform-Specific Topics

This appendix covers platform-specific topics—where to get distributions of Python for each specific platform (i.e., combination of hardware and operating system), and any important notes regarding compatibility or availability of tools specific to your platform.

Unix

Python's largest user base is most likely Unix users these days, although the number of Windows users is growing steadily. There are several distributions available for Unix. The standard method of obtaining Python is to download the source distribution (*http://www.python.org/download/download_source.html*), and configure, build, and install Python yourself. There was an effort a while back to keep at the Python web site a set of precompiled binaries of Python for most of the major Unix platforms, but this effort has mostly been dropped, because there was no way to make it maintainable; there are too many different versions of Unix and too many ways to configure Python for each one.

We haven't mentioned configurations of Python in this book; that's because we've mostly covered the most standard part of the Python distribution. Someone who downloads the source distribution, however, will soon notice a references to a file called *Setup* in the *Modules* directory. This file allows you to configure which modules are compiled, either for static or for dynamic linking. The set of available optional modules changes with each release and can be augmented by downloading third-party extensions.

There is an exception to the "no binary distributions" rule, and that is for Linux. Most versions of Linux come with Python already installed, and some use it extensively in their configuration management system. The version on the Linux distributions may not be the latest version available. Oliver Andrich maintains a set of RPMs (which are packages in a standard format for Red Hat Linux) of the latest distributions of Python, including the most popular extensions. These are available at *http://www.python.org/ download/download_linux.html.*

Unix-Specific Extensions

Several extensions are available on most if not all Unix versions. These include:

Standard distribution

There are interfaces to most well-established services on Unix. For example, there is a pwd module for interacting with the password file, a grp module for manipulating the Unix group database, as well as modules allowing one to interface to the crypt library functions (crypt), the *dbm/ndbm/gdbm* database libraries (dbm and gdbm), the tty I/O control calls (termios), the file descriptor I/O interface (fcntl), a module for measuring and controlling system resources (resources), a module for interfacing with the system logging tools (syslog), a wrapper module around the popen call that makes interfacing with shell commands easier (commands), and finally a module that gives access to the stat system call for finding such things as modification times of files and the like (stat).

The standard library also includes modules that operate on specific Unix flavors, such as SGI and SunOS/Solaris:

SGI-specific extensions

On Silicon Graphics systems, the standard distribution includes modules for interfacing with the AL audio library (al and AL), the CD library (cd), the FORMS Library by Mark Overmas (fl, flp and FL), the font manager (fm), the old IRIX GL library (gl, GL and DEVICE),* and the imglib image file format (imgfile).

SunOS-specific extensions

On SunOS/Solaris, the standard distribution includes one module, sunaudiodev, that allows an interface to the audio device.

Other Unix resources

Many modules have been published for support of various Unix tools or have been tested on Unix. These include interfaces to audio subsystems, scanners, and

---

* The OpenGL interface is supported cross-platform by a set of modules currently maintained by one of your authors (David Ascher), and is available at *http://starship.python.net/~da/PyOpenGL/.* It currently works on SGI systems as well as other Unix platforms and Windows, and can be linked with either OpenGL or the compatible Mesa toolkit.

cameras, the X Window System interface and its layered toolkits, and many others; search the Python web site if you're looking for a specific extension you think might have been interfaced already.

Windows-Specific Information

The Windows platform (Windows 95, 98, and NT) is one of the most active areas of growth for Python, both in terms of the number of users and in the number of extensions being built. While the standard distribution from *www.python.org* works just fine on Windows, there are a set of Windows-specific extensions that are available as part of the *win32all* package, from Mark Hammond. The *win32all* package is available at *http://www.python.org/windows/win32all/* and includes several powerful programs and extensions.

The most visible is the *Pythonwin* program, which is an integrated development environment for Python, providing an interactive interpreter interface (with keyboard shortcuts, font coloring, etc.), an editor, and an object browser (see Figure B-1). *Pythonwin* is, in fact, using several large packages that allow Python to drive a great deal of the libraries available as part of Windows, such as the Microsoft Foundation Classes, the ODBC database interface, NT-specific services such as logging, performance monitoring, memory-mapped files, pipes, timers, and, most importantly, all of COM, Microsoft's Common Object Model. This means that, as we mentioned in Chapter 10, *Frameworks and Applications*, most modern software written for Windows should be scriptable from Python if it supports any scripting at all. In general, almost anything you can do in heavily marketed scripting languages such as Visual Basic, you can do in Python with COM support. Python can also be used as an ActiveX scripting host in such programs as Internet Explorer.

Macintosh-Specific Information

The Macintosh platform also supports Python fully, thanks mostly to the efforts of Jack Jansen. There are a few Mac-specific features worth knowing about. First, you can make applets out of scripts, so that dropping a file on the script is the same as running the script with the dropped file's name in *sys.argv*. Also, Just van Rossum (yes, Guido's brother) wrote an Integrated Development Environment for Python on the Mac. It is included in the distribution, but the latest version can always be found at *http://www.python.org/download/download_mac.html*. A sample screenshot of Just's debugger in action is shown in Figure B-2.

Also, there are several modules that provide interfaces to Mac-specific services available as part of the MacPython distribution. These include interfaces to Apple Events, the Component, Control, Dialog, Event, Font, List, and Menu Managers,

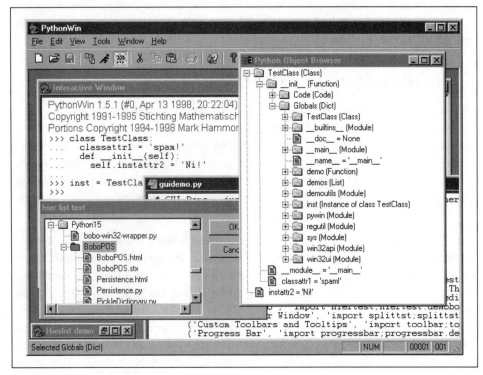

Figure B-1. The Pythonwin program in action

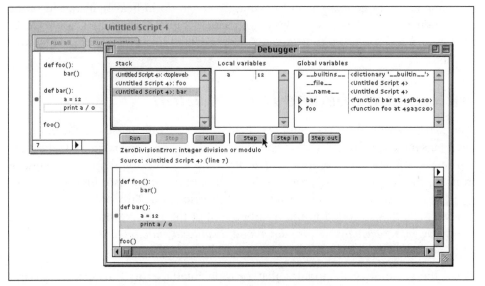

Figure B-2. Screenshot of the Macintosh IDE's debugger in action

QuickDraw, QuickTime, the Resource, Scrap and Sound managers, TextEdit, and the Window Manager. Also covered (and documented in a supplement to the library reference available at *http://www.python.org/doc/mac/*) are interfaces implementing the `os` and `os.path` modules, interfaces to the Communications Tool Box, the domain name resolver, the FSSpec, Alias Manager, finder aliases, and the Standard File package, Internet Config, MacTCP, the Speech Manager, and more.

Java

As we described in Chapter 10, JPython is a complete implementation by Jim Hugunin of Python for Java. It's the most different port mentioned in this appendix, since it shares none of the C code base (but most of the Python code base) of the reference implementation of Python. The home page for JPython is *http://www.python.org/jpython/*. The set of extensions to JPython is the same as the set of Java libraries that are available. In other words, it's a huge list. A good place to look for Java information is at Sun's web site: *http://java.sun.com.*

Other Platforms

Finally, many enterprising souls have ported Python more or less completely to a variety of other platforms. Table B-1 lists each port we know about, each platform, the author or maintainer of the port, and the URL from which more information can be gleaned.

Table B-1. Sources of Information

Platform	Author/ Maintainer	URL
Amiga	Irmen De Jong	*http://www.geocities.com/ResearchTriangle/Lab/ 3172/python.html*
BeOS	Chris Herborth	*http://www.qnx.com/~chrish/Be/software/ #programming*
Windows CE	Brian Lloyd	*http://www.digicool.com/~brian/PythonCE/ index.html*
DOS/Windows 3.1	Hans Novak	*http://www.cuci.nl/~hnowak/python/python.htm*
QNX	Chris Herborth	*ftp://ftp.qnx.com/usr/free/qnx4/os/language/ python-1.5.tgz*
Psion Series 5	Duncan Booth	*http://dales.rmplc.co.uk/Duncan/PyPsion.htm*
OpenVMS	Uwe Zessin	*http://decus.decus.de/~zessin/*
VxWorks	Jeff Stearns	*mailto:jeffstearns@home.com*

Solutions to Exercises

Chapter 1, Getting Started

1. *Interaction.* Assuming your Python is configured properly, you should partici-pate in an interaction that looks something like this:

```
% python
copyright information lines...
>>> "Hello World!"
'Hello World!'
>>>                          # <Ctrl-D or Ctrl-Z to exit>
```

2. *Programs.* Here's what your code (i.e., module) file and shell interactions should look like:

```
% cat module1.py
print 'Hello module world!'

% python module1.py
Hello module world!
```

3. *Modules.* The following interaction listing illustrates running a module file by importing it. Remember that you need to reload it to run again without stop-ping and restarting the interpreter. The bit about moving the file to a different directory and importing it again is a trick question: if Python generates a *module1.pyc* file in the original directory, it uses that when you import the module, even if the source code file (*.py*) has been moved to a directory not on Python's search path. The *.pyc* file is written automatically if Python has access to the source file's directory and contains the compiled bytecode ver-sion of a module. We look at how this works in more detail in Chapter 5, *Modules.*

```
% python
>>> import module1
```

```
Hello module world!
>>>
```

4. *Scripts.* Assuming your platform supports the **#!** trick, your solution will look like the following (though your **#!** line may need to list another path on your machine):

```
% cat module1.py
#!/usr/local/bin/python          (or #!/usr/bin/env python)
print 'Hello module world!'

% chmod +x module1.py

% module1.py
Hello module world!
```

5. *Errors.* The interaction below demonstrates the sort of error messages you get if you complete this exercise. Really, you're triggering Python *exceptions*; the default exception handling behavior terminates the running Python program and prints an error message and stack trace on the screen. The stack trace shows where you were at in a program when the exception occurred (it's not very interesting here, since the exceptions occur at the top level of the interactive prompt; no function calls were in progress). In Chapter 7, *Exceptions*, you will see you can catch exceptions using **try** statements and process them arbitrarily; you'll also see that Python includes a full-blown source-code debugger for special error detection requirements. For now, notice that Python gives meaningful messages when programming errors occur (instead of crashing silently):

```
% python
>>> 1 / 0
Traceback (innermost last):
  File "<stdin>", line 1, in ?
ZeroDivisionError: integer division or modulo
>>>
>>> x
Traceback (innermost last):
  File "<stdin>", line 1, in ?
NameError: x
```

6. *Breaks.* When you type this code:

```
L = [1, 2]
L.append(L)
```

you create a *cyclic* data-structure in Python. In Python releases before Version 1.5.1, the Python printer wasn't smart enough to detect cycles in objects, and it would print an unending stream of [1, 2, [1, 2, [1, 2, [1, 2, and so on, until you hit the break key combination on your machine (which, technically, raises a keyboard-interrupt exception that prints a default message at the top level unless you intercept it in a program). Beginning with Python Version 1.5.1, the printer is clever enough to detect cycles and prints [[...]] instead.

The reason for the cycle is subtle and requires information you'll gain in Chapter 2, *Types and Operators*. But in short, assignment in Python always generates references to objects (which you can think of as implicitly followed pointers). When you run the first assignment above, the name L becomes a named reference to a two-item list object. Now, Python lists are really arrays of object references, with an **append** method that changes the array in-place by tacking on another object reference. Here, the **append** call adds a reference to the front of L at the end of L, which leads to the cycle illustrated in Figure C-1. Believe it or not, cyclic data structures can sometimes be useful (but not when printed!).

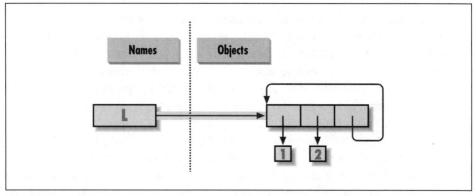

Figure C-1. A cyclic list

Chapter 2, Types and Operators

1. *The basics.* Here are the sort of results you should get, along with a few comments about their meaning:

Numbers

```
>>> 2 ** 16              # 2 raised to the power 16
65536
>>> 2 / 5, 2 / 5.0       # integer / truncates, float / doesn't
(0, 0.4)
```

Strings

```
>>> "spam" + "eggs"      # concatenation
'spameggs'
>>> S = "ham"
>>> "eggs " + S
'eggs ham'
>>> S * 5                # repetition
'hamhamhamhamham'
>>> S[:0]                # an empty slice at the front--[0:0]
''
>>> "green %s and %s" % ("eggs", S)  # formatting
```

'green eggs and ham'

Tuples

```
>>> ('x',)[0]                    # indexing a single-item tuple
'x'
>>> ('x', 'y')[1]                # indexing a 2-item tuple
'y'
```

Lists

```
>>> L = [1,2,3] + [4,5,6]        # list operations
>>> L, L[:], L[:0], L[-2], L[-2:]
([1, 2, 3, 4, 5, 6], [1, 2, 3, 4, 5, 6], [], 5, [5, 6])
>>> ([1,2,3]+[4,5,6])[2:4]
[3, 4]
>>> [L[2], L[3]]                 # fetch from offsets, store in a list
[3, 4]
>>> L.reverse(); L               # method: reverse list in-place
[6, 5, 4, 3, 2, 1]
>>> L.sort(); L                  # method: sort list in-place
[1, 2, 3, 4, 5, 6]
>>> L.index(4)                   # method: offset of first 4 (search)
3
```

Dictionaries

```
>>> {'a':1, 'b':2}['b']          # index a dictionary by key
2
>>> D = {'x':1, 'y':2, 'z':3}
>>> D['w'] = 0                   # create a new entry
>>> D['x'] + D['w']
1
>>> D[(1,2,3)] = 4               # a tuple used as a key (immutable)
>>> D
{'w': 0, 'z': 3, 'y': 2, (1, 2, 3): 4, 'x': 1}
>>> D.keys(), D.values(), D.has_key((1,2,3))        # methods
(['w', 'z', 'y', (1, 2, 3), 'x'], [0, 3, 2, 4, 1], 1)
```

Empties

```
>>> [[]], ["",[],(),{},None]                        # lots of nothings
([[]], ['', [], (), {}, None])
```

2. *Indexing and slicing.*

     a. Indexing out-of-bounds (e.g., L[4]) raises an error; Python always checks to make sure that all offsets are within the bounds of a sequence (unlike C, where out-of-bound indexes will happily crash your system).

     b. On the other hand, slicing out of bounds (e.g., L[-1000:100]) works, because Python scales out-of-bounds slices so that they always fit (they're set to zero and the sequence length, if required).

c. Extracting a sequence in reverse—with the lower bound > the higher bound (e.g., L[3:1])—doesn't really work. You get back an empty slice ([]), because Python scales the slice limits to makes sure that the lower bound is always less than or equal to the upper bound (e.g., L[3:1] is scaled to L[3:3], the empty insertion point after offset 3). Python slices are always extracted from left to right, even if you use negative indexes (they are first converted to positive indexes by adding the length).

```
>>> L = [1, 2, 3, 4]
>>> L[4]
Traceback (innermost last):
  File "<stdin>", line 1, in ?
IndexError: list index out of range
>>> L[-1000:100]
[1, 2, 3, 4]
>>> L[3:1]
[]
>>> L
[1, 2, 3, 4]
>>> L[3:1] = ['?']
>>> L
[1, 2, 3, '?', 4]
```

3. *Indexing, slicing, and del.* Your interaction with the interpreter should look something like that listed below. Note that assigning an empty list to an offset stores an empty list object there, but assigning it to a slice deletes the slice. Slice assignment expects another sequence, or you'll get a type error.

```
>>> L = [1,2,3,4]
>>> L[2] = []
>>> L
[1, 2, [], 4]
>>> L[2:3] = []
>>> L
[1, 2, 4]
>>> del L[0]
>>> L
[2, 4]
>>> del L[1:]
>>> L
[2]
>>> L[1:2] = 1
Traceback (innermost last):
  File "<stdin>", line 1, in ?
TypeError: illegal argument type for built-in operation
```

4. *Tuple assignment.* The values of X and Y are swapped. When tuples appear on the left and right of an assignment operator (=), Python assigns objects on the right to targets on the left, according to their positions. This is probably easiest to understand by noting that targets on the left aren't a real tuple, even though they look like one; they are simply a set of independent assignment targets. The items on the right *are* a tuple, which get unpacked during the

assignment (the tuple provides the temporary assignment needed to achieve the swap effect).

```
>>> X = 'spam'
>>> Y = 'eggs'
>>> X, Y = Y, X
>>> X
'eggs'
>>> Y
'spam'
```

5. *Dictionary keys.* Any immutable object can be used as a dictionary key—integers, tuples, strings, and so on. This really is a dictionary, even though some of its keys look like integer offsets. Mixed type keys work fine too.

```
>>> D = {}
>>> D[1] = 'a'
>>> D[2] = 'b'
>>> D[(1, 2, 3)] = 'c'
>>> D
{1: 'a', 2: 'b', (1, 2, 3): 'c'}
```

6. *Dictionary indexing.* Indexing a nonexistent key (D['d']) raises an error; assigning to a nonexistent key (D['d'] = 'spam') creates a new dictionary entry. On the other hand, out-of-bounds indexing for lists raises an error too, but so do out-of-bounds assignments. Variable names work like dictionary keys: they must have already been assigned when referenced, but are created when first assigned. In fact, variable names can be processed as dictionary keys if you wish (they're visible in module namespace or stack-frame dictionaries).

```
>>> D = {'a':1, 'b':2, 'c':3}
>>> D['a']
1
>>> D['d']
Traceback (innermost last):
  File "<stdin>", line 1, in ?
KeyError: d
>>> D['d'] = 4
>>> D
{'b': 2, 'd': 4, 'a': 1, 'c': 3}
>>>
>>> L = [0,1]
>>> L[2]
Traceback (innermost last):
  File "<stdin>", line 1, in ?
IndexError: list index out of range
>>> L[2] = 3
Traceback (innermost last):
  File "<stdin>", line 1, in ?
IndexError: list assignment index out of range
```

7. *Generic operations.*

   a. The + operator doesn't work on different/mixed types (e.g., string + list, list + tuple).

   b. + doesn't work for dictionaries, because they aren't sequences.

   c. The **append** method works only for lists, not strings, and **keys** works only on dictionaries. **append** assumes its target is mutable, since it's an in-place extension; strings are immutable.

   d. Slicing and concatenation always return a new object of the same type as the objects processed.

   ```
   >>> "x" + 1
   Traceback (innermost last):
     File "<stdin>", line 1, in ?
   TypeError: illegal argument type for built-in operation
   >>>
   >>> {} + {}
   Traceback (innermost last):
     File "<stdin>", line 1, in ?
   TypeError: bad operand type(s) for +
   >>>
   >>> [].append(9)
   >>> "".append('s')
   Traceback (innermost last):
     File "<stdin>", line 1, in ?
   AttributeError: attribute-less object
   >>>
   >>> {}.keys()
   []
   >>> [].keys()
   Traceback (innermost last):
     File "<stdin>", line 1, in ?
   AttributeError: keys
   >>>
   >>> [][:]
   []
   >>> ""[:]
   ' '
   ```

8. *String indexing.* Since strings are collections of one-character strings, every time you index a string, you get back a string, which can be indexed again. S[0][0][0][0][0] just keeps indexing the first character over and over. This generally doesn't work for lists (lists can hold arbitrary objects), unless the list contains strings.

   ```
   >>> S = "spam"
   >>> S[0][0][0][0][0]
   's'
   >>> L = ['s', 'p']
   >>> L[0][0][0]
   's'
   ```

9. *Immutable types.* Either of the solutions below work. Index assignment doesn't, because strings are immutable.

```
>>> S = "spam"
>>> S = S[0] + '1' + S[2:]
>>> S
'slam'
>>> S = S[0] + '1' + S[2] + S[3]
>>> S
'slam'
```

10. *Nesting.* Your mileage will vary.

```
>>> me = {'name':('mark', 'e', 'lutz'), 'age':'?', 'job':'engineer'}
>>> me['job']
'engineer'
>>> me['name'][2]
'lutz'
```

11. *Files.*

```
% cat maker.py
file = open('myfile.txt', 'w')
file.write('Hello file world!\n')
file.close()                         # close not always needed

% cat reader.py
file = open('myfile.txt', 'r')
print file.read()

% python maker.py
% python reader.py
Hello file world!

% ls -l myfile.txt
-rwxrwxrwa   1 0        0              19 Apr 13 16:33 myfile.txt
```

12. *The dir function revisited:* Here's what you get for lists; dictionaries do the same (but with different method names).

```
>>> [].__methods__
['append', 'count', 'index', 'insert', 'remove', 'reverse', 'sort']
>>> dir([])
['append', 'count', 'index', 'insert', 'remove', 'reverse', 'sort']
```

Chapter 3, Basic Statements

1. *Coding basic loops.* If you work through this exercise, you'll wind up with code that looks like the following:

```
>>> S = 'spam'
>>> for c in S:
...     print ord(c)
...
115
112
```

```
97
109

>>> x = 0
>>> for c in S: x = x + ord(c)
...
>>> x
433

>>> x = []
>>> for c in S: x.append(ord(c))
...
>>> x
[115, 112, 97, 109]

>>> map(ord, S)
[115, 112, 97, 109]
```

2. *Backslash characters*. The example prints the bell character (\a) 50 times;
   assuming your machine can handle it, you'll get a series of beeps (or one long
   tone, if your machine is fast enough). Hey—we warned you.

3. *Sorting dictionaries*. Here's one way to work through this exercise; see
   Chapter 2 if this doesn't make sense:

```
>>> D = {'a':1, 'b':2, 'c':3, 'd':4, 'e':5, 'f':6, 'g':7}
>>> D
{'f': 6, 'c': 3, 'a': 1, 'g': 7, 'e': 5, 'd': 4, 'b': 2}
>>>
>>> keys = D.keys()
>>> keys.sort()
>>> for key in keys:
...     print key, '=>', D[key]
...
a => 1
b => 2
c => 3
d => 4
e => 5
f => 6
g => 7
```

4. *Program logic alternatives*. Here's how we coded the solutions; your results
   may vary a bit.

   a.

```
L = [1, 2, 4, 8, 16, 32, 64]
X = 5

i = 0
while i < len(L):
    if 2 ** X == L[i]:
        print 'at index', i
        break
```

```
            i = i+1
    else:
        print X, 'not found'
```

b.

```
    L = [1, 2, 4, 8, 16, 32, 64]
    X = 5

    for p in L:
        if (2 ** X) == p:
            print (2 ** X), 'was found at', L.index(p)
            break
    else:
        print X, 'not found'
```

c.

```
    L = [1, 2, 4, 8, 16, 32, 64]
    X = 5

    if (2 ** X) in L:
        print (2 ** X), 'was found at', L.index(2 ** X)
    else:
        print X, 'not found'
```

d.

```
    X = 5
    L = []
    for i in range(7): L.append(2 ** i)
    print L

    if (2 ** X) in L:
        print (2 ** X), 'was found at', L.index(2 ** X)
    else:
        print X, 'not found'
```

e.

```
    X = 5
    L = map(lambda x: 2**x, range(7))
    print L

    if (2 ** X) in L:
        print (2 ** X), 'was found at', L.index(2 ** X)
    else:
        print X, 'not found'
```

Chapter 4, Functions

1. *Basics.*

```
% python
>>> def func(x): print x
...
>>> func("spam")
```

```
spam
>>> func(42)
42
>>> func([1, 2, 3])
[1, 2, 3]
>>> func({'food': 'spam'})
{'food': 'spam'}
```

2. *Arguments.* Here's what one solution looks like. You have to use `print` to see results in the test calls, because a file isn't the same as code typed interactively; Python doesn't echo the results of expression statements.

% cat mod.py
```
def adder(x, y):
    return x + y

print adder(2, 3)
print adder('spam', 'eggs')
print adder(['a', 'b'], ['c', 'd'])
```

% python mod.py
```
5
spameggs
['a', 'b', 'c', 'd']
```

3. *varargs.* Two alternative **adder** functions are shown in the following code. The hard part here is figuring out how to initialize an accumulator to an empty value of whatever type is passed in. In the first solution, we use manual type testing to look for an integer and an empty slice of the first argument (assumed to be a sequence) otherwise. In the second solution, we just use the first argument to initialize and scan items 2 and beyond. The second solution is better (and frankly, comes from students in a Python course, who were frustrated with trying to understand the first solution). Both of these assume all arguments are the same type and neither works on dictionaries; as we saw in Chapter 2, + doesn't work on mixed types or dictionaries. We could add a type test and special code to add dictionaries too, but that's extra credit.

% cat adders.py

```
def adder1(*args):
    print 'adder1',
    if type(args[0]) == type(0):     # integer?
        sum = 0                      # init to zero
    else:                            # else sequence:
        sum = args[0][:0]            # use empty slice of arg1
    for arg in args:
        sum = sum + arg
    return sum

def adder2(*args):
    print 'adder2',
    sum = args[0]                    # init to arg1
```

```
        for next in args[1:]:
            sum = sum + next        # add items 2..N
        return sum

for func in (adder1, adder2):
    print func(2, 3, 4)
    print func('spam', 'eggs', 'toast')
    print func(['a', 'b'], ['c', 'd'], ['e', 'f'])
```

```
% python adders.py
adder1 9
adder1 spameggstoast
adder1 ['a', 'b', 'c', 'd', 'e', 'f']
adder2 9
adder2 spameggstoast
adder2 ['a', 'b', 'c', 'd', 'e', 'f']
```

4. *Keywords.* Here is our solution to the first part of this one. To iterate over keyword arguments, use a `**args` for in the function header and use a loop like:

   `for x in args.keys(): use args[x]`

```
% cat mod.py
def adder(good=1, bad=2, ugly=3):
    return good + bad + ugly

print adder()
print adder(5)
print adder(5, 6)
print adder(5, 6, 7)
print adder(ugly=7, good=6, bad=5)
```

```
% python mod.py
6
10
14
18
18
```

5. and 6. Here are our solutions to Exercises 5 and 6, but Guido has already made them superfluous; Python 1.5 includes new dictionary methods, to do things like copying and adding (merging) dictionaries. See Python's library manual or the *Python Pocket Reference* for more details. X[:] doesn't work for dictionaries, since they're not sequences (see Chapter 2). Notice that if we assign (e = d) rather than copy, we generate a reference to a shared dictionary object; changing d changes e too.

```
% cat dict.py

def copyDict(old):
    new = {}
    for key in old.keys():
        new[key] = old[key]
    return new
```

```
def addDict(d1, d2):
    new = {}
    for key in d1.keys():
        new[key] = d1[key]
    for key in d2.keys():
        new[key] = d2[key]
    return new
```

```
% python
>>> from dict import *
>>> d = {1:1, 2:2}
>>> e = copyDict(d)
>>> d[2] = '?'
>>> d
{1: 1, 2: '?'}
>>> e
{1: 1, 2: 2}

>>> x = {1:1}
>>> y = {2:2}
>>> z = addDict(x, y)
>>> z
{1: 1, 2: 2}
```

7. *More argument matching examples.* Here is the sort of interaction you should get, along with comments that explain the matching that goes on:

```
def f1(a, b): print a, b              # normal args

def f2(a, *b): print a, b             # positional varargs

def f3(a, **b): print a, b            # keyword varargs

def f4(a, *b, **c): print a, b, c     # mixed modes

def f5(a, b=2, c=3): print a, b, c    # defaults

def f6(a, b=2, *c): print a, b, c     # defaults + positional varargs
```

```
% python
>>> f1(1, 2)                 # matched by position (order matters)
1 2
>>> f1(b=2, a=1)             # matched by name (order doesn't matter)
1 2

>>> f2(1, 2, 3)             # extra positionals collected in a tuple
1 (2, 3)

>>> f3(1, x=2, y=3)         # extra keywords collected in a dictionary
1 {'x': 2, 'y': 3}

>>> f4(1, 2, 3, x=2, y=3)   # extra of both kinds
1 (2, 3) {'x': 2, 'y': 3}
```

```
>>> f5(1)                        # both defaults kick in
1 2 3
>>> f5(1, 4)                     # only one default used
1 4 3

>>> f6(1)                        # one argument: matches "a"
1 2 ()
>>> f6(1, 3, 4)                  # extra positional collected
1 3 (4,)
```

Chapter 5, Modules

1. *Basics, import.* This one is simpler than you may think. When you're done, your file and interaction should look close to the following code; remember that Python can read a whole file into a string or lines list, and the `len` built-in returns the length of strings and lists:

```
% cat mymod.py

def countLines(name):
    file = open(name, 'r')
    return len(file.readlines())

def countChars(name):
    return len(open(name, 'r').read())

def test(name):                              # or pass file object
    return countLines(name), countChars(name)  # or return a dictionary

% python
>>> import mymod
>>> mymod.test('mymod.py')
(10, 291)
```

On Unix, you can verify your output with a **wc** command. Incidentally, to do the "ambitious" part (passing in a file object, so you only open the file once), you'll probably need to use the **seek** method of the built-in file object. We didn't cover it in the text, but it works just like C's **fseek** call (and calls it behind the scenes); **seek** resets the current position in the file to an offset passed in. To rewind to the start of a file without closing and reopening, call *file.seek(0)*; the file read methods all pick up at the current position in the file, so you need to rewind to reread. Here's what this tweak would look like:

```
% cat mymod2.py
def countLines(file):
    file.seek(0)                     # rewind to start of file
    return len(file.readlines())

def countChars(file):
    file.seek(0)                     # ditto (rewind if needed)
    return len(file.read())
```

```
def test(name):
    file = open(name, 'r')                  # pass file object
    return countLines(file), countChars(file)   # only open file once
```

```
>>> import mymod2
>>> mymod2.test("mymod2.py")
(11, 392)
```

2. *from/from**. Here's the `from*` bit; replace * with `countChars` to do the rest:

```
% python
>>> from mymod import *
>>> countChars("mymod.py")
291
```

3. *__main__*. If you code it properly, it works in either mode (program run or module import):

```
% cat mymod.py
def countLines(name):
    file = open(name, 'r')
    return len(file.readlines())

def countChars(name):
    return len(open(name, 'r').read())

def test(name):                            # or pass file object
    return countLines(name), countChars(name)   # or return a dictionary

if __name__ == '__main__':
    print test('mymod.py')
```

```
% python mymod.py
(13, 346)
```

4. *Nested imports.* Our solution for this appears below:

```
% cat myclient.py
from mymod import countLines
from mymod import countChars
print countLines('mymod.py'), countChars('mymod.py')
```

```
% python myclient.py
13 346
```

As for the rest of this one: *mymod*'s functions are accessible (that is, importable) from the top level of myclient, since from assigns just to names in the importer (it's as if `mymod`'s `defs` appeared in *myclient*). If *myclient* used import, you'd need to use a path to get to the functions in `mymod` from *myclient* (for instance, `myclient.mymod.countLines`). In fact, you can define *collector* modules that import all the names from other modules, so they're available in a single convenience module. Using the following code, you wind up with three different copies of name `somename`: `mod1.somename`, `collector.`

somename, and __main__.somename; all three share the same integer object initially.

```
% cat mod1.py
somename = 42
```

```
% cat collector.py
from mod1 import *      # collect lots of names here
from mod2 import *      # from assigns to my names
from mod3 import *
```

>>> **from collector import somename**

5. *Reload.* This exercise just asks you to experiment with changing the *changer.py* example in the book, so there's not much for us to show here. If you had some fun with it, give yourself extra points.

6. *Circular imports.* The short story is that importing recur2 first works, because the *recursive* import then happens at the import in recur1, not at a from in recur2. The long story goes like this: importing recur2 first works, because the recursive import from recur1 to recur2 fetches recur2 as a whole, instead of getting specific names. recur2 is incomplete when imported from recur1, but because it uses import instead of from, you're safe: Python finds and returns the already created recur2 module object and continues to run the rest of recur1 without a glitch. When the recur2 import resumes, the second from finds name Y in recur1 (it's been run completely), so no error is reported. Running a file as a script is not the same as importing it as a module; these cases are the same as running the first import or from in the script interactively. For instance, running recur1 as a script is the same as importing recur2 interactively, since recur2 is the first module imported in recur1. (E-I-E-I-O!)

Chapter 6, Classes

1. *The basics.* Here's the solution we coded up for this exercise, along with some interactive tests. The __add__ overload has to appear only once, in the superclass. Notice that you get an error for expressions where a class instance appears on the right of a +; to fix this, use __radd__ methods also (an advanced topic we skipped; see other Python books and/or Python reference manuals for more details). You could also write the add method to take just two arguments, as shown in the chapter's examples.

```
% cat adder.py

class Adder:
    def add(self, x, y):
        print 'not implemented!'
    def __init__(self, start=[]):
```

```
            self.data = start
    def __add__(self, other):
        return self.add(self.data, other)    # or in subclasses--return type?

class ListAdder(Adder):
    def add(self, x, y):
        return x + y

class DictAdder(Adder):
    def add(self, x, y):
        new = {}
        for k in x.keys(): new[k] = x[k]
        for k in y.keys(): new[k] = y[k]
        return new
```

```
% python
>>> from adder import *
>>> x = Adder()
>>> x.add(1, 2)
not implemented!
>>> x = ListAdder()
>>> x.add([1], [2])
[1, 2]
>>> x = DictAdder()
>>> x.add({1:1}, {2:2})
{1: 1, 2: 2}

>>> x = Adder([1])
>>> x + [2]
not implemented!
>>>
>>> x = ListAdder([1])
>>> x + [2]
[1, 2]
>>> [2] + x
Traceback (innermost last):
  File "<stdin>", line 1, in ?
TypeError: __add__ nor __radd__ defined for these operands
```

2. *Operator overloading.* Here's what we came up with for this one. It uses a few operator overload methods we didn't say much about, but they should be straightforward to understand. Copying the initial value in the constructor is important, because it may be mutable; you don't want to change or have a reference to an object that's possibly shared somewhere outside the class. The routes method `__getattr__` calls to the wrapped list:

```
% cat mylist.py

class MyList:
    def __init__(self, start):
        #self.wrapped = start[:]         # copy start: no side effects
        self.wrapped = []                # make sure it's a list here
        for x in start: self.wrapped.append(x)
    def __add__(self, other):
```

```
            return MyList(self.wrapped + other)
        def __mul__(self, time):
            return MyList(self.wrapped * time)
        def __getitem__(self, offset):
            return self.wrapped[offset]
        def __len__(self):
            return len(self.wrapped)
        def __getslice__(self, low, high):
            return MyList(self.wrapped[low:high])
        def append(self, node):
            self.wrapped.append(node)
        def __getattr__(self, name):          # other members--sort/reverse/etc.
            return getattr(self.wrapped, name)
        def __repr__(self):
            return `self.wrapped`

if __name__ == '__main__':
    x = MyList('spam')
    print x
    print x[2]
    print x[1:]
    print x + ['eggs']
    print x * 3
    x.append('a')
    x.sort()
    for c in x: print c,
```

```
% python mylist.py
['s', 'p', 'a', 'm']
a
['p', 'a', 'm']
['s', 'p', 'a', 'm', 'eggs']
['s', 'p', 'a', 'm', 's', 'p', 'a', 'm', 's', 'p', 'a', 'm']
a a m p s
```

3. *Subclassing.* Our solution appears below. Your solution should appear similar.

```
% cat mysub.py

from mylist import MyList

class MyListSub(MyList):
    calls = 0                                  # shared by instances

    def __init__(self, start):
        self.adds = 0                          # varies in each instance
        MyList.__init__(self, start)

    def __add__(self, other):
        MyListSub.calls = MyListSub.calls + 1  # class-wide counter
        self.adds = self.adds + 1              # per instance counts
        return MyList.__add__(self, other)

    def stats(self):
        return self.calls, self.adds           # all adds, my adds
```

```
if __name__ == '__main__':
    x = MyListSub('spam')
    y = MyListSub('foo')
    print x[2]
    print x[1:]
    print x + ['eggs']
    print x + ['toast']
    print y + ['bar']
    print x.stats()
```

```
% python mysub.py
a
['p', 'a', 'm']
['s', 'p', 'a', 'm', 'eggs']
['s', 'p', 'a', 'm', 'toast']
['f', 'o', 'o', 'bar']
(3, 2)
```

4. *Metaclass methods.* We worked through this exercise as follows. Notice that operators try to fetch attributes through __getattr__ too; you need to return a value to make them work.

```
>>> class Meta:
...     def __getattr__(self, name):          print 'get', name
...     def __setattr__(self, name, value): print 'set', name, value
...
>>> x = Meta()
>>> x.append
get append
>>> x.spam = "pork"
set spam pork
>>>
>>> x + 2
get __coerce__
Traceback (innermost last):
  File "<stdin>", line 1, in ?
TypeError: call of non-function
>>>
>>> x[1]
get __getitem__
Traceback (innermost last):
  File "<stdin>", line 1, in ?
TypeError: call of non-function

>>> x[1:5]
get __len__
Traceback (innermost last):
  File "<stdin>", line 1, in ?
TypeError: call of non-function
```

5. *Set objects.* Here's the sort of interaction you should get; comments explain which methods are called.

```
% python
>>> from set import Set
```

```
>>> x = Set([1,2,3,4])              # runs __init__
>>> y = Set([3,4,5])

>>> x & y                            # __and__, intersect, then __repr__
Set:[3, 4]
>>> x | y                            # __or__, union, then __repr__
Set:[1, 2, 3, 4, 5]

>>> z = Set("hello")                 # __init__ removes duplicates
>>> z[0], z[-1]                      # __getitem__
('h', 'o')

>>> for c in z: print c,             # __getitem__
...
h e l o
>>> len(z), z                        # __len__, __repr__
(4, Set:['h', 'e', 'l', 'o'])

>>> z & "mello", z | "mello"
(Set:['e', 'l', 'o'], Set:['h', 'e', 'l', 'o', 'm'])
```

Our solution to the multiple-operand extension subclass looks like the class below. It needs only to replace two methods in the original set. The class's documentation string explains how it works:

```
from set import Set

class MultiSet(Set):
    """
    inherits all Set names, but extends intersect
    and union to support multiple operands; note
    that "self" is still the first argument (stored
    in the *args argument now); also note that the
    inherited & and | operators call the new methods
    here with 2 arguments, but processing more than
    2 requires a method call, not an expression:
    """

    def intersect(self, *others):
        res = []
        for x in self:                   # scan first sequence
            for other in others:         # for all other args
                if x not in other: break # item in each one?
            else:                        # no:  break out of loop
                res.append(x)            # yes: add item to end
        return Set(res)

    def union(*args):                    # self is args[0]
        res = []
        for seq in args:                 # for all args
            for x in seq:                # for all nodes
                if not x in res:
                    res.append(x)        # add new items to result
        return Set(res)
```

Assuming the new set is stored in a module called *multiset.py*, your interaction with the extension will be something along these lines; note that you can intersect by using & or calling `intersect`, but must call `intersect` for three or more operands; & is a binary (two-sided) operator:

```
>>> from multiset import *
>>> x = MultiSet([1,2,3,4])
>>> y = MultiSet([3,4,5])
>>> z = MultiSet([0,1,2])

>>> x & y, x | y                                # 2 operands
(Set:[3, 4], Set:[1, 2, 3, 4, 5])

>>> x.intersect(y, z)                           # 3 operands
Set:[]
>>> x.union(y, z)
Set:[1, 2, 3, 4, 5, 0]

>>> x.intersect([1,2,3], [2,3,4], [1,2,3])      # 4 operands
Set:[2, 3]
>>> x.union(range(10))                          # non-MultiSets work too
Set:[1, 2, 3, 4, 0, 5, 6, 7, 8, 9]
```

6. *Class tree links.* Here's the way we extended the `Lister` class and a rerun of the test to show its format. To display class attributes too, you'd need to do something like what the `attrnames` method currently does, but recursively, at each class reached by climbing `__bases__` links.

```
class Lister:
    def __repr__(self):
        return ("<Instance of %s(%s), address %s:\n%s>" %
                        (self.__class__.__name__,       # my class's name
                         self.supers(),                 # my class's supers
                         id(self),                      # my address
                         self.attrnames()) )            # name=value list
    def attrnames(self):
        Unchanged...
    def supers(self):
        result = ""
        first = 1
        for super in self.__class__.__bases__:          # one level up from class
            if not first:
                result = result + ", "
            first = 0
            result = result + super.__name__
        return result

C:\python\examples> python testmixin.py
<Instance of Sub(Super, Lister), address 7841200:
        name data3=42
        name data2=eggs
        name data1=spam
>
```

7. *Composition.* Our solution is below, with comments from the description mixed in with the code. This is one case where it's probably easier to express a problem in Python than it is in English:

```
class Lunch:
    def __init__(self):
        # make/embed Customer and Employee
        self.cust = Customer()
        self.empl = Employee()
    def order(self, foodName):
        # start a Customer order simulation
        self.cust.placeOrder(foodName, self.empl)
    def result(self):
        # ask the Customer what kind of Food it has
        self.cust.printFood()

class Customer:
    def __init__(self):
        # initialize my food to None
        self.food = None
    def placeOrder(self, foodName, employee):
        # place order with an Employee
        self.food = employee.takeOrder(foodName)
    def printFood(self):
        # print the name of my food
        print self.food.name

class Employee:
    def takeOrder(self, foodName):
        # return a Food, with requested name
        return Food(foodName)

class Food:
    def __init__(self, name):
        # store food name
        self.name = name

if __name__ == '__main__':
    x = Lunch()
    x.order('burritos')
    x.result()
    x.order('pizza')
    x.result()
```

```
% python lunch.py
burritos
pizza
```

Chapter 7, Exceptions

1. *try/except.* Our version of the **oops** function follows. As for the noncoding questions, changing **oops** to raise **KeyError** instead of **IndexError** means

that the exception won't be caught by our try handler (it "percolates" to the top level and triggers Python's default error message). The names `KeyError` and `IndexError` come from the outermost built-in names scope. If you don't believe us, import `__builtin__` and pass it as an argument to the `dir` function to see for yourself.

```
% cat oops.py

def oops():
    raise IndexError

def doomed():
    try:
        oops()
    except IndexError:
        print 'caught an index error!'
    else:
        print 'no error caught...'

if __name__ == '__main__': doomed()

% python oops.py
caught an index error!
```

2. *Exception lists.* Here's the way we extended this module for an exception of our own:

```
% cat oops.py
MyError = 'hello'

def oops():
    raise MyError, 'world'

def doomed():
    try:
        oops()
    except IndexError:
        print 'caught an index error!'
    except MyError, data:
        print 'caught error:', MyError, data
    else:
        print 'no error caught...'

if __name__ == '__main__':
    doomed()

% python oops.py
caught error: hello world
```

3. *Error handling.* Finally, here's one way to solve this one; we decided to do our tests in a file, rather than interactively, but the results are about the same.

```
% cat safe2.py
import sys, traceback
```

```
def safe(entry, *args):
    try:
        apply(entry, args)                        # catch everything else
    except:
        traceback.print_exc()
        print 'Got', sys.exc_type, sys.exc_value

import oops
safe(oops.oops)
```

% python safe2.py
```
Traceback (innermost last):
  File "safe2.py", line 5, in safe
    apply(entry, args)                            # catch everything else
  File "oops.py", line 4, in oops
    raise MyError, 'world'
hello: world
Got hello world
```

Chapter 8, Built-in Tools

1. *Describing a directory.* There are several solutions to this exercise, naturally.
   One simple solution is:

```
import os, sys, stat

def describedir(start):
    def describedir_helper(arg, dirname, files):
        """ Helper function for describing directories """
        print "Directory %s has files:" % dirname
        for file in files:
            # find the full path to the file (directory + filename)
            fullname = os.path.join(dirname, file)
            if os.path.isdir(fullname):
                # if it's a directory, say so; no need to find the size
                print '  '+ file + ' (subdir)'
            else:
                # find out the size, and print the info.
                size = os.stat(fullname)[stat.ST_SIZE]
                print '  '+file+' size=' + `size`

    # Start the 'walk'.
    os.path.walk(start, describedir_helper, None)
```

which uses the **walk** function in the **os.path** module, and works just fine:

```
>>> import describedir
>>> describedir.describedir2('testdir')
Directory testdir has files:
  describedir.py size=939
  subdir1 (subdir)
  subdir2 (subdir)
Directory testdir\subdir1 has files:
  makezeros.py size=125
```

```
    subdir3 (subdir)
Directory testdir\subdir1\subdir3 has files:
Directory testdir\subdir2 has files:
```

Note that you could have found the size of the files by doing
`len(open(fullname, 'rb').read())`, but this works only when you have
read access to all the files and is quite inefficient. The `stat` call in the `os`
module gives out all kinds of useful information in a tuple, and the `stat`
module defines some names that make it unnecessary to remember the order
of the elements in that tuple. See the *Library Reference* for details.

2. *Modifying the prompt.* The key to this exercise is to remember that the `ps1`
   and `ps2` attributes of the `sys` module can be anything, including a class
   instance with a `__repr__` or `__str__` method. For example:

```
import sys, os
class MyPrompt:
    def __init__(self, subprompt='>>> '):
        self.lineno = 0
        self.subprompt = subprompt
    def __repr__(self):
        self.lineno = self.lineno + 1
        return os.getcwd()+'|%d'%(self.lineno)+self.subprompt

sys.ps1 = MyPrompt()
sys.ps2 = MyPrompt('... ')
```

This code works as shown (use the `-i` option of the Python interpreter to
make sure your program starts right away):

```
h:\David\book> python -i modifyprompt.py
h:\David\book|1>>> x = 3
h:\David\book|2>>> y = 3
h:\David\book|3>>> def foo():
h:\David\book|3...     x = 3            # the secondary prompt is supported
h:\David\book|3...
h:\David\book|4>>> import os
h:\David\book|5>>> os.chdir('..')
h:\David|6>>>                          # note the prompt changed!
```

3. *Avoiding regular expressions.* This program is long and tedious, but not especially complicated. See if you can understand how it works. Whether this is
   easier for you than regular expressions depends on many factors, such as your
   familiarity with regular expressions and your comfort with the functions in the
   `string` module. Use whichever type of programming works for you.

```
import string
file = open('pepper.txt')
text = file.read()
paragraphs = string.split(text, '\n\n')

def find_indices_for(big, small):
    indices = []
    cum = 0
    while 1:
```

```
            index = string.find(big, small)
            if index == -1:
                return indices
            indices.append(index+cum)
            big = big[index+len(small):]
            cum = cum + index + len(small)

    def fix_paragraphs_with_word(paragraphs, word):
        lenword = len(word)
        for par_no in range(len(paragraphs)):
            p = paragraphs[par_no]
            wordpositions = find_indices_for(p, word)
            if wordpositions == []: return
            for start in wordpositions:
                # look for 'pepper' ahead
                indexpepper = string.find(p, 'pepper')
                if indexpepper == -1: return -1
                if string.strip(p[start:indexpepper]) != '':
                    # something other than whitespace in between!
                    continue
                where = indexpepper+len('pepper')
                if p[where:where+len('corn')] == 'corn':
                    # it's immediately followed by 'corn'!
                    continue
                if string.find(p, 'salad') < where:
                    # it's not followed by 'salad'
                    continue
                # Finally! we get to do a change!
                p = p[:start] + 'bell' + p[start+lenword:]
                paragraphs[par_no] = p          # change mutable argument!

    fix_paragraphs_with_word(paragraphs, 'red')
    fix_paragraphs_with_word(paragraphs, 'green')

    for paragraph in paragraphs:
        print paragraph+'\n'
```

We won't repeat the output here; it's the same as that of the regular expression solution.

4. *Wrapping a text file with a class.* This one is surprisingly easy, if you understand classes and the **split** function in the **string** module. The following is a version that has one little twist over and beyond what we asked for:

```
import string

class FileStrings:
    def __init__(self, filename=None, data=None):
        if data == None:
            self.data = open(filename).read()
        else:
            self.data = data
        self.paragraphs = string.split(self.data, '\n\n')
        self.lines = string.split(self.data, '\n')
```

```
            self.words = string.split(self.data)
        def __repr__(self):
            return self.data
        def paragraph(self, index):
            return FileStrings(data=self.paragraphs[index])
        def line(self, index):
            return FileStrings(data=self.lines[index])
        def word(self, index):
            return self.words[index]
```

This solution, when applied to the file *pepper.txt*, gives:

```
>>> from FileStrings import FileStrings
>>> bigtext = FileStrings('pepper.txt')
>>> print bigtext.paragraph(0)
This is a paragraph that mentions bell peppers multiple times.  For
one, here is a red Pepper and dried tomato salad recipe.  I don't like
to use green peppers in my salads as much because they have a harsher
flavor.
>>> print bigtext.line(0)
This is a paragraph that mentions bell peppers multiple times.  For
>>> print bigtext.line(-4)
aren't peppers, they're chilies, but would you rather have a good cook
>>> print bigtext.word(-4)
botanist
```

How does it work? The constructor simply reads all the file into a big string (the instance attribute **data**) and then splits it according to the various criteria, keeping the results of the splits in instance attributes that are lists of strings. When returning from one of the accessor methods, the data itself is wrapped in a **FileStrings** object. This isn't required by the assignment, but it's nice because it means you can chain the operations, so that to find out what the last word of the third line of the third paragraph is, you can just write:

```
>>> print bigtext.paragraph(2).line(2).word(-1)
'cook'
```

Chapter 9, Common Tasks in Python

1. *Redirecting stdout.* This is simple: all you have to do is to replace the first line with:

```
import fileinput, sys, string    # no change here
sys.stdout = open(sys.argv[-1], 'w')  # open the output file
del sys.argv[-1]                 # we've dealt with this argument
...                              # continue as before
```

2. *Writing a simple shell.* Mostly, the following script, which implements the Unix set of commands (well, some of them) should be self-explanatory. Note that we've only put a "help" message for the **ls** command, but there should be one for all the other commands as well:

```
import cmd, os, string, sys, shutil

class UnixShell(cmd.Cmd):
    def do_EOF(self, line):
        """ The do_EOF command is called when the user presses Ctrl-D (unix)
            or Ctrl-Z (PC). """
        sys.exit()

    def help_ls(self):
        print "ls <directory>: list the contents of the specified directory"
        print "                 (current directory used by default)"

    def do_ls(self, line):
        # 'ls' by itself means 'list current directory'
        if line == '': dirs = [os.curdir]
        else: dirs = string.split(line)
        for dirname in dirs:
            print 'Listing of %s:' % dirname
            print string.join(os.listdir(dirname), '\n')

    def do_cd(self, dirname):
        # 'cd' by itself means 'go home'
        if dirname == '': dirname = os.environ['HOME']
        os.chdir(dirname)

    def do_mkdir(self, dirname):
        os.mkdir(dirname)

    def do_cp(self, line):
        words = string.split(line)
        sourcefiles,target = words[:-1], words[-1] # target could be a dir
        for sourcefile in sourcefiles:
            shutil.copy(sourcefile, target)

    def do_mv(self, line):
        source, target = string.split(line)
        os.rename(source, target)

    def do_rm(self, line):
        map(os.remove, string.split(line))

class DirectoryPrompt:
    def __repr__(self):
        return os.getcwd()+'> '

cmd.PROMPT = DirectoryPrompt()
shell = UnixShell()
shell.cmdloop()
```

Note that we've reused the same trick as in Exercise 2 of Chapter 8 to have a prompt that adjusts with the current directory, combined with the trick of modifying the attribute PROMPT in the cmd module itself. Of course those weren't part of the assignment, but it's hard to just limit oneself to a simple thing when a full-featured one will do. It works, too!

```
h:\David\book> python -i shell.py
h:\David\book> cd ../tmp
h:\David\tmp> ls
Listing of .:
api
ERREUR.DOC
ext
giant_~1.jpg
icons
index.html
lib
pythlp.hhc
pythlp.hhk
ref
tut
h:\David\tmp> cd ..
h:\David> cd tmp
h:\David\tmp> cp index.html backup.html
h:\David\tmp> rm backup.html
h:\David\tmp> ^Z
```

Of course, to be truly useful, this script needs a lot of error checking and many more features, all of which is left, as math textbooks say, as an exercise for the reader.

3. *Understanding map, reduce and filter.* The following functions do as much of the job of *map, reduce,* and *filter* as we've told you about; if you're curious about the differences, check the reference manual.

```
def map2(function, sequence):
    if function is None: return list(sequence)
    retvals = []
    for element in sequence:
        retvals.append(function(element))
    return retvals

def reduce2(function, sequence):
    arg1 = function(sequence[0])
    for arg2 in sequence[1:]:
        arg1 = function(arg1, arg2)
    return arg1

def filter2(function, sequence):
    retvals = []
    for element in sequence:
        if (function is None and element) or function(element):
            retvals.append(element)
    return retvals
```

Chapter 10, Frameworks and Applications

1. *Faking the Web.* What you need to do is to create instances of a class that has the fieldnames attribute and appropriate instance variables. One possible solution is:

```
class FormData:
    def __init__(self, dict):
        for k, v in dict.items():
            setattr(self, k, v)
class FeedbackData(FormData):
    """ A FormData generated by the comment.html form. """
    fieldnames = ('name', 'address', 'email', 'type', 'text')
    def __repr__(self):
        return "%(type)s from %(name)s on %(time)s" % vars(self)

fake_entries = [
    {'name': "John Doe",
     'address': '500 Main St., SF CA 94133',
     'email': 'john@sf.org',
     'type': 'comment',
     'text': 'Great toothpaste!'},
    {'name': "Suzy Doe",
     'address': '500 Main St., SF CA 94133',
     'email': 'suzy@sf.org',
     'type': 'complaint',
     'text': "It doesn't taste good when I kiss John!"},
    ]

DIRECTORY = r'C:\complaintdir'
if __name__ == '__main__':
    import tempfile, pickle, time
    tempfile.tempdir = DIRECTORY
    for fake_entry in fake_entries:
        data = FeedbackData(fake_entry)
        filename = tempfile.mktemp()
        data.time = time.asctime(time.localtime(time.time()))
        pickle.dump(data, open(filename, 'w'))
```

As you can see, the only thing you really had to change was the way the constructor for `FormData` works, since it has to do the setting of attributes from a dictionary as opposed to a `FieldStorage` object.

2. *Cleaning up.* There are many ways to deal with this problem. One easy one is to modify the *formletter.py* program to keep a list of the filenames that it has already processed (in a pickled file, of course!). This can be done by modifying the `if __main__ == '__name__'` test to read something like this (new lines are in bold):

```
if __name__ == '__main__':
    import os, pickle
```

```
CACHEFILE = 'C:\cache.pik'
from feedback import DIRECTORY#, FormData, FeedbackData
if os.path.exists(CACHEFILE):
    processed_files = pickle.load(open(CACHEFILE))
else:
    processed_files = []
for filename in os.listdir(DIRECTORY):
    if filename in processed_files: continue   # skip this filename
    processed_files.append(filename)
    data = pickle.load(open(os.path.join(DIRECTORY, filename)))
    if data.type == 'complaint':
        print "Printing letter for %(name)s." % vars(data)
        print_formletter(data)
    else:
        print "Got comment from %(name)s, skipping printing." % \
            vars(data)
pickle.dump(processed_file, open(CACHEFILE, 'w'))
```

As you can tell, you simply load a list of the previous filenames if it exists (and use an empty list otherwise) and compare the filenames with entries in the list to determine which to skip. If you don't skip one, it needs to be added to the list. Finally, at program exit, pickle the new list.

3. *Adding parametric plotting to grapher.py.* This exercise is quite simple, as all that's needed is to change the drawing code in the Chart class. Specifically, the code between xmin, xmax = 0, N-1 and graphics.fillPolygon(...) should be placed in an if test, so that the new code reads:

```
if not hasattr(self.data[0], '__len__'):   # it's probably a number (1D)
    xmin, xmax = 0, N-1

                                           # code from existing program, up to
                                           #    graphics.fillPolygon(xs, ys, len(xs))
elif len(self.data[0]) == 2:               # we'll only deal with 2-D
    xmin = reduce(min, map(lambda d: d[0], self.data))
    xmax = reduce(max, map(lambda d: d[0], self.data))

    ymin = reduce(min, map(lambda d: d[1], self.data))
    ymax = reduce(max, map(lambda d: d[1], self.data))

    zero_y = y_offset - int(-ymin/(ymax-ymin)*height)
    zero_x = x_offset + int(-xmin/(xmax-xmin)*width)

    for i in range(N):
        xs[i] = x_offset + int((self.data[i][0]-xmin)/(xmax-xmin)*width)
        ys[i] = y_offset - int((self.data[i][1]-ymin)/(ymax-ymin)*height)
    graphics.color = self.color
    if self.style == "Line":
        graphics.drawPolyline(xs, ys, len(xs))
    else:
        xs.append(xs[0]); ys.append(ys[0])
        graphics.fillPolygon(xs, ys, len(xs))
```

Index

Symbols

A

B

About the Authors

Mark Lutz is a software developer and a Python writer and trainer. He is the author of *Programming Python* and *Python Desktop Reference*, both published by O'Reilly & Associates. Mark has programmed a variety of Python systems, teaches courses about Python, and has been involved with the Python community since 1992.

David Ascher is a hybrid scientist/software engineer/trainer. By day, he is a vision researcher. By night, he spends a fair bit of time learning about computer science. He also teaches Python regularly.

Colophon

Our look is the result of reader comments, our own experimentation, and feedback from distribution channels. Distinctive covers complement our distinctive approach to technical topics, breathing personality and life into potentially dry subjects.

The animal on the cover of *Learning Python* is a wood rat (*Neotoma*, family *Muridae*). The wood rat lives in a wide range of living conditions (mostly rocky, scrub, and desert areas) over much of North and Central America, generally at some distance from humans, though they occasionally damage some crops. They are good climbers, nesting in trees or bushes up to six meters off the ground; some species burrow underground or in rock crevices or inhabit other species' abandoned holes.

These greyish-beige, medium-sized rodents are the original pack rats: they carry anything and everything into their homes, whether or not it's needed, and are especially attracted to shiny objects such as tin cans, glass, and silverware.

Mary Anne Weeks Mayo was the production editor and copyeditor of *Learning Python*; Sheryl Avruch was the production manager; Jane Ellin, Melanie Wang, and Clairemarie Fisher O'Leary provided quality control. Robert Romano created the illustrations using Adobe Photoshop 4 and Macromedia FreeHand 7. Mike Sierra provided FrameMaker technical support. Ruth Rautenberg wrote the index, with input from Seth Maislin.

Edie Freedman designed the cover of this book, using a 19th-century engraving from the Dover Pictorial Archive. The cover layout was produced with Quark XPress 3.32 using the ITC Garamond font. Whenever possible, our books use RepKover™, a durable and flexible lay-flat binding. If the page count exceeds RepKover's limit, perfect binding is used.

The inside layout was designed by Alicia Cech and implemented in FrameMaker 5.5 by Mike Sierra. The text and heading fonts are ITC Garamond Light and Garamond Book. This colophon was written by Nancy Kotary.